# UK-EU POLICE AND JUDICIAL COOPERATION POST-BREXIT

This unique open access collection offers an in-depth understanding of UK-EU police and judicial cooperation post-Brexit, an under-explored field.

It considers the legal and political operation of the Trade and Cooperation Agreement (TCA) and its implications for a wide number of policy areas. As well as critiquing its operation, contributors suggest reforms that would improve police and judicial cooperation between the UK and the EU.

This scholarly discussion is balanced against practical considerations, with short chapters setting out practitioners' perspectives on the TCA. It ends by reflecting on the future development of the UK-EU relationship and review of the TCA.

**Volume 24 in the series Hart Studies in European Criminal Law**

**Hart Studies in European Criminal Law**

Series Editors: Professor Valsamis Mitsilegas, Queen Mary University of London; Professor Katalin Ligeti, University of Luxembourg; Professor Anne Weyembergh, Brussels Free University

Since the Lisbon Treaty, European criminal law has become an increasingly important field of research and debate. Working with the European Criminal Law Academic Network (ECLAN), the series will publish works of the highest intellectual rigour and cutting edge scholarship which will be required reading for all European criminal lawyers.

The series is happy to consider both edited and single authored titles. The series defines 'European' and 'criminal law' in the broadest sense so books on the European criminal law, justice and policy will be considered. The series also welcomes books which offer different methodological approaches.

**Volume 1**: *EU Criminal Law after Lisbon: Rights, Trust and the Transformation of Justice in Europe*
Valsamis Mitsilegas

**Volume 2**: *Challenges in the Field of Economic and Financial Crime in Europe and the US*
Edited by Vanessa Franssen and Katalin Ligeti

**Volume 3**: *Chasing Criminal Money: Challenges and Perspectives On Asset Recovery in the EU*
Edited by Katalin Ligeti and Michele Simonato

**Volume 4**: *Limits to EU Powers: A Case Study of EU Regulatory Criminal Law*
Jacob Öberg

**Volume 5**: *The Needed Balances in EU Criminal Law: Past, Present and Future*
Edited by Chloé Brière and Anne Weyembergh

**Volume 6:** *Redefining Organised Crime: A Challenge for the European Union?*
Edited by Stefania Carnevale, Serena Forlati and Orsetta Giolo

**Volume 7**: *White Collar Crime: A Comparative Perspective*
Edited by Katalin Ligeti and Stanislaw Tosza

**Volume 8**: *Criminal Liability of Managers in Europe: Punishing Excessive Risk*
Stanisław Tosza

**Volume 9**: *The European Union and Deprivation of Liberty: A Legislative and Judicial Analysis from the Perspective of the Individual*
Leandro Mancano

**Volume 10**: *The Legitimacy of EU Criminal Law*
Irene Wieczorek

**Volume 11**: *The Fight Against Impunity in EU Law*
Edited by Luisa Marin and Stefano Montaldo

**Volume 12**: *Controlling Immigration Through Criminal Law: European and Comparative Perspectives on 'Crimmigration'*
Edited by Gian Luigi Gatta, Valsamis Mitsilegas, and Stefano Zirulia

**Volume 13**: *The Principle of Mutual Trust in EU Criminal Law*
Auke Willems

**Volume 14**: *Surveillance and Privacy in the Digital Age: European, Transatlantic and Global Perspectives*
Edited by Valsamis Mitsilegas and Niovi Vavoula

**Volume 15**: *The External Dimension of the EU's Policy against Trafficking in Human Beings*
Chloé Brière

**Volume 16**: *Criminal and Quasi-criminal Enforcement Mechanisms in Europe: Origins, Concepts, Future*
Edited by Vanessa Franssen and Christopher Harding

**Volume 17**: *Data protection, Migration and Border Control: The GDPR, the Law Enforcement Directive and Beyond*
Teresa Quintel

**Volume 18**: *Corporations and the Privilege against Self-Incrimination*
Stijn Lamberigts

**Volume 19**: *EU Enforcement Authorities: Punitive Law Enforcement in a Composite Legal Order*
Edited by Michiel Luchtman, Katalin Ligeti and John Vervaele

**Volume 20**: *Admissibility of Evidence in EU Cross-Border Criminal Proceedings: Electronic Evidence, Efficiency and Fair Trial Rights*
Edited by Lorena Bachmaier Winter and Farsam Salimi

**Volume 21**: *Proportionality of Criminal Penalties in EU Law*
Edited by Stefano Montaldo, Valsamis Mitsilegas and Lorenzo Grossio

**Volume 22**: *Stronger Victims' Rights in EU Law?: Assessment and Prospects*
Edited by Julia Burchett and Anne Weyembergh

**Volume 23**: *Proportionality of Criminal Offences and Penalties in EU Law: A Hybrid Principle*
Lorenzo Grossio

**Volume 24**: *UK-EU Police and Judicial Cooperation Post-Brexit: Implementing the Trade and Cooperation Agreement*
Edited by Gemma Davies and Helena Carrapico

# UK-EU Police and Judicial Cooperation Post-Brexit

## *Implementing the Trade and Cooperation Agreement*

Edited by
Gemma Davies
and
Helena Carrapico

•HART•
OXFORD • LONDON • NEW YORK • NEW DELHI • SYDNEY

HART PUBLISHING

Bloomsbury Publishing Plc

Kemp House, Chawley Park, Cumnor Hill, Oxford, OX2 9PH, UK

1385 Broadway, New York, NY 10018, USA

Bloomsbury Publishing Ireland Limited, 29 Earlsfort Terrace, Dublin 2, D02 AY28, Ireland

HART PUBLISHING, the Hart/Stag logo, BLOOMSBURY and the Diana logo are trademarks of Bloomsbury Publishing Plc

First published in Great Britain 2025



A catalogue record for this book is available from the British Library.

A catalogue record for this book is available from the Library of Congress.

Library of Congress Control Number: 2025933514

ISBN: HB: 978-1-50996-644-8
ePDF: 978-1-50996-646-2
ePub: 978-1-50996-645-5

Typeset by Compuscript Ltd, Shannon

For product safety related questions contact productsafety@bloomsbury.com

To find out more about our authors and books visit www.hartpublishing.co.uk. Here you will find extracts, author information, details of forthcoming events and the option to sign up for our newsletters.

This book is dedicated to one of the authors of this volume, Dr Vicky Conway (1980–2022), whose fearless spirit, academic brilliance and unwavering commitment to justice transformed Irish law and policing and championed the voices of those silenced and overlooked. Her legacy continues to inspire us all.

# FOREWORD

One of the many challenges of Brexit has been the potentially negative impact of the UK's withdrawal from the European Union in the field of security and criminal justice. Gemma Davies and Helena Carrapico have edited a rich, comprehensive and authoritative volume addressing the impact of Brexit on the field of police and judicial cooperation in criminal matters. A key strength of this volume is its focus not only on the structure and provisions of the Trade and Cooperation Agreement (TCA), but also, and predominantly, on the implementation of the TCA from an operational perspective. The editors ask a number of key questions in their introduction to the volume: How was cooperation under the TCA working? Was the reduced level of cooperation having an impact on criminal justice outcomes in the UK and EU? Have institutions been able to effectively mitigate the reduction in cooperation? Is there room to further strengthen or expand this cooperation to maintain public safety on both sides? The volume succeeds in providing insightful answers to these questions by bringing together scholars from different disciplines, including law, international relations and criminology.

The volume is structured in four main parts. In Part I, the volume editors provide a contextual and legal analysis of the evolution of the UK's participation in EU police and judicial cooperation in criminal matters mechanisms before and after Brexit. They focus in detail on the background, context behind and content of the TCA. Part II of the book is devoted to police cooperation. It includes chapters on the UK post-Brexit position with regard to EU databases, including the Schengen Information System, with regard to Europol, and with regard to mechanisms enabling the collection and transfer of passenger name record (PNR) data. The impact of Brexit on UK policing is addressed directly. Part III examines the impact of Brexit on judicial cooperation in criminal matters, focusing in particular on extradition and the transfer of prisoners. Part IV of the volume contains a comprehensive analysis of the impact of Brexit on cooperation on various areas of crime, including terrorism, organised crime, human trafficking, migrant smuggling, counterfeiting, environmental crime and cybercrime.

In their concluding chapter, the editors evaluate the implementation of the TCA as being a success, due largely to the dedication of practitioners working in the field. They further highlight the opportunities offered for improvement in cooperation through the planned review of the TCA. At the same time, improvement in the UK's position vis-à-vis the EU faces recurrent challenges arising from the position of the UK as a third country, including limited access to EU agencies, databases and cooperation mechanisms, requirements for meeting TCA benchmarks and evolving EU standards (notably in the field of data protection), and ultimately the reduced level of trust offered to the UK by the EU, as demonstrated recently by the CJEU ruling in *Alchaster*. The present volume is an indispensable guide to navigate the legal and operational challenges underpinning EU–UK cooperation in criminal matters, and is essential reading for academics, practitioners and policy makers in the field.

Valsamis Mitsilegas
*Liverpool*
*25 January 2025*

# CONTENTS

# LIST OF CONTRIBUTORS

**Paul Arnell** is Reader in Law within the Law School, Robert Gordon University, Aberdeen, Scotland. His research centres upon extradition, criminal jurisdiction and human rights. In recent times his research has focused upon areas including the political offence exception and the forum bar to extradition. His monograph, *Law Across Borders*, was published in 2012, and he has published widely on his areas of interest in law journals and the popular press.

**Chloé Brière** is Associate Professor of EU Law and Director of the Institute for European Studies at the Université Libre de Bruxelles since 2023. Her research notably addresses the EU's external relations in criminal matters. She published a monograph in 2021, building upon her PhD, entitled *The External Dimension of the EU's Policy against Trafficking in Human Beings*, and has also worked on the consequences of the UK's withdrawal from the EU for the EU area of criminal justice.

**Helena Carrapico** is Professor of International Relations and European Politics at Northumbria University (Social Sciences Department). Her research focuses on the governance of the EU Area of Freedom, Security and Justice. Her research is published in high-ranking social sciences journals, such as the *Journal of Common Market Studies*, the *Journal of European Integration*, *Geopolitics*, *European Security* and *International Affairs*. She is also the author of *Brexit and Internal Security – Political and Legal Concerns in the Context of the Future UK–EU Relationship* (2019).

**Fabrizio Costantino** is Lead Managing Consultant at ICF. He has undertaken coordination and scientific advisory roles for various national and international organisations. He is also the author of several publications in high-ranking international scientific journals and book series.

**Vicky Conway** was Associate Professor of Law at Dublin City University. Her research focused on police oversight, accountability and corruption. She authored several books and articles on topics of policing and criminal justice, including *Policing Twentieth Century Ireland: A History of An Garda Síochána* (2013). She held a BCL and LLM from University College Cork, a Masters in Criminology and Criminal Justice from the University of Edinburgh, and a PhD from Queen's University Belfast. Dr Conway passed away during the development of this edited volume.

**Clara Cotroneo** is a doctoral candidate at the University of Leiden's Institute of Security and Global Affairs. She is also an associate fellow at the Global Governance Institute, working on AI foresight, and a consultant in security and digital policies in Brussels. Her academic and policy research focus on hybrid threats and new technologies.

**Gemma Davies** is Associate Professor of Criminal Law at Durham University, School of Law. Her research interests and expertise lie in the field of transnational criminal law. Her work aims to understand barriers to criminal justice cooperation, particularly between the UK and other states, and seeks to facilitate better cooperation that also adequately protects the privacy and fundamental rights of citizens. In recent years her work has focused on the implications of Brexit and considered the growing need for cooperation in policing of the Dark Web. She is President of the European Criminal Law Association (UK).

**Shelley Deane** is a researcher in the Department of Law and Government at DCU, and co-editor of *Irish Studies in International Affairs* with the ARINS (Analysing and Researching Ireland North and South) project for the Royal Irish Academy and the Keough-Naughton Institute at the University of Notre Dame. She specialises in conflict-to-peace transitions, security, mediation and negotiation efforts in peace processes in Northern Ireland and the Middle East.

**Elaine Fahey** is Professor of Law at the Institute for the Study of European Law (ISEL), City Law School, City, University of London and Deputy Head of Department (Academic Programmes). Her research interests span the relationship between EU law and global governance, trade, transatlantic relations and the EU's Area of Freedom, Security and Justice. Her publications include a monograph, *The EU as a Global Digital Actor*, and the *Routledge Research Handbook on Transatlantic Relations* (as editor).

**Benjamin Farrand** is Professor in Law & Emerging Technologies at Newcastle University. His research focuses on the law and politics of technology regulation in areas of uncertainty, including topics such as regulatory approaches to cybersecurity, the sale of counterfeit goods online and the combating of disinformation on social media. He is currently leading on the Regulation & Governance Theme of the ESPRC project AGENCY: Assuring Citizen Agency in a World with Complex Online Harms.

**Katy Hayward** is Professor of Political Sociology at Queen's University Belfast, a Fellow of the Senator George J Mitchell Institute for Global Peace, Security and Justice, and a Senior Fellow in the UK in a Changing Europe think tank. The author of over 300 publications, Professor Hayward has written and presented to media, policy, civic and academic audiences worldwide on the subject of Brexit and its effect on Ireland/Northern Ireland. She was a co-investigator on the AHRC Network for UK–Ireland Criminal Justice Cooperation after Brexit (2018–21).

**Daniela Irrera** is Professor of Political Science and International Relations at the Centre for High Defence Studies, National Defence University, Rome. She is also Visiting Professor of Political Violence and Terrorism at the OSCE Academy in Bishkek. She is Chair of the European Consortium for Political Research Executive Committee. She has authored and co-edited 11 books and more than 70 publications in the fields of political science and international relations.

**Christian Kaunert** is Professor of International Security at Dublin City University, Ireland. He is also Professor of Policing and Security at the University of South Wales. In addition, he is Jean Monnet Chair, Director of the Jean Monnet Centre of Excellence and Director of the Jean Monnet Network on EU Counter-Terrorism (www.eucter.net). He is currently the Editor of the *Journal of Contemporary European Studies*,

*International Conflict and Cooperation* and the book series *European Security and Justice Critiques.*

**Alex MacKenzie** is a Senior Lecturer in International Politics at the University of Liverpool. He completed his PhD in European Politics at the University of Salford in 2012 and has published extensively on EU counter-terrorism in many prestigious journals since then. He is currently working on projects concerned with EU–UK security relations after Brexit, foreign fighters in Ukraine and the rise of the far right.

**Conall Mallory** is a Senior Lecturer in Law at Queen's University Belfast. His teaching and research interests lie within the fields of constitutional and international law. His work has a particular focus on human rights and judicial studies. He has published widely on the extraterritorial application of human rights law, the application of human rights during conflict and the extension of obligations to nationals in distress abroad. He holds a PhD from Northumbria University and an LLM in Human Rights Law from Queen's University Belfast.

**Estelle Marks** is lecturer in Criminology in the School of Law, Politics and Sociology, University of Sussex. A policing researcher focusing on policing powers as they transcend the boundaries of the state, she has conducted research projects on the police role in extradition, the role of trust in cross-border police relationships and the legal frameworks for mutual legal assistance.

**Jerry Pearson** is Senior Lecturer in Policing in the School of Social Sciences, University of Sunderland. Prior to the UK's exit from the EU, Dr Pearson led the UK police contingency planning team, working alongside colleagues from the National Crime Agency (NCA), the Home Office and policing agencies across Europe. He is a former Head of the National Police Chiefs' Council (NPCC) International Crime Coordination Centre (ICCC) and contributed to community safety across the UK by delivering innovative strategic solutions to the national threat posed by international criminality.

**Agathe Piquet** is a post-doctoral researcher (*chargée de recherches* FRS-FNRS) at the Institute for European Studies, UCLouvain Saint-Louis Bruxelles. Her main research interests are police cooperation and internal security in the EU, and she has published her research in high-ranking academic journals (*Journal of European Integration*, *Journal of Common Market Studies*, *Comparative European Politics*). Her current project aims to compare different EU Member State strategies to fight against environmental crime in Europe with that in the UK.

**Andrea Ryan** is Emerita Associate Professor and Co-Director of the Centre for Crime, Justice and Victim Studies at the School of Law, University of Limerick. Her research expertise lies in the areas of EU criminal justice, the European Convention on Human Rights, criminal evidence, comparative criminal procedure, criminal law and sentencing. She has published widely in these areas, including a book, *Towards a System of European Criminal Justice – The Problem of Admissibility of Evidence.*

**Christopher Thomson** is a Lecturer in Policing at Sunderland University. Prior to this position, he was Northeast Regional Liaison Officer with the International Crime Co-Ordination Centre and previously a Detective Chief Superintendent, Head of Northumbria Police's Professional Standards and Crime Departments.

**Niovi Vavoula** is Associate Professor in Cyber Policy at the University of Luxembourg, Department of Law. She publishes in the fields of EU immigration law, EU criminal law and privacy law. She is the author of the monograph *Immigration and Privacy in the Law of the EU: The Case of Information Systems* (2022) that examines the compatibility of information systems set up for immigration control purposes with the right to respect for private life.

**Matilde Ventrella** is Senior Lecturer in Law at Liverpool John Moores University. She has written two books on smuggling of migrants and human trafficking, and different articles published in, amongst others, the *European Law Journal*; *European Journal of Crime, Criminal Law and Criminal Justice*; *the New Journal of European Criminal Law*; and the *Marmara Journal of European Studies*. Matilde has recently completed the editing of a multidisciplinary book entitled *A Cultural History of Slavery and Human Trafficking (Volume 6)* (Bloomsbury Publishing, 2024). She has also recently been funded by the Society of Legal Scholars to undertake research activities on the role of EU agencies in protecting victims of human trafficking.

**Marianne L. Wade** is a Reader in Criminal Justice at the University of Birmingham, Birmingham Law School. Dr Wade also leads the Violence, Crime and Justice Research Theme there, and is a fellow of the Institute for Global Innovation and a member of West Midlands Police Counter-Terrorism Reference Group. Her activities focus on cross-border criminal justice cooperation and, particularly, related developments within the EU, including crimes of terrorism and trafficking human beings and their prevention, investigation and prosecution at national, regional and global levels.

**Amy Weatherburn** is a post-doctoral researcher (*chargée de recherches* FRS-FNRS) at the Université Libre de Bruxelles and Doctor of Law (VUB & Tilburg, 2019). Her post-doctoral research focuses on the normalisation of exploitation in the labour market and the development of law and policy that tackles exploitation beyond criminal law. Her main research areas are modern slavery, human trafficking, migration and fundamental rights. She has published a monograph entitled *Labour Exploitation in Human Trafficking Law* (2021).

**Tim J Wilson** is Professor Emeritus at Northumbria University Law School. His academic interests and internationally funded research have covered aspects of criminal justice and interrelated ecosystems at the interface of science, technology, economics and politics. He has contributed to parliamentary inquiries about the impact of Brexit on criminal justice and, more recently, electronic border management. Before his academic career, Professor Wilson was a member of the Senior Civil Service, where his work included a range of penal and forensic science policy issues.

PART I

# UK–EU Police and Judicial Cooperation: From Ad Hoc Cooperation to the Trade and Cooperation Agreement

# 1

# Introduction

GEMMA DAVIES AND HELENA CARRAPICO

In the years before the United Kingdom (UK) left the European Union (EU), a body of literature emerged that demonstrated the risks to public safety if cross-border cooperation in criminal matters between the UK and EU Member States were to be severed.[1] This literature contributed to the fast-emerging field of 'Brexit Studies'[2] and fed in to parliamentary committee reports and parliamentary briefings.[3] Concerns mainly focused on the potential loss of efficiency in cooperation, linked to reduced access to EU databases, instruments and mutual legal assistance. Questions were also raised regarding alignment with data protection, judicial oversight and human rights standards – which so often came up in the Trade and Cooperation Agreement (TCA)[4] negotiations – as well as concerns over the UK's diminished influence in shaping the direction of the Area of Freedom, Security and Justice. Overall, this literature lamented the changes to a relationship that was understood by most as having served the UK's interests in police and judicial cooperation in criminal matters particularly well.[5] The opt-in/opt-out framework, which was introduced with the Treaty of Amsterdam,[6] was seen not only as well

[1] See, eg, A Weyembergh, 'Consequences of Brexit for European Union criminal law' (2017) 8(3) *New Journal of European Criminal Law* 284; V Mitsilegas, European criminal law without the United Kingdon? The triple paradox of Brexit (2017) 8(4) *New Journal of European Criminal Law* 437; H Carrapico, 'Future Security Relations between the EU and the UK: a view of the past three years', *UK in a Changing Europe* (26 June 2019) available at https://ukandeu.ac.uk/future-security-relations-between-the-eu-and-the-uk-a-view-of-the-past-three-years/ (last accessed 8 November 2024).

[2] For wider Brexit-related literature, see F Figueira and B Martill (2020) 'Bounded rationality and the Brexit negotiations: why Britain failed to understand the EU' (2020) 28(12) *Journal of European Public Policy* 1871; B Martill 'Deal or no Deal: Theresa May's Withdrawal Agreement and the Politics of (Non-)Ratification' (2021) 59(6) *Journal of Common Market Studies* 1607.

[3] See, eg, House of Lords European Union Committee, *Beyond Brexit: policing, law enforcement and security* (25th Report of Session 2019–21, HL 250) available at https://committees.parliament.uk/publications/5298/documents/52902/default/ (last accessed 8 November 2024).

[4] Trade and Cooperation Agreement between the European Union and the European Atomic Energy Community, of the one part, and the United Kingdom of Great Britain and Northern Ireland, of the other part [2021] OJ L149/10.

[5] H Carrapico, A Niehuss and C Berthelemy *Brexit and Internal Security- Political and Legal Concerns on the Future UK–EU Relationship* (Palgrave Macmillan, 2019).

[6] Treaty of Lisbon amending the Treaty on European Union and the Treaty establishing the European Community, signed at Lisbon, 13 December 2007 [2007] OJ C306/01.

aligned with UK political priorities, but also as essential to addressing modern security challenges.

With only a week between the release of the final text of the TCA and the end of the transition period, there was little opportunity for debate, academic or political, on the text of Part Three of the Agreement. In the months that followed, academics and practitioners were able to offer preliminary commentary on the legal text[7] and on the detail of the negotiations,[8] while practitioners grappled with the implementation of the TCA's numerous implications for policing and criminal justice.[9] Whilst Part Three of the TCA provided welcome access to important mechanisms for sharing information, coordinating investigations and supporting prosecutions in cases with a cross-border dimension, there were significant changes to the relationship. Key instruments like the European Arrest Warrant (EAW) and the European Investigation Order (EIO), which previously enabled seamless extradition and evidence collection, were no longer available to the UK. Furthermore, the loss of access to critical databases, most notably the Second Generation Schengen Information System (SIS II), posed challenges for UK law enforcement's ability to promptly access and exchange information on wanted individuals, missing persons and stolen goods across the EU. The operational impact of these losses remained unclear, however, and many questions lingered: How was cooperation under the TCA working? Was the reduced level of cooperation having an impact on criminal justice outcomes in the UK and EU? Have institutions been able to effectively mitigate the reduction in cooperation? And, importantly, is there room to further strengthen or expand this cooperation to maintain public safety on both sides?

This edited collection seeks to answer these pressing questions by examining them through a multidisciplinary lens. By drawing together perspectives from Law, International Relations and Criminology, the volume provides a comprehensive analysis of the legal, social and political challenges that Brexit has introduced, not only in the field of police and judicial cooperation, but also in criminal justice broadly. The aim of this volume, which gathers together some of the most important authors in this field, is to contribute to the existing literature by focusing on how the changes introduced by the TCA are being implemented in practice, how practitioners are experiencing these changes, and how implementation is affecting public safety, governance and the prevention of cross-border crime.

In Part I of the volume, the editors map UK–EU police and judicial cooperation, from the time of the Maastricht Treaty right through to the signing of the TCA. More specifically, chapter 2 analyses the UK's selective participation throughout the development of a police and judicial cooperation framework within the Union from its inception until the 2014 opt-out decision, made possible by the Lisbon Treaty. It demonstrates how this history both foreshadowed Brexit and helps explain the eventual relationship that emerged in the TCA. Chapter 3 focuses on the negotiations leading to

[7] See, eg, the special issue by W Scholmburg and A Oehmichen 'Brexit: First observations on the EU-UK Trade and Cooperation Agreement in criminal law' (2021) 21(2) *New Journal of European Criminal Law* 193; O Garner, 'Justice and Home Affairs' in F Fabbrini (ed), *The Law and Politics of Brexit: Volume III: The Framework of New EU-UK Relations* (Oxford University Press, 2021), ch 8.

[8] M Pencheva, *EU–UK Police and Judicial Cooperation in Criminal Matters* (Palgrave Macmillan, 2021).

[9] R Davison, 'Everything is different but nothing has changed: The new post-Brexit extradition arrangements between the UK and the EU' (2021) 6 *Criminal Law Review* 427.

the Withdrawal Agreement and the Political Declaration. It highlights how the political landscape spilled over into the discussions on police and judicial cooperation. Chapter 4 further explores the political context to understanding the direction of travel taken by the TCA negotiations. The chapter maps the final text of Part Three of the TCA, which is then explored further in the rest of the volume.

Part II focuses on police cooperation under the TCA. In chapter 5, Marks maps the UK's participation in EU law enforcement networks and considers the impact of shifting to third-country status and the consequent loss of strategic influence. The chapter sets out what is known about the UK's changed status in many of the networks post-Brexit, and identifies trust-based interpersonal relationships as a key facilitator of cross-border police networks. The author argues that the role of networks in building trust-based relationships between transnational officers must not be overlooked and that interpersonal operational trust between criminal justice practitioners is essential. The UK must maximise its participation in law enforcement and criminal justice networks and not underestimate their importance in facilitating trust-based relationships. This is particularly important post-Brexit, as these relationships compensate for operational gaps created by reduced access to formal mechanisms and databases. In chapter 6, Pearson focuses on the impact of loss of access to the SIS II for UK policing, explaining why this created a risk to public safety. The UK took comprehensive action to address the loss of SIS II and the chapter assesses the effectiveness of these mitigation strategies to date. In Chapter 7, Fahey examines the provisions for the exchange of Passenger Name Records (PNRs) and provides legal analysis in light of the growing body of case law surrounding air passenger data. The chapter evidences the legalisation and institutional growth of PNR regulation and explores the actors and oversight provisions framing PNR in the TCA. Fahey concludes that, to date, the oversight mechanisms have indicated unimpressive effectiveness, with many layers of non-transparent and difficult-to-decipher governance. She concludes that PNR law has many shortcomings, which are not easily remedied or ameliorated by the TCA. In Chapter 8, Vavoula focuses on the development of centralised and decentralised information exchange systems – including those currently under development – by the EU, and on their future interoperability. She considers the extent to which the UK participated in these systems pre-Brexit, and examines the provisions in the TCA providing for access to DNA and fingerprints, criminal records and PNRs. Whilst the provisions appear largely similar to the existing EU rules, some discrepancies are argued to be problematic. The author highlights the ongoing importance of the UK's maintenance of its data adequacy decision and demonstrates that the forthcoming reforms, which will expand the interoperability framework, will require amendment of the TCA and create opportunities that the UK will miss out on. In Chapter 9, Conway, Deane and Hayward consider the case of the post-Brexit Irish border in order to reveal the achievements and vulnerabilities of cooperation between the two police services on either side of it. The authors demonstrate that the challenges are acute. Not all are caused by Brexit: some others are new, forged in part by renewed criminal exploitations of pre-existing blind spots on the border. Recommendations aimed at strengthening cross-border policing across the island of Ireland focus on improving communication, training and liaison. In Chapter 10, Costantino and Cotroneo explore, from a practitioner's perspective, the working and administrative arrangement signed between the UK's National Crime Agency and Europol, as provided for in the TCA. They consider the strengths and limitations of the current arrangements. They argue that Brexit has led to a general increase in bureaucracy affecting the speed and effectiveness of police cooperation. Chapter 11, by Thomson, also provides a police practitioner's view of Brexit. It maps law enforcement's preparations for Brexit, which included the creation of the International Crime Coordination Centre and the National Extradition Unit. The author argues that the improvements in UK policing structures resulted in a significant increase in capacity, which can be seen as a positive outcome of Brexit.

Part III of the volume focuses on judicial cooperation and fundamental rights under the TCA. In chapter 12, Wade considers judicial cooperation between the UK and EU post-Brexit, focusing on the collaboration that is taking place via Eurojust. At first glance, the provisions evoke an impression of business as usual. However, on analysis, the TCA provides only for the aspects of cooperation the UK considers necessary, with little attention paid to defence rights passed under the Stockholm Programme. Wade analyses statistics revealing the UK's engagement with Eurojust to date. Overall, there is clear evidence of UK practitioners working hard to maintain the criminal justice legacy of EU membership. However, the author questions how durable this cooperation can be, highlighting important gaps in the TCA that reveal a refusal to acknowledge the reality of the EU as a criminal justice governance polity. The extent to which the UK can ignore the European Public Prosecutors Office (EPPO), particularly if the proposal for a counterterrorism EPPO comes to fruition, is also considered. In chapter 13, Arnell considers the surrender/extradition provisions in the TCA and discusses whether these provisions will function effectively and efficiently, but also in a way that is fair and just. Extradition has always had competing purposes: the facilitation of criminal justice cooperation between jurisdictions and the protection of requested persons. Arnell argues that the rules under the TCA are notably less cooperative than those that existed under the EU Framework Decision establishing the EAW. He suggests that the TCA can be said to have moved the pendulum towards the protection of requested persons, at the expense of transnational criminal cooperation. In chapter 14, Ryan considers extradition between the UK and Ireland. This is an important focus, as the close historic and geographical connections between the jurisdictions mean that there is a high level of extradition 'traffic' between the two states. The chapter examines the differences between the EAW and an arrest warrant under the TCA. The issues of proportionality, delay, trial readiness, fundamental rights and abuse of process are also explored. In chapter 15, Wilson considers a noticeable omission from the TCA, namely, prisoner transfer provisions. Such provisions were initially sought by the UK but do not appear in the final text. The chapter addresses the complexity of including prisoner transfer within the scope of the TCA. In contrast, the author argues that a new EU–UK prisoner transfer cooperation arrangement could make use of common international obligations, so that transfer arrangements would be part of a suite of anti-discriminatory and rehabilitative measures. In chapter 16, Mallory considers the protection of human rights and fundamental freedoms under Part Three of the TCA. The chapter notes that the TCA binds the UK to human rights protection under the European Convention on Human Rights (ECHR), highlighting that both parties have committed to shared values of democracy, the rule of law and human rights. It also underlines, however, that there has been a track record on the side of UK politicians of questioning whether it would be in the UK's interest to remain in the ECHR. If a UK government was to take action in that direction, the TCA includes extensive provisions that enable suspension or termination of the cooperation.

Part IV of the volume focuses on the impact of the TCA implementation on different forms of crime and insecurity. Authors in this section look more broadly at how the UK–EU relationship has impacted the fight against specific criminal threats. In chapter 17, MacKenzie and Kaunert consider the impact on the fight against terrorism, a field in which the UK was often at the forefront of efforts to strengthen European cooperation. To date, Brexit and the implementation of the TCA do not seem to have seriously affected either side's ability to combat terrorism. However, the threat landscape is constantly evolving, and a key question will be whether perceptions of terrorism continue to be shared between London and other European capitals. Alignment is essential, as there appears to be little appetite in Brussels for much deeper engagement with the EU. The authors argue for a new EU–UK forum on terrorism to be created. In chapter 18, Irrera considers the impact of the TCA on the fight against organised crime. Similarly to MacKenzie and Kaunert, she also argues there is no clear framework for effectively addressing the multifaceted global and regional security challenges that the UK and EU face from organised crime. The TCA's focus on police and judicial cooperation has been at the expense of policy coordination. In chapter 19, Farrand focuses on combating the dissemination of counterfeit goods. The author demonstrates the risks that the circulation of counterfeit goods presents to security, and argues that clearer rules on access to important tools such as the IP Enforcement Database of the EU's Intellectual Property Office (EUIPO) would ensure that UK authorities have up-to-date knowledge regarding trends, transit routes and best practices regarding the combating of counterfeit goods. In chapter 20, Ventrella focuses on migrant smuggling by sea. She highlights that the TCA is thin on measures that would enhance cooperation on the smuggling of migrants. The impact of changes in migration law since 2022 are set out, and the author argues that an agreement with the EU on migration and asylum, going beyond the existing working agreement with Frontex and, as a minimum, establishing safe and legal routes to the UK and setting out fair rules on redistribution, is essential. In chapter 21, Brière and Weatherburn focus on the fight against human trafficking. Although the UK played a leading role in developing this field pre-Brexit, it was not singled out as an area for thematic cooperation. The impact of both withdrawal from the EU and the resulting shift in status at regional and global levels in anti-trafficking developments are analysed. The authors argue that while Brexit may have had, so far, a limited impact on EU–UK cooperation – thanks to the close pre-existing ties and mitigating measures – its main consequence might be a displacement of UK authorities' focus in favour of wider international cooperation. In chapter 22, Piquet focuses on the fight against environmental crime. The chapter explores the unprecedented politicisation of environmental issues seen throughout Brexit negotiations. Post-Brexit, three main challenges are identified: legal framework divergence, loss of police and judicial cooperation, and risks to the specialised National Wildlife Crime Intelligence Unit now the UK is not subject to EU pressure to maintain it. In chapter 23, Farrand focuses on cybercrime. The chapter outlines the growing importance of bodies such as the European Cybercrime Centre (EC3) within Europol, the Computer Security Incident Response Team (CERT-EU), the European Union Agency for Cybersecurity (ENISA) and the European Defence Agency, and demonstrates the increased need for cooperation in the field. Although cybersecurity is a distinct area for thematic cooperation in Part Four of the TCA, Farrand concludes that there is a knock-on effect for police and judicial cooperation, given Part Four's relatively few substantive and unambitious provisions dedicated to the topic. The risks presented by potential regulatory divergence are further explored. The author argues that the UK should rethink regulatory reforms that take it out of the 'European privacy family', as well as taking up the opportunities to engage with ENISA, CERT-EU and the Cooperation Group on the basis of mutual interest in combating cybercrime and ensuring cybersecurity.

In Part V, the editors, Davies and Carrapico, bring together the key findings of the book alongside the findings of their research commissioned by the Scottish Parliament in the context of the Scottish Parliament Information Centre (SPICe).[10] The chapter summarises the key operational deficits caused by Brexit for police and judicial cooperation and their impact. It demonstrates that Brexit has led to impunity for serious crime, although quantifying and evidencing this impact remains challenging. Understanding the operational deficits caused by the implementation of the TCA is vital if we are to address issues in the future. On this basis, the chapter sets out the priorities for the future enhancement of the UK–EU relationship. Davies and Carrapico argue there is a need for a comprehensive and ambitious review of the TCA in 2026 to ameliorate current risks to public safety. The upcoming review of the TCA presents a valuable opportunity to assess the impact of its implementation, address issues within the Agreement's scope and explore complementary agreements to tackle unresolved challenges. Looking even further down the road, the TCA needs to ensure it stands the test of time. In practice, it is not a living document, as it only captures important aspects of police and judicial cooperation as they existed in December 2020. The tools available under the TCA will soon become obsolete. Further development of the governance structures of the TCA is also needed to ensure greater transparency and accountability, and to guarantee that the TCA evolves in parallel with UK and EU domestic development.

[10] Davies and Carrapico were awarded a Fellowship with the Scottish Parliament, which enabled them to explore the impact of the implementation of the TCA on the criminal justice system in Scotland by seeking to understand how cooperation has continued to take place and what operational challenges have emerged. The Fellowship resulted in the publication of the following policy paper: G Davies and H Carrapico, *UK–EU Law Enforcement and Judicial Cooperation in Criminal Matters in Part Three of the Trade and Cooperation Agreement: The Impact on Scotland*, Scottish Parliament Policy Paper (2024). The latter relied on data collected through a roundtable with 14 representatives of the Scottish criminal justice system, the Scottish Government and academics, which took place in March 2023; 23 semi-structured interviews conducted between July 2023 and January 2024 with members of the Scottish Police, the Crown Office and Procurator Fiscal Service, the Scottish Parliament, the Scottish Government and EU-based police and judicial cooperation practitioners; and an academic literature review carried out between July 2023 and January 2024. The editors would sincerely like to thank all participants involved in this research for their contribution towards both the development of the policy paper and the writing of this edited volume.

# 2

# The UK's Uneasy Participation in EU Police and Judicial Cooperation: The Road from Maastricht to Lisbon

GEMMA DAVIES AND HELENA CARRAPICO

## I. Introduction

Although the roots of police and judicial cooperation stretch back to 1976 and the Trevi Group,[1] it took until 1993 for cooperation in the field of criminal law to be formalised under the pillar structure. Whilst Member States recognised the need for police and judicial cooperation, they were hesitant to embrace the supranational machinery of the Community Pillar (the first pillar). The Second and Third Pillars gave the Member States an institutionalised forum in which to discuss these matters, without subjecting themselves to supranational controls. Mitsilegas describes a process of 'gradual, contested evolution of EU criminal law'[2] that eventually led to a transfer of competence from Member States to the Union level, culminating with the Lisbon Treaty in 2009.[3] This chapter maps the United Kingdom's (UK's) participation throughout the development of a police and judicial cooperation framework within the Union from its inception until the 2014 opt-out decision, made possible by the Lisbon Treaty. As will be seen, the UK has been at times the driving force and at others the opposing force in the development of police and judicial cooperation. It is, in part, the UK's uneasy participation in European Union (EU) criminal law that led to the development of a 'variable geometry'[4] that permitted states to have differing levels of association with the emerging Area of Freedom, Justice and Security (AFSJ).[5] This history both foreshadows Brexit

[1] TREVI was formally established following a resolution adopted by the EC Ministers of Justice and Home Affairs in 1976. It was not based on any formal Treaty provisions and operated outside the formal Community law framework. See V Mitsilegas, *EU Criminal Law* (Hart Publishing, 2009) ch 4.

[2] Mitsilegas (n 1) 31.

[3] Treaty of Lisbon amending the Treaty on European Union and the Treaty establishing the European Community, 13 December 2007 [2007] OJ C306/01.

[4] For discussion of this concept, see B De Witte 'The future of variable geometry in a post-Brexit European Union' (2017) 24(2) *Maastricht Journal of European and Comparative Law* 153.

[5] A Enge, 'Opting in or opting out? The EU's variable geometry in the area of freedom, security and justice' in R Pereira et al (eds), *The Governance of Criminal Justice in the European Union* (Edward Elgar, 2020) 39.

and is necessary to understand the eventual relationship that emerges in the Trade and Cooperation Agreement.[6] The final section of the chapter maps the development of the external dimension to the AFSJ in police and judicial cooperation, and considers how this has further developed fertile ground from which the UK–EU relationship has emerged post-Brexit.

## II. The Development of an Institutional Framework

Cooperation in criminal justice matters had long existed outside of the EU within the framework of the Council of Europe, but as new areas of transnational criminality developed, drivers towards cooperation within the Union increased.[7] The emergence of the EU internal market, resulting in the abolition of internal borders and facilitating free movement of goods, services, people and capital, provided a driver towards increased institutional cooperation.[8] The 1990 Schengen Implementing Convention included provisions primarily on immigration, asylum and border controls, but also on police cooperation.[9] This included the establishment of the Schengen Information System (SIS). The stated driver was that the increased freedoms granted to citizens and businesses had to be balanced by increasing the powers of states and their apparatus to detect, investigate and prosecute crime. This Schengen 'logic'[10] has driven the subsequent development of EU criminal law and can still be seen in the decisions of the Court of Justice of the European Union (CJEU) when interpreting the operation of the European Arrest Warrant (EAW).[11] It has also been argued, however, that the compensatory measures rationale[12] does not fully explain or justify the restrictiveness of the policies subsequently adopted, and that the driving force behind the AFSJ has been security.[13] Costello argues that 'the lie that this system is required by the internal free market movement is revealed in relation to the UK and Ireland's participation in a range of external border control measures without any commitment to the abolition of internal border controls'.[14]

[6] Trade and Cooperation Agreement between the European Union and the European Atomic Energy Community, of the one part, and the United Kingdom of Great Britain and Northern Ireland, of the other part [2020] OJ L149/10.

[7] Mitsilegas (n 1).

[8] Treaty establishing the European Economic Community, 25 March 1957, 294 UNTS 3 (entry into force 1 January 1958), Art 3.

[9] The Schengen acquis – Convention implementing the Schengen Agreement of 14 June 1985 between the Governments of the States of the Benelux Economic Union, the Federal Republic of Germany and the French Republic on the gradual abolition of checks at their common borders [2000] OJ L239/19.

[10] Mitsilegas (n 1) 7.

[11] For discussion, see S Alegre and M Leaf, 'Mutual Recognition in European Judicial Co-operation: A Step Too Far Too Soon? Case Study – The European Arrest Warrant' (2004) 10(2) *European Law Journal* 200.

[12] S Lavenex and W Wallace, 'Justice and Home Affairs: Towards a "European Public Order"?' in H Wallace et al (eds), *Policy-Making in the European Union*, 5th edn (Oxford University Press, 2005) 460.

[13] D Bigo, 'Border Regimes, Police Cooperation and Security in an Enlarged European Union' in J Zielonka (ed), *Europe Unbound: Enlarging and Reshaping the Boundaries of the European Union* (Routledge, 2003) 213.

[14] C Costello, 'Administrative Governance and the Europeanisation of Asylum and Immigration Policy' in H Hofmann and A Turk (eds), *EU Administrative Governance*. (Edward Elgar, 2006) 287, 289.

A major criticism of the Maastricht Treaty[15] was that, unlike foreign and security policy under the Second Pillar, the Third Pillar involved subjects that touched on fundamental human rights. It was therefore argued that the need for accountability in this policy field was much greater, requiring a full role for the European Parliament and review jurisdiction for the European Court of Justice. In the Treaty of Amsterdam, the Third Pillar areas of immigration, asylum, borders and civil law were 'communitarised', forming part of Title IV of the EC Treaty.[16] The Third Pillar was renamed 'provisions on police and judicial cooperation in criminal matters'.

The objective was to provide 'citizens with a high level of safety within the AFSJ by developing common action among the Member States in the fields of police and judicial cooperation in criminal matters and by preventing and combatting racism and xenophobia'.[17] The Treaty of Amsterdam provided express reference to the development of the Union as an 'Area of Freedom, Security and Justice'. This was accompanied by the incorporation of the Schengen acquis into Community/Union law. The Treaty also endorsed the principle of mutual recognition, which 'should become the cornerstone of judicial cooperation … in criminal matters within the Union'.[18]

## III. The UK as a Driver Towards Cooperation

The late 1990s saw a shift to the principle of mutual recognition. Concern about the slow pace of integration post-Maastricht, coupled with Member States' wariness of EU harmonisation, served as a catalyst for this shift. It was the UK, during its Presidency in 1998, that first suggested that mutual recognition might be the way forward.[19] Jack Straw, then Home Secretary, argued for a situation 'where each Member State recognises the validity of decisions of courts from other Member States in criminal matters with a minimum of procedure and formality'.[20] It was not a new concept, having already been used to attain the internal market. This suggestion was endorsed by the European Council in the Tampere Programme, and by the Commission in 1999. Mutual recognition requires states to recognise other norms as equivalent to their own, but they accept because of the need to cooperate in the enforcement of another state's systems of law. It was seen as a 'shortcut' that avoided the 'more legally demanding and politically complicated method of harmonising criminal law systems'.[21] Mutual recognition was underpinned by the high level of trust that existed between Member States and was argued to be a 'panacea' for lack of convergence in domestic law.[22]

[15] Treaty on European Union (Consolidated Version) ('Treaty of Maastricht') [2002] OJ C325/5.

[16] Treaty of Amsterdam amending the Treaty on European Union, the Treaties establishing the European Communities and certain related acts [1997] OJ C 340/01.

[17] Treaty of Maastricht (n 15) Art 29(1).

[18] According to the Conclusions of the Tampere European Council of 15 and 16 October 1999, point 33.

[19] Cardiff European Council of 15–16 June 1998, para 39.

[20] Quoted by Mitsilegas (n 1) 116.

[21] L Marin, 'The European Arrest Warrant and Domestic Legal Orders. Tensions Between Mutual Recognition and Fundamental Rights: The Italian Case' (2008) 15(4) *Maastricht Journal of European and Comparative Law* 473, 475.

[22] ibid 483.

The Framework Decision on the EAW was the first judicial cooperation instrument to implement the principle of mutual recognition of judicial decisions in criminal matters.[23] European institutions, including the Court of Justice in these early years, were accused of viewing mutual recognition as requiring 'blind' trust as transplanted from the internal market.[24] Criticisms of this approach and the risks it posed to fundamental rights quickly followed.[25] Despite its early problems, and significant media criticism,[26] the UK embraced the use of the EAW and its impact was profound.[27] Sir Julian King, then European Commissioner responsible for security, estimated that the UK surrendered to other states a total of 8,000 wanted people and received 1,000 using the EAW between 2004 and 2017.[28] The UK also embraced using EU mechanisms, databases and institutions to their operational fullest. The UK was said to use Europol more than any other EU country.[29] For example, the UK was one of the biggest contributors to the Europol Information System and led on many European Multidisciplinary Platform Against Criminal Threats (EMPACT) projects.[30] Evidence to the Home Affairs Committee confirmed that the UK had, at the time, 160,000 alerts on the Schengen Information System II (SIS II) platform[31] and participated extensively in Joint Investigation Teams.[32]

The shift from a focus on military threats to a broader understanding of security hastened after the 9/11 attacks in 2001 in the USA, which led to stronger calls for a coordinated international response to terrorism in Europe.[33] Although political integration was always viewed with caution by the UK (as discussed in more detail section IV), from an operational perspective, cooperation was viewed as highly desirable.[34] The UK led, not only in driving mutual recognition, but also in the development of many EU tools and a broader model of intelligence-led policing:[35] UK law enforcement embraced

[23] Council Framework Decision of 13 June 2002 on the European arrest warrant and the surrender procedures between Member States – Statements made by certain Member States on the adoption of the Framework Decision (2002/584/JHA) [2002] OJ L 190.

[24] A Willems, 'The Court of Justice of the European Union's Mutual Trust Journey in EU Criminal law: From a Presumption to (Room for) Rebuttal' (2019) 20 *German Law Journal* 468.

[25] E Guild (ed), *Constitutional Challenges to the European Arrest Warrant* (Wolf Legal Publishers, 2006).

[26] As an example, see S Chakrabarti, 'It's not just Eurosceptics who think the European arrest warrant is rotten' *The Guardian* (10 November 2015).

[27] L Mancano, 'You'll never work alone: A systemic assessment of the European Arrest Warrant and judicial independence' (2021) 58(3) *Common Market Law Review* 683; T Christou and K Weis, 'The European Arrest Warrant and Fundamental Rights' (2020) 1(1) *New Journal of European Criminal Law* 31.

[28] D Boffey, 'Brexit: UK may have to recognise ECJ court rulings to keep security cooperation' *The Guardian* (30 April 2017), cited by House of Lords European Union Select Committee, 'Brexit: Judicial oversight of the European Arrest Warrant', HL Paper 16 (27 July 2017).

[29] HM Government, 'The UK's cooperation with the EU on justice and home affairs, and on foreign policy and security issues' (9 May 2016) para 1.16.

[30] House of Lords, *Select Committee on the European Union, Home Affairs Sub-Committee, Corrected oral evidence: Brexit: Future UK–EU Security and Policing Co-operation* (12 October 2016) Q19.

[31] ibid Q86.

[32] See evidence of A Saunders, House of Lords EU Committee, *Brexit: Future UK-EU Security Cooperation* (7th Report of Session 2016–17, HL Paper 77) paras 74 and 75.

[33] A Shepherd, 'EU counterterrorism, collective securitization, and the internal-external security nexus' (2021) 7(5) *Global Affairs* 733.

[34] V Mitsilegas and E Guild, 'Police and criminal justice co-operation after Brexit'.(2023) 30(11) *Journal of European Public Policy* 2519.

[35] V Mitsilegas, 'European criminal law after Brexit' (2017) 28(2) *Criminal Law Forum* 219.

participation in the EU architecture as vital to the security of the UK.[36] The inaugural Presidency of Eurojust was held by a UK prosecutor, Michael Kennedy, from 2002 to 2007, followed immediately by another UK prosecutor, Aled Williams, until 2012. The Directorship of Europol was held by UK civil servant Rob Wainright from 2009 until 2018 during a critical time of development, as it became a formal EU agency in 2010. Throughout this period, the ambitious Hague Programme was implemented. This foresaw law enforcement as being readily able to access and exchange evidence with colleagues around the Union.[37] This was continued through implementation of the Swedish Initiative, which introduced the 'Principle of Availability'.[38] The UK also led from 2001 onwards in the development of the Data Retention Directive.[39] During its Presidency of the European Council in 2005, using the political momentum that followed the 7/7 bombings, the Directive was pushed through. The UK Government was said to have used European momentum to secure the data retention regime that it wanted at home, where the domestic Parliament was resistant to far-reaching surveillance laws.[40] Its efforts were, however, in vain, as the CJEU shortly afterwards annulled the Directive in the *Digital Rights Ireland* judgment, holding that the Directive 'entailed an interference with the fundamental rights of practically the entire European population'.[41]

## IV. The Lisbon Treaty – The Beginning of the End for UK Participation

The Lisbon Treaty, which came into force in December 2009, had a marked impact on the AFSJ. The previous three-pillar system was demolished and instead integrated into the main body of the Treaties under Title V of Part Three of the Treaty on the Functioning of the European Union as an area of shared competence revealing its centrality to EU policy.[42] The ordinary legislative procedure was now to be the norm – which meant an

[36] J Evans and J Sawers, 'The EU can't dictate to us on security but staying in it can keep us safer' *The Sunday Times* (8 May 2016).

[37] 'Communication from the Commission to the Council and the European Parliament of 10 May 2005 – The Hague Programme: ten priorities for the next five year The Partnership for European Renewal in the Field of Freedom, Security and Justice' COM(2005) 184 final, [2005] OJ C236.

[38] Council Framework Decision 2006/960/JHA of 18 December 2006 on simplifying the exchange of information and intelligence between law enforcement authorities of the Member States of the European Union [2006] OJ L386/89.

[39] Directive 2006/24/EC of the European Parliament and of the Council of 15 March 2006 on the retention of data generated or processed in connection with the provision of publicly available electronic communications services of public communications networks and amending Directive 2002/58/EC [2006] OJ L105/54.

[40] LawFare, 'The history of DRIPA 2014 – data retention in the UK' (19 August 2021). Also see V Mitsilegas, 'The privatisation of surveillance in the digital age' in V Mitsilegas and N Vavoula (eds), *Surveillance and privacy in the digital age. European, transatlantic and global perspectives* (Hart Publishing, 2021) 104.

[41] Joined Cases C-293/12 and C-594/12 *Digital Rights Ireland Ltd v Minister for Communications, Marine and Natural Resources and Others and Kärntner Landesregierung and Others*, ECLI:EU:C:2014:238, para 53.

[42] Consolidated versions of the Treaty on European Union and the Treaty on the Functioning of the European Union Consolidated version of the Treaty on European Union Consolidated version of the Treaty on the Functioning of the European Union Protocols Annexes to the Treaty on the Functioning of the European Union Declarations annexed to the Final Act of the Intergovernmental Conference which adopted the Treaty of Lisbon, signed on 13 December 2007 Tables of equivalences [2016] OJ C 202/1.

end to Framework Decisions, replaced by Directives and Regulations within the competency of the CJEU. Member States could now refer a question of law to the Court under the preliminary rulings process. The Commission was empowered to bring enforcement proceedings if a state did not implement a measure or did so incorrectly.

These constitutional changes compounded fears that ever-increasing integration would undermine British sovereignty. In response to this, in 1997, the UK secured EU agreement to the right to choose whether to participate in any new EU legislation covering asylum and judicial cooperation in civil matters. In 2007, this right to 'opt in' was extended to cooperation in policing and criminal justice. During the negotiation, the UK had also insisted on inserting Article 10 of Protocol 36 to the EU Treaties. This permitted the UK Government a five-year 'grace' period to decide whether to be bound by the police and criminal justice and mutual recognition measures, which were adopted before the Treaty of Lisbon entered into force. By May 2014, the UK had to decide on whether to stay 'in' the Justice and Home Affairs (JHA) measures or to exercise its right to opt out. In the background, there was a growing swell of Conservative Euroscepticism, which resulted, amongst other things, in the UK's passing of the European Union Act 2011 that stated any expansion of EU powers would require a UK referendum.

Although the opt-out was negotiated by the Labour Government, it was a Conservative Government that had to decide whether to make use of it. The then Prime Minister, David Cameron, was said to be under pressure to 'repatriate criminal justice', and it was rumoured that this opt-out might be offered as a less troublesome alternative to those calling for a referendum on 'pulling out of Europe'.[43] Of primary concern for the Conservative Government was the risk that the jurisdiction of the CJEU might result in 'judicial activism', which could undermine the UK's common law systems and result in loss of national control. The House of Lords European Union Committee, however, found no evidence to support these concerns.[44] The Government also stated that the opt-in negotiation should be used to secure reform to the EAW, which had been heavily criticised. The issue of the UK's opt-in, and the EAW in particular, had become increasingly politicised. In several commentaries in the media, 'the EAW was seen as emblematic of arguments about the EU more generally, divisions with the Conservative Party and the rising popularity of UKIP'.[45] It was clear that mutual recognition, supposedly the answer to avoiding harmonisation, still had significant repercussions for UK criminal justice. Wieczorek has argued that the EU had emerged inevitably as a 'primary policy actor' over time, and could be seen pursuing a normative agenda in areas in which Member States were capable of acting on their own.[46]

On 24 July 2013, the UK notified the Council that it would make use of the blank opt-out option. This amounted to over 130 measures, although not all were still actively

[43] A Hinarejos, J Spencer and S Peers, 'Opting Out of EU Criminal Law – What is Actually Involved?' *University of Cambridge Faculty of Law Research Paper No 25/2012*.

[44] House of Lords European Union Committee, *EU Police and Criminal Justice Measures: The UK's 2014 Opt-out Decision* (13th Report of Session 2012–13, HL Paper 159) para 89.

[45] House of Lords, 'The European Arrest Warrant Opt-in'. Select Committee on Extradition law' (1st report of Session 2014–15, HL Paper 63) para 9.

[46] I Wieczorek, 'The emerging role of the EU as a primary normative actor in the EU Area of Criminal Justice' (2021) 27(4-6) *European Law Journal* 378.

used. The UK began to negotiate back in to 35 measures, which it considered were in the 'national interest', by the end of 2013.[47] The process depended on whether the measure was a Schengen or non-Schengen measure. For Schengen measures, whether the UK could re-participate was decided by a unanimous vote of the European Council.[48] For non-Schengen measures, the decision lay with the Commission. If the UK was unhappy with the Commission's decision, it could be referred to the Council and decided by Qualifying Majority Vote. Initially, some Member States said that the UK would have to opt back in to more measures, but in the end the UK was allowed to take the cherry-picking approach it wished.[49]

The operational imperative for continued participation in EU criminal law was clearly articulated. Theresa May, as Home Secretary, declared that EU measures were vital to 'stop foreign criminals coming to Britain, deal with European fighters coming back from Syria, stop British criminals evading justice abroad, prevent foreign criminals evading justice by hiding here, and get foreign criminals out of our prisons'.[50] The House of Lords European Union Committee argued that the Government's decision not to rejoin a number of measures, including the European Judicial Network and implementing measures relating to Europol, risked substantive and reputation damage.[51] McCartney highlighted that the degree of parliamentary involvement in the opt-out and opt-in decisions also resulted in significant debate around transparency and accountability.[52] The UK Government held a debate in Parliament on the 35 opt-in measures only once it had already concluded negotiations with the EU institutions and Member States. Theresa May defended this position, stating it would be 'a poor negotiating strategy to reveal one's hand in public while a deal is still being done'.[53] In the end, by opting out and then successfully opting in to the most important measures, the UK was able to reconcile the 'sovereignty-effectiveness paradox'.[54] It could say it had maintained sovereignty by opting out of the whole of the EU pre-Lisbon acquis, but that it had also taken on board operational concerns of practitioners and ensured national security was not compromised by participating in key measures.

The EU also now had explicit competence over criminal procedure on condition that it was necessary to facilitate mutual recognition of judgments and judicial decisions and police and judicial cooperation in criminal matters having a cross-border dimension. This was an unwelcome reverberation of mutual recognition from the UK's perspective.

[47] Foreign and Commonwealth Office, *Decision pursuant to Article 10 of Protocol 36 to The Treaty on the Functioning of the European Union* (Cm 8671, 2013).

[48] ibid for discussion of the operation of Art 10(5) of Protocol 36.

[49] C McCartney, 'Opting in and Opting Out: Doing the Hokey Cokey with EU Policing and Judicial Cooperation' (2013) 77(6) *The Journal of Criminal Law* 543.

[50] House of Lords (n 30) 2.

[51] House of Lords, *Follow-up report on EU police and criminal justice measures: The UK's 2014 opt-out decision* (European Union Committee, 5th Report of Session 2013–14, HL Paper 69).

[52] European Scrutiny Committee, *The UK's opt-out of pre-Lisbon criminal law and policing measures*, 21st report (7 November 2013). Also see comments by B Cash, HC Deb 7 April 2014, vol 579, col 26, 'It is not just a question of whether Parliament is given the opportunity to deliberate before decisions are taken behind closed doors, but a question of whether Parliament is, in effect, being asked to rubber stamp something that has already been decided in negotiations behind those closed doors. The problem is one of the matter therefore being hidden from the searching gaze of the public and Parliament itself.'

[53] HC Deb 7 April 2014, vol 579, col 27.

[54] Mitsilegas and Guild (n 34).

It was argued that without approximation of procedural rights, human rights were subordinated to the efficiency of mutual recognition. The AFSJ is marked by its direct impact on individual rights. Whilst most other areas of the EU acquis provide rights to individuals, the EU's increasing competence in criminal justice provided power to the state.

The second concession negotiated by the UK was Protocol 21 to the Lisbon Treaty.[55] The latter provided the UK and Ireland with the right to opt in to subsequent provisions in the AFSJ, which included criminal law measures. The UK Government could now decide measure by measure what it would opt in to. The UK took a variable approach to whether it would opt in to post-Lisbon measures. Surprisingly, the UK participated in the European Investigation Order (EIO).[56] This is an example of operational imperatives outweighing Euro-scepticism. The Home Secretary gave evidence that 'When I looked at this issue of the European Investigation Order, there was one thing driving my thinking, which was a desire to ensure that we could give the police the powers that they need to catch criminals.'[57] The decision to opt in to the EIO was a 'recognition of the functional necessity of being "in the system" of EU-wide cooperation, which superseded political sovereignty concerns'.[58]

Controversially the UK did not opt into several defence procedural rights instruments. The suite of measures formed a 'roadmap' of rights designed to address concerns that mutual recognition and mutual trust were undermining fundamental rights.[59] As an alternative, the UK tabled a non-legally binding resolution, which was eventually rejected.[60] Whilst the UK opted in to the first measures on the rights of suspects and defendants in criminal procedure, it did not participate in others. These included, for example, the Directive on the right to access to a lawyer.[61] This approach led to criticisms that the UK's participation followed an 'à la carte' model, which had the potential to 'de-legitimise' police and judicial cooperation.[62] The primary driver for non-participation was not that the instruments would result in unwanted domestic change, but that they would be open to the interpretation of their terms in the CJEU.[63] The UK's strategy was to opt in post-adoption only if the measure in its final form was

[55] Consolidated version of the Treaty on the Functioning of the European Union PROTOCOL (No 21) on the Position of the United Kingdom and Ireland in Respect of the Area Of Freedom, Security and Justice [2016] OJ C202/295.

[56] Directive 2014/41/EU of the European Parliament and of the Council of 3 April 2014 regarding the European Investigation Order in criminal matters [2014] OJ L130/1.

[57] House of Commons European Scrutiny Committee, *The European Investigation Order and Parliamentary Scrutiny of Opt-in Decisions, Oral Evidence* (6 July 2011, HC 1416) Q1.

[58] Mitsilegas and Guild (n 34).

[59] A Tinsley, 'Protecting Criminal Defence Rights through EU Law: Opportunities and Challenges' (2013) 4(4) *New Journal of European Criminal Law* 461.

[60] House of Lords European Union Committee, *Breaking the Deadlock: what future for EU procedural rights?* (2nd Report of Session 2006-07, HL Paper 20) paras 21–24.

[61] Directive 2013/48/EU of the European Parliament and of the Council of 22 October 2013 on the right of access to a lawyer in criminal proceedings and in European arrest warrant proceedings, and on the right to have a third party informed upon deprivation of liberty and to communicate with third persons and with consular authorities while deprived of liberty [2013] OJ L 294/1. Also see D Giannoulopoulos, 'Fair trial rights in the UK post Brexit: Out with the charter and EU law, in with the ECHR?' (2016) 7(4) *New Journal of European Criminal Law* 389.

[62] Mitsilegas (n 1) 56.

[63] Mitsilegas and Guild (n 34).

considered acceptable. This was clear in the late adoption of the Directive on trafficking in human beings,[64] where Damian Green stated the UK had opted in once it was 'absolutely sure that the text would not change during those negotiations in a way that would be detrimental to the integrity of the UK's criminal justice system'.[65]

Protocol 21 was negotiated partly because of the grave concerns the UK had about the EU's plans to develop a European Public Prosecutors Office (EPPO). The body would be responsible for the investigation and prosecuting of crimes against the financial interest of the EU. In the end, the UK would not need Protocol 21 to opt out of the EPPO. Article 86 TFEU introduced an exception to the ordinary decision-making procedure when it proposed the establishment of the EPPO. Eurosceptics viewed the EPPO, first set out in the Corpus Juris Project in 1997, with alarm. Exceptionally, the UK Government was so concerned that it introduced a requirement for a referendum into UK law before the UK could specifically participate in the EPPO, via the European Union Act 2011.[66] Spencer argues that the EPPO was rejected 'not on the basis of what the proposal actually contains, but a conception of it that bears no relation to what was actually proposed; a distorted version propagated by the Eurosceptic press and then internalised by the Conservative party'.[67] Mainstream newspapers ran with headlines such as 'Alarm over Euro-wide justice plan' and 'Freedom's flame flickers'.[68] The People's Pledge was a political campaign aiming to bring about a referendum on the UK's membership of the EU. It argued in a blog that the EPPO would be the end of 'Britain's most ancient and hallowed liberties', adding 'Could there be a better reason to vote for withdrawal from the EU?'[69]

## V. The Development of the EU's External Dimension in Police and Judicial Cooperation

The rapid development of internal EU action in criminal matters has been accompanied by a strong emphasis on external action, particularly since the entry into force of the Treaty of Amsterdam.[70] To fully understand the relationship negotiated between the UK and EU on the UK's exit from the Union, it is important to consider how the EU has cultivated its external relationships and the way it has developed as an actor on the

[64] Directive 2011/36/EU on preventing and combating trafficking in human beings and protecting its victims, and replacing Council Framework Decision 2002/629/JHA, [2011] OJ L101/1.

[65] HC Deb 9 May 2011, vol 527, col 977.

[66] European Union Act 2011, s 6(5)(c). For further comment, see J Spencer, 'The UK and EU criminal law: Should we be leading, following or abstaining?' in V Mitsilegas, P Alldridge and P Cheliotis (eds), *Globalisation, Criminal Law and Criminal Justice. Theoretical, comparative and transnational perspectives* (Hart Publishing, 2015).

[67] J Spencer, 'Who's Afraid of the Big, Bad European Public Prosecutor?' (2011) 14 *Cambridge Yearbook of European Legal Studies* 363.

[68] House of Lords Select Committee on the European Communities, *Prosecuting Fraud on the Communities' Finances: The Corpus Juris* (9th Report of Session 1998-99, HL Paper 62).

[69] Cited in Spencer (n 61). Website no longer active.

[70] Treaty of Amsterdam amending the Treaty on European Union, the Treaties establishing the European Communities and certain related acts [1997] OJ C340/1. See for further discussion V Mitsilegas, 'The External Dimension of EU Action in Criminal Matters' (2007) 12(4) *European Foreign Affairs Review* 457.

international stage. Strengthening borders within the AFSJ is perceived as one of the most obvious ways for the EU to deliver on its mandate to provide a 'high level of security', to be achieved through measures in the field of police and judicial cooperation.[71] The shock of 9/11 brought another paradigm shift when terrorism was recognised as a key threat requiring 'better coordination between EU external action and JHA policies'.[72] This was followed in 2005 by the creation of Frontex, which has since rapidly grown. The expansions of the EU in 2004 and 2007 also required increased efforts to foster reform and increase capacity prior to accession. Attempts to foster judicial reforms in Central and Eastern European countries have resulted in a successful programme of 'policy transfer' through development of transnational networks that 'socialise judicial staff'.[73] For example, the EUROMED project aims to enhance capacity of the Southern Partner Countries to fight serious and organised crime and to strengthen strategic cooperation between national law enforcement authorities.[74] Such projects are not limited to the EU's immediate borders. For instance, the EU contributed to the anti-terrorism programmes of the Jakarta Centre for Law Enforcement and in supporting law enforcement and intelligence cooperation to fight cocaine trafficking from Latin America.[75] The 2005 external AFSJ strategy acknowledges the growing importance of the external dimension, recognising that 'internal and external aspects of EU security are intrinsically linked'.[76] In shaping the fight against crime in other states, the EU has incrementally consolidated its role as a 'global crime fighter'.[77]

From the early 2000s, the EU also launched itself as an international actor capable of negotiating agreements with third countries on behalf of Member States. The first to be agreed were the EU–US agreements on extradition and mutual legal assistance.[78] These were followed by several negotiated Passenger Name Record (PNR) agreements with the US, Canada and Australia, to deal with conflict-of-laws issues arising after legislative changes were brought in following 9/11 to improve security. These agreements have been highly controversial and resulted in multiple challenges through the CJEU.[79] Throughout this period the EU was criticised for allowing its own standards to be compromised in order to achieve its broader political aims of cooperation.

[71] J Monar, 'The Integration of Police and Judicial Cooperation in Criminal Matters into EU external Relations. Achievements and Problems' in C Fijnaut and J Ouwerkerk (eds), *The Future of Police and Judicial Cooperation in the EU* (Brill, 2010) 49.

[72] Council of the European Union, *European Security Strategy – A Secure Europe in a Better World* (Brussels, 8 December 2003) 15895/03: 15.

[73] D Piana, 'Unpacking Policy Transfer, Discovering Actors: The French Model of Judicial Education Between Enlargement and Judicial Cooperation in the EU' (2007) 5 *French Politics* 33.

[74] European Commission, *EURO-MED Partnership*, Regional Strategy Paper 2002–2006 (Brussels, 2002) 33–35.

[75] Monar (n 66).

[76] Communication from the Commission, 'A Strategy for the External Dimension the area of Freedom, Security and Justice' COM(2005) 491.

[77] A Russo and E Stambol, 'The external dimension of the EU's fight against transnational crime; Transferring political rationalities of crime control' (2022) 48(2) *Review of International Studies* 326.

[78] Council Decision 2003/516/EC of 6 June 2003 concerning the signature of the Agreements between the EU and the USA on extradition and mutual legal assistance in criminal matters [2003] OJ L181/25; V Mitsilegas, 'The New EU-US Co-operation on Extradition, Mutual Legal Assistance and the Exchange of Police Data' (2003) 8(4) *European Foreign Affairs Review* 515.

[79] E De Capitani, 'Passenger name records (PNR) data: How the EU is promoting (virtual) security by actually limiting Passengers' fundamental rights' (2003) 29(1-2) *European law Journal* 212.

The EU in these negotiations, on its own admission, opted for a more moderate and cooperative approach.[80] The EU has also been involved in the development of transnational law through participation in international treaties.[81] For example, in 2006 the EU reached an agreement with the International Criminal Court on cooperation and assistance.[82] The EU also acceded to multiple UN instruments such as the UN Protocol to Prevent, Supress and Punish Trafficking in Persons in 2004 and in 2005 the UN Convention against Corruption.[83] It has been a key actor in UN Security Council matters and in other international institutions, such as the Financial Action Task Force, leading to what is described as the 'global production of norms in criminal matters'.[84] This can be seen most recently during the negotiation of the Second Protocol to the Budapest Convention, where the EU sought to shape the treaty to ensure compatibility with EU law.[85]

## VI. Conclusion

From intergovernmental cooperation, EU criminal law has grown to an established policy field at the core of the European project. The AFSJ plays an important role in ensuring the safety of people across Europe but has had contested impacts on fundamental rights. As a policy field, it has been one of the most difficult to develop. All Member States have battled with the contradictory pressures to address rising cross-border crime through removing barriers to cooperation whilst maintaining sovereignty and control over their own national criminal law and procedures.[86] The development of the AFSJ has required concessions some states have been more easily able to make than others.

Tensions between sovereignty and operational need have been particularly present in the UK's cooperation in the field. As we have seen, the UK has at time been the driver towards further integration, particularly on matters of practical cooperation, but also deeply mistrusting of losing sovereignty in the criminal sphere. The EU responded

[80] Communication from the Commission to the Council and the Parliament, 'Transfer of Air Passenger Name Record (PNR) Data: A Global EU Approach, COM (2003) 826 final, 5.

[81] According to Arts 18 and 37 TEU, the Presidency represents the EU as far as Title VI matters are concerned, and may express the position of the EU in international organisations and at international conferences. By virtue of Arts 19 and 37, Member States are also under an obligation to coordinate their actions within international organisations and at international conferences and to defend the common positions adopted under Title VI TEU.

[82] Council Decision 2006/313/CFSP of 10 April 2006 concerning the conclusion of the Agreement between the International Criminal Court and the European Union on cooperation and assistance [2006] OJ L115/49; Council Decision 2009/426/JHA of 16 December 2008 [2009] OJ L138/27.

[83] Protocol to Prevent, Suppress and Punish Trafficking in Persons, Especially Women and Children, Supplementing the United Nations Convention against Transnational Organized Crime (entered into force 15 November 2000) 2237 UNTS 319; United Nations Convention Against Corruption (entered into force 14 December 2005) 2349 UNTS vol 41.

[84] V Mitsilegas, 'The European Union and the Globalisation of Criminal Law' (2010) 12 *Cambridge Yearbook of European Legal Studies* 337.

[85] Second Additional Protocol to the Convention on Cybercrime on enhanced co-operation and disclosure of electronic evidence 2022 (CETS No 224).

[86] H Wallace, W Wallace and M Pollack (eds), *Policy-Making in the European Union*, 5th edn (Oxford University Press, 2005).

flexibly, allowing the UK to participate on a case-by-case basis post Lisbon, despite criticisms that this could undermine the legitimacy and coherence of the AFSJ. There is doubt over whether the UK's pick-and-choose approach would have been sustainable in the long term.[87] The UK trod a cautious path, mediating between the clear operational need for cooperation, voiced by senior practitioners and academics through parliamentary committees and the Eurosceptic backbenchers and popular press who 'systematically misinformed' the British public about the risks posed by integration in the field.[88] This led to the 'opt-in-opt-out' saga, described by Yvette Cooper, then Shadow Home Secretary, as a 'massive game of hokey-cokey'.[89] The EPPO project and fears of a path towards a fully centralised European prosecutor, for example, were well articulated to the British public and undoubtedly contributed to the 2016 referendum and its outcome. This history also explains why, despite its ultimate exit from the Union, the UK continued to have a clear focus on preserving operational and practical cross-border cooperation to the greatest extent possible.[90]

At the same time, police and criminal justice in the AFSJ has developed a strong external dimension, leading to the EU's emergence as an important actor on the international stage. Institutions such as Europol have embraced third-party cooperation as the EU developed its strategy to export its own police and judicial standards, with success. The response of the CJEU to external agreements in the field of police and judicial cooperation because of data protection and fundamental rights concerns has curtailed or slowed the Commission's aspirations, but has also provided a justification for the further exporting of EU standards within international agreements. The EU's increased willingness to extend operational cooperation to third states has provided fertile ground for cooperation with the UK. On the other hand, as will be seen throughout this volume, it means that UK action is, and will continue to be, dictated by the need to ensure alignment with EU data protection legislation and fundamental rights.

[87] Mitsilegas (n 1) 56.
[88] Spencer (n 61).
[89] HC Deb 15 July 2013, vol 566 (36), col 791.
[90] House of Lords (n 27).

# 3

# From the Brexit Referendum to the Withdrawal Agreement

HELENA CARRAPICO AND GEMMA DAVIES

## I. Introduction – The Political Context of the Brexit Referendum

Following a long track record of internal disagreements within the Conservative Party as to the ideal direction of the relationship between the United Kingdom (UK) and the European Union (EU), as well as the growing politicisation of the relationship in the media more widely, David Cameron promised, in 2013, to organise a referendum on the UK's membership of the EU.[1] This promise, which set the wheels in motion in a process that would eventually result in the UK's leaving the EU, should be considered in its wider political context. Although criticism of the EU had been present in the UK's political landscape since before the UK's accession in 1973, it considerably accelerated from the late 1990s onwards, a period that was characterised by Conservative Party apprehensions about the significant EU policy and institutional expansion that accompanied the signing of the Maastricht and Amsterdam Treaties,[2] as well as by the consolidation of strongly Eurosceptic fringe parties, such as UKIP and the BNP.[3] When David Cameron assumed the leadership of the Conservative Party in 2005, he sought to put these concerns to rest[4] by enacting several changes aimed at appeasing the Eurosceptic members of his Party. The 2013 referendum promise and its inclusion

[1] D Cameron, EU speech at Bloomberg (23 January 2013) available at www.gov.uk/government/speeches/eu-speech-at-bloomberg (last accessed 16 January 2025).

[2] A Alexandre-Collier, 'Euroscepticism under Margaret Thatcher and David Cameron: From Theory to Practice' (2015) 17 *Observatoire de la société Britannique* 115 available at doi.org/10.4000/osb.1778; Treaty of Maastricht amending the Treaty on the European Union, the Treaties establishing the European Communities and certain related acts [1992] OJ C191/1; Treaty of Amsterdam amending the Treaty on European Union, the Treaties establishing the European Communities and certain related acts [1997] OJ C340/1.

[3] T Bale, 'Why David Cameron called the 2016 referendum – and why he lost it, UK in a changing Europe' (2022) available at https://ukandeu.ac.uk/why-david-cameron-called-the-2016-referendum/ (last accessed 16 January 2025).

[4] D Cameron, Leader's Speech in Bournemouth (2006) available at www.britishpoliticalspeech.org/speech-archive.htm?speech=314 (last accessed 16 January 2025).

in the 2015 Conservative Party electoral manifesto are therefore part of a longer process of politicisation of the UK–EU relationship.

Following an unexpected 2015 electoral result that saw the Conservative Party win a majority of seats, the Government enacted its electoral promises by putting forward the legal basis for a consultative referendum through the European Union Referendum Act 2015.[5] During this period, the Prime Minister also made use of his electoral mandate to renegotiate the UK's membership of the EU,[6] namely, by proposing to introduce (i) an emergency break, preventing EU citizens residing in the UK from claiming benefits for the first four years of residence, (ii) a red card system, aimed at further increasing EU subsidiarity, and (iii) guarantees that no EU competences would be introduced to realise an 'ever-closer union'. Encouraged by the concessions obtained by the UK during the 2015/2016 renegotiation, David Cameron announced the referendum for the 23 June 2016, when he hoped the UK population would vote 'Remain'.[7]

During the referendum campaign, key Eurosceptic politicians, supported by a panoply of pro-leave movements (such as Vote Leave, Leave.eu, and Grassroots Out), associated the EU with the UK's lack of funding for public services, its increased number of immigrants, a reduced capacity to enact its own legislation and trade agreements, costs that outweighed its benefits and being out of sync with UK priorities.[8] In the words of one of these movements, 'the EU is undermining democracy, prosperity, and international cooperation. … It is hostile to the combination of world-class universities, technological innovation, and venture capital that is fundamental to technological innovation.'[9] Pro-remain movements (including Britain Stronger in Europe, British Influence, and European Movement UK), on the other hand, attempted to highlight the important risks to the economy, to the trade relationship with the EU, and ultimately to the UK's leadership role within the EU and beyond.[10] These movements' lack of strategy and difficulty in conveying the advantages of EU membership in accessible ways would, however, severely impact the referendum result.[11]

Bearing in mind both this background and chapter 2's analysis of the historical development of UK–EU police and judicial cooperation in criminal matters, this chapter proposes to explore, first, how these topics were discussed during the referendum campaign and its immediate aftermath, followed by an analysis of the negotiations leading to the endorsement of the Withdrawal Agreement and of the Political Declaration. The chapter makes the argument that the referendum result led to considerable upheaval and polarisation within the UK political landscape, which partly spilled

[5] For the complete text of the European Union Referendum Act 2015, see at www.legislation.gov.uk/ukpga/2015/36/contents/enacted (last accessed 16 January 2025).

[6] House of Commons, *UK Government's Renegotiation of EU Membership: Parliamentary Sovereignty and Scrutiny* (14th Report of Session 2015–16) available at https://publications.parliament.uk/pa/cm201516/cmselect/cmeuleg/458/458.pdf (last accessed 16 January 2025).

[7] T Bale, *The Conservative Party After Brexit: Turmoil and Transformation*, 1st edn (Polity, 2023).

[8] N Farage, 'Nigel Farage makes Victory Speech' *You Tube, The Guardian News* (24 June 2016) available at www.youtube.com/watch?v=MPbDONLZwXQ (last accessed 16 January 2025).

[9] Vote Leave, '"Leave" looks like …, Vote Leave' (2016) available at www.voteleavetakecontrol.org/briefing_newdeal.html (last accessed 16 January 2025).

[10] Britain Stronger in Europe, 'Why Britain is Stronger in Europe' (2016) available at https://nawo.org.uk/wp-content/uploads/2016/01/Britain-Stronger-In-Europe-Key-Briefings.pdf (last accessed 16 January 2025).

[11] A Fagan and S van Kessel, *The Failure of Remain- Anti-Brexit Activism in the United Kingdom* (McGill-Queen's University Press, 2023).

over into discussions on police and judicial cooperation. Despite initially harbouring optimistic visions for the future of the UK–EU relationship, successive rounds of negotiation ultimately led to a more limited approach by the UK Government, which is reflected in both the Withdrawal Agreement and the Political Declaration. The conclusion of the chapter examines the domestic challenges encountered in securing a successful vote on these two documents and transitioning to the negotiation of the future relationship.

## II. Law Enforcement and Judicial Cooperation in the Referendum Campaign

Law enforcement and judicial cooperation topics were present during campaign discussions, although to a considerably more limited extent than other higher-profile subjects such as the economy or immigration.[12] Leave proponents, such as Michael Gove and Dominik Raab, made the case that EU membership was weakening the UK's border control capability, affecting the UK's surveillance powers and threatening its security more generally.[13] More specifically, free movement of EU citizens, and EU citizens themselves, were portrayed as a security risk to the UK: 'It is now the EU and the Luxembourg Court that present the clear and present danger to our security. They put their ivory tower dogma of EU free movement ahead of the safety of our citizens.'[14] Given the country's perceived inability to control EU citizens entering and settling in the UK, this risk was based on speculation regarding free movement as facilitating the circulation of criminals and terrorists.[15] Pro-Leave movements also made the case that the UK's capacity to decide on the powers of law enforcement and intelligence agencies, as well as on extradition, was controlled by the Court of Justice of the European Union (CJEU) and hindered by the Charter of Fundamental Rights.[16] Brexit, on the other hand, was presented as enabling the UK 'to regain control of our borders, including far stronger powers over who we can deport, and [implement] proper preventative checks at the border'.[17]

Practitioners also expressed their views on the impact of Brexit for their work. One of the former Heads of MI6, Richard Dearlove, argued that the view that the UK would be less secure outside of the EU was not a credible one because the UK would still

[12] H Carrapico, A Niehuss and C Berthelemy, *Brexit and Internal Security- Political and Legal Concerns on the Future UK–EU Relationship* (Palgrave Macmillan, 2019).

[13] Vote Leave (2016) 'Gove and Raaab: EU membership makes us less safe' (2016) available at www.voteleave-takecontrol.org/gove_and_raab_eu_membership_makes_us_less_safe.html (last accessed 21 March 2024).

[14] R Dearlove, Interview on *BBC World* (2016) available at www.voteleavetakecontrol.org/sir_richard_dear-love_speech_at.html (last accessed 2 April 2024).

[15] Vote Leave, Press Release, 'EU's Open Border System is like hanging a sign welcoming terrorists to Europe' (2015) available at ww.ukpol.co.uk/press-release-eus-open-border-system-is-like-hanging-a-sign-welcoming-terrorists-to-europe/ (last accessed 16 January 2025).

[16] Vote Leave, Briefing, 'Security – Vote Leave is the Safer Option' (2016) available at www.voteleavetakecon-trol.org/briefing_safety.html (last accessed 21 March 2024); Charter of Fundamental Rights of the European Union [2012] OJ C326/391.

[17] Vote Leave (n 13).

remain a leader in counter-terrorism, and in security more generally, and that the quality of cooperation with EU countries was not dependent on EU membership:

> [T]he urgency of counter terrorist work, the quality of the EU's expertise, the practical and moral imperatives that drive liaison exchanges and the shared revulsion when terrorist violence is unleashed on innocent citizens is what binds the UK into excellent intelligence and security relations with every individual EU member.[18]

Vote Leave also made use of other practitioners' views, even if they were not originally related to Brexit, to further support their campaign. The case of Ron Noble, former Secretary-General of Interpol, is a particularly good example, with his views on Schengen being used to undermine trust in EU databases and instruments: the EU's open borders are 'like hanging a sign welcoming terrorists to Europe'.[19]

Remain proponents, such as Theresa May, on the other hand, made the case that the UK would be less safe if it left the EU.[20] She emphasised the enhanced efficiency brought by these instruments in combating international crime and underscored the significant benefits the UK had derived from them. Drawing upon crime and law enforcement statistics, as well as historical cases such as the extraditions of Hussain Osman and Rachid Ramda, she contemplated the potential impact of withdrawing from EU instruments such as the European Arrest Warrant (EAW), the Schengen Information System II (SIS II) or the Passenger Name Record (PNR) Agreement. Echoing the arguments she had engaged with during the mass opt-out discussions of 2012/2014 in her role as Secretary of State for the Home Department (see chapter 2), she argued that addressing transnational threats necessitated more than merely closing borders; it demanded increased cooperation with EU partners. These arguments were also reflected in the Government's Brexit campaign leaflet[21] and widely circulated by the Britain Stronger in Europe movement,[22] which added that leaving the EU would also have a detrimental effect on the UK's security leadership in the EU, in particular on the capacity to influence the direction of the Area of Freedom, Security and Justice (AFSJ).

It was not only the political community that was divided over law enforcement and judicial cooperation matters, the practitioner community was equally split. Among the most vocal was the former Europol Director, Rob Wainwright, who responded to Richard Dearlove's remarks by highlighting that UK law enforcement saw the advantages of working with Europol and with EU instruments on a daily basis.[23] The former heads of MI6 and MI5, John Sawers and Jonathan Evans, joined him and added that

[18] Dearlove (n 14).

[19] R Noble, 'Europe's Welcome Sign to Terrorists' *New York Times* (19 November 2015) available at www.nytimes.com/2015/11/19/opinion/europes-welcome-sign-to-terrorists.html (last accessed 2 April 2024).

[20] T May, 'Home Secretary's Speech on the UK, EU and Our Place in the World' (2016) available at www.gov.uk/government/speeches/home-secretarys-speech-on-the-uk-eu-and-our-place-in-the-world (last accessed 20 March 2024).

[21] UK Government, 'Why the Government believes that voting to remain in the European union is the best decision for the UK' (2016) available at https://assets.publishing.service.gov.uk/media/5a8055a4e5274a2e87db9392/why-the-government-believes-that-voting-to-remain-in-the-european-union-is-the-best-decision-for-the-uk.pdf?ref=quillette.com (last accessed 20 March 2024).

[22] See n 10.

[23] R Mason, 'Europol Chief: Brexit would be a mistake for UK security' *The Guardian* (24 March 2016) available at www.theguardian.com/uk-news/2016/mar/24/europol-chief-rob-wainwright-brexit-mistake-uk-security-richard-dearlove (last accessed on 2 April 2024).

'the reason we would be less safe is that we would be unable to take part in the decisions that frame the sharing of data, which is a crucial part of counter-terrorism and counter-cyber work that we do these days'.[24]

Reflecting the rest of the campaign, Remain arguments often attempted to highlight specialist knowledge, make use of statistics and make appeals to reason. While there is evidence suggesting that such discourse resonated positively within communities with particular security apprehensions (Bove et al, for example, discuss how these arguments played out in areas affected by terrorist violence[25]), the strategy of emphasising the advantages of European internal security and the potential risks associated with its diminution did not sway a significant proportion of the electorate. Instead, this segment tended to prioritise other more pressing concerns, prove more responsive to emotional appeals and overlook the immediate benefits of the EU.[26] Conversely, the Leave campaign was particularly successful at creating a coherent dual romantic narrative,[27] which it also applied to the law enforcement and judicial cooperation field. On the one hand, it framed Brexit in particularly positive and optimistic terms, projecting a nation-building vision, where the UK would be able to fulfil its perceived potential and become a world leader. Richard Dearlove's views on the UK's counter-terrorist capabilities and leadership potential are particularly representative of this narrative. On the other hand, the Leave campaign was successful at stirring up feelings of distrust and anger against the Establishment, in particular the EU Establishment, which was framed in negative terms, as being inefficient, overbearing, in crisis and threatening.[28] The views expressed by Michael Gove and Dominik Raab on the security threat posed by free movement are particularly illustrative of the narrative's duality. Ultimately, the coherence of the Leave campaign narrative, bolstered by sustained political and media disparagement of the EU, along with a call for immediate action against the perceived status of the UK within the EU, proved to be a winning strategy, as 52 per cent of the electorate voted to leave on the 23 June 2016.

## III. The Aftermath of the Referendum

Following the Brexit vote, the UK entered a soul-searching, if not topsy turvy, phase. From June 2016 until the invocation of Article 50, the Government was focused on trying to understand how to interpret and implement the referendum result, and how to define its position ahead of upcoming negotiations with the EU.[29] The result came as

[24] 'Row as ex-intelligence chiefs say EU membership protects UK security' *BBC News* (8 May 2016) available at www.bbc.co.uk/news/uk-36239741 (last accessed 2 April 2024).

[25] V Bove, G Efthyvoulou and H Pickard, 'Did Terrorism Affect Voting in the Brexit Referendum?' (2022) 52(3) *British Journal of Political Science* 1133, doi:10.1017/S0007123420000927.

[26] T Coutto, 'Half-full or half-empty? Framing of UK–EU relations during the Brexit referendum campaign' (2020) 42(5) *Journal of European Integration* 695.

[27] A Spencer and K Oppermann, *The Brexit Policy Fiasco* (Routledge, 2021).

[28] B Bennett, '"Crisis" as a discursive strategy in Brexit referendum campaigns' (2019) 16(4) *Critical Discourse Studies* 449.

[29] B Martill, 'Deal or no Deal: Theresa May's Withdrawal Agreement and the Politics of (Non-)Ratification' (2021) 59(6) *Journal of Common Market Studies* 1607; Treaty of Lisbon Amending the Treaty on European Union and the Treaty Establishing the European Community [2007] OJ C306/1.

a surprise to most political actors, including the UK Government, and limited thought had in practice been given to the different political options involved in exiting the EU. This initial phase is marked by significant political uncertainty, evident not only in the resignation of Prime Minister David Cameron and his replacement by Theresa May, but also in the challenge of reaching a compromise on how to implement Brexit and develop a shared vision for the future UK–EU relationship. Not wishing to be perceived as supporting a Remain agenda and sensing the urgency in delivering on her referendum mandate, the new Prime Minister promised to rise to the challenge at 'a time of great national change',[30] claiming that 'Brexit means Brexit – and we're going to make a success of it'. In her first key speech on the relationship with the EU, May prioritised developing an ambitious global vision for the UK after Brexit, as a 'fully-independent, sovereign country' that would be able to control its borders, make its own laws and create its own relationship with the EU without the need to follow pre-existing models.[31]

Despite considerable political impetus to move forward, little progress was made specifically in relation to law enforcement and judicial cooperation. In her Lancaster speech, in January 2017, the Prime Minister attempted to sketch the Government's vision of the future relationship and its objectives for the negotiations.[32] She announced that the UK would strive for the inclusion of law enforcement and judicial cooperation in criminal matters in the future UK–EU relationship, recognising the significance of cooperation within the current challenging security landscape. The shared interests and shared values of the UK and EU would be at the heart of the future partnership, which would be key to addressing crime and terrorism. In line with some of the principal concerns expressed during the referendum discussions, Theresa May also announced the Government's intention to terminate free movement, thereby extending migratory controls to EU citizens, and to cease the jurisdiction of the CJEU, seen as encroaching upon the UK's sovereignty. At this stage, however, little detail was provided as to what that law enforcement and judicial partnership would entail, and how it could be accomplished outside of the Court's jurisdiction. As such, important questions regarding law enforcement and judicial cooperation remained unanswered at this stage, namely, what access the UK would be able to obtain to Europol or Eurojust if it rejected the Court's jurisdiction, whether EU Member States would be willing to extradite suspects if the UK no longer had access to the EAW, or even what would happen to this area of cooperation if a deal could not be reached with the EU? This is despite the existence of important instances of reflection, including a thorough report by the House of Lords on the future law enforcement relationship.[33]

[30] T May, 'Statement from the new Prime Minister Theresa May' *gov.uk* (2016) available at www.gov.uk/government/speeches/statement-from-the-new-prime-minister-theresa-may (last accessed on 2 April 2024).

[31] T May, 'Read Theresa May's keynote speech to the Conservative conference in full' *The Independent* (5 October 2016) available at www.independent.co.uk/news/uk/politics/theresa-may-speech-tory-conference-2016-in-full-transcript-a7346171.html (last accessed 2 April 2024).

[32] T May, 'The Government's Negotiating Objectives for Exiting the EU: PM Speech' *gov.uk* (2017) available at www.gov.uk/government/speeches/the-governments-negotiating-objectives-for-exiting-the-eu-pm-speech (last accessed 3 April 2024).

[33] House of Lords, *Brexit: Future UK-EU Security and Police Cooperation. European union Committee* (7th Report of Session 2016–17) available at https://publications.parliament.uk/pa/ld201617/ldselect/ldeucom/77/77.pdf (last accessed 3 April 2024).

Bringing this initial phase to a close, Theresa May triggered Article 50 of the Treaty of Lisbon, on 29 March 2017, through a letter addressed to the European Council.[34] The document laid out the UK's broad priorities for its future relationship with the EU, namely a 'deep and special partnership' covering both economic and security cooperation. It clearly states that 'in security terms, a failure to reach agreement would mean our cooperation in the fight against crime and terrorism would be weakened'. While the letter represents a significant historical milestone, formally commencing the countdown on the two-year negotiation window, its primary significance lies in reflecting domestic pressures within the UK, rather than indicating substantial progress in establishing a detailed negotiation position. In fact, over the nine months that had elapsed since the referendum, the UK Government had been preoccupied not only with delivering Brexit, but also with healing the deep rifts that had emerged within the Conservative Party and, more importantly, within the country itself.[35] Confronted with the genuine prospect of a dis-United Kingdom, the Government sought to navigate a delicate balance between fulfilling its perceived Brexit mandate and mitigating tensions between Leave and Remain voters. Additionally, it aimed to prevent increased political conflict between the countries that voted to remain in the EU (Scotland and Northern Ireland) and those that did not (England and Wales). The potential for constitutional disruption was particularly visible following the Scottish Parliament's symbolical vote to reject the triggering of Article 50.[36] This difficult balancing act, coupled with limited reflection on the different Brexit modalities and their policy impact, drew repeated international criticism regarding the vagueness of the Government's plans, as well as pressure to start negotiations.[37]

## IV. The Divorce Negotiations – The Withdrawal Agreement

This phase of the Brexit negotiations presented itself as a particularly challenging one, given the objectives set by the UK Government and the two-year timeframe defined by Article 50 (which included not only the negotiation of an agreement but also its ratification). The Government hoped to settle on a specific negotiation position, secure a withdrawal agreement (also often referred to as the divorce agreement), obtain the support of Parliament for that agreement, define the parameters and legal format of the future UK–EU post-Brexit relationship, and launch a new foreign policy looking

[34] T May, Prime Minister's Letter to Donald Tusk Triggering Article 50 (2017) available at https://assets.publishing.service.gov.uk/media/5a7481c140f0b646cbc40610/Prime_Ministers_letter_to_European_Council_President_Donald_Tusk.pdf (last accessed 2 April 2024).

[35] L McGowan (2018) *Preparing for Brexit: Actors, Negotiations and Consequences*. Cham, Switzerland: Palgrave macmillan.

[36] S Carrell, 'Scottish Parliament Backs Symbolic Motion Rejecting Article 50' *The Guardian* (7 February 2017) available at www.theguardian.com/uk-news/2017/feb/07/scottish-parliament-backs-symbolic-motion-rejecting-article-50 (last accessed 3 April 2024).

[37] C Stoddard, 'Donald Tusk: Brexit talks should start soon' *Politico* (8 September 2016) available at www.politico.eu/article/donald-tusk-brexit-talks-should-start-soon-theresa-may-referendum-europe-future-consequences/ (last accessed 3 April 2024).

beyond the EU, aimed at framing Britain as truly global.[38] As this section argues, during this phase, the UK Government's stance on law enforcement and judicial cooperation in criminal matters began to crystallise, as this policy domain gained prominence within the withdrawal negotiations and the development of the Political Declaration. This development occurred, however, and as outlined in section III, against a backdrop of ongoing domestic and international pressures, which continued to increase throughout this phase.

The primary objective of the initial phase of negotiations, which commenced in June 2017, was to reach an agreement on the UK's exit terms, ultimately named the Withdrawal Agreement.[39] It was established with the EU that once broad exit terms were agreed, both negotiation teams would start a parallel process where they would start putting forward proposals for the future UK–EU relationship post-Brexit (which would in time become known as the second UK–EU agreement, the Trade and Cooperation Agreement (TCA)).[40] The underlying purpose of the Withdrawal Agreement was to ensure that the UK's exit would take place in an orderly manner, one that would create a transition period able to reduce political and legal uncertainty for citizens and businesses. Following on from the EU's adoption of the Brexit negotiation procedures and guidelines,[41] three main issues were positioned at the heart of the withdrawal negotiations: citizens' rights (would EU citizens residing in the UK and UK citizens residing in the EU continue to have a right to remain and, if so, under what conditions?); the financial settlement (what financial commitments had the UK made to the EU as a Member State?); and the Northern Ireland border (how to ensure that the Good Friday Agreement would be respected and that no physical border would be built). In addition to these particularly pressing issues, other separation matters were identified, including Euratom, goods placed on the market before Brexit, on-going Union procedures and, more importantly for this volume, law enforcement and judicial cooperation in criminal matters.

On this last specific issue, both the UK and the EU aimed to clarify the expected outcome of ongoing procedures in police and judicial cooperation in criminal matters. These included the issuing of EAWs, mutual legal assistance requests, freezing or confiscation orders, and access to databases. Unlike the three main issues driving the Withdrawal Agreement negotiations, there was general consensus on both sides regarding the law enforcement and judicial cooperation one, namely on the idea that structured and formalised cooperation procedures ongoing at the time of withdrawal should be allowed to continue and eventually be completed. It was also quickly agreed that the CJEU would remain the competent body to oversee those procedures. Despite

[38] May (2016) (n 31).

[39] Agreement on the Withdrawal of the United Kingdom of Great Britain and Northern Ireland from the European Union and the European Atomic Energy Community [2020] OJ L29/7.

[40] Trade and Cooperation Agreement between the European Union and the European Atomic Energy Community, of the one part, and the United Kingdom of Great Britain and Northern Ireland, of the other part [2021] OJ L444/14.

[41] European Council, 'European Council (Art 50) guidelines for Brexit negotiations' (2017) available at www.consilium.europa.eu/en/press/press-releases/2017/04/29/euco-brexit-guidelines/ (last accessed 5 April 2024).

agreement on the broad principles, some details required lengthier negotiation.[42] For instance, by December 2017 (after six rounds of negotiations), the precise list of instruments or procedures permitted to continue had not yet been finalised, nor had the duration for which they would be permitted to continue been determined. In addition, by the end of August 2018, it was still unclear what standards should be applied to personal data transmitted to the UK in the context of police investigations. The time taken to reach an agreement in law enforcement and judicial cooperation, however, was largely influenced by the prioritisation of other, more challenging issues (specifically, the Northern Ireland border), rather than by any significant difficulties encountered in negotiating this area. Any remaining disagreements in this field were finally settled by October 2018,[43] with the remainder of the Withdrawal Agreement completed by 18 November 2018.

Where law enforcement and judicial cooperation in criminal matters was concerned, the text of the Agreement provided that 'the elements of the Justice and Home Affairs policy will continue to apply to the United Kingdom during the transition period, and the UK will remain bound by EU acts applicable to it upon its withdrawal'.[44] It warned, however, that at the end of the transition, the UK would be disconnected from all EU databases and networks, unless a new agreement provided otherwise. While this implied that the majority of the UK's involvement in the AFSJ would persist unchanged until the end of the transition, certain exemptions underscored that, even before Brexit formally occurred, the UK–EU relationship was no longer business as usual. In other words, it involved the loss of the right to opt into entirely new AFSJ measures (under Protocols 19 and 21 to the Treaty of Lisbon) and Member States' ability to refuse the extradition of their own nationals to the UK in the context of EAWs.[45]

## V. The Divorce Negotiations – The Political Declaration

If the main objective of this phase of Brexit negotiations was for both parties to agree on a legal text that would enable the UK's orderly withdrawal from the EU, the secondary objective was to start a conversation about what the UK–EU relationship could look like post-Brexit. The latter was to be summarised in a document, which would in time become known as the Political Declaration, and which would serve as a broad framework for the negotiation of the future relationship (the TCA negotiations). Having

[42] European Commission, 'Communication from the Commission to the European Council (Art 50) on the state of progress of the negotiations with the United Kingdom under article 50 of the Treaty on European Union' COM(2017) 784 final (8 December 2017) available at file:///Users/kcpw6/Downloads/COM(2017)784_0.pdf (last accessed 5 April 2024).

[43] T May, 'PM's Statement on European Council: 22 October 2018' available at www.gov.uk/government/speeches/pms-statement-on-european-council-22-october-2018 (last accessed 6 April 2024).

[44] Agreement on the Withdrawal of the United Kingdom of Great Britain and Northern Ireland from the European Union and the European Atomic Energy Community, Part Three, Title V available at https://commission.europa.eu/strategy-and-policy/relations-non-eu-countries/relations-united-kingdom/eu-uk-withdrawal-agreement_en (last accessed 6 April 2024).

[45] M Pencheva, *EU–UK Police and Judicial Cooperation in Criminal Matters* (Palgrave Macmillan, 2021).

considered that sufficient progress had been achieved on the Withdrawal Agreement by December 2017, the EU proposed starting a parallel process where both parties would start discussing their visions for their post-Brexit relationship.[46]

Although the prioritisation of this policy field had already been established by the Prime Minister in her January 2017 speech on the UK's negotiation objectives and in her letter triggering Article 50, a first comprehensive position would be published in September, two months after the EU released its own position on this topic. In 'Security, law enforcement and criminal justice: a future partnership paper',[47] the UK Government expanded on its original idea that continued cooperation was key to ensuring the safety and security of both UK and EU citizens. Recognising that it would no longer be able to benefit from the AFSJ's toolkit in the same way as Member States, the UK Government was, nonetheless, focused on negotiating a substantially more ambitious future agreement than the ones in force with third countries. As part of this ambition, it proposed that the post-Brexit relationship should prioritise (i) the facilitation of data-driven law enforcement (including accessing databases such as Prüm, ECRIS, PNR and the SIS II); (ii) provision of practical assistance to operations (through instruments such as the European Investigation Order, Joint Investigation Teams and the EAW); and (iii) access to EU law enforcement and judicial cooperation agencies (Europol and Eurojust). This future cooperation would not only be bespoke but would also not be subject to the direct jurisdiction of the CJEU, with a dispute resolution mechanism needing to be negotiated.

These ambitious objectives were subsequently echoed by the Prime Minister in landmark speeches, such as the September 2017 Florence speech and the February 2018 Munich speech. In the first, Theresa May struck an amicable tone, reiterating the UK's unconditional commitment to European security in the face of shared threats, highlighting the shared values of liberty, democracy, human rights and the rule of law, and outlining the UK's contribution to this area: '[T]he United Kingdom has outstanding capabilities … world class security, intelligence and law enforcement services.'[48] In Munich, following several arduous negotiation rounds, her tone turned ominous as she sought to further defend the UK's proposal for a creative and unique approach aimed at replicating most of the existing cooperation. The Prime Minister expanded on the UK's contributions to the AFSJ in considerable detail, while also cautioning that failure to pursue a more ambitious agreement would amount to demagoguery, with 'damaging real-world consequences for the security of all our people'.[49] This was a warning

[46] D Tusk, 'Statement by President Donald Tusk on the draft guidelines for the second phase of the Brexit negotiations' (2017) available at www.consilium.europa.eu/en/press/press-releases/2017/12/08/statement-by-president-donald-tusk-on-second-phase-brexit/ (last accessed 6 April 2024).

[47] HM Government, 'Security, law enforcement and criminal justice: a future partnership paper' (2017) available at https://assets.publishing.service.gov.uk/media/5a820450e5274a2e8ab570f1/Security__law_enforcement_and_criminal_justice_-_a_future_partnership_paper.PDF (last accessed 4 April 2024).

[48] T May, 'PM's Florence speech: a new era of cooperation and partnership between the UK and the EU' *gov.uk* (2017) available at www.gov.uk/government/speeches/pms-florence-speech-a-new-era-of-cooperation-and-partnership-between-the-uk-and-the-eu (last accessed on 2 April 2024).

[49] T May, 'PM speech at Munich Security Conference: 17 February 2018' (2018) available at www.gov.uk/government/speeches/pm-speech-at-munich-security-conference-17-february-2018 (last accessed 7 April 2024).

that the UK Government would frequently reiterate, principally in its paper 'The Future Relationship between the United Kingdom and the European Union' (July 2018),[50] where it responded to the EU's view that the future relationship would always need to take into account the fact that the UK would become a third country outside of Schengen and could not enjoy the same benefits as Member States. It is clear from this document that the negotiation rounds had been challenging and that the UK had had to reconsider its original objective of replicating pre-Brexit access to law enforcement and judicial cooperation instruments. Instead, by the summer of 2018, the UK's position had shifted towards prioritising the development of operational processes closely aligned with EU tools and databases. The Political Declaration was eventually agreed on 22 November 2018, shortly after the Withdrawal Agreement. The text reflects a more tempered vision of the UK–EU relationship, where the UK and the EU propose to continue comprehensive cooperation in law enforcement and judicial cooperation, but one that takes into account the UK's future status as a non-Schengen third country.[51] The Declaration foresees cooperation in three main areas: (i) data exchange; (ii) operational cooperation between authorities; and (iii) anti-money laundering and counterterrorism financing, making explicit reference to instruments such as PNR, Prüm, Europol, Eurojust and Joint Investigation Teams, and the creation of streamlined procedures for the surrender of suspected and convicted individuals. While these three areas broadly align with the UK's original September 2017 proposal, the scope of cooperation is significantly constrained by the UK's future status, restricting its access to several instruments and databases, including SIS II. Importantly, the Political Declaration also stipulates that cooperation in this field is contingent upon adherence to the European Convention on Human Rights,[52] a notable point considering that the UK negotiation team initially requested its omission.[53]

## VI. Conclusion – Moving on to the Negotiation of the Future Relationship?

With both the Withdrawal Agreement and the Political Declaration agreed by the UK and the EU, this phase of the Brexit negotiations ended with their endorsement by the

[50] UK Government, 'The Future Relationship between the United Kingdom and the European Union' (2018) available at https://assets.publishing.service.gov.uk/media/5c8f805440f0b640d60882b1/The_Future_Relationship_between_the_United_Kingdom_and_the_European_Union_120319.pdf (last accessed 7 April 2024).

[51] UK Government and European Commission, 'Political Declaration setting out the Framework for the Future Relationship between the European Union and the United Kingdom' (2018) available at https://assets.publishing.service.gov.uk/media/5bfa8708e5274a2aeac7b4a0/25_November_Political_Declaration_setting_out_the_framework_for_the_future_relationship_between_the_European_Union_and_the_United_Kingdom__.pdf (last accessed 7 April 2024).

[52] European Convention for the Protection of Human Rights and Fundamental Freedoms (European Convention on Human Rights, as amended) (adopted 4 November 1950, entered into force 3 September 1953) ETS 5.

[53] Pencheva (n 43).

European Council on 25 November 2018. After an unexpected and polarising referendum result, and amid a politically turbulent post-referendum period, negotiations were marked by a swift acknowledgement by both parties of the significance of law enforcement and judicial cooperation in criminal matters. This was also a phase marked by the continued commitment of the UK to the AFSJ, not only rhetorically but also in practice, with the Government making the decision to continue to opt in to numerous JHA initiatives.[54] However, it was also characterised by a prolonged negotiation process regarding the details of withdrawal and the future relationship.

So what does Brexit mean in this policy area? Despite a degree of domestic contestation, the UK Government started negotiations on a particularly optimistic note, pushing for a transition period that would enable on-going procedures to be completed and for a future relationship that would replicate the kind of cooperation from which it had benefitted pre-Brexit. It soon realised, however, that its future non-Schengen third-country status was understood by the EU as an important limitation to the kind of cooperation that could take place post-Brexit. While the Withdrawal Agreement ensured that cooperation would largely remain unchanged during the transition phase, it also served as an indication of challenges ahead, with Member States gaining the ability to reject UK-issued EAW requests for their own nationals. Building on this, the Political Declaration has set the tone for the negotiation of the future relationship, clearly signalling that Brexit would significantly alter UK–EU law enforcement and judicial cooperation. While it offers the prospect of some access to EU databases, instruments and agencies, it excludes others, such as the SIS II and the EAW, in which the UK had expressed interest.

While the European Council's endorsement of the Withdrawal Agreement and the Political Declaration was significant, it did not automatically lead to their entry into force. Both documents needed to be voted on by the UK Parliament, and the actual withdrawal had to take place. However, more than a year would pass before this occurred – a year marked by an escalation in domestic political conflict, stemming not only from the Opposition[55] but also from Conservative Party members themselves. Although most of this conflict was related to the Northern Ireland arrangement, the law enforcement and judicial cooperation elements of the documents were also a target of criticism. Richard Dearlove, for example, tried to lobby for the rejection of Theresa May's deal on national security grounds: 'the prime minister's Brexit deal would surrender the UK's forces and intelligence services to EU control … it would damage the UK's relationship with NATO, the US, and the leading Commonwealth security and intelligence partners'.[56]

[54] Home Office and Ministry of Justice, 'JHA (Title V) opt-in and Schengen opt-out decisions taken between the 1 December 2009 and the present' (2018) available at https://assets.publishing.service.gov.uk/media/5aba786bed915d78bc23496e/Opt-in_webpage_update_-_data_-_March_2018.pdf (last accessed 8 April 2024).

[55] K Starmer, 'Britain after Brexit: Speech at Leeds Beckett University' (2017) available at www.youtube.com/watch?v=V3Ng7z9PHXo (last accessed 4 April 2024).

[56] J Craig, 'Ex-MI6 and defence chiefs warn Tory MPs to vote down Brexit deal that threatens national security' *Sky News* (10 January 2019) available at https://news.sky.com/story/theresa-mays-brexit-deal-threatens-national-security-ex-mi6-chief-sir-richard-dearlove-warns-11603738 (last accessed 8 April 2024).

As a result of this upheaval, MPs rejected both documents not just once but three times – in January and twice in March 2019 – in one of the largest defeats in Parliament's history. This led to the Prime Minister's stepping down and to the election of a new Conservative Party leader. Chapter 4 will examine how the UK Government addressed the lack of agreement to move forward with negotiations on the future relationship, as well as how this phase progressed and ultimately resulted in the TCA.

# 4

# The Trade and Cooperation Agreement – Preparation, Negotiation and Outcomes for Police and Judicial Cooperation in Criminal Matters

HELENA CARRAPICO AND GEMMA DAVIES

## I. Introduction

The signing of the Withdrawal Agreement[1] and of the Political Declaration[2] by the United Kingdom (UK) and the European Union (EU) in November 2018 took place during yet another politically fraught period in the UK.[3] As mentioned in chapter 3, the year that followed the signing of the documents was characterised by an escalation in domestic political tensions, fuelled equally by members of Opposition parties and by members of the Conservative Party. This internal conflict would reveal the existence of different UK approaches to the future relationship with the EU, including the future police and judicial cooperation relationship, and pave the way for a new UK Government, led by Boris Johnson. This chapter starts by discussing this relevant political context, which is key to understanding the direction of travel in the Trade and Cooperation Agreement[4] (TCA) negotiations. It aims to discuss the impact of the governmental changes on UK negotiation positions, as well as the resulting strain on the UK–EU relationship, which grew increasingly tense over the course of the negotiations. Ultimately, the chapter analyses both the UK and EU negotiation positions on

[1] Agreement on the Withdrawal of the United Kingdom of Great Britain and Northern Ireland from the European Union and the European Atomic Energy Community [2020] OJ L29/7.

[2] European Union and United Kingdom, 'Political Declaration Setting Out the Framework for the Future Relationship Between the European Union and the United Kingdom' (adopted 17 October 2019) [2019] OJ C384 I/191.

[3] F Fabbrini, 'The Brexit Negotiations and the May Government' (2019) Special Issue 2 *European Journal of Legal Studies* 1.

[4] Trade and Cooperation Agreement between the European Union and the European Atomic Energy Community, of the one part, and the United Kingdom of Great Britain and Northern Ireland, of the other part [2021] OJ L444/14.

police and judicial cooperation, and presents the changes brought about by the TCA in this field. The latter serve as a basis for the detailed discussions in the remainder of this edited volume, which explore the issues that have emerged since the TCA began to be implemented.

In section II, the chapter explores the intensified preparations that were carried out for a 'no-deal Brexit' scenario, following the repeat rejection of the Withdrawal Agreement and Political Declaration. It highlights the assumed implications for police and judicial cooperation in criminal matters, as well as the mitigating plans that were put in place to address such implications. Section III then explores the political fallout from the repeated rejection, and the consequent changes both to the UK Government and to its approach to the negotiations. It highlights that the new Prime Minister, Boris Johnson, adopted a tougher stance, insisting on the renegotiation of the Withdrawal Agreement and threatening a 'no-deal Brexit', which eventually resulted in the approval of a revised agreement and allowed for the negotiations on the future relationship to start. Section IV analyses the specific negotiation of police and judicial cooperation, during which the UK sought to maintain access to law enforcement agencies and information systems, as well as to develop new mutual legal assistance and extradition mechanisms. The chapter points out that, unlike other policy areas, the new UK Government's position on police and judicial cooperation was fairly well aligned with that of the previous Government, despite the changes in overall rhetoric. Section V is dedicated to the outcome of the negotiation for this policy field. It underlines that although the UK and the EU were able to secure an important level of cooperation, which respects the red lines of both parties, the relationship has, nevertheless, changed significantly. It is now a slimmed-down relationship, where the UK may have maintained some access to EU agencies, information-sharing systems and mutual legal assistance, but where its role and influence have now been considerably reduced.

## II. The Pre-TCA Negotiations' Context: The Fallout from the Withdrawal Agreement Rejections and the Acceleration of 'No-deal' Preparations

Debate and scrutiny of the Withdrawal Agreement and of the Political Declaration documents began in the UK Parliament on 9 January 2019, with concerns over the feasibility of the Agreement quickly intensifying. The points of contention, raised by both Remain and Leave Members of Parliament (MPs), primarily revolved around the uncertainty created by the Agreement and the accompanying Declaration. Remain MPs, particularly those in Opposition, viewed the negotiated outcome as falling far short of the level of cooperation the UK had previously enjoyed, with some still harbouring hopes of steering the process towards a second referendum.[5] Leave MPs, on the other

[5] J Corbyn, HC Deb 15 January 2019, vol 652, cols 1108–1109, available at https://hansard.parliament.uk/commons/2019-01-15/debates/2504FA7B-45BE-423D-8971-E451EF0594A9/EuropeanUnion(Withdrawal)Act (last accessed 1 October 2024).

hand, perceived the Withdrawal Agreement and the Political Declaration as a betrayal of the 2016 referendum result, as the documents implied that Northern Ireland would partly be kept in the Single Market (this part of the Agreement is also known as the Irish backstop).[6] The debate also covered police and judicial cooperation in considerable detail, with disagreements focusing on the extent to which the Withdrawal Agreement and the governmental red lines regarding the future UK–EU relationship were expected to impact on citizens' safety and security.[7] Despite the guarantees provided by Prime Minister Theresa May, which included letters of assurance from the EU institutions[8] and from EU Member States, Parliament voted to reject the Withdrawal Agreement and the Political Declaration on 15 January 2019 (432 votes against, 202 votes for).

Following the rejection, Theresa May pursued further talks with the EU, which remained supportive of the Prime Minister's efforts to ratify the negotiated documents but firmly stated that there would be no renegotiation.[9] This support was provided in the form of further legal assurances[10] (including a new legal instrument[11] and a statement supplementing the Political Declaration[12]) clarifying that the backstop would only be a temporary measure and that negotiations on the future relationship would start as soon as the Agreement and the Declaration were ratified. However, these assurances again proved insufficient to dissuade MPs, and the UK Government suffered new defeats on 12 March 2019 (391 votes against, 242 for) and 29 March 2019 (344 votes against, 286 for). The unexpected results sent shockwaves through the UK and EU political landscapes, leading the UK Government to ask for repeated extensions to the Article 50 period[13] and for the 'no-deal Brexit' scenario to gain prominence among possible future avenues.

[6] J Rees-Mogg, Letter urging MPs to oppose the draft Withdrawal Agreement (14 November 2018) available at https://brexitcentral.com/text-jacob-rees-moggs-letter-urging-mps-oppose-draft-withdrawal-agreement/ (last accessed 1 October 2024).

[7] D Abbott, HC Deb 11 January 2019, vol 652, col 708, available at https://hansard.parliament.uk/commons/2019-01-11/debates/DBEB14BC-9AE7-4965-9DC9-3C5B273B8CE7/EuropeanUnion(Withdrawal)Act (last accessed 1 October 2024).

[8] D Tusk and JC Junker, Joint Letter of President Tusk and President Junker to Theresa May, Prime Minister of the United Kingdom (14 January 2019) available at www.consilium.europa.eu/en/press/press-releases/2019/01/14/joint-letter-of-president-tusk-and-president-juncker-to-theresa-may-prime-minister-of-the-united-kingdom/ (last accessed 1 October 2024).

[9] F Figueira and B Martill, 'Bounded rationality and the Brexit negotiations: why Britain failed to understand the EU' (2020) 28(12) *Journal of European Public Policy* 1871 available at https://doi.org/10.1080/13501763.2020.1810103.

[10] JC Junker, Letter to President Tusk (11 March 2019) available at www.consilium.europa.eu/media/41013/20190311-letter-president-juncker-tusk.pdf (last accessed 1 October 2024).

[11] Council of the European Union, Instrument relating to the agreement on the withdrawal of the United Kingdom of Great Britain and Northern Ireland from the European Union and the European Atomic Energy Community, XT 21014/19 (20 March 2019) available at https://data.consilium.europa.eu/doc/document/XT-21014-2019-INIT/en/pdf (last accessed 1 October 2024).

[12] Council of the European Union, Joint Statement supplementing the Political Declaration setting out the framework for the future relationship between the European Union and the United Kingdom of Great Britain and Northern Ireland, XT 21018/19 (20 March 2019) available at https://data.consilium.europa.eu/doc/document/XT-21018-2019-INIT/en/pdf (last accessed 1 October 2024).

[13] T May, Request by the United Kingdom for an extension under Article 50 TEU (20 March 2019), available at https://data.consilium.europa.eu/doc/document/XT-20005-2019-INIT/en/pdf; and T May, Request by the United Kingdom for a new extension under Article 50 TEU (5 April 2019) available at https://assets.publishing.service.gov.uk/government/uploads/system/uploads/attachment_data/file/793058/PM_letter_to_His_Excellency_Mr_Donald_Tusk__1_.pdf (last accessed 1 October 2024).

Although preparations for a 'no-deal' scenario had been underway on both sides, especially since the summer of 2018, there was a noticeable increase in the pace of preparations following the repeated rejections of the negotiated agreement.[14] Where police and judicial cooperation was concerned, 'no deal' planning clearly indicated that the UK and the EU would become entirely disconnected from each other in terms of access to information systems and databases, and that the UK would become reliant on Council of Europe and on United Nations Conventions, as well as on multilateral organisations, such as Interpol, in order to liaise with EU Member States.[15] The EU Commission ensured that EU Member States had access to the necessary information in order to build contingency plans and fallback options. The UK also allocated substantial resources to expedite ongoing police investigations, and worked closely with partner countries to strengthen bilateral relations and understand the implications of Brexit from their institutional and legislative standpoints.[16] For example, as part of its collaboration with Europol liaison officers, a document was drafted to specify how cooperation would operate with each partner EU Member State.[17] Partner countries were advised to revise their Secure Information Exchange Network Application (SIENA) matrix to guarantee that the UK would still receive alerts usually designated for EU countries. Investigations already in progress were fast tracked, and priority cases were flagged.[18] Efforts were made to resolve pending requests and warrants while uploading relevant information to the Interpol I-24/7 system in preparation for the potential loss of access to the Schengen Information System (SIS II). This was supported through the creation of the UK-wide International Crime Coordination Centre (ICCC),[19] which offered training and resources, and through the secondment of officers. Established in September 2018, with temporary Brexit funding, the ICCC was intended to minimise Brexit's impact on policing in the UK and has proved to be a valuable asset (see Pearson, chapter 6). Its primary focus was on identifying EU policing tools to which the UK was expected to lose access, creating contingency plans for each, and promoting awareness of the tools that would remain available post-Brexit. The ICCC also developed and delivered training for officers, established connections with EU partner agencies, enhanced the use of international tools within UK policing and established a 24/7 helpline (see Thomson,

[14] Council of the European Union, General Affairs Council (Art 50) 19/03/2019, 19 March 2019, available at www.consilium.europa.eu/en/meetings/gac-art50/2019/03/19/ (last accessed 1 October 2024); and Department for Exiting the European Union, 'UK government's preparations for a "no-deal" scenario' (21 December 2018) available at www.gov.uk/government/publications/uk-governments-preparations-for-a-no-deal-scenario/uk-governments-preparations-for-a-no-deal-scenario (last accessed 7 October 2024).

[15] European Commission, 'A No-Deal Brexit: Police and Judicial Cooperation' (April 2019) available at https://brexit.com.cy/assets/img/PDF/ALLA/factsheet_police_and_judicial_coordination_final.pdf (last accessed 7 October 2024).

[16] S Fella, 'Planning for a no-deal Brexit' Briefing Paper no 8733 (2019) (House of Commons Library_ available at https://commonslibrary.parliament.uk/research-briefings/cbp-8733/ (last accessed 7 October 2024).

[17] G Davies and H Carrapico, UK–EU Law Enforcement and Judicial Cooperation in Criminal Matters under Part Three of the Trade and Cooperation Agreement: the impact on Scotland, Policy Paper of the Scottish Parliament (2024).

[18] G Davies, 'Facilitating Cross-Border Criminal Justice Cooperation Between the UK and Ireland After Brexit: "Keeping the Lights On" to Ensure the Safety of the Common Travel Area' (2021) 85(2) *The Journal of Criminal Law* 77, doi.org/10.1177/0022018320977528.

[19] National Police Chiefs Council, 'UK Policing as Prepared as Possible for a Potential no-deal Exit' (11 October 2019) available at https://news.npcc.police.uk/releases/uk-policing-as-prepared-as-possible-for-a-potential-no-deal-eu-exit (last accessed 7 October 2024).

chapter 11). A major initiative of the ICCC was to train and expand the number of officers authorised to use the Interpol I-24/7 system as a substitute for SIS II. Furthermore, it developed an application for frontline officers, offering clear instructions on managing cases involving foreign nationals. The ICCC has since been merged into the National Crime Agency (NCA) and the United Kingdom International Crime Bureau (UKICB), and has been renamed the Joint International Crime Centre (JICC), currently operating as a fully funded unit with permanent personnel.

## III. Negotiation Preparations – Different UK Administration, Different Priorities?

Faced with the EU's refusal to renegotiate the Withdrawal Agreement, the failure to find a compromise with Opposition parties, a poor performance of the Conservative Party at the European Parliament elections and growing calls from her own party to stand down, Theresa May announced her resignation, effective from 7 June 2019.[20] The resignation prompted a Conservative Party leadership contest, resulting in Boris Johnson's achieving his leadership aspirations, being declared the new Prime Minister in July 2019.[21] The election marked an important shift in the UK's approach to its relationship with the EU, the Prime Minister adopting a considerably less cooperative stance regarding the ratification of the Withdrawal Agreement and Political Declaration.[22]

Boris Johnson resumed talks with the EU, highlighting that the negotiated deal in its current form would not gain approval by Parliament. He called for a renegotiation of the Withdrawal Agreement that would include the deletion of the Irish backstop, and made it clear that he was prepared to pursue a no-deal Brexit if the EU refused to revisit the Agreement.[23] The weeks that followed were characterised by considerable conflict and paralysis, with both sides accusing each other of bad faith and ideological blindness. The situation was ultimately resolved through a UK proposal to replace the Irish backstop with a single regulatory zone covering the entire island of Ireland, thereby introducing regulatory checks between Great Britain and Northern Ireland. This proposal, which modified around 5 per cent of the Withdrawal Agreement, left the section on police and judicial cooperation unchanged. Although the European Commission was initially sceptical of the UK's proposal, viewing it as an untested approach that could undermine the integrity of the Single Market and as lacking legal feasibility,[24] bilateral discussions

[20] F Biermann and S Jagdhuber, 'Take it *and* leave it! A postfunctionalist bargaining approach to the Brexit negotiations' (2021) 45(4) *West European Politics* 793, doi.org/10.1080/01402382.2021.1901039; and 'Theresa May quits: UK set for new PM by end of July' *BBC News* (24 May 2019) available at www.bbc.co.uk/news/uk-politics-48395905 (last accessed 7 October 2024).

[21] T Bale, The Conservative Party After Brexit: turmoil and transformation (Polity 2023).

[22] J Curtis et al, 'The October 2019 EU–UK Withdrawal Agreement' Briefing Paper no CB8713 (2019) (House of Commons Library) available at https://researchbriefings.files.parliament.uk/documents/CBP-8713/CBP-8713.pdf (last accessed 7 October 2024).

[23] B Johnson, HC Deb 3 October 2019, vol 664, cols 1383- 1384, available at https://hansard.parliament.uk/commons/2019-10-03/debates/585F872D-9372-4448-A32F-5CEC0FD49FB7/BrexitNegotiations (last accessed 8 October 2024).

[24] M Barnier, Statement by Michel Barnier at the European Parliament Plenary Session (9 October 2019) available at https://ec.europa.eu/commission/presscorner/detail/en/STATEMENT_19_6055 (last accessed 8 October 2024).

between the UK and the Republic of Ireland facilitated a compromise, ultimately leading to a revised Agreement. Securing domestic approval in the UK, however, proved to be more challenging, prompting the Prime Minister to call a General Election to gain the mandate he believed was necessary to pass the Withdrawal Agreement through Parliament. Following a Conservative Party's decisive victory with a strong majority, the Withdrawal Agreement and Political Declaration were approved by the House of Commons (358 votes in favour and 234 against) on 20 December 2019. Upon ratification by both parties, the UK's departure from the EU was made effective on 31 January 2020.

The UK's exit from the EU, and the implementation of the Withdrawal Agreement, initiated a transition period (also referred to as 'implementation period' by the UK Government) during which the two parties agreed to negotiate their future relationship. The period, the end date of which was set as 31 December 2020, aimed to provide both parties with the necessary stability to explore different alternatives regarding the future relationship, by temporarily retaining numerous features of the UK's membership. The Withdrawal Agreement foresaw keeping the UK as a member of the Single Market and of the Customs Union during that phase, as well as maintaining free movement, citizens' rights, and most of Justice and Home Affairs' cooperation. With regard to police and judicial cooperation, as outlined in chapter 3, although much of the relationship remained intact, it could no longer be treated as business as usual. The UK lost its right to opt in to new measures in the Area of Freedom, Security and Justice (AFSJ) (under Protocols 19 and 21 of the Treaty of Lisbon),[25] and Member States also gained the ability to deny the extradition of their own nationals to the UK under the framework of the European Arrest Warrant (EAW).[26]

Negotiations on the future relationship started on 2 March 2020, following the Council of the European Union's adoption of the negotiation mandate and of the European Commission's negotiation directives.[27] Given the unusually short length of the transition period (11 months from the date of exit), both parties agreed to meet every two to three weeks for negotiation rounds.[28] Although UK–EU relations had been experiencing a significant degree of turbulence and politicisation for some years, the arrival of Boris Johnson in the UK Government, as mentioned above, represented an important rhetorical shift in the way the UK administration engaged with the EU, as well as a change in political priorities.[29] Boris Johnson had established a history of vocal criticism towards the EU, in his roles both as a politician and a journalist, which became

[25] Protocol (No 19) on the Schengen Acquis Integrated into the Framework of the European Union' [2007] OJ C306/158; Protocol (No 21) on the Position of the United Kingdom and Ireland in Respect of the Area of Freedom, Security and Justice' [2007] OJ C306/160.

[26] Withdrawal Agreement (n 1). See also M Pencheva, *EU–UK Police and Judicial Cooperation in Criminal Matters* (Palgrave Macmillan, 2021).

[27] Council of the European Union, 'EU-UK Relations – Council gives the go-ahead for talks to start and adopts negotiating directives' Press Release (25 February 2020) available at www.consilium.europa.eu/en/press/press-releases/2020/02/25/eu-uk-relations-council-gives-go-ahead-for-talks-to-start-and-adopts-negotiating-directives/ (last accessed 9 October 2024).

[28] For more information on the negotiation terms, see 'Terms of Reference on the UK–EU Future Relationship Negotiations' available at https://commission.europa.eu/document/download/6c4e341c-10ed-4c9a-a9f7-824513f37a63_en?filename=terms-of-reference-eu-uk-future-relationship.pdf.

[29] M Brusenbauch Meislova and B Bujard, 'Prime ministerial political leadership and the domestic politics of Brexit: Theresa May and Boris Johnson compared' (2024) 19 *British Politics* 268.

especially visible when he emerged as central figure within the Leave campaign.[30] Not only had he recurrently discussed what he considered to be the 'anti-democratic absurdities' of the EU through a particularly populist rhetorical style,[31] but he also often expressed British exceptionalist views, characterised by a British superiority stance and the expectation of special treatment from the EU.[32] Johnson's comments on May's negotiated Withdrawal Agreement illustrate his views particularly well: 'It is a humiliation. We look like a seven-stone weakling being comically bent out of shape by a 500lb gorilla. We have wrapped a suicide vest around our constitution and handed the detonator to Brussels.'[33] It is therefore unsurprising that his views and political approach led to a tougher UK negotiation stance, efforts to backtrack on previously agreed commitments, a move away from regulatory alignment, a reduction in the scope of the envisioned UK–EU relationship, and a shift towards increased confrontation, diminished trust and heightened diplomatic tension.[34] Under the Johnson Premiership, Brexit was understood as the ultimate priority of the Government and articulated through anti-EU rhetoric: hard exit was presented in a positive light and dissent was labelled as treason to the will of the British people.[35]

Overall, the intention to create a comprehensive relationship envisaged by Theresa May's Government was replaced with the desire to pursue a much more slimmed-down partnership. Soon after stepping into No 10 Downing Street, Boris Johnson argued that the 'proposed future relationship [contained in the Political Declaration] is not the goal of the current UK Government. The Government intends that the future relationship should be based on a Free Trade Agreement in which the UK takes control of its own regulatory affairs and trade policy.'[36] In addition to the Free Trade Agreement, he proposed that additional international agreements be signed on a more ad hoc basis, namely on fisheries, internal security, aviation and civil nuclear cooperation. His justification was based on the understanding that a thicker relationship with the EU was not to the UK's advantage from the perspective of the country's sovereignty.[37] This approach was defined as the ability of UK institutions to shape the country's legal framework

[30] B Johnson, 'Voting to stay in the EU is the risky option', *Vote Leave* (6 June 2016) available at www.voteleavetakecontrol.org/voting_to_stay_in_the_eu_is_the_risky_option.html (last accessed 8 October 2024).

[31] B Farrand and H Carrapico, '"People like that cannot be trusted": populist and technocratic political styles, legitimacy, and distrust in the context of Brexit negotiations' (2021) 17(2) *Journal of Contemporary European Research* 1, available at www.jcer.net/index.php/jcer/article/view/1186/909 (last accessed 16 January 2025).

[32] A MacKenzie, S Léonard and C Kaunert, '"They Need Us More than We Need Them": British Exceptionalism, Brexit, and Justice and Home Affairs' (2020) 25(4) *European Foreign Affairs Review* 573.

[33] 'Boris Johnson and Jeremy Hunt debate the Chequers deal' *Mail Online* (8 September 2018) available at www.dailymail.co.uk/news/article-6146853/BORIS-JOHNSON-JEREMY-HUNT-debate-Chequers-deal.html (last accessed 7 October 2024).

[34] T Wille and B Martill, 'Trust and calculation in international negotiations: how trust was lost after Brexit' (2023) 99(6) *International Affairs* 2405, doi.org/10.1093/ia/iiad243.

[35] S Wolff, H Carrapico and A Piquet, 'Out of Sight, Out of Mind? UK–EU Member States Bilateralism as an Enabler of Europeanisation' *Journal of Common Market Studies* (29 September 2024), doi.org/10.1111/jcms.13690.

[36] B Johnson, 'A Fair and Reasonable Compromise: UK Proposals for a New Protocol on Ireland/Northern Ireland' (2 October 2019) available at https://assets.publishing.service.gov.uk/media/5d94b55b40f0b6422ce2df8d/PM_letter_to_Juncker_WEB.pdf (last accessed 11 October 2024).

[37] B Johnson, 'The Future Relationship between the UK and the EU. Written Statement to Parliament' (3 February 2020) available at www.gov.uk/government/speeches/the-future-relationship-between-the-uk-and-the-eu (last accessed 11 October 2024).

independently, ruling out any form of regulatory alignment, jurisdiction of the Court of Justice of the European Union (CJEU) or supranational oversight in any policy area. However, there appeared to be little consideration of the viability of such a strategy, both in terms of the EU's negotiating stance with third countries and its willingness to make concessions, as well as the practical challenges of navigating a disentangled economic, social and security relationship on the basis of a Free Trade Agreement and supplementary ad hoc international agreements.

## IV. The Negotiation of Police and Judicial Cooperation in Criminal Matters in the Context of the TCA

While this shift was notably reflected in the Government's overall rhetoric towards the EU, it is interesting to observe that it was not as apparent within the negotiations on police and judicial cooperation. A closer analysis of negotiations in this field reveals that although there is a clear change in political tone towards a more aggressive stance – highlighting the UK's central role in European internal security and need to achieve sovereignty in this area – as well as efforts to secure a separate agreement for this field, the broad objectives remained aligned with those identified by Theresa May's Government in 2017.[38] As outlined in chapter 3, Theresa May initially sought to replicate the UK's pre-Brexit police and judicial cooperation framework as closely as possible. However, following discussions with the Commission on what the EU was ready to negotiate, she had then settled on a more limited bespoke toolkit that aimed at facilitating data-driven law enforcement, practical assistance to operations, access to EU law enforcement and judicial cooperation agencies, and border management cooperation. Boris Johnson's Government aimed to pursue these same operational ambitions, highlighting that any future agreement would need to have its own proportionate governance system, with no role assigned to the CJEU.[39] More specifically, the Government proposed to negotiate four key elements:

1. Access to data:
   (a) the exchange of criminal records, including equivalent access to the European Criminal Records Information System (ECRIS);
   (b) the sharing of DNA, fingerprint and vehicle registration data through the Prüm database;
   (c) access to PNR data; and
   (d) real-time alerts on missing persons and objects, akin to SIS II.

[38] HM Government, 'Security, Law enforcement and Criminal justice – a Future Partnership Paper' (18 September 2017) available at https://assets.publishing.service.gov.uk/media/5a820450e5274a2e8ab570f1/Security__law_enforcement_and_criminal_justice_-_a_future_partnership_paper.PDF (last accessed 4 October 2024).

[39] HM Government, 'The Future Relationship with the EU – The UK's Approach to Negotiations' (February 2020) available at https://assets.publishing.service.gov.uk/media/5e579695e90e07110306a2f5/The_Future_Relationship_with_the_EU.pdf (last accessed 8 October 2024).

2. In terms of law enforcement cooperation, it sought to establish an operational partnership with Europol under a third-country arrangement, similar to that with the United States (US).
3. For judicial cooperation in criminal matters, it aimed at creating a comparable agreement with Eurojust – aligned with that sought for Europol – developing a surrender system that would replace the EAW, introducing new mutual legal assistance mechanisms and enabling the transfer of prisoners.
4. Additionally, the Government aimed to negotiate a separate agreement on asylum and migrant returns, which, although not part of police and judicial cooperation, would have a significant impact on police cooperation addressing illegal migration.

The EU, on the other hand, proposed a narrower form of cooperation, arguing that the UK was a non-Schengen country that should not 'enjoy the same rights and facilities as a Member State'.[40] If the EU recognised the importance of the shared security interests and geographical proximity of both parties, it also considered that the UK should not be allowed direct access to EU information systems (including SIS II), or take part in the management of EU agencies. The exchange of PNR data, DNA, fingerprint and vehicle registration data, as well as future cooperation with Europol and Eurojust, was presented as being open to negotiation, provided that access would be subject to strict data protection and oversight. The EU also proposed the streamlining of mutual legal assistance in criminal matters, including joint investigations and the exchange of criminal records – taking Council of Europe conventions as a basis. In addition, it suggested the creation of surrender procedures, on condition that Member States be allowed to declare that their own nationals would not be surrendered. Finally, the EU also expressed an interest in developing a single, more comprehensive agreement, as opposed to separate deals.

Analysing these two sets of proposals, we observe a willingness on both sides to develop a strong police and judicial cooperation relationship, albeit with some notable differences. Namely, the contrasting of the two sets of proposals reveals, on the one hand, a pragmatic interest on the side of the UK in negotiating an agreement that went beyond what other third countries had (in terms of access to data, databases and instruments) and, on the other hand, a more cautious EU approach in what it was willing to offer. First, regarding data exchange, there was a clear indication, from the EU, that the UK would not be allowed to access SIS II. This refusal was presented on both legal and political grounds: not only was there no legal route for a non-EU and non-Schengen country to access this database, but the European Parliament was also adamant that the UK had proved untrustworthy when dealing with SIS II data in the past.[41] Second,

[40] European Parliament, 'Resolution of 12 February 2020 on the Proposed Mandate for Negotiations for a New Partnership with the United Kingdom of Great Britain and Northern Ireland' [2020] OJ C294/29, available at www.europarl.europa.eu/doceo/document/TA-9-2020-0033_EN.pdf (last accessed 12 October 2024). Also see Council of the European Union, Annex to Council Decision authorising the opening of negotiations with the United Kingdom of Great Britain and Northern Ireland for a new partnership agreement, 5870/20, ADD 1 REV 3, 25 February 2020 available at www.consilium.europa.eu/media/42736/st05870-ad01re03-en20.pdf (last accessed 12 October 2024).

[41] The UK was accused of illegally copying SIS II personal information and sharing it with US companies. For more information, see N Nielsenm 'UK Unlawfully Copying Data From EU Police System' *EU Observer* (28 May 2018) available at https://euobserver.com/justice/141919 (last accessed 14 October 2024).

regarding judicial cooperation, two important differences stand out, namely, the proposed replacement of the EAW with a more limited surrender mechanism and no possibility of prisoner exchange. Third, migration and asylum did not feature in the EU's proposal, with the exception of references to a possible partnership with Europol to tackle organised immigration crime and to a dialogue on shared objectives to tackle irregular migration upstream, namely in third countries.

In addition to these significant differences, several challenges were expected to emerge over the course of negotiations, in particular regarding data adequacy and the risk of a UK exit from the European Convention on Human Rights (ECHR), both of which directly impacted the police and judicial cooperation policy area. Although UK discussions on a possible departure from the ECHR were not new and had never been acted on before,[42] the EU considered that such a possibility – or any changes to domestic human rights law impacting the implementation of the Convention – could endanger any future cooperation with the UK. In order to minimise such possibility, the EU's negotiation mandate clarified that a UK departure from the ECHR would automatically result in the termination of any future police and judicial cooperation, given the centrality of safeguarding human rights and fundamental freedoms, democratic principles and the rule of law in this field.[43] The EU also proposed introducing an important element of conditionality in the future relationship, requiring a data adequacy decision from the Commission, to confirm that the UK would continue to offer the level of data protection necessary to exchange criminal justice data. The adequacy decision would therefore not only dictate the level of ambition of the future agreement but would also serve as a ground for the latter's suspension.

Between March and December 2020, the UK and the EU met over the course of nine rounds of negotiations, all of which included police and judicial cooperation discussions.[44] Although both parties departed from the objective to develop a strong relationship in this policy field, progress was painstakingly slow and punctuated by serious friction. As expected, alignment with fundamental and individual rights and data protection issues would re-emerge at regular intervals during the negotiations (see Mallory, chapter 16). The EU recurrently attributed the lack of progress in police and judicial cooperation to the UK's refusal 'to provide firm guarantees – rather than vague principles – on fundamental rights and individual freedoms', as well as its insistence on 'lowering current standards and deviating from agreed mechanisms of data protection'.[45] Following the third round of negotiations, it would even accuse the UK

[42] During her tenure as Secretary of State for the Home Department (2010–16), Theresa May repeatedly argued in favour of departing from the ECHR, as she considered the Convention incompatible with Conservative legislative proposals in the area of immigration and counter-terrorism (for an example, see 'Theresa May: UK should quit European Convention on Human Rights' *BBC News* (25 April 2016) available at www.bbc.co.uk/news/uk-politics-eu-referendum-36128318 (last accessed 15 October 2024).

[43] See European Parliament (2020) and Council of the European Union (2020) (n 36).

[44] For an example of the negotiation agenda, see the agenda of the first round here at https://commission.europa.eu/publications/agenda-first-round-uk-eu-future-relationship-negotiations-02-05-march-2020_en (last accessed 15 October 2024).

[45] M Barnier, Press Statement by Michel Barnier following the Second Round of Future Relationship Negotiations with the United Kingdom (24 April 2020) available at https://ec.europa.eu/commission/presscorner/detail/en/statement_20_739 (last accessed 15 October 2024).

of 'asking the Union to ignore its own [data protection] law and the jurisprudence of the European Court of Justice on passenger data'.[46] It was only with the fourth round of negotiations that constructive discussions were reported in this area, following the UK's commitment to the ECHR. And even then, numerous questions remained as to how this commitment could be reflected, in practice, in the future agreement. This was particularly the case considering the UK's expressed negotiation red lines, namely, the refusal to provide the CJEU with a role in protecting fundamental rights in the context of the future relationship.[47]

Whereas the UK's negotiation statements were generally neutral in tone and avoided providing details as to the progress achieved on specific topics,[48] the EU declarations were often more candid, providing a deeper insight into the mounting friction within the relationship. In particular, the EU would more than once accuse the UK of back-tracking on the substance of the Political Declaration and on the ambition expressed in previous negotiations,[49] as well as acting in bad faith,[50] a view that culminated with the Commission's opening an infringement procedure against the UK for breaching its obligations under the Withdrawal Agreement.[51] Politicians in the UK, on the other hand, would also express their displeasure as to the EU's negotiation stance, when addressing domestic audiences. Ten weeks prior to the transition period deadline, the UK Prime Minister declared that trade and security negotiations would not continue unless the EU was willing to fundamentally change its approach, and that the country should prepare itself for a no-deal scenario on 1 January 2021.[52] This political tension would only start to dissipate with an increase in the intensity of negotiations from October onwards. Within two months, an agreement would be reached that included an important section on law enforcement and judicial cooperation in criminal matters, and which addressed the issues of fundamental rights and of data protection in a way that felt acceptable to both parties. Section V of this chapter summarises the outcome of the negotiations for this policy field, the implementation of which is then discussed in the remainder of the volume.

[46] M Barnier, Remarks by Michel Barnier following Round 3 of Negotiations for a New Partnership between the European Union and the United Kingdom (15 May 2020) available at https://ec.europa.eu/commission/presscorner/detail/en/speech_20_895 (last accessed 15 October 2024).

[47] M Barnier, Statement by Michel Barnier following Round 6 of Negotiations for a New Partnership between the European Union and the United Kingdom (23 July 2020) available at https://ec.europa.eu/commission/presscorner/detail/en/STATEMENT_20_1400 (last accessed 16 October 2024).

[48] D Frost, Statement following the Conclusion of Round 1 Negotiations with the EU (5 March 2020) https://no10media.blog.gov.uk/2020/03/05/statement-on-the-conclusion-of-the-first-round-of-negotiations/ (last accessed 16 October 2024).

[49] M Barnier, Statement by Michel Barnier following Round 4 of Negotiations for a New Partnership between the European Union and the United Kingdom (5 June 2020) available at https://ec.europa.eu/commission/presscorner/detail/en/SPEECH_20_1017 (last accessed 15 October 2024).

[50] See Barnier (15 May 2020) (n 42).

[51] European Commission, 'Withdrawal Agreement: European Commission sends letter of formal notice to the United Kingdom for breach of its obligations' Press Release (1 October 2020) available at https://ec.europa.eu/commission/presscorner/detail/en/ip_20_1798 (last accessed 16 October 2024).

[52] L O'Carroll et al, 'Boris Johnson tells UK: prepare for a no-deal Brexit' *The Guardian* (16 October 2020) available at www.theguardian.com/politics/2020/oct/16/boris-johnson-tells-uk-prepare-for-a-no-deal-brexit (last accessed 17 October 2024).

# V. TCA Outcomes in Police and Judicial Cooperation in Criminal Matters – A Steady but Downgraded Cooperation

Following the conclusion of TCA negotiations at the end of December 2020, Part Three of the Agreement reassured policymakers and practitioners that the UK and the EU would maintain an important level of cooperation on law enforcement and criminal justice. While the Withdrawal Agreement ensured that ongoing investigations remained uninterrupted during the transition period, the TCA ended the uncertainty that professionals in the field had been facing regarding the future relationship. Part Three of the TCA consists of 13 titles that cover three main areas: (i) continued access, from a third-country perspective, to EU agencies and information-sharing systems; (ii) mutual legal assistance; and (iii) a mechanism for surrendering wanted individuals. While the TCA represents the most comprehensive and in-depth agreement the EU has with any non-Member State in the area of police and judicial cooperation, the current arrangements also reveal an important departure from the pre-Brexit relationship the UK enjoyed. In addition to reduced access to EU tools, information and agencies, new challenges have arisen, such as declining UK strategic and operational influence, as well as maintaining mutual trust among the various actors involved (see Marks, chapter 5; Conway, Deane and Hayward, chapter 9).[53]

## A. Continued Access to EU Agencies and Information-sharing Systems

Titles V and VI of Part Three of the TCA allow UK authorities to maintain access to some EU agencies involved in police and judicial cooperation. While several agencies operate within the EU's AFSJ, such as the European Union Drugs Agency and the European Union Agency for Law Enforcement Training (CEPOL), the TCA restricts the UK's access to the two primary agencies in this field: Europol, the EU's law enforcement cooperation agency; and Eurojust, the EU agency for criminal justice cooperation (see Wade, chapter 12).[54] Titles V and VI are further supported by specific working arrangements with both agencies (see Cotroneo and Costantino, chapter 10).[55] Despite this positive outcome, however, the UK no longer participates in Europol and Eurojust's Management Boards or coordination structures, leaving it without any direct influence over the organisations' future direction. In addition, UK officers can no longer be employed at Europol's Operational and Analysis Centre. Officers who

[53] O Garner, 'Justice and Home Affairs' in F Fabbrini (ed), *The Law and Politics of Brexit*, vol III: *The Framework of New EU–UK Relations* (Oxford University Press, 2021) 157.

[54] House of Lords (2021) *Beyond Brexit- Policing, Law Enforcement and Security* available at https://lordslibrary.parliament.uk/beyond-brexit-policing-law-enforcement-and-security/ (last accessed 19 October 2024).

[55] A Working and Administrative Arrangement between the National Crime Agency and Europol was signed in September 2021 (see www.nationalcrimeagency.gov.uk/news/nca-and-europol-sign-up-to-a-new-working-arrangement), and a Working Arrangement between Eurojust and the Home Office was signed in December 2021 (see www.eurojust.europa.eu/news/eurojust-and-uk-home-office-sign-working-arrangement).

were in key roles, including strategic managers overseeing analysis projects, had to leave their posts when the UK exited the EU in 2021. The TCA has also had an impact on the UK's capacity to conduct police investigations with Member States. While the UK can still participate in Joint Investigation Teams (JITs), UK agencies can not initiate a JIT. Additionally, participation in JIT meetings and in training opportunities for British police officers are no longer funded by the EU or EU agencies. Furthermore, the UK also now faces limitations in terms of accessing the Europol databases on which it previously relied. Any information request now needs to be submitted to Europol for consideration, as no direct access to the databases has been granted. Although the SIENA is still available for sensitive data exchange, the UK only receives messages marked 'EU Restricted' and is excluded from information labelled 'EU Confidential', which includes intelligence data.

With regard to other information systems, the TCA provides access to DNA, fingerprint and vehicle registration data, as well as to PNRs, and partial access to criminal convictions. No access to SIS II has been negotiated. More specifically, Title II of Part Three allows for the automated transfer of DNA, fingerprint and vehicle registration data between the UK and EU, similar to the Prüm framework. When a query matches data in another state's database, further details can be requested through mutual legal assistance. The TCA ensures that the UK and EU Member States grant access to their data under the same conditions as for domestic authorities. Although vehicle registration data is foreseen, the UK has not yet signalled its readiness for the evaluation of this type of data. Under the TCA, countries are required to use a version of the European Vehicle and Driving Licence Information System (EUCARIS) to conduct automated searches of vehicle registration data, to which the UK currently does not have access. Interim cooperation was allowed until 30 June 2022, and since then the UK has reportedly been engaged in technical preparations to implement the vehicle registration data component of the Prüm system. Where Passenger Name Records (PNRs) are concerned, access to EU air travel departure data is provided for in Title III of Part Three, with rules largely mirroring the EU PNR Directive,[56] but with one notable exception. The UK is now required to delete PNR data after passengers depart from the UK, unless objective evidence demonstrates that specific individuals pose a risk in relation to terrorism or serious crime (see Fahey, chapter 7).[57] Regarding access to criminal convictions, the UK has lost access to ECRIS, although new provisions, in Title IX of Part Three, closely replicate its functions by facilitating the exchange of criminal conviction information. A notable difference from ECRIS is the extended reporting time, with monthly updates and a response window of 20 days, compared to ECRIS's prompt communications and 10-day response. Finally, despite its critical importance, the UK lost access to SIS II at the end of the Brexit transition, leading to the deletion of approximately 40,000 alerts on dangerous criminals and wanted suspects by December 2020. Additionally, by the end of 2021, 5.7 million alerts generated by the UK were removed from this system

[56] E Fahey, E Guild and E Kuskonmaz, 'The Novelty of EU Passenger Name Records (PNR) in EU Trade Agreements: on shifting uses of data governance in light of the EU–UK Trade and Cooperation Agreement PNR provisions' (2023) 8(1) *European Papers* 273; Directive (EU) 2016/681 of the European Parliament and of the Council of 27 April 2016 on the use of passenger name record (PNR) data for the prevention, detection, investigation and prosecution of terrorist offences and serious crime [2016] OJ L119/132.

[57] This takes into account *Opinion 1/15 EU–Canada PNR Agreement*, ECLI:EU:C:2017:592.

(see Pearson, chapter 6). Although the UK joined SIS II relatively late, in 2015, and its use was limited to law enforcement, the system quickly became a key tool for UK policing. In 2019 alone, UK officers accessed SIS II 603 million times.[58] It was considered crucial for officers to make informed decisions, such as custody-related matters, to maintain public safety. The UK is now relying on the Interpol I-24/7 system, which has more limited functionality (see Thomson, chapter 11). Related to the loss of access to the SIS II and the piecemeal access to the above-mentioned systems, it is also important to highlight that the TCA rests on information systems' development as it stood in 2021, making it unable to adapt to recent changes to the systems or instruments. This is particularly the case as regards the EU's current push towards interoperability between systems for information exchange (see Vavoula, chapter 8).

## B. Mutual Legal Assistance and the Surrender Mechanism

The TCA has also had an impact on the scope for mutual legal assistance between the UK and the EU, and on the surrender of suspects. The UK is no longer able to participate in the EAW system,[59] but, under Title VII of Part Three of the Agreement, it is subject to new surrender arrangements that retain many of the EAW's features, such as time limits and grounds for mandatory refusal (see Arnell, chapter 13; Ryan, chapter 14). The key differences between the EAW and the TCA surrender arrangements include the introduction of proportionality as an overarching principle, and the addition of three new grounds for refusal: (i) political offences; (ii) nationality; and (iii) dual criminality.[60] The TCA explicitly incorporates proportionality, allowing it to be assessed both when a warrant is issued and during its execution. If the provided information is insufficient to judge proportionality, the executing authority must request further details from the issuing state. The TCA also reintroduces the political offence exception in UK–EU surrender arrangements, though EU Member States can limit this exception to specific offences, like those outlined in the 1977 European Convention on the Suppression of Terrorism.[61] Since the end of the transition period, 12 Member States have reinstated a limited political offence exception with the UK.[62] Member States can also notify the UK that they will not extradite their own nationals. Ten Member States have already invoked this provision,[63] exceeding UK Home Office expectations, and 13 others have

[58] House of Lords, *Beyond Brexit – Policing, Law Enforcement and Security* (26 March 2021) available at https://committees.parliament.uk/publications/5298/documents/52902/default/ (last accessed on 16 January 2025).

[59] Council Framework Decision of 13 June 2002 on the European arrest warrant and the surrender procedures between Member States [2002] OJ L190/1 available at https://eur-lex.europa.eu/legal-content/EN/TXT/?uri=celex%3A32002F0584 (last accessed 20 October 2024).

[60] G Davies and P Arnell, 'The new UK–EU extradition arrangements' (2021) 6 *Scots Law Times* 21.

[61] European Convention on the Suppression of Terrorism (adopted 27 January 1977, entered into force 4 August 1978) ETS 90.

[62] Belgium, Czech Republic, Denmark, France, Croatia, Italy, Cyprus, Poland, Portugal, Slovakia, Finland and Sweden. For the complete list of notifications and conditionality of surrender, see https://assets.publishing.service.gov.uk/media/65438f5bd36c91000d935c47/2023-07-27_EU_Notifications_to_the_UK.pdf.

[63] Poland, Croatia, Finland, France, Germany, Greece, Latvia, Slovakia, Slovenia and Sweden. For the complete list of notifications and conditionality of surrender, see https://assets.publishing.service.gov.uk/media/65438f5bd36c91000d935c47/2023-07-27_EU_Notifications_to_the_UK.pdf.

set conditions for surrender, such as reciprocity or temporary surrender. The definition of 'national' has also been broadened. The Court of Justice's *Petruhhin* ruling[64] further impacts surrender arrangements by requiring Member States to prioritise EAWs over third-country requests for their nationals. In line with international extradition norms, the TCA also requires 'dual criminality', meaning the crime must be an offence in both the issuing and executing states. While the EAW previously assumed dual criminality for a list of offences, the TCA removes this assumption. Dual criminality now needs to be proved, unless both parties formally waive it (the UK has not made such a waiver), potentially resulting in more challenges based on dual criminality. Furthermore, post-Brexit, human rights considerations play a larger role in surrender decisions. Without the mutual trust previously inherent in EU cooperation, courts in Member States are more inclined to scrutinise the human rights implications of extraditing individuals to the UK, especially regarding prison conditions. Related to this specific point, it is also important to highlight that prisoner transfer between the two parties has not been included in the TCA (see Wilson, chapter 15).

Finally, before Brexit, the UK could issue a European Investigation Order (EIO), a legally binding request for other EU Member States to collect evidence or conduct investigative actions within a specified timeframe. However, with the entry into force of the TCA, this option is no longer available. The UK now relies on the 1959 European Convention on Mutual Assistance in Criminal Matters,[65] alongside Title VII of the TCA, for cooperation with EU Member States.[66] The TCA introduced a standardised form for mutual assistance requests, but it was only finalised in the first half of 2023.

## VI. Conclusion

This chapter aimed to explore the complexities and outcomes of TCA negotiations, focusing on their impact on UK–EU police and judicial cooperation. The chapter highlighted the political context leading up to the TCA negotiations, starting with the repeated rejections of the Withdrawal Agreement and Political Declaration under Theresa May's Government. It discussed how the rejections by the UK Parliament led to the acceleration of 'no-deal' Brexit preparations, particularly highlighting the potential impact on police and judicial cooperation. The chapter underlined that under a no-deal scenario, the UK claimed to have been ready to forgo its cooperation with the EU and replace it instead with bilateral relations with EU Member States, grounded on Council of Europe and United Nations conventions. The chapter then discussed how this phase of political turbulence paved the way for changes in the UK government and in the UK–EU relationship. The new Prime Minister's tougher stance, including the threat of a 'no-deal' exit, eventually led to a revised Withdrawal Agreement, which, in turn, enabled

[64] Case C-182/15 *Petruhhin v Latvijas Republikas Ģenerālprokuratūra*, EU:C:2016:630 available at https://curia.europa.eu/juris/document/document.jsf?text=&docid=177901&pageIndex=0&doclang=EN&mode=lst&dir=&occ=first&part=1&cid=4293987 (last accessed 17 October 2024).

[65] European Convention on Mutual Assistance in Criminal Matters (adopted 20 April 1959, entered into force 12 June 1962) ETS 30.

[66] G Davies et al, 'Police Cooperation and Exchange of Information under the EU–UK Trade and Cooperation Agreement (TCA)' (2021) 12(2) *New Journal of European Criminal Law* 262.

its approval in Parliament. Despite the change in political leadership, and in approach towards the EU, the chapter noted that Boris Johnson's Government's approach to police and judicial cooperation was aligned with that of Theresa May's Government. It continued to aim for a robust partnership while emphasising UK red lines, namely, respect for sovereignty and the independence of the UK legal system from the CJEU. The chapter then progressed to analysis of the specific negotiation process and positions, where it highlighted the UK's desire for continued access to EU law enforcement agencies, to information databases and to mutual legal assistance, and contrasted it with the EU's narrower offer of cooperation (which was based on concerns over the UK's status as a non-Schengen country, as well as over fundamental rights and data protection). The text explicitly underlined the recurrent friction between the two parties and the difficulties in reaching an agreement. The final section of the chapter outlined the TCA's outcomes for police and judicial cooperation, painting a picture of a workable but diminished framework for this policy field in the post-Brexit era.

This chapter completes Part I of this volume, dedicated to the historical, political and legal analysis of the evolution of the UK–EU police and judicial cooperation in criminal matters, starting from the roots of that cooperation in the 1970s up to the TCA's entry into force in 2021. The following chapters of the volume explore the multiple legal and political challenges currently stemming from the implementation of the Agreement.

# PART II

# Police Cooperation under the Trade and Cooperation Agreement

# 5

# The Importance of Trust-based Networks in Police and Judicial Cooperation

ESTELLE MARKS*

## I. Introduction

Within the European Union's (EU's) Area of Freedom, Security and Justice, there are many police and judicial cooperation networks that facilitate person-to-person contact between national law enforcement and prosecuting authorities. These networks take various forms: some are organised through formal EU institutions such as Europol or in support of formal systems such as the SIRENE network, which operates the Schengen Information System (SIS); others are focused on specific areas of work, such as cybercrime; or around strategically important locations; whilst others operate in a general cross-border context via a network of national contact points. Before Brexit, the United Kingdom (UK) participated fully in these networks.

Following Brexit, the UK has retained operational access to EU law enforcement networks through third-country agreements but has lost its strategic influence. Other networks have fallen away entirely, even though they pre-dated EU cooperation frameworks. The UK has left SIS and closed its SIRENE Bureau, relying instead on its Interpol National Central Bureau (NCB). To compensate, the UK has expanded its network of International Liaison Officers (ILOs) and Liaison Magistrates, who are placed in embassies on a bilateral basis. The UK has also centralised much of its international policing capabilities, launching the International Crime Coordination Centre (ICCC) and a National Extradition Unit in 2020 (see Thomson, chapter 11). Subsequently, in 2023, these resources were merged with the UK International Crime Bureau (UKICB) at the National Crime Agency (NCA), which acts as the Interpol NCB, hosts the UK's Europol National Unit (ENU) and oversees the UK network of ILOs. This newly launched Joint International Crime Centre (JICC) creates a hub for much of the UK cross-border capability, which was previously distributed locally across all 43 police forces, a fragmentation that was particularly costly in the extradition field.[1]

* This research was supported by the Economic and Social Research Council (grant numbers 1614694 and ES/W006766/1).

[1] E Marks, 'Policing the European Arrest Warrant: An Empirical Study of a Transnational Policing Tool', PhD thesis, King's College London, 2020.

This chapter sets out what is known about the UK's changed status in many of the networks following Brexit and identifies trust-based interpersonal relationships as a key facilitator of cross-border police work. Transnational officers work in cross-border settings, whether as national contact points, bilateral ILOs or liaisons to EU justice institutions. These officers act as the 'oil and glue' that keep the wheels of transnational justice turning.[2] The role of networks in building trust-based relationships between transnational officers must not be overlooked.

Interpersonal operational trust is closely related to, but distinct from, the principle of mutual trust. The principle of mutual trust between states as a prerequisite to mutual recognition has been a core focus of the EU's agenda during the expansion of mechanisms for police and judicial cooperation in criminal matters. Mutual trust is based on normative considerations, such as proportionality, human rights protections and fair trial rights. This chapter focuses, instead, on the role of trust between criminal justice practitioners. Operational trust is more practical, based on mutual understanding and a good and predictable service between partners. This level of trust is central to effective day-to-day cooperation and should be a key concern when developing policy in this area.

Transnational officers are experts in bridging gaps between systems and fostering trust. Access to counterparts via networks and the opportunity to wield strategic influence so that priorities are aligned is key to their work. The impact of Brexit on the UK's access to and participation in these networks is only partly understood and more research is needed. Other chapters in this volume demonstrate that Brexit has hampered police cooperation despite the existence of the Trade and Cooperation Agreement (TCA). This chapter emphasises the need for the UK to maximise its participation in law enforcement and criminal justice networks wherever possible and not underestimate their importance in facilitating trust-based relations. Particularly in the post-Brexit era, as the UK relies on these trust-based relationships to compensate for gaps created by reduced access to formal mechanisms and databases.

## II. Building Operational Trust Through Transnational Networks

Scholars studying transnational policing have long observed that much cross-border cooperation takes place through informal channels and that, given the choice, officers prefer informal routes.[3] Official mechanisms for cooperation, whether for criminal

[2] EA Nadelmann, 'Cops across Borders: Transnational Crime and International Law Enforcement' (Harvard University, 1987).

[3] L Guille, 'The Proliferation of Parallel Tracks in Police and Judicial Cooperation in Europe: The Current "Chaos"' *Journal of Police Studies* (2010) 16; B Bowling and J Sheptycki, 'Introduction: The Structures of Global Policing and Transnational Law Enforcement' in B Bowling and J Sheptycki (eds), *Global Policing and Transnational Law Enforcement* (Sage, 2015) vii; P Swallow, 'European Police Cooperation: A Comparative Analysis of European Level Institutional and Organisational Developments and National Level Policies and Structures', PhD thesis, University of Southampton, 1998; M Anderson et al, *Policing the European Union 'Theory, Law, and Practice'* (Clarendon Press, 1996); D Bigo, 'Liaison Officers in Europe: New Officers in the European Security Field' in J Sheptycki (ed), *Issues in Transnational Policing* (Routledge, 2000) 67.

records checks, intelligence sharing, mutual legal assistance or evidence exchange, are notoriously slow and cumbersome.[4] Although EU mechanisms, including the European Arrest Warrant (EAW) and the European Investigation Order (EIO), have increased the speed and reduced the complexity of some formal requests, a significant volume of police work falls outside of their scope. This is true within the EU and even more so outside of it.

Much of the literature assumes a self-evident distinction between formal and informal cooperation, but in reality no clear division exists. Rather, mechanisms and routes for cooperation sit on a spectrum. Sheptycki[5] offers three distinctions for thinking about the formal–informal nexus: (i) 'Formal practices' with a capital 'F', which are time-consuming and often slow, such as evidence exchange via mutual legal assistance; (ii) 'formal practices' with a small 'f', which work faster than most formal routes but are still subject to some formal accountability within an organisation; and (iii) informal practices, which are not subject to any formal accountability.[6]

Whether a practice is subject to formal accountability offers one tool for placing it on the formal–informal spectrum. Another is to consider the formality required to initiate and respond to requests. Much work on informal cooperation stresses direct contact and reliance on personal relationships.[7] This kind of cooperation might be initiated through a simple phone call with no formal requirements at all. At the most formal end of the scale, on the other hand, the institutionalised nature of arrangements is stressed.[8] At its extreme, a request may require judicial approval, prescribed content and transmission through designated channels. In between these extremes lie systems for information exchange that do not require approval and place little restriction on the format of requests but provide a prescribed route, for example via national bureaux.

Although much work on transnational policing focuses on either end of this formal–informal scale, some scholars acknowledge that they are not mutually exclusive.[9] Others suggest that informal cooperation persists even after formal institutions are created,[10] and in some cases 'informal EU practitioner forums' have inspired and supported formal developments.[11] It is unlikely that one will replace the other because 'the two forms are complementary, both required to achieve success'[12] and there is no bright line that divides them.

[4] B Bowling and C Kopf, 'Transnational Policing in Europe and Its Local Effects' *European Law Enforcement Research Bulletin* (2017).

[5] J Sheptycki, *In Search of Transnational Policing* (Ashgate, 2002).

[6] M Shellaker, S Tong and P Swallow, 'UK–EU Law Enforcement Cooperation Post-Brexit: A UK Law Enforcement Practitioner Perspective' (2023) 24(4) *Criminology & Criminal Justice* 841.

[7] Anderson et al (n 3) 74.

[8] Bowling and Kopf (n 4).

[9] B Bowling, R Reiner and J Sheptycki, *The Politics of the Police*, 5th edn (Oxford University Press, 2019) 196.

[10] E Herschinger and M Jachtenfuchs, 'Informell Oder Institutionalisiert? Die Internationalisierung Der Inneren Sicherheit' (2012) 53 *Politische Vierteljahresschrift* 493.

[11] S Hufnagel, *Policing Cooperation across Borders: Comparative Perspectives on Law Enforcement within the EU and Australia* (Routledge, 2016); S Hufnagel, 'Police Cooperation in Europe, China and Australia: Does Trust Depend on the Political System?' in S Hufnagel and C McCartney (eds), *Trust in International Police and Justice Cooperation* (Hart Publishing, 2017).

[12] Anderson et al (n 3) 76.

As discussed above, operational trust is a practical concern. From a public policy perspective, inter-organisational trust is seen 'as the expectation that a cooperating partner will act in a predictable, reliable, and fair manner';[13] and for individual officers or prosecutors, trust is based on 'expectations and predictions of future behaviour' that allow them take a 'leap of faith' in conditions of uncertainty.[14] Whilst the EU has identified trust as a key feature in police cooperation, it has not clearly identified what it means by trust or 'who should be trusting whom, and why'.[15] Referencing the sociological literature on trust, Block explores the relationship between trust and risk, noting that investing time and resources in cooperating or conveying information entails the risk that the partner will fail to fulfil their side of the bargain. They may fail to deliver a reciprocal commitment or deviate from mutually understood norms. A decision to cooperate despite this risk requires trust that the partner will not fall short. The more formal a mechanism, the less risk is involved, and the less personal trust is required to act.

However, trust is not just an act of reliance; it is a belief or feeling of confidence in so acting. Much of the literature conflates the act of cooperation with the feeling of trust, but truly understanding trust means identifying not only why actors cooperate but why they feel confident in doing so. This kind of trust is based on prior knowledge and mutual understanding,[16] which is best developed through personal contact.[17]

As Walker suggests, 'police officers can find solidarity, trust and empathy with foreign colleagues born of similar working conditions and priorities'.[18] Other scholars speak of a transnational policing subculture, 'a global civil society in the policing sector'[19] that 'provides the oil and glue of international law enforcement'.[20] But differences in feelings of fraternity towards international colleagues are felt by nationally rooted officers cooperating transnationally, on the one hand, and those officers whose role is fundamentally transnational, on the other.[21] It is key that those transnational officers and prosecutors, whose role is focused on bridging the gaps between national systems, are given sufficient opportunities to build trust with their counterparts.

The structure of transnational policing is 'polycentric, fluid and complex',[22] where global and supranational infrastructure links the national and the local through legal

[13] A Efrat, 'Assessing Mutual Trust among EU Members: Evidence from the European Arrest Warrant' (2019) 26 *Journal of European Public Policy* 656.

[14] Hufnagel and McCartney (eds) (n 11).

[15] L Block, 'Establishing Trust despite the Risk? An Analysis of the Need for Trust in Police Cooperation' in Hufnagel and McCartney (eds) (n 11) 13.

[16] K Nicolaïdis, 'Trusting the Poles? Constructing Europe through Mutual Recognition' (2007) 14 *Journal of European Public Policy* 682.

[17] Marks (n 1).

[18] N Walker, 'The Pattern of Transnational Policing' in T Newburn (ed), *Handbook of Policing*, 2nd edn (Willan, 2008) 119, 123.

[19] N Walker, 'Defining Core Police Tasks: The Neglect of the Symbolic Dimension?' (1996) 6(1) *Policing and Society* 53, 53; J Sheptycki, 'The Constabulary Ethic and the Transnational Condition' in A Goldsmith and J Sheptycki (eds), *Crafting transnational policing, police capacity building and global policing reform* (Hart Publishing, 2007) 31.

[20] P Andreas and E Nadelmann, *Policing the Globe: Criminalization and Crime Control in International Relations* (Oxford University Press, 2006) 232.

[21] B Bowling and J Sheptycki, *Global Policing* (Sage, 2012) 84–85; Marks (n 1).

[22] Bowling and Sheptycki (n 21) 63.

frameworks, databases and networks, whether formal, informal or somewhere in between. Networks form a central part of the transnational policing infrastructure[23] not just because they are operationally effective in supporting the execution of formal requests (or bypassing them when necessary), but because they provide opportunities for person-to-person contact that supports the development and maintenance of trust. Full participation in the governance structure of networks also allows states to align their priorities with others, which further improves cooperation.

The rest of this chapter draws on a 2017 pre-Brexit case study of police cooperation between the UK and other EU states in EAW cases.[24] This snapshot of law enforcement cooperation demonstrates how much is at risk if UK access and influence in these networks are not sufficiently safeguarded. The EU has been a key driver in establishing networks,[25] but it has not been the only influence. Sadly, as well as diminishing UK influence in EU networks, Brexit has led to the dissolution of the Cross Channel Intelligence Conference (CCIC), one of the first cross-border police networks established in the UK.

## III. European Criminal Justice Cooperation Networks

### A. Schengen, SIRENE and SIS-VIS

SIS is the EU's largest security and border management database. It contains alerts on missing persons, vehicles, stolen identity documents and persons wanted for judicial purposes.[26] Alerts can contain a wide range of data, from personal details to photographs or biometric information. The database is linked to police national computers and updates in real time across the Continent. Each Member State has a national SIRENE bureau that administers the national system. These bureaux are embedded in national police agencies and staffed by police officers, civilian police staff and immigration or border officials in some states. In the UK, the SIRENE bureau was part of the NCA's UK International Crime Bureau (UKICB).[27] Communication via SIS is standardised via a system of numbered alerts and forms that have specific purposes and prescribed content. Only SIRENE officers can send transnational communication via SIS, although other users, including local police and courts, can create and populate alerts for transmission by the Bureau.

[23] J Sheptycki, 'The Global Cops Cometh: Reflections on Transnationalization, Knowledge Work and Policing Subculture' (1998) *British Journal of Sociology* 57; Marks (n 1).

[24] Marks (n 1).

[25] M Bayer, 'Making International Law Enforcement Networks More Efficient: Time to Reposition the Liaison Officer' in M den Boer and L Block (eds), *Liaison Officers: Essential actors in transnational policing* (Eleven International Publishing, 2013) 119.

[26] There is also a portion of the database related to visas and border crossing which the UK did not access as it was not a member of the Schengen Area.

[27] Marks (n 1) 106.

Although staff in SIRENE bureaux usually communicate through the highly formalised database, they occasionally speak on the phone, and senior officers do meet in person. The Directorate General for Migration and Home Affairs (DG Home) is responsible for SIS and coordinates the SIS Working Groups. This includes the SIS-VIS group, an operational steering group that meets every six weeks and works on small- and large-scale system issues, from the addition of new vehicle codes to the wholesale redrafting of regulations. There is also a SIS-SIRENE group, which meets every six months. It acts as a strategic steering group, led by current Commission priorities, and chaired by the Member State that holds the EU presidency. Working group meetings give national bureaux members important opportunities to meet counterparts and to raise and resolve operational issues in a face-to-face forum.

The Directorate General for Migration and Home Affairs (DG Home) provides training to new SIRENE officers, and works with the European Agency for Law Enforcement Training (CEPOL) to provide ongoing training and development via short residential courses and webinars. These courses provide opportunities for national SIRENE officers to meet international counterparts and aid the development of mutual understanding, allowing officers to informally discuss their practices and better understand other systems.

The UK was disconnected from SIS in 2021 and now relies on Interpol as an alternative means for cross-border information exchange. The UK has actively encouraged EU states to enter all SIS alerts into Interpol systems, a process referred to as 'double keying'.[28] This is especially important in European extradition cases, as the UK has no sight of EAWs circulated via SIS. In some states, Interpol systems are operated by the same officers administering SIS. In other countries, the systems are not linked, and data cannot always be shared across platforms. Whilst many European states report complying with the UK's request to double key, this is not universal, and it is difficult to monitor. It leaves the possibility of blind spots for UK law enforcement: a wanted person may enter or reside in the UK with impunity if a wanted notice has not been circulated via Interpol.

Interpol is an international agency with 194 Member States. Each country hosts an NCB: in the UK, the NCB is situated in the NCA's UKICB, which previously hosted the SIRENE bureau. The Interpol network does give officers some opportunities to meet their international counterparts. A yearly general assembly includes all member states, and there are annual European conferences, regular Heads of Bureau meetings, working groups and steering groups. Member states regularly send officers on secondment to Interpol's headquarters in Lyon to aid the development of national expertise. However, opportunities for operational officers to develop personal relationships are more frequent within the SIRENE network. The UK has therefore lost the operational capabilities of SIS (see Pearson, chapter 6) and its network value. The loss of the UK's SIRENE Bureau deprives transnational officers in the UK of opportunities to come together with counterparts and form personal trust-based relationships that support the functioning of even the most formal of cooperation mechanisms.

[28] European Union Committee, *Beyond Brexit: Policing, Law Enforcement and Security* (HL 2019-21, 250).

## B. Europol and Eurojust

Europol is the EU's Agency for Law Enforcement Cooperation and Eurojust is the Agency for Criminal Justice Cooperation. They have complementary functions and work together, providing 'support to national authorities during transnational criminal investigations'.[29] For example, cross-border investigations beginning with Europol queries may progress to Joint Investigation Teams (JITs) established with the support of Eurojust. Both Agencies provide similar network capabilities for police and prosecutors respectively, via member country desks in their Netherlands-based headquarters. All EU Member States have country desks, staffed by seconded law enforcement professionals at Europol and prosecutors at Eurojust. Staff on national desks can liaise with their international counterparts directly, face-to-face in their offices, meeting spaces and canteens. Raising a specific query is as simple as walking down the corridor to the office of the relevant country.

At Eurojust, the National Members seconded to country desks form the College of Eurojust, which is responsible for the Agency's operational work. There is no formal route for domestic prosecutors to raise queries with Eurojust, they can simply pick up the phone and speak to their National Member. It would not, however, be acceptable for domestic prosecutors to contact the National Member of another state, queries must be funnelled through their own country desk.[30] A small number of non-EU states also have liaison prosecutors stationed at Eurojust Headquarters, who have the same face-to-face access to international counterparts, but they are not members of the College of Eurojust and cannot be appointed to the Executive Board to vote on organisational matters or wield managerial influence.

At Europol, each Member State has a liaison desk with seconded liaison officers from domestic law enforcement agencies. These liaison desks are not operationally controlled by Europol, which has its own growing workforce of analysts, specialists, database operators and operational support teams addressing an ever-expanding mandate.[31] Rather, the liaison desks are employed by their nation-state and linked directly to their domestically situated ENU, which acts as a liaison between Europol and the domestic law enforcement agencies. In 2017, the UK liaison desk included staff seconded from the NCA, the Metropolitan Police, Regional Organised Crime Units and Police Scotland.

These Agencies sit somewhere in the middle of the formal/informal scale: there is some organisational accountability as requests are counted and reported in the agencies' activity monitoring. At Europol there is some formality in making a request to the national desk, as requests should be routed through the domestic ENU, but there is nothing to stop a domestic officer from contacting a Europol liaison directly if they know them. There is less formality involved in contacting Eurojust; prosecutors can call or email directly. However, in both Agencies, requests must be routed through the

[29] Eurojust, 'Eurojust Partners' available at www.eurojust.europa.eu/states-and-partners/eu-partners/europol (2023) (last accessed 11 October 2023).

[30] Marks (n 1) 111.

[31] M Busuioc and M Groenleer, 'Beyond Design: The Evolution of Europol and Eurojust' in C Kaunert, S Leonard and J Occhipinti (eds), *Justice and Home Affairs Agencies in the European Union* (Routledge, 2016).

national desk of the officer or prosecutor making the query. It is unacceptable to make enquiries direct to other country's desks. Once a query is made, there is no formality in the discussions between country desks; officers and prosecutors can simply talk in person, by email or on the phone with no restrictions or formal requirements.

After Brexit, the UK and EU concluded third-country working agreements, under the terms permitted by the TCA, with both Europol and Eurojust. Retaining physical desks was of vital operational importance, and without the TCA, UK liaisons would have been forced to relocate to the British embassy in The Hague. The UK Liaison Bureau at Europol has continuing access to the secure email system and remains a multi-agency team, which has expanded since 2017 to include officers from eight domestic enforcement agencies, making it the second largest third-country desk after that of the United States. In many ways, cooperation with both Agencies has continued smoothly with little additional friction.[32] The UK can still participate in JITs but cannot initiate one.

However, current arrangements mean that the UK has lost strategic influence. The UK no longer participates in the management and coordination structures of either body. The long-term implications of this loss of influence have yet to be felt. Additionally, UK officers can no longer be employed directly by Europol in its Operational and Analysis Centres: those in post had to leave when the UK left the EU in 2021. The working arrangements do allow invitations to be extended to UK representatives to associate with operational analysis projects in relevant cases. For example, UK officers are no longer employed by EC3, which provides operational support in cybercrime investigations, but UK liaison officers can still participate in the Joint Cybercrime Action Taskforce (J-CAT) analysis projects.

The UK should prioritise further developing the operational relationship with Europol by facilitating better use of the network by domestic law enforcement. Despite contributing a large volume of data to the Europol intelligence database,[33] UK practitioners did not utilise the network capacity of these agencies to their fullest extent even before Brexit, often preferring alternative routes for requests.

## C. Informal European Networks – EN-FAST and the EJN

Two key elements of European infrastructure for fugitive cases are the police and prosecutor networks established at a European level, which create person-to-person links via national contact points. The European Network of Fugitive Active Search Teams (EN-FAST), used by law enforcement, is dedicated solely to fugitive work, while the European Judicial Network (EJN), used by prosecutors, has a much broader remit, supporting cross-border cooperation more generally. Direct contact with counterparts through casework or conferences and training events is key to relationship and trust building in these highly informal structures.

Established in 2013 under a Memorandum of Association, EN-FAST links national police working in Fugitive Active Search Teams across the EU. The network

[32] House of Lords (n 28) para 111.

[33] Home Affairs Committee, *UK–EU Security Cooperation after Brexit* (HC 2017–19, 635).

is comprised of domestic police professionals actively engaged in fugitive and extradition work. Europol hosts the EN-FAST public-facing 'most wanted' platform and CEPOL collaborates with the network to provide training. EN-FAST teams deal mostly with high-profile, high-risk or extremely urgent fugitive cases, but they are not officially limited in their remit. Cooperation through EN-FAST is direct, informal and fast. The network is built on high levels of trust and personal relationships. Conferences are held regularly, and because staff turnover is low, contact points get to know each other personally over time. There is an expectation that queries and cases from EN-FAST partners will be prioritised and that the network will not be used for trivial or speculative matters.

Most EN-FAST contact points are operational police officers. Before Brexit, the UK's EN-FAST contacts were non-operational officers situated in the UKICB. Some partners noted that the lack of an operational team in the UK, compounded by the fact that not all NCA staff have a police background, and that UK contacts changed more regularly than their partners, was a barrier to trust. Since UK extradition policing was centralised, the operational teams in the National Extradition Unit have taken on the EN-FAST role. It seems likely that this will improve operational cooperation and support trust building by providing better continuity in relationships.

For prosecutors, the EJN[34] forms a network of national prosecutorial and judicial contact points working in roles related to international cooperation. The network has a small secretariat that is responsible for its functioning and continuity. Each state has a nominated corresponding member who plays a coordination role, disseminating information relating to the EJN, promoting training courses and liaising with the secretariat. Contact points provide practical support to professionals in other states, forwarding specific queries to the correct national authority, following up on delayed responses or advising on making successful requests. Contacts are listed on the EJN's secure online platform, which also contains country-specific information on cooperation tools. The network hosts biannual meetings, allowing national members to meet international counterparts and build relationships. Although not all UK prosecutors use the EJN, those that do speak highly of it and appreciate opportunities for direct personal contact.[35]

EN-FAST and the EJN represent the most informal end of the spectrum in terms of cross-border cooperation. Although the EJN does compile European-level data on the volume of work that contact points handle, there are no oversight or accountability mechanisms for individual cases. There is no formality in contacting EJN contact points; a prosecutor can raise queries with overseas counterparts by email or phone.

Similarly, the EN-FAST network has no oversight mechanism or public data about the way in which the network is used or the volume of cases. The high levels of trust involved in the relationships create informal restrictions on how police utilise them. Contact points from the UK were clear they would only use the network for high-risk or urgent cases, and were at pains to provide a good service. Police within the network contact each other directly, by email, phone and even WhatsApp, often making contact

[34] Established in 1998 under Regulation (EU) 2018/1727 of the European Parliament and of the Council of 14 November 2018 [2018] OJ L295/138.

[35] Marks (n 1).

via officers from other countries with whom they have established relationships. Making contact in this way gives an informal endorsement of the officer making a request, leveraging the trust built between others to lend to their own credibility. Direct person-to-person contact helps to quickly resolve or progress complex and urgent cases. Transnational officers are clear that positive experiences via informal channels help build trust, and they are aware that misusing these channels or failing to give good service could negatively impact the wider cooperative relationship.

The UK has retained operational access to the EJN and EN-FAST, but only through third-party or observer agreements. The UK continues to have access to EJN contact points, but it is unclear if UK prosecutors can participate in training and relationship-building events alongside those from EU Member States. With observer status in the EN-FAST network, the UK can access the network of contact points and cooperate on individual cases. But it is not clear how much strategic influence has been lost, whether the UK can form part of the core group that manages the network or what its position in the general assembly is. Moving forward, ensuring that operational officers and prosecutors are well-resourced to make the best use of, and provide the best service to, these networks should be a key priority. Practitioners should also be encouraged to participate in opportunities for face-to-face relationship building wherever possible.

## D. European Networks Focused on Specific Areas of Work

The European Commission also funds, in whole or in part, several networks focused on specific areas of police work.[36] These networks do not fall under the Europol structure, although Europol is often an associate member and some do use Europol systems. Covering a diverse range of policing priorities, these networks include Road Policing (Roadpol), Counter-Terrorism (ATLAS and EUHRSN), Water Policing (Aquapol), Rail Policing (Railpol), Law Enforcement Technology Services (ENLETS) and Airport Policing (Airpol). These networks link local and national police working on specific priorities and serve a diverse range of functions. Some networks operate single points-of-contact lists for operational purposes; many have working groups focused on strategic development and improving cross-border cooperation in their field. Some of these networks have capacity-building and training functions or facilitate the development of best-practice guidance and the rollout of new technologies.[37]

Very little is known about the specific operations of these networks or the way in which they are utilised by the UK. The UK's status in these networks has probably shifted due to Brexit, but the result of that shift is unclear. Nevertheless, opportunities for direct and face-to-face contact afforded by membership of these networks are valuable for the development and maintenance of trust across a range of policing priorities. More research is needed to better understand the workings of these networks and the UK's current position in them.

[36] European Commission, 'Law Enforcement Cooperation' (2021) available at www.ec.europa.eu/newsroom/pps/items/715174/en (last accessed 18 October 2023).

[37] S Antonius, 'Building trust and more: the importance of police cooperation networks in the European Union' in Hufnagel and McCartney (eds) (n 11) 149.

## IV. Networks Associated with Strategically Important Locations

There are other common types of cross-border network besides those established at an EU level. Perhaps the earliest example of formally structured cross-border policing agreements are those associated with strategically important locations, particularly in border regions. These networks are often established in response to the relaxation of border controls, for example in the Benelux region in the 1960s or across the Franco-German Border in 1977.[38] For the UK, the most significant of these networks has been the CCIC. Established in 1968, the annual conference brought together police personnel operating in the Channel region from the UK, France, Belgium and the Netherlands. A key network for the transnational exchange of criminal intelligence in the pre-digital age, this conference also operated as an early policy network, where officers who developed personal relationships laid the foundations for the transnational policing infrastructure for the Channel Tunnel. At the very first meeting, the Chief Constable of Kent Police clearly outlined his aim to 'encourage closer personal relationships between officers in his Force and Belgian and French police officers stationed adjacent to the English Channel'.[39]

Even though the CCIC pre-dates the UK's membership to the EEC, the Brexit vote in 2016 resulted in France's withdrawal of its delegation from the conference and the CCIC has been disbanded.[40] This loss of person-to-person networking for senior officers in the Channel Region is a blow to trust building and a clear example of how distrust at a political level can impact operational trust on the ground.[41]

## V. Bilateral Networks

On a bilateral basis, the UK has a global network of ILOs based in British embassies across Europe and around the world. These officers form personal trust-based relationships with local law enforcement, especially those working in areas that are high-priority for the UK. These officers are well placed to get things done outside of the official channels in urgent and complex cases, and are experts in bridging the gaps between legal systems, helping UK police and those in their host state to shape requests so they can be actioned promptly. The ILOs report to the NCA and can be contacted through the JICC but also directly by local police officers; there is little to no formality involved in requesting their assistance, but their position is constrained by what is appropriate in the specific relationship and the relevant domestic law.

The UK's ILO network is mirrored by the Foreign Law Enforcement Community (FLEC) network, comprised of foreign officers based in embassies in London. When viewed from this perspective, the foreign ILOs based in London themselves form a

[38] Anderson et al (n 3) 60.
[39] Sheptycki (n 5).
[40] Shellaker, Tong and Swallow (n 6).
[41] Marks (n 1).

network that establishes personal, trust-based relationships with UK law enforcement and with each other. They get to know each other through consular events and in other social settings, as well as working together as the need arises.

The workload of an ILO will depend on the nature of the relationship between the UK and the host state. For example, there are ILOs in Spain whose work is almost exclusively dedicated to fugitive manhunts, whilst the ILO in Poland rarely dealt with an EAW case before Brexit. The strength of the ILO network relies on the personal relationships that officers build in their host state and on the lack of formality involved in making requests for information. This means that the need for trust and confidence is high, and the effectiveness of the relationship relies heavily on credibility and a good service.

The Crown Prosecution Service (CPS) also has a network of Liaison Prosecutors bilaterally placed in embassies around the world. Much like ILOs these Liaison Magistrates build specialist knowledge of their host legal system and help to shape and progress requests. The expansion of the Liaison Prosecutor network in Europe has been a key element of the CPS response to Brexit and the complications introduced by the reintroduction of the nationality bar in surrender cases under the TCA and the loss of the EIO (see Arnell, chapter 13). In 2017, the UK had liaison magistrates in Spain, France and Italy within the EU. At a minimum, this network has now expanded to include Romania, Portugal, Belgium, the Netherlands and Germany in response to Brexit.

These officers and prosecutors work in a semi-diplomatic context, representing their state from their embassy base, acutely aware that their job relies on goodwill and trust-based relationships to get things done. A key part of planning for Brexit was to expand and strengthen these bilateral relationships to respond to any complications that arose under whatever agreement was reached. One drawback of relying on these individual relations over the long term is that the continuity of relationships can be damaged as personnel change. Encouraging the sharing of local knowledge among transnational officers could help mitigate this risk, and wherever possible new ILOs should be placed concurrently with the officers they are to replace, to allow for in-depth and meaningful handover.

## VI. Conclusion

Networks are vital operational and strategic tools. Cooperation relies on high levels of trust to work well, and strategic alignment can bring organisational priorities and resources into line with practitioners working on the ground. Networks across the spectrum, from formal to informal, provide vital forums to build institutional and personal trust. This trust is practical, based on prior and continued knowledge and repeated operational contact, which strengthens the ties that bind.[42] Positive experiences of cooperation build goodwill, and opportunities to meet outside of operations create

[42] Nicolaïdis (n 16).

spaces to foster mutual understanding. Direct face-to-face contact is key to developing, maintaining and repairing trust, and these opportunities should be maximised.

Officers whose role is largely focused on transnational work are often part of networks such as EN-FAST or SIRENE working groups. They may also be ILOs. These officers explicitly see themselves as representatives of their state and understand their diplomatic role in developing mutual understanding and trust. There is evidence of a developing subculture of transnational policing (the norms, beliefs, attitudes and routines of this specific policing specialism), where officers, linked to international counterparts on a daily basis, work together in pursuit of shared occupational goals.[43] It is this developing 'transnational identity – based on the notion that a cop is a cop, and a criminal is a criminal, no matter what their respective national identities – that provides the oil and glue of contemporary international law enforcement'.[44] These officers tend to be more understanding of practical problems with other Member States' practices and are generally more conscious of the reputational risks associated with their own operational failures. They are also experts in building understanding and managing expectations within their own state, helping domestically situated officers to mould requests to fit the requirements of other systems. As the European Commission states, 'the work of the networks is fundamental for the creation of trust among law enforcement officials and agencies, for energizing the channels of communication and cooperation and for conceiving a genuine EU law enforcement community'.[45] As the UK has left the EU it has lost access to some of the most formal mechanisms for streamlined cooperation, including SIS and the SIRENE network, the EAW and the EIO. It remains an operational member of the EU criminal justice institutions and of the policing networks, but mostly as a third party, and has lost at least some strategic influence. At least one network that pre-dates UK membership of the EU has been negatively impacted by the Brexit vote. This has left the UK heavily reliant on bilateral cooperation and its ILO network to try to fill the gaps left by formal mechanisms.

Now that UK law enforcement find themselves as outsiders looking in on the EU community, it is imperative that access to trust-based networks is maintained, that this work is sufficiently resourced and that the impact of Brexit on UK influence is fully understood. Building and maintaining trust is more challenging from outside of the EU, and policymakers should be mindful that political mistrust can undercut operational trust in unexpected ways. Gaining a better understanding of the scope and value of low-visibility person-to-person contacts should be a key priority, and policies should be developed to ensure the continuity of trust in an ever-changing political landscape.

[43] Bowling and Sheptycki (n 21) 84–85.

[44] E Nadelmann, *Cops across Borders: The Internationalization of US Criminal Law Enforcement* (Penn State Press, 2010) 468.

[45] European Commission (n 36).

# 6

# Loss of Access to Schengen Information System II: UK Policing Perspectives

JERRY PEARSON

## I. Introduction

Following the European Union (EU) exit referendum on 23 June 2016, the exact conditions of the United Kingdom's (UK's) withdrawal from the EU were negotiated against a tense backdrop of domestic instability, characterised by political division and public protest. During this period, the Brexit debate understandably dominated the media, with commentators frequently referring to the risks associated with any loss of access to the Schengen Information System (SIS II) by UK law enforcement agencies.[1] A 2016 report from the House of Lords Home Affairs Sub-Committee reported that 'Britain will be less safe after leaving the EU unless integral EU security arrangements and law enforcement databases are retained or adequately replaced'.[2]

The potential inability of British police officers to access the SIS and other law enforcement databases was signalled as a significant threat to public safety and representative of the need for a comprehensive post-exit security agreement between the UK and the EU. Given that few of the British public had heard of SIS II before the Brexit debate, it quickly entered public consciousness as an important policing tool that would leave us all less safe, if lost. This view was not exclusively held within the UK, as some politicians within the EU also publicly warned of the security threat represented by the UK's future exclusion from law enforcement systems such as SIS II. In 2018, Horst Seehofer, the German Interior Minister, broke ranks with other EU politicians and declared that 'it is obvious that the UK will no longer be a member of the union after its withdrawal but that must not lead to less security for our citizens'. Mr Seehofer went on

[1] M Bulman, 'UK risks being left 'less safe' after Brexit, peers warn' *The Independent* (16 December 2016) available at www.independent.co.uk/news/uk/home-news/brexit-uk-less-safe-security-lords-report-policing-a7478241.html (Last accessed 3 April 2023).

[2] House of Lords, Brexit: future UK–EU security and police cooperation (2016).

to insist that the 'full security partnership with the UK must encompass the entire EU security architecture'.[3]

Despite the numerous calls for the UK to retain access to SIS II after leaving the EU, the final settlement agreement confirmed that that access to the SIS II database would be lost following formal exit and at the conclusion of the agreed implementation period. Notwithstanding the many mutual operational benefits of continued UK access to SIS II, the EU 'resolutely adhered to the view that access to the benefits of EU membership (such as SIS II) was restricted to members of the EU'.[4] While this view may well have been politically motived and designed to maintain the integrity of the EU project, by 2018, reports of UK mismanagement of SIS II were beginning to circulate.[5] On that basis, it is possible to speculate that the EU may have felt disinclined to make a special case for UK retention of SIS II, based on previous failures to rigidly adhere to the rules governing usage of the system by Member States.

What was also less readily understood by the public, was that British access to SIS II was still a relatively new development, and that UK law enforcement agencies were already working hard to mitigate the risks of a 'no deal' Brexit by ensuring that contingency arrangements were in place. It could be argued that the response of UK policing to the potential loss of access to EU policing tools such as SIS II was both comprehensive and decisive in nature. This chapter will assess the operational effectiveness of the UK response to that loss and will additionally examine and explore the operational features of SIS II and the ongoing consequences of its loss.

## II. Background

The SIS was initially conceived in 1995 as an alert-based system, allowing law enforcement agencies across Europe to collaborate quickly and easily following the abolition of internal borders between some countries within the EU. It has been described as 'one of the most important large-scale databases used for immigration and border controls in the European Union'.[6] However, of equal if not greater importance than border control, was the ability of Member States to use SIS and other EU databases to conduct 'real-time data sharing between law enforcement agencies'.[7]

In 2013, a second-generation version of the system (SIS II) was launched with a range of enhanced functionalities, such as the possibility of adding fingerprints and photographs to alerts. Policing agencies in the UK were not early adopters of the

[3] G Chazan and A Barker (2018) 'EU rigidity on Brexit putting lives at risk, says German minister' *FT.com* (2018) available at www.proquest.com/docview/2071761212/citation/5B49EC62CC474A5DPQ/1 (last accessed 3 April 2023).

[4] J Pearson (2021) 'Policing capabilities lessened after Brexit' *UK in a Changing Europe* (2021) available at https://ukandeu.ac.uk/policing-capabilities-lessened-after-brexit/ (last accessed on 3 April 2023).

[5] N Neilson, 'UK unlawfully copying data from EU police system' *EU Observer* (28 May 2018) available at https://euobserver.com/rule-of-law/141919 (last accessed 3 April 2023).

[6] J Parkin, 'The Difficult Road to the Schengen Information System II: The legacy of "laboratories" and the cost for fundamental rights and the rule of law' *CEPS* (2011) available at www.ceps.eu/wp-content/uploads/2011/04/SIS_II_paper_liberty_security_formatted1.pdf (last accessed 3 April 2023).

[7] K Ditcham, 'Brexit Day' *RUSI News* (2020) available at www.rusi.org/news-and-comment/rusi-news/brexit-day-rusi-experts-look-ahead (last accessed 3 April 2023).

SIS databases, only connecting in 2015, a full 20 years after their first introduction. An alert entered in SIS by one country becomes available in real time in all other countries that use SIS. This helped to facilitate law enforcement, immigration and border control. As the UK had opted out of the common travel area called the Schengen Zone, the UK could only ever participate in the law enforcement aspects of SIS II.[8]

While SIS included only seven EU Member States as database users upon its initial launch in 1995, it steadily expanded to the extent that at the point of the UK's exit from the EU in 2020, SIS II users included all EU Member States (other than Ireland and Cyprus) together with four other countries that were not EU Member States but were members of the Schengen Common Travel Zone. Since that time, Ireland has now become a SIS II user and plans are in place for Cyprus to join the system. During 2019 (which provided the last full year of statistics prior to Brexit), UK law enforcement agencies accessed SIS II a total of 571,697,394 times, making them the third largest user of the system behind only Spain and France.[9] With 9 per cent of all SIS II transactions made by UK law enforcement agencies, British police forces were enthusiastic and important users of the system.

The huge number of SIS II transactions regularly undertaken by UK policing agencies can largely be explained by the database's substantial integration with the Police National Computer (PNC). The practical consequence of this integration was to cause every person checked by police officers within the UK to be simultaneously checked against the SIS II database. In many cases, the police officer conducting the checks had not sought SIS II checks to be made, or was even aware that they had been conducted. However, the SIS II database did provide a safety net, which ensured that British police officers would be made aware of fugitives or missing persons, stolen property and vehicles, as well as important items of intelligence, should they relate to the inquiry being conducted. The National Police Chiefs' Council (NPCC) took the view that access to SIS II was essential for mainstream policing, noting that

> the ability to understand whether somebody is wanted in another country, whether they are missing, whether the vehicle they are driving is stolen and so on … is critical in allowing officers on the street to make decisions (for instance in relation to custody) to safeguard the welfare of people across the country.[10]

Despite the considerable benefits for both EU and UK policing agencies of access to a mutual intelligence-sharing mechanism like SIS II, access to the database was viewed by the EU as one of the blue-ribbon benefits of EU membership. To enjoy the benefits of membership (argued the EU), you had to be a full member, or an associate member, of

[8] Home Office, 'Second generation Schengen Information System (SISII)' *gov.uk* (2015) available at www.assets.publishing.service.gov.uk/government/uploads/system/uploads/attachment_data/file/421540/SISII_General_Information_document.pdf (last accessed 3 April 2023).

[9] EULisa, European Union Agency for the Operational Management of Large-Scale IT Systems in the Area of Freedom, Security and Justice (SIS ll – 2019 Statistics) (2020) available at www.eulisa.europa.eu/sites/default/files/documents/SIS%20II%20-%202019%20-%20Statistics.pdf?utm_source=chatgpt.com (last accessed 16 January 2025).

[10] House of Lords, *Corrected oral evidence: Brexit: Future UK–EU Security and Policing Co-operation* (2016) available at www.data.parliament.uk/writtenevidence/committeeevidence.svc/evidencedocument/eu-home-affairs-subcommittee/brexit-future-ukeu-security-and-policing-cooperation/oral/41072.html (last accessed 3 April 2023).

the club. On that basis, the UK's access to SIS II was removed following its exit from the EU, and at the conclusion of the transition period on 31 December 2020. Senior figures within UK policing subsequently confirmed that 'the loss of SISII will have a major operational impact' and cause forces to 'circulate far fewer persons and objects'.[11]

# III. Operational Consequences

The SIS II is an alert-based system that allows policing agencies to circulate the details of persons, vehicles, property and specific items of intelligence to colleagues in countries across Europe. Prior to the loss of access to SIS II, its operational benefits were openly acknowledged by senior officers within UK policing, who described it as 'an absolute game-changer',[12] stating that 'it allows our officers to immediately see in front of them if somebody is wanted, if there is stolen property or if somebody needs to be arrested and extradited'.[13] In order to assess the impact of the loss of SIS II upon operational policing, we will examine in turn, the most widely used and useful alerts (or 'articles' as they are known within SIS II).

## A. Wanted Persons

An Article 26 alert allows the circulation of fugitives from justice (wanted persons) who are suspected of having committed a crime and are being actively sought by a policing agency. The circulation of a wanted person on SIS II is invariably accompanied by the creation of a European Arrest Warrant (EAW), which allows the arrest, detention and speedy extradition of that person if located within another Member State's jurisdiction. In practical terms, if a British police officer (pre-Brexit) had conducted a PNC check on a person, SIS II would have been checked simultaneously. If that person was circulated as wanted from any other SIS II-user country, the officer would have been able to immediately arrest and detain that person. The operational functionality afforded to officers by this feature is extremely useful when attempting to locate fugitives; and due to the integrated nature of the PNC and SIS II, creation of a wanted person domestically within the UK would automatically generate a Europe-wide SIS II Article 26 alert. Equally importantly, should British fugitives flee the UK and travel to Europe, a SIS II circulation could result in their detection and arrest. An example of this was provided in the case of a male wanted for the double murder of an elderly couple in the UK, whose vehicle was located at Dover. This led police to believe that the male had travelled to

[11] M Hewitt, NPCC Letter to Yvette Cooper (2020) available at www.committees.parliament.uk/publications/3466/documents/33316/default/; Home Office, 'Second generation Schengen Information System (SISII)' *gov.uk* (2015) available at www.assets.publishing.service.gov.uk/government/uploads/system/uploads/attachment_data/file/421540/SISII_General_Information_document.pdf (last accessed 3 April 2023).

[12] Hewitt (n 11).

[13] House of Commons, *Oral evidence: Progress of the negotiations on the UK's Future Relationship with the EU* (HC 203, 2020) available at https://committees.parliament.uk/oralevidence/694/pdf/ (last accessed 3 April 2023).

Europe; and following a SIS II circulation of the wanted person, the suspect was located in Luxembourg a few days later.[14]

## B. Missing Persons

Additionally, SIS II allows the circulation of missing persons using an Article 32 alert, which can greatly assist policing agencies in tracing often vulnerable persons across Europe's open internal borders. Given that human trafficking is an increasingly prevalent crime within Europe, circulations of this nature are an important feature of modern policing. A further useful application of this alert concerns cases of international child abduction, which make up the second largest category of missing children within the EU.[15] These incidents often feature parents of different nationalities, where one parent attempts to travel to their home country with their child, often in contravention of court orders and the wishes of the other parent.

## C. Sought for Judicial Purposes

Circulations under Article 34 tend to involve witnesses or suspects whose location is sought as part of an ongoing criminal investigation or judicial proceedings. Typically, a suspect in the early stages of an investigation might abscond before a police force has collated sufficient evidence to justify an arrest or initial interview. To properly proceed with the investigation, it might become necessary to speak with the suspect and an Article 34 alert would be created in an attempt to establish their location. Similarly witnesses who, having initially cooperated with an investigation, might subsequently disengage with the judicial process and abscond. Once again, an Article 34 alert would be the most appropriate method of attempting to determine their location.

## D. Discrete Checks

Article 36 alerts are created by investigating agencies that wish to collate intelligence on the movements of organised criminals without making them aware of an ongoing policing interest in their activities. An example of how this might work in practical terms would be if the police in the Netherlands created an alert involving a Dutch drug dealer. Should this person then travel to southern Spain to arrange the importation of controlled drugs, an Article 36 alert would allow the requesting agency in the Netherlands to be supplied with information that might include travel details, hotel check-in information, vehicles, and details of travelling companions and other associates. All this information would be provided to the requesting agency, without the

[14] A Saunders, 'Brexit: future UK–EU security and police cooperation' (2016) available at www.publications.parliament.uk/pa/ld201617/ldselect/ldeucom/77/77.pdf (last accessed 3 April 2023).

[15] Missing Children Europe, 'International Child Abduction' (2023) available at www.missingchildreneurope.eu/international-child-abduction/ (last accessed 3 April 2023).

suspect's awareness of any police interest in them or their movements. Clearly, alerts of this nature are extremely useful to investigating agencies when attempting to develop the intelligence picture around organised crime groups.

### E. Vehicles

Circulations using Article 36(2) alerts are important in allowing police officers to quickly identify stolen vehicles that have been transported across international borders. The benefits of a system that can quickly identify vehicles stolen from anywhere within the EU are obvious, and are particularly useful within Continental Europe, given the nature of the border-free Schengen Area.

### F. Objects

Article 38 alerts allow policing agencies to circulate details of lost or stolen objects in order that they might be subsequently located, if found elsewhere within the EU. These objects typically include items such as firearms or passports, and may also relate to items that are sought for evidential purposes.

### G. Borders

The SIS II allows law enforcement agencies employed in border control duties to be able to determine immediately if alerts relating to a potential entrant to the country indicate that they represent a threat to the safety and security of the nation. With such clear operational benefits, the border represents another area where the loss of SIS II was keenly felt. Shellaker et al have shown that 'the loss of the EAW and SIS II is significant, as police officers at UK borders will not be able to know if they are missing offenders'.[16]

## IV. Mitigation Strategies

As early as 2017, the National Crime Agency (NCA) and the NPCC began planning for the potential loss of access to European policing tools following exit from the EU. Unusually, the police services of both Scotland and Northern Ireland agreed to collaborate with the NPCC to provide a UK-wide solution, which illustrates the gravity with which the situation was viewed by police leaders. A joint NPCC/NCA team of international policing experts was quickly formed to work on the project, and they were supported in their work by the Home Office.

[16] M Shellaker, S Tong and P Swallow, 'UK–EU law enforcement cooperation post-Brexit: A UK law enforcement practitioner perspective' (2023) 24(4) *Criminology & Criminal Justice* 841.

Despite its huge operational value, due to various political and legal considerations, continued UK access to SIS II was quickly identified as one of the least likely EU policing tools to be retained. If SIS II access was indeed lost, the UK recognised that the Interpol I-24/7 database would be the only viable system of international circulations and alerts that would be available to UK officers. However, the wholescale adoption of I-24/7 as a replacement for SIS II was not without practical difficulties as several obstacles presented themselves. Although also an alert-based database system, the Interpol I-24/7 system lacks much of the functionality and ease of use associated with SIS II. This view was identified and publicly articulated by senior NPCC figures, who stated that 'if we lost SIS II, we would rely on the Interpol database. The Interpol database has some capability that is similar. It does not have all the capability that SIS has'.[17]

A further significant issue was the lack of integration between the PNC and I-24/7. While the seamless integration of SIS II and the PNC had allowed officers to automatically check both UK and EU-wide systems simultaneously, this was not possible with I-24/7. Similarly, the creation of a wanted or missing person on PNC, which would automatically create the appropriate alert on SIS II, was not possible with I-24/7. In practical terms, the long-awaited introduction of a new version of the PNC meant that the UK Government was unwilling to commit significant funds to upgrade the existing IT architecture within PNC, to allow automatic integration with I-24/7. Although work to semi-automate some Interpol circulations was undertaken prior to Brexit, the IT solutions that were put in place were relatively primitive and failed to fully replace SIS II functionality. 'Interpol is not linked to national systems and … it will be slower and lack the capability of SISII. Because of the differences between SISII and Interpol, forces will circulate far fewer persons and objects.'[18]

Prior to 2017, the Interpol I-24/7 system was chronically underused by UK police forces, which had quickly become reliant on SIS II as their principal tool for international circulations and alerts. Some forces had conducted little or no I-24/7 activity in recent years. In response, the NPCC established the International Crime Coordination Centre (ICCC) in March 2019, funded by the Home Office. The ICCC was established with a mandate to 'support and advise UK policing to better use international instruments, especially through the UK's withdrawal from the EU'.[19]

During 2019, one of the immediate priorities for the newly created ICCC was to address the persistent underuse of the Interpol I-24/7 system by police forces. As the main contingency system for loss of access to SIS II, the need was urgent to increase both the number of I-24/7 users and system transactions. In real terms at that time, some forces held very few I-24/7 user licences, and those that did exist were usually located within specialist units such as Force Intelligence Bureaux. The practical implications of this arrangement were that an officer requiring an urgent out-of-hours I-24/7 check on a suspect was unlikely to be able to obtain one. Using a comprehensive communication campaign during 2019, the ICCC began to make policing aware of the potential

[17] House of Commons (n 13).
[18] Hewitt (n 11).
[19] College of Policing, *Authorised Professional Practice – International Investigation* (2019) available at www.college.police.uk/app/investigation/international (last accessed 3 April 2023).

changes to operational capability that Brexit might bring. The ICCC network of regional 'single points of contact' (SPOCs) was then able to work with forces to significantly increase the number of trained I-24/7 users and to make sure that 24-hour coverage was provided to operational officers by ensuring that force control-room and custody staff were also trained to conduct I-24/7 checks. Ultimately, this work resulted in the issuing of around 6,000 additional I-24/7 user licences to staff within UK police forces and a significant increase in police usage of Interpol systems.[20]

A further challenge facing forces lay in the lack of integration between the PNC and the I-24/7 system. This resulted in the need for alerts and circulations, first, to have to be created on the PNC by operational officers, then for a form to be completed, containing the relevant details, which was forwarded to the NCA's International Crime Bureau, where the information was checked, and finally for an alert or circulation to be created on I-24/7 by NCA staff. Unsurprisingly, this process was described as 'clunky' and 'more bureaucratic, slower and complex'.[21] Given these problems, the ICCC also began work to alleviate some of the more bureaucratic parts of the process, and subsequently had some success in partially automating alerts by using 'smart forms' that ended some of the double keying of data that was required under the existing system. However, senior police leaders were keen to point out to politicians that the loss of SIS II, and its replacement with Interpol alerts, was far from satisfactory.[22]

The Interpol I-24/7 system itself does have some similarities with SIS II in that they are both alert-based systems that can be used for the circulation of persons and objects. For example, the SIS II Article 32 Missing Persons alert is equivalent to an Interpol Yellow (Missing Persons) Notice. However, despite the considerable efforts of UK policing to ensure that the Interpol I-24/7 system provided a workable replacement for SIS II, a further issue existed that threatened to undermine operational capability. Following the loss of access to SIS II, British policing was heavily committed to ensuring that the Interpol system was used for all UK alerts and circulations. To be effective, this arrangement also depends upon a degree of reciprocity from police forces in each EU country. For I-24/7 to be a truly effective replacement for SIS II, the UK is dependent upon EU countries' creating their alerts and circulations on both SIS II (to which they have full access) and I-24/7. Faced with the same double-keying issues as the UK, in many cases EU countries chose not to spend time and energy in populating I-24/7 as comprehensively as SIS II. To address this issue, the UK expended considerable effort in attempting to persuade EU policing agencies to increase their use of I-24/7 alerts and to encourage them to undertake this 'double-keying process'.[23]

Despite these efforts, the operational consequence of this inconsistency of approach is that a European criminal who might be circulated as wanted throughout the EU on SIS II, could travel to the UK undetected, if not also circulated as wanted on

[20] House of Lords, *Uncorrected oral evidence: Post-Brexit UK-EU security cooperation* (2023) available at www.committees.parliament.uk/oralevidence/12848/pdf/ (last accessed 3 April 2023).

[21] A France, 'Catching criminals "may take longer under no-deal Brexit", says senior Met officer Richard Martin' *Evening Standard* (19 December 2020) available at www.standard.co.uk/news/crime/richard-martin-police-criminals-nodeal-brexit-b384510.html (last accessed 3 April 2023).

[22] Hewitt (n 11).

[23] House of Lords (n 20).

an Interpol Red (Wanted Person) Notice. Invariably, this has caused a degree of 'operational blindness', which could mean that

> British police officers are now unable to determine whether or not a foreign national might in fact be a dangerous offender that represents a threat to British communities. Of course, this highly unsatisfactory arrangement is a two-way street, and European policing agencies will be similarly unsighted on whether dangerous British offenders are at large in continental Europe.[24]

The final issue confronting UK police officers when seeking to replace SIS II with the I-24/7 system concerns the arrest of wanted persons. While the circulation of a wanted person using and Article 26 SIS II alert is inevitably accompanied by an EAW, which allows for that person's immediate arrest, in UK law an Interpol Red Notice does not provide officers with the same power. On that basis, an officer checking a foreign national might (if indeed an Interpol check is requested) be informed that a Red Notice exists for that person and be told that they are a fugitive, wanted in another country. Unless the officer has grounds for an immediate arrest on suspicion of a crime committed in the UK, they would be obliged to allow that person to go on their way, as there is no mechanism in law for officers to arrest on a Red Notice unless in possession of a warrant issued by a British court. This was addressed prior to Brexit in legislation that introduced a power to arrest based on a Red Notice.[25] However, the power of arrest associated with the new Extradition (Provisional Arrest) Act 2020 is limited and only applies to specified countries in which the UK has a high degree of judicial trust. These include EU members and countries such as Australia, Canada, New Zealand, Switzerland and the United States.[26]

## V. Measuring the Loss of SIS II

Measurement of the true impact of the loss of SIS II is complicated by several factors, including a lack of empirical data and the disruptive effect of the Covid-19 pandemic restrictions on free movement. Crime statistics show that the police in England and Wales recorded a 13 per cent fall in total recorded crime between 2020 and 2021, while offences involving theft fell by 32 per cent, with a 10 per cent reduction in sexual offending.[27] Therefore, it is unlikely that the true impact of the loss of European policing tools during the immediate post-EU exit period will ever be known. Consequently, we must look to the experiences of practitioners to add context to any discussion of the impact of the loss of SIS II.

Research conducted with police officers in the months following loss of access to SIS II illustrates some of the views of practitioners and the operational challenges they face. Shellaker et al report that, without access to SIS II, officers consistently

[24] Pearson (n 4).

[25] Shellaker, Tong and Swallow (n 16).

[26] Extradition (Provisional Arrest) Act 2020 Ch 18.

[27] Home Office, *Crime Outcomes in England and Wales 2020–2021* (2021) available at www.gov.uk/government/statistics/crime-outcomes-in-england-and-wales-2020-to-2021/crime-outcomes-in-england-and-wales-2020-to-2021 (last accessed 3 April 2023).

described their inability to properly identify foreign criminals entering the country, with one officer stating 'we now have individuals crossing the border, and we haven't got a clue who they are: it's ridiculous'.[28] Further concerns were expressed about the inability of police officers to properly understand and control the threat represented by foreign national offenders once they have entered the country: 'So, they could be in this country doing whatever they want, and we wouldn't even know where they are.'[29] These views are a powerful indicator of the levels of dissatisfaction felt by operational officers when questioned about post-Brexit reductions in operational capability.

More recent interviews conducted by Davies and Farrand-Carrapico have identified that although the UK introduced a power to arrest based on Red Notices circulated via I-24/7, in practice there is a reluctance to arrest on this basis, and officers prefer to wait until an Arrest Warrant issued under the Trade and Cooperation Agreement (TCA) (known as a TCA warrant) is certified by the UK Central Authority (UKCA). This can lead to delay or even loss of an opportunity to arrest a wanted person (see Davies and Carrapico, chapter 4). Although many states are double keying alerts onto I-24/7 as requested by the UK, a TCA warrant is issued only if there is a known connection to the UK. If a person is wanted by the UK, an alert will be issued, but as Member State police databases do not automatically link to I-24/7, this is much less likely to be picked up than if an EAW were to be circulated via SIS II.[30] Although we have yet to know the statistical implications of these changes, for some time senior officers have acknowledged that there is a 'significant loss of capability in terms of access to data, which is automated and integrated within our systems'.[31]

As well as the loss of access to previous SIS II capabilities, the UK is now forced to observe from the sidelines future enhancements to the SIS II operating platform. These involve making significantly increased amounts of biometric data available to law enforcement agencies, including photographs, fingerprints, palm prints and DNA. Developments such as these will enable EU countries to share more information than ever before, and enhance the capabilities of their law enforcement agencies to circulate preventative alerts aimed at protecting vulnerable persons and disrupting terrorist activity. The UK will not benefit from these developments.

## VI. Potential Solutions

Law enforcement agencies in the UK remain hopeful that future revisions to Part Three of the TCA might yet be negotiated with the EU. A mechanism exists within the TCA that allows its provisions to be reviewed on a five-year basis,[32] including those

[28] Shellaker,Tong and Swallow (n 16).

[29] ibid.

[30] G Davies and H Carrapico, *Police and Judicial Cooperation Post Brexit* (Scottish Parliament, 2024).

[31] Shellaker,Tong and Swallow (n 16)/.

[32] C Coleman and N Newson, *UK–EU Trade and Cooperation Agreement* (2021) available at www.lordslibrary.parliament.uk/uk-eu-trade-and-cooperation-agreement/ (last accessed 10 May 2023).

relating to law enforcement and security. There is no doubt that law enforcement professionals, within both the EU and the UK, would welcome reconsideration of UK access to SIS II:

> Given the wider security environment, the strong shared interests in tackling what are largely shared threats, and the engagement of security and law enforcement professionals in finding ways to make the projected arrangements work, we must hope they will provide the basis for building cooperation in the future.[33]

However, the chances that the UK will quickly negotiate post-Brexit access to SIS II appear to be diminishing, with most commentators accepting that a further extended period of exclusion is likely.[34]

There is a recognition, within UK policing, that strengthening existing bilateral agreements with EU Member States might assist in bridging some of the operational gaps caused by the loss of SIS II. It is already the case that the TCA contains a 'legal basis for exchanging security alerts bilaterally'.[35] Police officers understand that close collaboration on matters related to transnational criminality is highly desirable and that strengthening bilateral working arrangements provides a quick win for the UK and the EU. The ICCC quickly identified, following its launch, that the foreign law enforcement community (FLEC) in London, which includes numerous EU police officers seconded to their various embassies, could prove useful. Mechanisms such as the FLEC and Europol (to which the UK retained access as a third country) are extremely useful in allowing UK officers to liaise and exchange information with EU agencies during dynamic crime and security investigations.[36] The 2022 bilateral agreement between the UK and Portugal provides evidence of a willingness among some EU Member States to further develop the working relationship with the UK beyond the terms of the TCA.[37] Agreements such as these provide some cause for optimism that future bilateral agreements with EU partners on the exchange of data and other information may well serve to further enhance operational capability.

The development of new technologies and data-sharing mechanisms with EU partners provides another opportunity to address the loss of access to SIS II. The UK has invested heavily in the development of a new IT system called the International Law Enforcement Alerts Platform (I-LEAP). The I-LEAP programme has two phases, the first of which is enhancement of functionality and connectivity between UK policing and Interpol IT systems. It is anticipated that I-LEAP will allow forces to automate the creation and circulation of alerts, and will go some way to addressing the ongoing lack of direct connectivity between UK systems and Interpol. By September 2024 a

[33] J King and J Scarlet, 'The Future of UK–EU Security Cooperation, The Future of UK–EU Security Cooperation' *RUSI* (2021) available at www.rusi.orghttps://www.rusi.org (last accessed 10 May 2023).

[34] R Syaland, 'UK police and Border Force to remain locked out of EU database of criminals' *The Guardian* (1 March 2023) available at www.theguardian.com/politics/2023/mar/01/uk-police-and-border-force-to-remain-locked-out-of-eu-database-of-criminals (last accessed 10 May 2023).

[35] King and Scarlet (n 33).

[36] House of Lords (n 20).

[37] Prime Minister's Office, UK–Portugal Joint Declaration on Bilateral Cooperation (2022) available at UK–www.gov.uk (last accessed 10 May 2023).

total of 46 UK police forces including those in Scotland, Northern Ireland, England and Wales had connected to Phase 1 of the I-LEAP system.[38]

The second phase of the I-LEAP project is an attempt to replicate much of the functionality of SIS II by concluding an EU-wide multilateral information-sharing agreement. It is anticipated that upon delivery of the project, the UK and EU countries will be able to share real-time alerts that have been described as 'a return to a SIS II-type functionality'.[39] The UK Government also intends to negotiate separate bilateral agreements with selected partner countries. It is likely that partner countries will include '5-Eyes' partners such as Australia, New Zealand and Canada. However, despite the rosy optimism of senior officers, who have declared that 'phase 2 of I-LEAP will be a real stride forward and will mean we are back to where we were in a position of SIS II',[40] it is unlikely that phase 2 of the I-LEAP programme will be delivered before 2027, and even this is optimistic as there is currently no buy-in from the EU.

Despite the clear operational difficulties for UK police officers represented by the loss of access to SIS II and other EU policing tools, some improvements have flowed from the Brexit process. The creation of the ICCC, using temporary Brexit funding from HM Treasury, was initially conceived as a no-deal Brexit mitigation measure. However, it has served to considerably raise the profile of both international criminality and the use of I-24/7 among frontline officers. Additional developments, such as the establishment of the National Extradition Unit and national programmes of training for frontline officers, helped to burnish the reputation of the ICCC. Subsequently, UK law enforcement recognised the value of a central unit dedicated to international enquiries that could act as a national resource to officers. In 2023, the functions of ICCC were absorbed into the NCA and re-launched as the Joint International Crime Centre (JICC). This change established the JICC as a fully funded unit with a permanent cadre of skilled staff able to develop interpersonal relationships with EU officers to aid international policing cooperation (see Thomson, chapter 11).

## VII. Conclusion

While UK law enforcement agencies, supported by the Home Office, made considerable efforts to mitigate the operational risks represented by Brexit, there is no doubt that the loss of SIS II has caused a significant loss of capability. The creation of the ICCC, together with greater use of the Interpol I-24/7 system, has allowed policing to 'make do and mend' while attempting to develop longer-term solutions to bridge the SIS II capability gap. However, for frontline officers, 'the practical consequence of this situation is that British police officers are now unable to determine' in many cases 'whether or not a foreign national might in fact be a dangerous offender that represents a threat

[38] House of Lords. International Law Enforcement Alerts Platform (2024) available at: https://hansard.parliament.uk/Lords/2024-09-02/debates/42E4320C-7A83-4790-BA27-636A700C9113/InternationalLawEnforcementAlertsPlatform.

[39] ibid.

[40] ibid.

to British communities'.[41] Post-Brexit, the operational reality for officers is reliance on sub-optimal SIS II replacements while the UK remains locked out of a system that would mitigate risk to communities within both the UK and Continental Europe.

The future does hold the promise of significant improvements, and the delivery of Phase 1 of the I-LEAP system will greatly enhance the effectiveness of Interpol's I-24/7 as an operational system within the UK. Phase 2 of I-LEAP may solve many of the operational problems caused by the loss of SIS II, but this will only happen with the agreement of the EU. Until that time, operational officers will continue to be confronted by risk and attempt to manage it using less sophisticated systems than those previously available. Ultimately, the inability of politicians to reach agreement on the UK's continued access to SIS II has eroded the ability of police officers, in both the EU and the UK, to ensure the safety and security of their citizens.

[41] Pearson (n 4).

# 7

# The EU–UK Trade and Cooperation Agreement Passenger Name Records Provisions: Framing the Effectiveness of Degrees of Legalisation and Institutionalisation

ELAINE FAHEY*

## I. Introduction

The topic of Passenger Name Records (PNRs) constitutes one of the most long-term, evolving and consistently controversial areas of European Union (EU) law in the Area of Freedom, Security and Justice (AFSJ). It has resulted in several highly controversial international agreements, much litigation and a directive with extraordinary origins from the 9/11 era of law making.[1] This chapter focuses upon its most recent and significant inclusion in a trade agreement with the UK, the EU–UK Trade and Cooperation Agreement (TCA).[2] The law relating to PNRs is usually found externally in international agreements with third countries. The TCA is highly striking as a trade agreement, in which PNRs are found in a lengthy chapter. Several decades on since its introduction into EU law, PNR law shows no sign of abating. Most of all it has failed to quell concerns as to its evolution, increasingly normalising it into ordinary EU law – but largely following on from a series of controversial decisions of the Court of Justice of the EU (CJEU). The EU now has a range of transfer PNR agreements with many non-EU countries, with several under negotiation, and which continue to be complex to renegotiate and which evolve in line with case law. The AFSJ, which Article 3(2) of the Treaty on European

* Thanks to Ivanka Karaivanova for research assistance. Thanks also to the editors for helpful comments received. The chapter develops further arguments set out in the works cited in nn 1 and 2.

[1] E Fahey, 'The life cycle of passenger name records in European Union law – on the normalisation of crisis' (2023) 70 *Irish Jurist* 211.

[2] Trade and Cooperation Agreement between the European Union and the European Atomic Energy Community, of the one part, and the United Kingdom of Great Britain and Northern Ireland, of the other part (EU–UK TCA) [2021] OJ L149/10.

Union sets out as an 'area', has been gradually 'regularised' over time as a legal and institutional space and has had a booming legislative agenda since the entry into force of the Treaty of Lisbon.[3]

Passeger Name Records embody many of the key characteristics of shifts in AFSJ law over time, evolving into a significant but also multifarious morass of law. Arguably the high-water mark of PNR law is constituted by the PNR chapter in the TCA, which provides for a range of new legal parameters for the treatment of PNRs in EU law, dominated by shifts in oversight provisions that are implemented in the TCA unlike in any other international PNRs agreement of the EU.

Increasingly, PNR law is also subject to judicial review.[4] Most concerns and much litigation have centred heavily upon oversight. This is despite the proliferation of PNR law, first as external relations law then as internal EU law. The CJEU's capacity to ameliorate its oversight elements has increasingly become critical, over the past number of years, from a human rights perspective, as will be outlined further in section III. As the EU AFSJ increasingly securitises and witnesses shifts in the use of PNR data stemming from borders and migration control, PNR law has evolved. Somewhat paradoxically and ironically, PNR law appears to be engaged in both deepening and widening its ostensible institutionalisation, evident in the TCA. Data transfer law has been heavily court-centric, but has also witnessed the CJEU's prescribing detailed outcomes in the review of PNR law.[5] It invites the question as to the place of oversight of these provisions and their broader place.

The law applying to PNRs seems to be evolving, with an increasing number of actors becoming involved in its governance. This has generated many controversies and challenges. This is particularly well embodied by the EU–UK TCA provisions on PNRs, where oversight becomes a key feature in the wake of *Opinion 2/15*, arguably as a form of *institutionalisation*, witnessed through turns towards deepening structures, more efforts to develop transparency, accountability and to embed actors as part of a range of processes.[6] The law on PNRs arguably reflects other areas of the AFSJ in showing significant *legalisation and institutionalisation* tendencies. There are multiple agreements, instruments and rules in the form of legalisation. This shift is thus demonstrated in a morass of emerging law, particularly of instruments, actors and powers. In this regard, this shift may be said to provide evidence of legalisation, a legalisation that is paradoxical and ironic, where its proliferation is responsive yet also responding to multiple subjects and objects and pursuing more agendas, but not necessarily with fundamental rights and the rule of law in mind.

This chapter thus explores descriptively the recent evolution of PNR law in EU external relations law, evolving into a trade agreement, with a plethora of new actors and

[3] Consolidated version of the Treaty on European Union [2012] OJ C326/13; Treaty of Lisbon amending the Treaty on European Union and the Treaty establishing the European Community, signed at Lisbon, 13 December 2007 [2007] OJ C306/1.

[4] See further in E Fahey, E Guild and EM Kuskonmaz, 'The Novelty of EU Passenger Name Records (PNR) in EU Trade Agreements: On Shifting Uses of Data Governance in Light of the EU–UK Trade and Cooperation Agreement PNR Provisions' (2023) 8(1) *European Papers – A Journal on Law and Integration* 273.

[5] Fahey (n 1).

[6] See E Fahey, *The EU as a Global Digital Actor* (Hart Publishing, 2023) Introduction. See also *Opinion 1/15*, ECLI:EU:C:2017:592.

oversight provisions through the framing of this evolution as degrees of legalisation and institutionalisation. Oversight is a key means to examine these developments, as one of the most important legal issues arising in EU law for PNRs in this period. It considers legalisation in section II, situating PNRs as an evolution of the AFSJ through law initially, moving now in the TCA into a trade agreement. Section III, on institutionalisation, sets out the many actors involved in PNRs oversight, and section IV discusses the early outcomes of that oversight, which appear to indicate unimpressive effectiveness, despite the many layers of governance (which are also non-transparent and difficult to decipher). The chapter concludes, in section V, that PNRs law generally appears to have many shortcomings that are not easily remedied or ameliorated by the TCA, however significant their presence there might be.

## II. On (Over)Legalisation?

The AFSJ was estimated to account for approximately 30 per cent of the EU's legislative output just a few years ago.[7] The AFSJ still suffers, despite this normalisation, from contradictions in practice.[8] First, there is a reasonable amount of legislation but few Court decisions until recently. Second, it is also a highly complex area, with significantly more treaty law/protocols/decisions on the AFSJ than on legislative matters, not necessarily reflecting more law and policy but rather the incomplete nature of integration, differentiation practices and partial institutionalisation. Third, where there is case law with respect to the AFSJ, some of it is characterised as generating extraordinary levels of injustice, as opposed to the history of free-movement law as a provider of rights and redress. Yet, fourth, at the same time, much substantive AFSJ law making is now conducted using maximalist harmonisation and nearly always increasingly using external norms. More law making in substantive areas of policy beyond procedural rules has also coincided with a period characterised by a plethora of soft law instruments and instruments designed to evade judicial review, deployed to manage core aspects of AFSJ migration policy in times of crisis. In such times, there is an increasing number of soft law tools in EU external migration, used to enable flexibility, deploying management lexicon, principles and tools as a means to avoid or minimalise the need for 'hard' binding law (eg, codes, frameworks, compacts, action plans).

[7] E De Capitani, 'Progress and Failure in the Area of Freedom, Security and Justice' in F Bignami (ed), *EU Law in Populist Times* (Cambridge University Press, 2020) 387; R Dehousse and O Rosenburg 'There Has Been a Substantial Drop in EU Legislative Output Since 2010'. *LSE EUROPP* (3 February 2015) available at https://blogs.lse.ac.uk/europpblog/2015/02/03/there-has-been-a-substantial-drop-in-eu-legislative-output-since-2010/ (last accessed 4 April 2024). See also A Ripoll Servent and F Trauner (eds), *The Routledge Handbook of Justice and Home Affairs Research* (Routledge, 2017); E Fahey, 'The Evolution of Transatlantic Legal Integration: Truly, Madly, Deeply? EU–US Justice and Home Affairs' in Ripoll Sarvant and Trauner (eds) ibid 336; E Fahey (2021) 'The Rise and Fall of International Law in the Post-Lisbon AFSJ Legislation Cycles' (2021) 1 *Groningen Journal of European Law* 1.

[8] Fahey, 'The Rise and Fall of International Law in the Post-Lisbon AFSJ Legislation Cycles' (n 7); E Fahey (2019) 'Hyper-legalisation and delegalisation in the AFSJ: on contradictions in the external management of EU migration' in J Santos Vara et al (eds), *Constitutionalising the External Dimensions of EU Migration Policies in Times of Crisis: Legality, Rule of Law and Fundamental Rights Reconsidered* (Edward Elgar, 2019).

Part Three, Title III of the TCA expressly states that it deals with the transfer, use and processing of 'passenger name record data' gleaned from flights between the Union and the UK, and provided to the UK's 'competent authority'; it also establishes 'specific safeguards' governing the data's use. All such data must be processed 'strictly' for the purposes of 'preventing, detecting, investigating or prosecuting terrorism or serious crime' or, in 'exceptional cases', where it is necessary 'to protect the vital interests of any natural person'. The processing of PNR data has 'become a widely used essential law enforcement tool, in the EU and beyond, to prevent and fight terrorism and other forms of serious crime, such as drugs-related offences, human trafficking, and child sexual exploitation'.[9] It thus evinces a wide array of legal purposes, methods and actions to engage in the regulation of PNRs. It is significant that it has evolved as a legal subject area to this point.

The TCA represents a high-water mark of EU third-country engagement in the area of PNRs because, unlike any other agreement, it contains a PNR-dedicated chapter. Agreements on PNRs usually tend to be found within/alongside trade agreements with third countries or on foot thereof, as evidence of deepening justice and home affairs collaborations. The evolution of PNR law into a trade agreement might be understood to be esoteric for some reasons. For some, Part Three of the TCA – the section dealing with law enforcement and judicial cooperation in criminal matters – indicates a spectrum of continuity/discontinuity in cooperation from 1 January 2021 onwards.[10] Although it constitutes an initial loss of operational efficiency and a diminution of formal British government influence over the strategic development of EU criminal justice law, institutions and operational priorities, it makes provision for 'business as usual' in PNR law as to general continuity for data sharing (biometric and vehicle data via the Prüm arrangements and criminal records), PNR screening and confiscation measures. Yet the placement of PNR law in a trade agreement, that is the TCA, labelled as a 'cooperation' agreement, is noticeable as a significant evolution of the legalisation of PNR law – and a very obvious form of *less* business as usual, marking significant change and legal form development.[11] In this regard, the operational nature of the TCA is one genre of study, whereas the substantive locus of PNR law constitutes another.

The placement of PNRs provisions in a trade agreement in the TCA is argued here to be a very noticeable effort at institutionalisation and legalisation in the face of other-country rejection thereof. The UK as a leader in PNR developments has been a key driver of PNR law and innovations, which makes the TCA all the more remarkable. This is because the trajectory of PNRs appears to have soured somewhat, given

[9] European Commission, 'Migration and Home Affairs' available at https://home-affairs.ec.europa.eu/policies/law-enforcement-cooperation/passenger-data_en (last accessed 4 April 2024).

[10] eg TJ Wilson, 'EU–UK criminal justice and security cooperation after Brexit: A perspective' (2021) 3 *Forensic Science International: Synergy* 100144; S Wolff, A Piquet and H Carrapico, 'UK's withdrawal from Justice and Home Affairs: a historical institutionalist analysis of policy trajectories' (2022) 20 *Comparative European Politics* 604.

[11] On terminology, see P Van Elsuwege 'A new legal framework for EU-UK relations: some reflections from the perspective of EU external relations law' (2021) 6(1) *European Papers* 785.

lesser interest from other third countries perhaps, where PNR negotiations have been simply abandoned (ie with Japan).[12] The view has been expressed in the United States (US) that the stringency of CJEU case law has reached its peak, subjecting countries like the US to standards not applicable within the EU itself. This situation makes the amelioration of EU–US PNRs difficult.[13] The TCA arguably represents a significant legalisation of PNRs developments, and this is no surprise in an era where PNRs are used for multiple purposes arguably beyond their original design – in particular in border control.[14]

More broadly, however, the controversy surrounding PNR law continues unbated given the evolution of crisis law post-9/11, and is thus carried over into external relations more centrally.[15] The entrenchment of crisis law making as to PNRs, first as external relations law, subsequently as internalised EU law in the form of a directive, has entailed its increasing legalisation, deepening securitisation in EU law and the controversial concept of the crisis in the AFSJ.[16] The difficulty with the legalisation emerging then, reaching into the EU's strongest competences externally in a trade agreement, controversially also is that it adds a veneer of respectability and legitimisation to the evolution of PNR law. This is because of the lack of direct effect of EU trade agreements (explicitly provided for in the TCA)[17] and the lack of transparent reporting regimes surrounding the implementation of trade agreements, irrespective of their bureaucratisation.[18] Thus the enhanced sophistication of the expression of the PNR provisions may provide evidence of the AFSJ as an area of law, but its proliferation of sources, instruments and outcomes is not per se something of consequence from a positive perspective. Even with more layers of oversight, legalisation does not in itself present a positive trajectory. Ironically, better governance and enhanced reporting, and more actors inside this new placement of PNR law, may simply indicate its over-legalisation, without any benefits whatsoever, and may thus follow the trajectory of much AFSJ law despite the PNR law's placement in the TCA *qua* trade chapter.

Section III examines the TCA PNR actors; we will return to the early evaluation of the TCA in section IV.

[12] For background, see E Fahey and I Wieczorek 'The European Parliament as a Defender of EU Values in EU–Japan Agreements: What Role for Soft Law and Hard Law Powers?' (2022) 47 *European Law Review* 331.

[13] For reasons of space, it is not possible to consider these issues further, but see K Propp, 'Why sharing passenger data doesn't fly for the EU's top court' *Atlantic Council* Blog (7 July 2022) available at www.atlanticcouncil.org/blogs/new-atlanticist/why-sharing-passenger-data-doesnt-fly-for-the-eus-top-court/ (last accessed 4 April 2024).

[14] Fahey, Guild and Kuskonmaz (n 2).

[15] Fahey (n 1).

[16] V Mitsilegas, 'The Preventive Turn in European Security Policy. Towards a Rule of Law Crisis' in Bignami (ed) (n 7) 301.

[17] See P Eeckhout, 'Brexit Sovereignty and its Dead Ends' (2022) 13 *Global Policy* 98.

[18] W Weiß, 'Delegation to treaty bodies in EU agreements: Constitutional constraints and proposals for strengthening the European Parliament' (2018) 14(3) *European Constitutional Law Review* 532; C Eckes and P Leino-Sandberg, 'The EU-UK Trade and Cooperation Agreement – Exceptional Circumstances or a new Paradigm for EU External Relations?' (2022) 85 *Modern Law Review* 164.

## III. On Institutionalisation

**Table 7.1** The Actors in PNR Oversight

| Actor | Article |
|---|---|
| Competent authority | 543 |
| Passenger Information Units (PIU) | 543 |
| Specialised Committee on Law Enforcement and Judicial Cooperation (Specialised Committee) | 552 |
| Independent administrative body | 552 |
| Judicial review | 553, 544 |
| Partnership Council | 1.4h |

There are many actors involved in the PNR TCA provisions. These actors, several new, several committee-like, form an important web of protections for citizens, but perhaps also a murky morass of entities that do not uniformly have citizens at the forefront.

A plethora of actors are provided for in the TCA, involved in tasks such as governance, supervision, communication, transfer, review and accountability that can broadly be said to relate to oversight. These include a competent authority, Passenger Information Units (PIUs), the Specialised Committee on Law Enforcement and Judicial Cooperation ('the Specialised Committee'), independent reviews, a judicial review and the Partnership Council, which are variously provided for in Part Three, Title III TCA. This is in addition to the broader governance structure of the TCA.[19] Whether they are cumulatively significant remains to be seen. Whether the TCA PNR provisions are compatible with the CJEU's *Opinion 1/15*, particularly as to oversight, also remains to be seen.[20]

The concept of 'competent authority' is defined in Article 543 of the TCA. The phrase 'UK competent authority' means a UK authority competent for the prevention, detection, investigation or prosecution of terrorist offences or serious crime that has been notified to the European Commission in accordance with Article 7(3) of the Passenger Name Record Directive.[21] The competent authority is pivotal to the operation of PNRs, including being responsible for receiving and processing PNR data under the TCA. Under Article 543(d), the PIUs serve as the competent authority for the Member States:

> Passenger Information Units ('PIUs') means the Units established or designated by Member States that are responsible for receiving and processing PNR data.[22]

[19] See N Levrat, 'Governance: Managing Bilateral Relations' in F Fabbrini (ed), *The Law & Politics of Brexit, vol 3: The Framework of New EU–UK Relations* (Oxford University Press, 2021) 219.

[20] Statewatch, 'Brexit: Commission answers to EU member state questions on the Trade and Cooperation Agreement' (25 January 2021) available at www.statewatch.org/news/2021/january/brexit-commission-answers-to-eu-member-state-questions-on-the-trade-and-cooperation-agreement/ (last accessed 4 April 2024).

[21] Directive 2016/681 of the European Parliament and of the Council of 27 April 2016 on the use of passenger name record (PNR) data for the prevention, detection, investigation and prosecution of terrorist offences and serious crime [2016] OJ L119/132.

[22] In the UK this is the Home Office (National Border Targeting Centre Independent Compliance Governance Team).

The competent authorities and PIUs, in turn, must 'cooperate' with one another, which provides a rare instance of bilateral institutional cooperation provided for under the TCA. A list of competent authorities is provided for in law.[23]

The main powers of the competent authority to use PNR data are set out in Article 544 of the TCA, entitled 'Purposes of the use of PNR data', which provides:

> 2. In exceptional cases, the [UK] competent authority may process PNR data where necessary to protect the vital interests of any natural person, such as:
> (a) risk of death or serious injury; or
> (b) a significant public health risk, in particular as identified under internationally recognised standards.

Under Article 551, it is provided that the governing principles of the competent authority, outlining automated processing of PNR data, entail that:

> The [UK] competent authority shall ensure that any automated processing of PNR data is based on non-discriminatory, specific and reliable pre-established models and criteria ….

Article 552(3) on retention of PNR data finally provides for unmasking powers, to the effect that:

> The [UK] competent authority may unmask PNR data only if it is necessary to carry out investigations for the purposes set out in Article 544. Such unmasked PNR data shall be accessible only to a limited number of specifically authorised officials.

The competent authority entity or concept is to be distinguished from the 'independent administrative body', as referred to in Articles 552(7), 552(11)(d), 552(12)(a) and 553 of the TCA, since the latter body has explicitly to be independent from the UK competent authority (UK PIU) and perform governance. This independence is necessary to 'assess on a yearly basis the approach applied by the [UK] competent authority as regards the need to retain PNR data pursuant to paragraph 4'.[24] It is also the only entity expressly mandated to ensure 'oversight' in relation to PNR data pursuant to Article 554.[25] Thus, it ostensibly complies with the CJEU's *Opinion 1/15*. The independent authority is required to supervise compliance with and enforcement of data protection. It is therefore a key actor of change in the TCA, marking a shift away from the EU–Canada PNR Agreement. This follows not only from the TCA but also from Article 36 of the Law Enforcement Directive (LED),[26] as it requires the EU to monitor the compliance with the data protection conditions by third countries, including a periodic review to reassess the adequacy decision. Therefore, Article 525(3) of the TCA provides that the Specialised Committee will be responsible for overseeing the data protection rules applicable to the cooperation under Part Three.

[23] Competent authorities designated by the United Kingdom under Part Three of the Agreement: Law Enforcement and Judicial Cooperation in Criminal Matters [2021] OJ C117I/11 available at https://eur-lex.europa.eu/legal-content/EN/TXT/PDF/?uri=CELEX:22021X0406(02) (last accessed 4 April 2024).

[24] EU–UK TCA, Art 552(7).

[25] EU–UK TCA, Art 554(d).

[26] Directive 2016/680 of the European Parliament and of the Council of 27 April 2016 on the protection of natural persons with regard to the processing of personal data by competent authorities for the purposes of the prevention, investigation, detection or prosecution of criminal offences or the execution of criminal

Article 546(1)–(4) provide that the UK competent authority shall share data 'upwards' and 'horizontally' with Europol or Eurojust, or horizontally with the PIUs of the Member States 'as soon as possible in specific cases where necessary to prevent, detect, investigate, or prosecute terrorism or serious crime'.[27] However, pursuant to Article 546(6), the UK competent authority and the PIUs of the Member States are required to ensure that only the minimum amount of PNR data necessary is shared under paragraphs (1)–(4).

Beyond these bodies sits a Specialised Committee on Law Enforcement and Judicial Cooperation.[28] Here, the TCA establishes a committee to assist the parties in their endeavour to reach a consensual solution and to foster their cooperation when allegations of breach of their duties under the TCA arise. The agenda and minutes of the Specialised Committee are online but do not clarify its membership in these documents. It has powers to take reports and thus provides for reporting and accountability.[29] Article 552(12) of the TCA provides that the UK

> shall provide to the Specialised Committee on Law Enforcement and Judicial Cooperation, nine months after the entry into force of this Agreement and again a year later if the interim period is extended for a further year:
>
> (a) a report from the independent administrative body ….[30]

At the time of writing, the agenda and minutes of the Specialised Committee's meetings reference ongoing reviews of a wide range of activity, yet consistently featuring PNR issues.[31] There are few references to courts in the PNR provisions. The terms 'court

penalties, and on the free movement of such data, and repealing Council Framework Decision 2008/977/JHA [2016] OJ L119/89.

[27] Art 546(2) of the TCA provides 'At the request of Europol or Eurojust, … the United Kingdom competent authority shall share PNR data, the results of processing those data, or analytical information containing PNR data, in specific cases where necessary to prevent, detect, investigate, or prosecute terrorism or serious crime.'

[28] See Art 552(12) of the TCA; See the European Commission website on the minutes of the Specialised Committee on Law Enforcement and Judicial Cooperation, available at https://commission.europa.eu/strategy-and-policy/relations-non-eu-countries/relations-united-kingdom/eu-uk-trade-and-cooperation-agreement/meetings-eu-uk-partnership-council-and-specialised-committees-under-trade-and-cooperation-agreement/specialised-committee-law-enforcement-and_en (last accessed 4 April 2024).

[29] The provision of Art 552(12) further specifies that the report 'shall include the opinion of the [UK] supervisory authority referred to in Article 525(3) as to whether the safeguards provided for in paragraph 11 of this Article have been effectively applied'. The UK shall also provide to the Specialised Committee on Law Enforcement and Judicial Cooperation 'the assessment of the [UK] of whether the special circumstances referred to in paragraph 10 of [Art 552] persist, together with a description of the efforts made to transform the PNR processing systems of the [UK] into systems which would enable PNR data to be deleted in accordance with paragraph 4 of [Art 552]'. See Art 552(12)(a) and (b), respectively, of EU–UK TCA.

[30] Thus Art 549(4) read in conjunction with Art 552(12)(a) of the TCA develops the next layer of oversight: it provides that 'The [UK] competent authority shall promptly inform the Specialised Committee on Law Enforcement and Judicial Cooperation of any significant incident of accidental, unlawful or unauthorised access, processing or loss of PNR data.' See A Janet (2021) 'Dispute settlement and jurisdictional issues for law enforcement and judicial cooperation in criminal matters under the EU–UK trade and cooperation agreement'. New Journal of European Criminal Law. 12: 290.

[31] eg TCA implementation, Mutual Legal Assistance (Art 635), DNA-profiles and fingerprints (Prüm) ex ante evaluation (Art 540), Passenger Name Record Data – UK report and assessment (Art 552), Mutual assistance on traffic offences (Art 640(7) TCA), Passenger Name Record data – update and expiration of derogation on Article 552(4), Anti-Money Laundering – (Article 654 TCA), Exchanges of DNA, fingerprints and vehicle registration data under Title II of Part Three of the TCA (akin to intra-EU 'Prüm'); see European Commission Website (n 28).

or independent administrative body', as mentioned in Article 552(7), refer to and on their face comply with the requirements set out by the CJEU in *Opinion 1/15* on the use and disclosure of PNRs. *Opinion 1/15* found that such had to be 'subject to prior review either by a court or by an independent administrative body'.[32] However, courts play a much more limited role in just two instances. Articles 553 and 544 of the TCA reference the capacity of a court to conduct a prior review or compel oversight. For instance, the competent authority has to process data where compelled by a court. Yet, overall, there are few such instances. Thus, the term 'independent body' is, as a result, arguably highly confusing. The title overall puts more faith in an independent administrative body than in courts and other tribunals, since the court has only one review competence in Article 553(2). The independent administrative body has to be independent from the UK competent authority, as referred to in Article 552(7), which requires the body to conduct an assessment 'on a yearly basis [of] the approach applied by the United Kingdom competent authority as regards the need to retain PNR data pursuant to paragraph 4'. Article 553 provides that the use of PNR data is subject to prior review by a court or independent administrative body based on a reasoned request by the UK competent authority, in those cases when the UK competent authority will use PNR data

> retained in accordance with Article 552 for purposes other than security and border control checks, including any disclosure under Article 555 and Article 556, only where new circumstances based on objective grounds indicate that the PNR data of one or more passengers might make an effective contribution to the attainment of the purposes set out in Article 544.[33]

Article 552(7), in conjunction with Article 552(12)(a), also provides that the UK shall ensure that a domestic supervisory authority responsible for data protection will have the power to supervise compliance with and enforcement of data protection. The UK is required to inform the EU of implementation and compliance. On the face of it, these provisions operate as a series of multiple governances and accountability checks.

In addition to all the above, the TCA also establishes the Partnership Council – chaired by both the UK and EU – with overall responsibility to oversee the implementation, application and interpretation of the TCA. Article 7(1)(b) of Title Three on the Institutional Framework provides that it can make recommendations to the parties regarding the transfer of personal data in specific areas covered by this Agreement or any supplementing agreement. The Partnership Council also seeks to resolve any issues that may arise during the implementation of the TCA and can also delegate some of its powers to the Trade Partnership Specialised Committees. The Partnership Council can amend certain parts of the TCA, 'provided that such amendments are necessary to correct errors, or to address omissions or other deficiencies', and can take binding decisions regarding the implementation of the TCA.[34] The function of the Partnership

[32] *Opinion 1/15* (n 6) para 208.
[33] EU-UK TCA, Art 553(1).
[34] Agreement on the withdrawal of the United Kingdom of Great Britain and Northern Ireland from the European Union and the European Atomic Energy Community 2019/C 384 I/01 [2019] OJ C384I/1, Art 164.

Council becomes significant directly and indirectly to oversight issues. Under the terms of Part Three of the TCA, the UK has been permitted to derogate from the obligation to delete all PNR data after individuals leave the UK if it applies additional safeguards designed to protect PNR data for an interim period. These additional safeguards reflect the CJEU's *Opinion 1/15* of 26 July of 2017 on the legality of the EU/Canada PNR Agreement and are listed in Part Three. The law enforcement agreement states that the UK has been allowed to derogate from this principle on the basis of 'special circumstances' that prevent the Government from 'making the technical adjustments necessary to transform the PNR processing systems,' which the UK operated while EU law applied 'into the systems which would enable PNR data to be deleted' in accordance with paragraph 4. These 'special circumstances' are not explained further.[35] For instance, the PNR data of most travellers has to be deleted after their stay in the UK has ended, which is an important development in line with *Opinion 1/15*.[36] However, the UK did not have to apply this particular provision for at least one year, and this derogation could be extended for another year if the Partnership Council agreed to it pursuant to Article 552(13) of the TCA. This has occurred twice under the Agreement, pursuant to two decisions of the Partnership Council at the time of writing, discussed next.[37]

# IV. The Early Outcomes of Oversight in the TCA

## A. On Process and Procedure

The PNR data of travellers who are not suspected of crimes and whose information is not needed for law enforcement purposes could thus be kept by the UK for another two years before the deletion obligation comes into force. The application of this provision has been reviewed.[38] The scope for manoeuvre on such sensitive

[35] See House of Lords European Union Committee, *Beyond Brexit: policing, law enforcement and security* (25th Report of Session 2019–21, 26 March) available at https://committees.parliament.uk/publications/5298/documents/52902/default/ (last accessed 4 April 2024).

[36] EU–UK TCA, Art 552(4); *Opinion 1/15* (n 6) paras 205–206.

[37] Decision No 2/2021 of the Partnership Council established by the Trade and Cooperation Agreement between the European Union and the European Atomic Energy Community, of the one part, and the United Kingdom of Great Britain and Northern Ireland, of the other part of 21 December 2021 as regards the extension of the interim period during which the United Kingdom may derogate from the obligation to delete Passenger Name Record data of passengers after their departure from the United Kingdom [2021] OJ L467/6; Decision No 2/2022 of the Partnership Council established by the Trade and Cooperation Agreement between the European Union and the European Atomic Energy Community, of the one part, and the United Kingdom of Great Britain and Northern Ireland, of the other part of 21 December 2022 as regards the second and last extension of the interim period during which the United Kingdom may derogate from the obligation to delete Passenger Name Record data of passengers after their departure from the United Kingdom [2022] OJ L328/153.

[38] Council Decision (EU) 2021/2293 of 20 December 2021 on the position to be taken on behalf of the Union in the Partnership Council established by the Trade and Cooperation Agreement with the United Kingdom regarding the extension of the derogation from the obligation to delete passenger name record data of passengers after their departure from the United Kingdom [2021] OJ L458/514.

data is thus a matter of some concern, largely evading oversight, as it does. It has been argued that the EU should not be tied by any arbitrary deadline and consider the overall protection of data being transferred at every opportunity.[39] However, this decision was taken early in the relationship, with swift application. The first meeting of the Specialised Committee on Law Enforcement and Judicial Cooperation took place on 19 October 2021, with minutes published only several months later, where, pursuant to Article 552 of the TCA, the UK report and assessment of Passenger Name Record Data was considered. The Specialised Committee noted that the opinion of the UK supervisory authority, included with the report of the independent administrative body (IAB) provided under Article 552(12) of the TCA, was based only on the information contained in the report of the IAB. The UK indicated that in view of the unique situation arising as a result of Covid-19, the UK supervisory authority was prepared to provide a note to complement its opinion in November, following a review of the operation of the interim period safeguards undertaken directly by the UK supervisory authority.[40] It is difficult to see any legal provision for this 'note' or to evaluate its potential legal salience. Then, in the second decision of the TCA Partnership Council (Decision 2/2021), it agreed on the extension of the interim period on 21 December 2021.[41] The EU position, taken on the Union's behalf in the Partnership Council pursuant to Article 552(13) of the TCA, was to agree to extend the interim period during which the UK might derogate from the obligation to delete the PNR data of passengers after they depart from the United Kingdom by one year, until 31 December 2022, which was renewed again in 2022 until the end of 2023. The second Partnership Council decision extending this period until the end of 2023 was expressed conclusively and finitely as to its extension period.[42]

The House of Lords European Union Committee asked the Government to explain the 'special circumstances' that permitted the UK derogation under Part Three and it received a terse reply that

> the phrase 'special circumstances' reflects the position the UK is in. Formerly, as a member state, we were cooperating under the PNR directive. As a third country, the EU is now required to treat us as a third country and therefore the CJEU opinion in respect of the EU–Canada Agreement applies to the UK in this respect. At the moment, our technical systems are not set up in a way that can fully comply with the requirements in the Agreement.[43]

[39] E Massé, 'Access Now's memo on the data transfers and PNR provisions under the EU–UK Trade Agreement' *Access Now* (January 2021) available at www.accessnow.org/cms/assets/uploads/2021/01/EU-UK-Deal-Data-transfers-PNR.pdf (last accessed 4 April 2024).

[40] European Commission 'First Specialised Committee on Law Enforcement and Judicial Cooperation under the EU–UK Trade and Cooperation Agreement' (2022) available at https://ec.europa.eu/info/publications/first-specialised-committee-law-enforcement-and-judicial-cooperation_en (last accessed 4 April 2024).

[41] Decision No 2/2021 of 21 December 2021 (n 37).

[42] eg Art 1 of Decision No 2/2022 (n 34) provides 'The interim period during which the United Kingdom may derogate from the obligation under Article 552(4) of the Trade and Cooperation Agreement to delete Passenger Name Record data of passengers after their departure from the United Kingdom is extended for a second and last time until 31 December 2023 pursuant to Article 552(13) of that Agreement.'

[43] House of Lords European Union Committee (n 35).

It also asked the Minister to clarify the exact nature of the 'independent administrative body' that will annually police the UK's adherence to standards in relation to PNR data retention. Minister Kevin Foster MP replied:

> The National Border Targeting Centre's independent compliance governance team, a functionally independent part of the UK's passenger information unit, not involved in the operational use of PNR data, has been designated by the Home Secretary as the independent body to undertake this work.[44]

The depth of this independence remains to be seen and appears complex to evaluate. Thus far, non-governmental organisations (NGOs) remain concerned.[45] Notably, on 22 February 2021, the European Data Protection Supervisor also issued a non-binding Opinion questioning the legality of aspects of these arrangements, including the use of the TCA as the sole legal basis for exchanging PNR data with the UK, and the potential three-year length of the derogation, points that appear important to consider.[46] It is worth remarking that the previous derogations were granted on the basis that the UK would be complying and deleting such data as part of the EU position in the Council Decision.[47] The Home Secretary further wrote in late 2023 to the House of Lords Justice and Home Affairs Committee undertaking as much, and a recent European Commission report on the implementation and application of the TCA in 2023 mentions only, without more, the successful operation of the provisions:

> Implementation of the TCA in relation to law enforcement and judicial cooperation functioned smoothly … On the transfer of Passenger Name Record (PNR) data by air carriers to the UK for flights between the EU and the UK, in line with Article 552(15) of the TCA, the interim period expired on 31 December 2023. From 1 January 2024, the United Kingdom must delete a passenger's PNR data …, unless a risk assessment indicates a need to retain such data ….[48]

[44] House of Lords, European Union Committee, Security and Justice Sub-Committee, *Corrected oral evidence: Post-Brexit UK-EU security co-operation* (16 February 2021) available at https://committees.parliament.uk/oralevidence/1723/html/ (last accessed 4 April 2024).

[45] See T Bunyan and C Jones, 'Brexit: Goodbye and hello: The new EU-UK security architecture, civil liberties and democratic control'. *Statewatch* (20 January 2022) available at www.statewatch.org/brexit-goodbye-and-hello-the-new-eu-uk-security-architecture-civil-liberties-and-democratic-control (last accessed 4 April 2024).

[46] ibid 19; Opinion on the conclusion of the EU and UK trade agreement and the UK and EU exchange of classified information agreement (22 February) available at https://edps.europa.eu/system/files/2021-02/2021_02_22_opinion_eu_uk_tca_en.pdf (last accessed 4 April 2024).

[47] Council Decision (EU) 2022/2574 of 19 December 2022 on the position to be taken on behalf of the Union within the Partnership Council established by the Trade and Cooperation Agreement between the European Union and the European Atomic Energy Community, of the one part, and the United Kingdom of Great Britain and Northern Ireland, of the other part, as regards the extension of the interim period referred to in Article 552(11) of that Agreement during which the United Kingdom may derogate from the obligation to delete Passenger Name Record data of passengers after their departure from the United Kingdom [2022] OJ L334/98.

[48] Home Secretary, Letter to Baroness Sally Hamwee, Chair, House of Lords Justice and Home Affairs Committee (18 October 2023) available at https://committees.parliament.uk/publications/41869/documents/207633/default/ (last accessed 4 April 2024); European Commission COM(2024) 127 final on the implementation and enforcement of the Trade and Cooperation Agreement 1 January–31 December 2023 available at https://commission.europa.eu/document/download/def518e5-144b-4e73-a54a-5b078544da48_en?filename=COM-2024-127_0_en.pdf (last accessed 4 April 2024).

Despite the phraseology and emphasis upon the mandatory nature of the obligation, there is no other detail provided as to compliance with it or enforcement.

## B. Evaluating the TCA PNR Actors and Actions

There was scant information available at the time of writing as to *how* these decisions on the PNR derogation were arrived at and its implications. Their evaluation is thus more complex. The effectiveness of the Partnership Council, in particular, in securing effective oversight above and beyond the breath of the generous PNR provisions, generous to transfers more than oversight perhaps, has been a concern for many.[49] Nonetheless, while all such issues are essentially moot in the face of the expiry of the derogation, the procedures expose the breadth and latitude granted to the UK as to data transfer in the area of PNRs, irrespective of the framing of the latitude. They also show the veneer of oversight operating here, through layers of actions, actors and procedures.

The vast range of oversight actors provides an example of the layers of institutionalised governance emerging. However, their effectiveness and the actual 'reach' of the layers of governance remains to be seen.[50] Early analyses of the TCA are highly critical of the outcomes relative to the labyrinth of bodies and structures.[51] The TCA has an additional later layer of annual reporting that remains the substantive difference, along with the putative layer of courts engaging in judicial review. The opaqueness of the layers of TCA PNR governance will arguably continue to be problematic.

The extensive range of data transfers taking place therein unifies academics, civil liberties groups and NGOs alike in their opposition thereto, not dissimilar to most PNR law, which attracts wide-ranging and reasonably unified condemnation of its existence.[52] Notably, threats still existed at the time of writing on the part of the UK Government post-Brexit, to exit the Council of Europe European Convention on Human Rights and to allegedly 'reform' the General Data Protection Regulation in the Data Protection and Digital Information (No 2 Bill).[53]

# V. Conclusions

The topic of PNRs constitutes one of the most long-term, evolving and consistently controversial areas of EU law in the AFSJ. It has resulted in several highly controversial

[49] See, eg, the submissions and outline arguments of comments received throughout in House of Lords European Union Committee (n 35).

[50] See Levrat (n 19).

[51] See Bunyan and Jones (n 45).

[52] ibid; O Garner, 'Part Three of the EU–UK TCA – From a 'Disrupted' Area of Freedom, Security and Justice to "New Old" Intergovernmentalism in Justice and Home Affairs?' Brexit Institute Working Paper Series No 1/2021 (3 February 2021) available at https://papers.ssrn.com/sol3/papers.cfm?abstract_id=3778183 (last accessed 4 April 2024).

[53] UK Government, *The Benefits of Brexit: how the UK is taking advantage of leaving the EU* (January 2022) available at www.gov.uk/government/publications/the-benefits-of-brexit (last accessed 4 April 2024); European Convention on Human Rights of 1950; Regulation (EU) 2016/679 of the European Parliament and of the Council of 27 April 2016 on the protection of natural persons with regard to the processing of personal data and on the free movement of such data, and repealing Directive 95/46/EC (General Data Protection Regulation) [2016] OJ L119/1.

international agreements, much litigation and a directive with extraordinary origins from the 9/11 era of law making. Passenger Name Record law has become a victim of a constant cycle of litigation. This is evident most recently in relation to the PNR Directive challenge, where the CJEU sought to rewrite Belgian law in *Ligue des droits humains*.[54] Given the highly controversial nature of PNR law, its checks and balances have generated much concern. Various litigants, from the European Parliament to NGOs, have sought to litigate it. However, again paradoxically, a corpus of law has evolved from the CJEU that is not necessarily producing ameliorated outcomes. Legalisation and institutionalisation are argued here to be a core feature of PNR law embodying AFSJ, where it proliferates over a relatively short period of time. Whether it evolves to be an effective oversight system remains to be seen. The TCA provisions indicate a higher degree of legalisation of PNRs to date, which is important and worthwhile, particular in light of the significance of data in the TCA. Yet from a more specific perspective, PNR law shows an evolution here that is difficult to match when compared with other partners. There appear to be many shortcomings and challenges of PNR law generally that are not easily remedied or ameliorated by the TCA, however significant the TCA PNR provisions may be.

[54] Case C-817/19 *Ligue des droits humains*, ECLI:EU:C:2022:491.

# 8

# The UK's (Non-)Participation in Interoperable Centralised and Decentralised Systems for Information Exchange: Paying a Heavy Price for Brexit?

NIOVI VAVOULA

## I. Introduction

The departure of the United Kingdom (UK) from the European Union (EU) created shockwaves around law enforcement authorities, whose work heavily relies on the processing of personal data to prevent, detect and investigate criminal offences. This involved both the UK authorities, which relied on their counterparts in other EU Member States (EUMS), and law enforcement authorities located in the EU, as the UK has had a pioneering role in law enforcement. This chapter aims to analyse the UK's participation in centralised and decentralised information exchange mechanisms in the law enforcement context post-Brexit, and to highlight the exchange opportunities offered by the Trade and Cooperation Agreement (TCA) and what the UK is missing out on.

The chapter is structured as follows: section II provides a concise overview of the centralised and decentralised information exchange systems – operational and under development – in the EU Area of Freedom, Security and Justice (AFSJ), which concern police cooperation. Section III explains how variable geometry and the UK's extended opt outs from the AFSJ led to somewhat fragmented – yet particularly important – participation in centralised exchange systems, namely the Schengen Information System (SIS), and various decentralised exchange mechanisms, such as Prüm, the European Criminal Record Information System (ECRIS) and Passenger Name Records (PNRs). Section IV examines the participation of the UK in centralised and decentralised mechanisms in the post-Brexit era, looking into the limits and opportunities offered by the TCA. In section V it is concluded that the TCA enables the continuation of data exchanges in relation to the Prüm, PNR and ECRIS mechanisms under provisions largely similar to the existing EU rules, although some discrepancies with the EU rules may be seen as problematic. At the same time, the loss of access to SIS has had a significant impact on the operation of UK law enforcement authorities, as the alternative avenue via Interpol does not allow for the same functionalities as SIS.

## II. Centralised and Decentralised Information Exchange Systems: In a Nutshell

A central pillar of the development of EU criminal law has been the establishment of mechanisms aiming at facilitating the exchange and other forms of processing of personal data, particularly in the context of combating terrorism and serious crimes. These legislative initiatives have relied upon Article 87(2)(a) of the Treaty on the Functioning of the European Union (TFEU) and have been two-pronged.[1] On one hand, emphasis has been placed on the establishment of EU-wide *centralised* information systems for law enforcement purposes. On the other hand, legal instruments have aimed at eliminating obstacles to the exchange of personal data among national law enforcement authorities through *decentralised* mechanisms of information exchange.

With regard to centralised databases, the most emblematic instrument is the Schengen Information System (SIS), a centralised IT system operational since 1995.[2] The System has two branches, for immigration control[3] and law enforcement, and registers alerts on various categories of persons and objects. With regard to its law enforcement branch, governed by Regulation 2018/1862,[4] SIS stores alerts on persons wanted for arrest and extradition,[5] missing persons or vulnerable persons who need to be prevented from travelling,[6] persons sought to assist with a judicial procedure,[7] persons or objects subject to discreet inquiry or specific checks,[8] objects sought for the purpose of seizure or their use as evidence in criminal proceedings,[9] unknown wanted persons[10] and third-country nationals suspected of involvement in terrorist offences or other serious crimes (see Pearson, chapter 6).[11]

The System forms part of an elaborate network of IT systems that process personal data of third-country nationals.[12] These systems are: the operational Visa Information

[1] TFEU [2012] OJ C326/47. For an analysis, see V Mitsilegas and N Vavoula, 'Databases' In V Mitsilegas (ed), *EU Criminal Law*, 2nd edn (Hart Publishing, 2022) ch 5.

[2] See Art 93 of the Convention implementing the Schengen Agreement [2000] OJ L239/19 (CISA).

[3] Regulation 2018/1860 of the European Parliament and of the Council of 28 November 2018 on the use of the Schengen Information System for the return of illegally staying third-country nationals [2018] OJ L312/14.

[4] Regulation 2018/1862 of the European Parliament and of the Council of 28 November 2018 on the establishment, operation and use of the Schengen Information System (SIS) in the field of police cooperation and judicial cooperation in criminal matters, amending and repealing Council Decision 2007/533/JHA, and repealing Regulation (EC) No 1986/2006 of the European Parliament and of the Council and Commission Decision 2010/261/EU [2018] OJ L312/56.

[5] ibid Arts 26–31.

[6] ibid Arts 32–33.

[7] ibid Arts 34–35.

[8] ibid Arts 36–37.

[9] ibid Arts 38–39.

[10] ibid Arts 40–41.

[11] ibid Arts 37a–37b.

[12] See N Vavoula, *Immigration and Privacy in the Law of the EU: The Case of Information Systems* (Brill Nijhoff, 2022).

System (VIS)[13] and Eurodac,[14] the forthcoming Entry/Exit System (EES),[15] the European Travel Information and Authorisation System (ETIAS)[16] and the European Criminal Record Information System for Third-Country Nationals (ECRIS-TCN).[17] With the exceptions of Eurodac, which was set up to assist the Dublin system in determining the Member State responsible for examining an asylum application, and ECRIS-TCN, which has its origins in the decentralised ECRIS and is thus based on Article 82(1) TFEU, the rest of the systems form part of the Schengen *acquis*. Importantly, all these systems are accessible by law enforcement authorities, either for the fight against terrorism and serious crimes in accordance with specific conditions – that is the case for VIS, Eurodac, EES and ETIAS – or, in the case of ECRIS-TCN, for various purposes.[18] These systems are to become interoperable by 2027, in accordance with Regulations 2019/817[19] and 2019/818.[20] This means that the different data will be combined and interconnected in novel ways to pursue various aims, such as to facilitate quick access to all systems simultaneously (European Search Portal – ESP), identify multiple identities (Multiple Identity Detector – MID) and streamline law enforcement access (Common Identity Repository – CIR).

As for decentralised systems, various legal instruments have aimed at promoting police cooperation through exchanges of personal data. This is notwithstanding the

[13] Regulation (EC) No 767/2008 of the European Parliament and of the Council of 9 July 2008 concerning the Visa Information System (VIS) and the exchange of data between Member States on short-stay visas (VIS Regulation) [2008] OJ L218/60.

[14] Eurodac processes the fingerprints of asylum seekers and certain categories of irregular migrants for asylum-related purposes. Regulation 603/2013 of the European Parliament and of the Council of 26 June 2013 on the establishment of 'Eurodac' for the comparison of fingerprints for the effective application of Regulation (EU) No 604/2013 establishing the criteria and mechanisms for determining the Member State responsible for examining an application for international protection lodged in one of the Member States by a third-country national or a stateless person and on requests for the comparison with Eurodac data by Member States' law enforcement authorities and Europol for law enforcement purposes, and amending Regulation (EU) No 1077/2011 establishing a European Agency for the operational management of large-scale IT systems in the area of freedom, security and justice (recast) [2013] OJ L180/1.

[15] Regulation (EU) 2017/2226 of the European Parliament and of the Council of 30 November 2017 establishing an Entry/Exit System (EES) to register entry and exit data and refusal of entry data of third-country nationals crossing the external borders of the Member States and determining the conditions for access to the EES for law enforcement purposes, and amending the Convention implementing the Schengen Agreement and Regulations (EC) No 767/2008 and (EU) No 1077/2011 [2017] OJ L327/20.

[16] Regulation (EU) 2018/1240 of the European Parliament and of the Council of 12 September 2018 establishing a European Travel Information and Authorisation System (ETIAS) and amending Regulations (EU) No 1077/2011, (EU) No 515/2014, (EU) 2016/399, (EU) 2016/1624 and (EU) 2017/2226 [2018] OJ L236/1.

[17] Regulation (EU) 2019/816 of the European Parliament and of the Council of 17 April 2019 establishing a centralised system for the identification of Member States holding conviction information on third-country nationals and stateless persons (ECRIS-TCN) to supplement the European Criminal Records Information System and amending Regulation (EU) 2018/1726 [2019] OJ L135/1.

[18] N Vavoula, 'Consultation of EU Immigration Databases for Law Enforcement Purposes: A Privacy and Data Protection Assessment' (2020) 22 European Journal of Migration and Law 139.

[19] Regulation (EU) 2019/817 Regulation (EU) 2019/817 of the European Parliament and of the Council of 20 May 2019 on establishing a framework for interoperability between EU information systems in the field of borders and visa and amending Regulations (EC) No 767/2008, (EU) 2016/399, (EU) 2017/2226, (EU) 2018/1240, (EU) 2018/1726 and (EU) 2018/1861 of the European Parliament and of the Council and Council Decisions 2004/512/EC and 2008/633/JHA [2019] OJ L135/27.

[20] Regulation (EU) 2019/818 of the European Parliament and of the Council of 20 May 2019 on establishing a framework for interoperability between EU information systems in the field of police and judicial cooperation, asylum and migration and amending Regulations (EU) 2018/1726, (EU) 2018/1862 and (EU) 2019/816 [2019] OJ L135/85.

formidable challenges for legality and fundamental rights, due to the differences in the regulation of police authorities between EUMS, which are closely related to the position of the police in the criminal justice system and the domestic constitutional framework.[21] In particular, mutual legal assistance has been pushed with a view to exchanging national criminal records, DNA files or fingerprint data. ECRIS facilitates the exchange of criminal records amongst national authorities by interconnecting national criminal records databases.[22] Directive (EU) 2023/977 lays down the rules under which EUMS law enforcement authorities may exchange existing information and intelligence effectively and expeditiously for the purpose of conducting criminal investigations or criminal intelligence operations.[23] Finally, the Prüm regime, first developed outside the EU framework but subsequently incorporated into EU law, regulates the exchange of DNA, fingerprint and vehicle registration data between EU law enforcement authorities.[24] In March 2024, it was replaced by Prüm II, aimed at establishing a central router for exchanging biometric data, allowing automated searches of two new categories of data (facial images and police records), and including Europol and its databases in the Prüm system. In addition, through the router the latter will become part of the interoperability framework.[25] The objective of creating Prüm II is to further automate the cross-border sharing of personal (and often highly sensitive) data: people's faces, fingerprints and DNA data, vehicle registration data and police records. Europol will also be responsible for the development and technical management of a separate European Police Records Index System (EPRIS) – a central infrastructure that would be used to carry out automated searches of police records for those EUMS that decide to participate.

These initiatives are complemented by various other schemes co-opting the private sector in law enforcement. A major move to involve the private sector in cooperating with the state in the fight against crime has occurred in the field of anti-money laundering (AML), whereby dedicated Financial Information Units (FIUs) receive information on suspicious transactions by different entities in the private sector,[26] the retention of metadata by telecommunications companies, and the transfer of air travellers' data (PNR data) to national Passenger Information Units (PIUs) in accordance with the PNR Directive.[27]

[21] See Mitsilegas and Vavoula (n 1).

[22] Council Framework Decision 2009/315/JHA of 26 February 2009 on the organisation and content of the exchange of information extracted from the criminal record between Member States [2009] OJ L93/23; Directive (EU) 2019/884 [2019] OJ L151/143.

[23] Directive (EU) 2023/977 of the European Parliament and of the Council of 10 May 2023 on the exchange of information between the law enforcement authorities of Member States and repealing Council Framework Decision 2006/960/JHA [2023] OJ L134/1.

[24] Council Decision 2008/615/JHA of 23 June 2008 on the stepping up of cross-border cooperation, particularly in combating terrorism and cross-border crime [2008] OJ L210/1; Council Decision 2008/616/JHA of 23 June 2008 on the implementation of Decision 2008/615/JHA on the stepping up of cross-border cooperation, particularly in combating terrorism and cross-border crime [2008] OJ L210/12.

[25] Regulation (EU) 2024/982 of the European Parliament and of the Council of 13 March 2024 on the automated search and exchange of data for police cooperation, and amending Council Decisions 2008/615/JHA and 2008/616/JHA and Regulations (EU) 2018/1726, (EU) No 2019/817 and (EU) 2019/818 of the European Parliament and of the Council (the Prüm II Regulation) [2024] OJ L2024/982.

[26] V Mitsilegas, *Money Laundering Counter-measures in the European Union: A New Paradigm of Security Governance versus Fundamental Legal Principles* (Kluwer Law International, 2003).

[27] Directive (EU) 2016/681 of the European Parliament and of the Council of 27 April 2016 on the use of passenger name record (PNR) data for the prevention, detection, investigation and prosecution of terrorist offences and serious crime [2016] OJ L119/132.

# III. The UK's Participation in Large-scale IT Systems Pre-Brexit and Post-Brexit

## A. Variable Geometry in the EU Area of Freedom, Security and Justice

The UK's participation in the EU *acquis* in general and the AFSJ in particular has been underpinned by constitutional complexity, exemplified by extensive opt outs in the field of EU migration and criminal law since the Amsterdam Treaty.[28] The *sui generis* position of the UK as a non-Schengen EU Member State signified that not all IT systems were accessible to British authorities, considering that many of these formed part of the Schengen *acquis* in which the UK did not participate. Furthermore, with the adoption of the Lisbon Treaty,[29] the UK had the right not to participate in the whole of Title V TFEU, including criminal law matters. The block opt out also extended to legislation amending existing legal instruments that were binding upon the UK. Furthermore, Protocol No 36 on Transitional Provisions retained the pre-Lisbon limited powers of EU institutions regarding (former) third-pillar law for a transitional period of five years after the entry into force of the Lisbon Treaty.[30] When the transitional period came to an end on 1 December 2014, the UK exercised that block opt out, but rejoined 35 (former) third-pillar measures in the area of police and judicial cooperation in criminal matters, this having been 'thoroughly assessed', 'judged to be in the national interest' and deemed 'vital'.[31] In between the Treaty of Lisbon and the UK's departure from the EU, the UK opted to join a further 30 or more police and criminal justice measures, such as the PNR Directive.

## B. Limited and Problematic Participation in Centralised Databases

With regard to SIS, the UK participated in its law enforcement branch between 2015 and 2020.[32] Such participation was problematic, as the UK persistently breached

[28] Treaty of Amsterdam amending the Treaty on European Union, the Treaties establishing the European Communities and certain related acts [1997] OJ C340/1. J Monar, 'The "Area of Freedom, Security and Justice": "Schengen" Europe, Opt-Outs, Opt-Ins and Associates' in K Dyson and A Sepos (eds), *Which Europe? The Politics of Dierentiated Integration* (Palgrave Macmillan, 2010).

[29] Treaty of Lisbon amending the Treaty on European Union and the Treaty establishing the European Community, signed at Lisbon [2007] OJ C306/1.

[30] Consolidated version of the Treaty on European Union – PROTOCOLS – Protocol (No 36) on transitional provisions [2008] OJ C115/322.

[31] HL Deb 7 February 2017 vol 778, col 1669, available at www.parliament.uk/globalassets/documents/publications-records/house-of-lords-publications/hansard-bound-volumes/hl_bv778_index.pdf (last accessed 16 April 2024).

[32] Council Implementing Decision (EU) 2015/215 of 10 February 2015 on the putting into effect of the provisions of the Schengen acquis on data protection and on the provisional putting into effect of parts of the provisions of the Schengen acquis on the Schengen Information System for the United Kingdom of Great Britain and Northern Ireland [2015] OJ L36/8.

the SIS rules.[33] Internal documentation listed years of violations by British authorities, which were deemed to constitute 'serious and immediate risks to the integrity and security of SIS data as well as for the data subjects'.[34] The examples were numerous: the data copied was handed to border police even though some of the information was not only incorrect but also outdated, thus potentially meaning that innocent people visiting or living in the UK ran the risk of being flagged for violations they had never committed from data that was unlawfully copied and stored; the UK ignored alerts issued by other EUMS, to the extent that vehicles stolen in the territory of another Member State and located in the UK were not seized;[35] and the UK made numerous full and partial copies of SIS, increasing the risk of data breaches.

In turn, as the UK participated in the Dublin system for the allocation of the Member State responsible for the examination of applications for international protection, it also operated Eurodac and could consult that system for law enforcement purposes. The UK was not connected to the VIS, and its efforts to be connected to VIS solely for law enforcement purposes were in vain; in Case C-481/08 *UK v Council*, the Court of Justice of the European Union (CJEU) opined that the UK could not have a pick-and-choose policy regarding legislative instruments implementing the Schengen *acquis*.[36] The judgment clarified that the development of the common visa policy was the core objective, and any use of the database in the context of law enforcement must be treated as secondary and collateral. The CJEU took note of the specific conditions of law enforcement access that testify to its exceptional character. Thus, opening up VIS to criminal law agencies would go beyond the original purpose of the database, so it was necessary to specify rules and procedures to limit access. Moreover, the UK was equally excluded from the EES and ETIAS, which are also part of the Schengen *acquis* in which the UK did not participate. As for ECRIS-TCN, the UK had expressed its interest in participating, but following Brexit this was not possible.

## C. Extensive Use of Decentralised Systems

The extended opt outs of the UK from criminal justice cooperation caused significant delays in the implementation of the Prüm regime into the UK legal order. The UK was able to exchange DNA data between June 2019 until December 2020[37] and fingerprint data between August and December 2020;[38] it never put in place the cooperation system

[33] N Nielsen 'UK Unlawfully Copying Data from EU Police System' *Euobserver* (28 May 2019) (last accessed 16 April 2024).

[34] European Commission, *Report of re-evaluation visit to the UK on Schengen Information System* (2018). Also see European Commission (2020) COM(2020) 165 final, available at www.statewatch.org/media/documents/news/2020/may/eu-com-uk-sis-law-breaking-action-plan-assessment-com-2020-165-fin.pdf (last accessed 16 April 2024).

[35] N Nielsen, 'UK Taking "Steps" after Illegal copying of EU Schengen data' *Euobserver* (25 July 2019) available at www.euobserver.com/rule-of-law/145530 (last accessed on 16th April 2024). See Council Document 6003/20 (declassified 24 March 2023).

[36] Case C-482/08 *UK v Council*, ECLI:EU:C:2010:631.

[37] Council Implementing Decision (EU) 2019/968 of 6 June 2019 on the launch of automated data exchange with regard to DNA data in the United Kingdom [2019] OJ L156/8.

[38] Council Implementing Decision (EU) 2020/1188 of 6 August 2020 on the launch of automated data exchange with regard to dactyloscopic data in the United Kingdom [2020] OJ L265/1.

for vehicle registration data. Parliament wished to exclude biometric data held by UK authorities on individuals suspected of committing a criminal offence from Prüm searches, to only permit searches of data concerning recordable offences and to apply higher forensic science standards in the course of determining matches of DNA and fingerprint data. In June 2020, the then UK Government unilaterally decided to include suspects' data in its automated biometric data exchanges within the shareable Prüm dataset for all of the EU.[39] This move was seen as the UK's offering an olive branch to the EU in light of the negotiations for their future relationship on security aspects.[40] Furthermore, the UK benefited enormously from ECRIS; according to a Commission report, until 2019 the UK was the second most active user (after Germany) and was one of the EUMS requesting information considerably more often than it was requested to provide information.[41] Finally, the UK took part in the PNR system,[42] but in view of Brexit, the EU evaluation of the implementation of the PNR Directive, no specific information was provided as regards any implementation issues.[43]

# IV. Post-Brexit

In the post-Brexit era, the UK has lost access to centralised systems, particularly SIS, as well as the possibility to participate in the interoperability components in the future; however, the TCA enables exchange of personal data broadly mirroring the PNR and ECRIS rules.

## A. Losing Access to SIS

During the Brexit negotiations, it became clear quite early that continuation of benefitting from the wealth of personal data stored in the information systems, particularly with regard to SIS, was out of the question. British negotiators had sought to maintain access to SIS as part of a deal, following security-related concerns raised by police chiefs – after all, the UK was checking the system around 603 million times per year, thus making it a very significant pool of information.[44] This was notwithstanding the UK's stated negotiating position, seeking a future agreement on law enforcement cooperation between the UK and EU that provided 'capabilities similar to those delivered by SIS'. Indeed, SIS contains around 86 million alerts and is searched more

[39] See House of Commons European Scrutiny Select Committee, 'Cross-border police cooperation: the automated exchange of DNA and fingerprint data under Prüm' (9 September 2020) available at www.publications.parliament.uk/pa/cm5801/cmselect/cmeuleg/229-xv/22911.htm (last accessed 16 April 2024).

[40] 'UK Agrees to Share Suspects' DNA with EU Crime-fighting System' *The Guardian* (15 June 2020) available at www.theguardian.com/politics/2020/jun/15/britain-agrees-share-suspects-dna-eu-crime-fighting-system (last accessed 16 April 2024).

[41] European Commission, COM(2020) 778 final, 6.

[42] Passenger Name Record Data and Miscellaneous Amendments Regulations 2018 (SI 2018/598).

[43] European Commission, SWD(2020) 128 final.

[44] 'Priti Patel Claims Brexit Leaves UK Safer despite Losing Access to Key EU Databases' *The New European* (26 December 2020) available at www.theneweuropean.co.uk/brexit-news-westminster-news-priti-patel-on-brexit-deal-6870862/ (last accessed 16 April 2024).

than 86 billion times per year.[45] However, it has been legally impossible to offer access to any country not in the Schengen Area, including the UK. Therefore, enforcement officers can no longer immediately have access to real-time data about persons and objects of interest. To downplay the importance of this, the UK Government subsequently stressed that less than 0.5 per cent of SIS records relate to persons of interest to law enforcement, with most of them being immigration documents to which the UK never had access before Brexit.[46] As a result, around 40,000 alerts on dangerous criminals and wanted suspects had to be deleted by the end of December 2020 when the UK left the EU. Similarly, 5.7 million alerts originating from the UK were deleted at the end of 2021.[47]

Losing access to SIS has meant that the UK now relies on the sharing of information with EUMS through the Interpol I-24/7 system, which contains around 90 million Notices and Diffusions. This is the primary mechanism, but alternatives exist, that is, the UK Liaison Bureau in Europol and via the National Crime Agency's extensive network of International Liaison Officers. Assistant Chief Constable Ayling described this arrangement as falling 'a long way short of the benefits provided by SIS'.[48] Indeed, the effectiveness of the fall-back procedure depends on EUMS' 'double keying' alerts, in both SIS and the Interpol system. Furthermore, EUMS must make a decision, in each case, about whether to use this process, and each Member State has its own operational procedures and legislation in respect of Interpol to determine at what point an alert may be circulated on Interpol systems. This creates uncertainty and concerns as to whether the UK is missing out on SIS alerts that are not uploaded on to the Interpol database. Officials were originally optimistic that UK law enforcement bodies would still get access to the data they needed, with the number of red notices coming through Interpol said to be broadly the same as previously received through SIS – or around 90 per cent.[49] The most recent information on the effectiveness of the substitute solution is contradictory: whereas sources reveal that the Interpol system is working but it is considerably slower, and is therefore not being used as often to check on suspects' credentials, the Home Office has insisted that the use of Interpol data is working well and that there is no risk to public safety.[50] A key challenge in this respect affecting slowness is that the Interpol I-24/7 database provides data in a matter of hours, not seconds, therefore information to front-line officers is not provided in real time, as was the case with SIS, though work

[45] EU-LISA, 'SIS II 2022 – Annual Statistics'. available at www.eulisa.europa.eu/Publications/Reports/SIS%20II%202022%20Statistics%20-%20Report.pdf (2023) (last accessed 16 April 2024).

[46] 'UK not Missing out on Crime Intelligence' post-Brexit' *Police Professional* (8 June 2021) available at www.policeprofessional.com/news/uk-not-missing-out-on-crime-intelligence-post-brexit/ (last accessed on 16th April 2024).

[47] EU-LISA (n 45) 12.

[48] House of Lords European Union Committee, *Beyond Brexit: Policing, Law Enforcement and Security* (25 March 2021) 23 available at https://committees.parliament.uk/publications/5298/documents/52902/default/ (last accessed 16 April 2024).

[49] Police Professional (n 46).

[50] R Syal, 'UK Police and Border Force to Remain Locked out of EU Database of Criminals' *The Guardian* (1 March 2023) available at www.theguardian.com/politics/2023/mar/01/uk-police-and-border-force-to-remain-locked-out-of-eu-database-of-criminals (last accessed 16 April 2024).

has been underway to increase the speed at which Interpol Notices are available to UK frontline law enforcement officers.[51]

The UK aspires to improve the exchange of alert data between the UK, EU and third countries, through the development of the International Law Enforcement Alert Platform (ILEAP).[52] This will provide a single platform for UK law enforcement authorities to access and share alerts related to people, documents and objects with international partners on a reciprocal basis. It is to be implemented in two phases, whereby the first phase will deliver a direct and real-time connection to Interpol data; under the second phase, a longer-term goal is to provide reciprocal access to international alert data exchange with international partners, prioritising the EU. As such, ILEAP may be capable of replicating some of the functionality of SIS, subject to agreements with EU and international partners.[53] Gaining access to EU datasets is at a very early stage and is not expected to be completed before 2027/2028.[54] Partly, the timeline to implement the second phase of ILEAP is related to the emergence of an EU initiative to develop a framework for reciprocal access to security-related information for border guards in the EU and partner third countries to detect criminals and terrorists efficiently. Clearly, the proposal has been influenced by efforts to boost cooperation between the UK and the EU in the post-Brexit era, with the Home Office stating that it hopes to 'engage and influence EU partners' to ensure the Commission's proposal 'is aligned with UK requirements'.[55] Reference to the inadequacies of how criminal justice data is currently shared via Interpol's systems is also noted in the call for evidence.[56] An EU-wide solution could offer reciprocal, direct and real-time access to security-related alerts between the UK and all EUMS, but so far it has been heavily criticised, as potentially disregarding EU data protection law, which is one of the most robust data protection frameworks worldwide.[57] Of relevance to these initiatives is a Commission initiative for a framework for reciprocal access to security-related information for frontline officers between the EU and key third countries to counter shared security threats. The UK is likely to be one of these partners, allowing it to counterbalance the lack of access to SIS.[58]

[51] House of Lords European Union Committee (n 48) 24–25. See also Home Office, Letter from the UK Home Office to Baroness Hamwee (18 October 2023) available at www.committees.parliament.uk/publications/41869/documents/207633/default/ (last accessed 16 April 2024).

[52] Home Office, *International Law Enforcement Alerts Platform (I-LEAP) Programme* (February 2023) available at www.gov.uk/government/publications/home-office-major-programmes-accounting-officer-assessments/international-law-enforcement-alerts-platform-i-leap-programme (last accessed 16 April 2024).

[53] Statewatch, *International Police Data-sharing: What Are the UK and EU Cooking up?* (19 July 2023) available at www.statewatch.org/analyses/2023/international-police-data-sharing-what-are-the-uk-and-eu-cooking-up/ (last accessed 16 April 2024).

[54] Syal (n 50).

[55] Home Office (n 52).

[56] European Commission, *Security-related information sharing – reciprocal access for frontline officers in the EU and key partner countries* (2023) available at www.ec.europa.eu/info/law/better-regulation/have-your-say/initiatives/13243-Security-related-information-sharing-%E2%88%92-reciprocal-access-for-frontline-officers-in-the-EU-and-key-partner-countries_en (last accessed 16 April 2024).

[57] European Digital Rights *Have Your Say Initiative: Security Related Information Sharing* (2023) available at www.privacyinternational.org/sites/default/files/2023-03/Security%20Related%20Information%20Sharing%20-%20Joint%20Submission.pdf (last accessed 16 April 2024).

[58] For concerns, see Statewatch, *Submission to European Commission Consultation on "Security-related Information Sharing"* (29 March 2023) available at www.statewatch.org/analyses/2023/submission-to-european-commission-consultation-on-security-related-information-sharing/ (last accessed 16 April 2024).

## B. UK Nationals: From EU Citizens Excluded from the Personal Scope of Databases to Third-Country Nationals whose Data are Processed in Interoperable Databases

Exiting the EU has signified that British nationals' data will be checked against the information systems in question, as they have become third-country nationals. This concerns ETIAS, EES, VIS and ECRIS-TCN, and has the following consequences: regarding ETIAS, all UK nationals who wish to travel to the Schengen Area will be required to obtain a travel authorisation prior to their trip, thus their personal data will be stored in ETIAS. Similarly, EU nationals will be subject to equivalent requirements following the implementation of the UK Electronic Travel Authorisation Scheme. The latter was rolled out in October 2023 in respect of Qatari nationals, and in February 2024 it was expanded to nationals of Bahrain, Jordan, Kuwait, Oman, the United Arab Emirates and Saudi Arabia. However, the roll out will be further extended to nationals of the EU and North America by the end of 2024. Furthermore, as VIS will be used to store records of long-stay visa and residence permit applicants, UK nationals applying to any Schengen state for a longer visit will necessarily have their personal data stored and further processed therein. Moreover, as EES will monitor the entry and exit (place and time) of all short-stay travellers, irrespective of whether they need a visa or not, visa-free UK travellers' data will be stored in EES too. This is important, because, as mentioned above, these systems will also operate on an ancillary basis as law enforcement tools; therefore, UK nationals' data will be cross-checked for crime prevention or detection. Finally, personal data regarding the criminal records of British nationals who are convicted in an EU Member State, including dual nationals also holding the nationality of an EU Member State, will be stored in ECRIS-TCN.

## C. Prüm

Whereas access to SIS has been discontinued, exchanges of data via decentralised systems have largely remained intact. Title II of Part Three of the TCA enables the continuation of Prüm-based cooperation by allowing automated transfers of DNA profiles, fingerprints and vehicle registration data through detailed provisions that replicate the EU's current (Prüm I) rules.[59] This means that there is no direct, real-time access to sensitive personal data (DNA and dactyloscopic data); rather, access is through a decentralised system that confirms a match (hit/no-hit). The querying state is merely informed whether the profile sought is available in the other states' databases. In the case of a hit, further information may be obtained by contacting the state holding the data or initiating a request for mutual legal assistance. Furthermore, the TCA obliges the UK and EUMS to allow competent authorities of other states access to all categories of data available for search and comparison under the same conditions as those applicable to their domestic authorities. However, under Article 540 of the TCA, before any

[59] The procedural and technical details for the implementation of Title II are set out in Annex 39.

exchange of data can be carried out, the UK must submit an *ex ante* evaluation. Based on the evaluation report (and possibly a pilot run regarding vehicle data, an exchange that was not taking place before Brexit), the EU will decide the date on which personal data may be sent to the UK. This is confusing, given that the UK will have already been subject to an evaluation by means of which it will have already started exchanging DNA and dactyloscopic data. The provision provides that the UK and EUMS can only carry out exchanges based on the Prüm regime for nine months after entry into force of the TCA and the date an evaluation visit took place to extend exchanges.[60] Indeed, since 30 June 2022, such exchanges have taken place, but not on vehicle registration data.[61]

The substantive reform of the Prüm framework in 2024 has necessitated a formal amendment to Title II of Part Three of the TCA if the UK wishes to continue its participation. The TCA anticipates such amendment if the EU laws underpinning Prüm cooperation (the Prüm I rules) are 'substantially' amended or are 'in the process of being amended substantially'.[62] The process requires the EU to notify the UK that it wishes to agree a formal amendment of the relevant TCA provisions via the governance structures established in the TCA (the Specialised Committee for Law Enforcement and Judicial Cooperation ('the Specialised Committee')). The notification will trigger an initial nine-month period of consultations, which could lead to the suspension of Prüm cooperation (in full or in part) if the EU and UK are unable to agree on a formal amendment of the TCA. The suspension could be extended for a further nine months while consultations continue. If there is still no agreement, cooperation will then cease. The Prüm reform raises several important issues from the perspective of constitutional law and the protection of human rights. First, whether it will be possible, if negotiations do not progress well, to retain the status quo, as currently set out in the TCA. The wording of Article 541 of the TCA suggests that the UK will either have to agree to the new arrangements, with possible tweaks, or lose the cooperation that it currently enjoys.[63] This creates a situation whereby the UK, prior to Brexit, took part in the legislative process at EU level and could influence the adopted legislation, whereas in the post-Brexit era the UK has no such say. Second, Prüm II has been heavily criticised by the European Data Protection Supervisor (EDPS) and civil society actors as violating the rights to privacy and personal data protection, particularly by failing to demonstrate the necessity and proportionality of its measures, due to its vastly expanded categories of personal data. Unlawfully retained photos of millions of individuals who have

[60] P Arnell et al 'Police Cooperation and Exchange of Information under the EU–UK Trade and Cooperation Agreement' (2021) 12(2) *New Journal of European Criminal Law* 265.

[61] Council Decision (EU) 2022/1014 of 17 June 2022 on the position to be taken on behalf of the Union vis-à-vis the United Kingdom of Great Britain and Northern Ireland regarding the determination under Article 540(2) of the Trade and Cooperation Agreement between the European Union and the European Atomic Energy Community, of the one part, and the United Kingdom of Great Britain and Northern Ireland, of the other part, of the date from which personal data relating to DNA profiles and dactyloscopic data as referred to in Articles 530, 531, 534 and 536 of that Agreement may be supplied by Member States to the United Kingdom [2022] OJ L170/68.

[62] TCA, Art 541.

[63] House of Commons European Scrutiny Committee, *Sixteenth Report of Session 2022–23* (March 2023) 8–15. available at www.committees.parliament.uk/publications/34666/documents/190803/default/ (last accessed 16 April 2024).

never been charged with a crime, referred to as 'custody images', will likely be opened up to searches by police forces in EUMS.[64] As a result, the UK might wish to make tweaks to Prüm II to ensure compatibility with human rights and not uncritically accept the EU reforms. Third, the inclusion of Europol and its databases within the revised Prüm framework would enable EUMS to check biometric data shared with Europol by third countries (such as the UK), and Europol to check the same data received from these third countries against EUMS national databases. Fifth, in the UK, the negotiation of international treaties remains a prerogative of the executive, and the formal role reserved for parliamentary scrutiny is close to non-existent. In practice, some limited parliamentary oversight has been granted in recent years, but it is entirely within the Government's power to negotiate, sign and ratify treaties without informing Parliament of any the details beforehand.[65] This means that Parliament's views, including any concerns or criticisms, may be sidelined in this process for the sake of keeping up with the developments in the EU and maintaining access to EU-wide avenues of information exchange.

## D. Passenger Name Records

Title III of Part Three of the TCA provides for continued UK access to PNR data for flights departing from the EU, and vice versa, under rules largely reflecting those of the EU PNR Directive and taking into account *Opinion 1/15* of the CJEU regarding the draft EU–Canada PNR Agreement.[66] Here, there are two key issues of interest. First, the TCA includes a temporary derogation of one year for the UK to make necessary technical adjustments for the deletion of PNR files upon passengers' departure,[67] in accordance with Article 552(4) of the TCA and in compliance with *Opinion 1/15*.[68] The UK must report to the Specialised Committee after nine months, and if the technical issues persist, the Partnership Council may extend the interim period by another year, but this period must cease after three years.[69] The interim period for the derogation ended in December 2023, the UK confirming that it was on track to transform its data-processing systems into systems that would enable PNR data to be deleted.[70] However, before this date, PNR data of travellers whose information was not needed for law enforcement

[64] Statewatch, *UK Participation in 'Unnecessary' Police Facial Recognition System Needs Open, Thorough, Democratic Debate* (31 October 2023) available at www.statewatch.org/news/2023/october/uk-participation-in-unnecessary-police-facial-recognition-system-needs-open-thorough-democratic-debate/ (last accessed 16 April 2024).

[65] Statewatch, *Brexit: Goodbye and Hello – The New EU–UK Security Architecture, Civil Liberties and Democratic Control* (20 January 2022) available at www.statewatch.org/media/3050/eu-uk-brexit-goodbye-and-hello.pdf (last accessed 16 April 2024).

[66] *Opinion 1/15*, ECLI:EU:C:2017:592.

[67] TCA, Art 552(11).

[68] *Opinion 1/15* (n 66) paras 204–211.

[69] TCA, Art 552(12). For concerns, see EDPS, *EDPS Opinion on the conclusion of the EU and UK trade agreement and the EU and UK exchange of classified information agreement.* (2021) 12 available at www.edps.europa.eu/system/files/2021-02/2021_02_22_opinion_eu_uk_tca_en.pdf (last accessed 16 April 2024).

[70] LEJC, *EU–UK Trade and Cooperation Agreement (TCA): Third meeting of the Specialised Committee on Law Enforcement and Judicial Cooperation (LEJC)* (19 June (2023) available at www.commission.europa.eu/system/files/2023-06/Agenda%20-%20Third%20meeting%20of%20the%20Specialised%20Committee%20on%20Law%20Enforcement%20and%20Judicial%20Cooperation.pdf (last accessed 16 April 2024).

purposes could be kept by the UK before the deletion obligation came into force. In December 2023, the UK confirmed that it had completed the required technical adjustments to the UK's PNR data systems; thus, as from 1 January 2024, the UK must comply with the retention regime as with all other TCA requirements. The Commission must continue monitoring the UK's compliance with the PNR provisions in the context of the Specialised Committee, as established by the TCA. Second, the TCA allows the UK to use PNR for other purposes in 'exceptional cases' when it is 'necessary to protect the vital interests of any person'. Those exceptional cases can concern either 'a risk of death or serious injury' or, more controversially, 'a significant public health risk', in particular as identified under internationally recognised standards.[71] This was not foreseen in the UK legislation implementing the EU PNR Directive. According to the Commission, the use of PNR data does not contradict the prescriptions of the EU PNR Directive, as the provision applies only to the UK (not between Member States) in exceptional circumstances. Furthermore, similar agreements with third countries recognise that there may be exceptional circumstances where PNR data can be processed to protect the vital interests of any individual, such as a risk of death or serious injury or a significant public health risk, and the CJEU, in its *Opinion 1/15* has already accepted the exceptional use of PNR for such purposes.[72]

## E. European Criminal Record Information System

Title IX of Part Three of the TCA enables exchanges of information extracted from criminal records between the UK and EUMS to continue under rules close to the ECRIS legal framework. Its provisions supplement the relevant articles in the Council of Europe Mutual Legal Assistance (MLA) Convention and Protocols[73] and take precedence over the MLA provisions in the TCA. Accordingly, central authorities are obliged to inform one another of convictions handed down against nationals of other states, at least once per month ('as soon as possible' under the ECRIS rules), while requests must be replied to within 20 working days (10 days under the ECRIS rules). As mentioned, the TCA does not provide for the exchange of criminal records information on third-country nationals – that would not be possible given the nature of ECRIS-TCN as a centralised database. Instead, the UK can access such information by making 'bilateral requests' to EUMS for data about third-country nationals.[74] In practice, as EUMS continue to use ECRIS to cooperate with the UK, the UK has built its own infrastructure (UKRIS), compatible with ECRIS.[75]

[71] TCA, Art 544(2).

[72] See Council, WK 793/2021, available at www.statewatch.org/media/1759/eu-uk-agreement-questions-com-wk-793-21.pdf (last accessed 16 April 2024).

[73] Council of Europe, European Convention on Mutual Assistance in Criminal Matters (opened for signature 20 April 1959, entered into force 12 June 1962) ETS No. 30; Additional Protocol to the European Convention on Mutual Assistance in Criminal Matters (opened for signature 17 March 1978, entered into force 12 April 1982) ETS No. 99; Second Additional Protocol to the European Convention on Mutual Assistance in Criminal Matters (opened for signature 8 November 2001, entered into force 1 February 2004) ETS No. 182.

[74] House of Lords European Union Committee (n 48) 22.

[75] ibid 21.

## F. How Will Future Interoperability Affect UK–EU Police Cooperation?

The forthcoming interoperability of large-scale IT systems for third-country nationals will mean that law enforcement authorities and Europol will have to comply with 'streamlined', simplified rules for law enforcement access to immigration data. This would have been relevant to the UK only in connection with Eurodac, to which it had access, as both SIS and ECRIS-TCN have a strong law enforcement dimension and therefore law enforcement access is not subject to the specific conditions under which data in Eurodac, VIS, EES and ETIAS may be consulted. Besides, SIS will not be connected to the Common Identity Repository, one of the interoperability components, due to its complex architecture, allowing EUMS to operate national copies of SIS. Therefore, at first sight one might argue that the UK would not have missed out on the implementation of interoperability. This would be a short-sighted viewpoint, considering that the interoperability components are only the beginning of a long process of making not only centralised information systems but also decentralised ones interoperable. This has already started materialising in the case of Prüm, through its connection with the central router, which will be interconnected with CIR. Furthermore, PNR data and a sub-set of it, Advanced Passenger Information (API) data, will also become part of the interoperability framework, as a router similar to that envisaged in Prüm II will be developed to facilitate the transfer of API data by the air carriers to national competent authorities not only for border-control purposes but for law enforcement as well.[76] Therefore, the departure of the UK from the EU has significant implications for UK law enforcement authorities, as they miss out not only on the opportunities offered by an interoperability framework to speedily access relevant information stored in different systems and governed by different instruments, but importantly on the ability to quickly combine the information from these different sources. As for the interoperability of EU-wide IT systems, this does not hinder access of the UK to any decentralised systems under the TCA. Interoperability is merely a way to enable more efficient use of the data already stored in centralised or decentralised systems among EUMS, without affecting any transfers outside the EU. This is why Regulation (EU) 2024/982, regulating Prüm II, does not make any reference to the position of the UK.

# V. Conclusion

This chapter aimed to examine the challenges arising from the UK's participation (and non-participation) in centralised and decentralised mechanisms of exchange of law enforcement-related information in the post-Brexit era. The chapter highlighted that the TCA enables the continuation of access to Prüm, PNR and ECRIS mechanisms under provisions largely similar to the existing EU rules, although some discrepancies have raised eyebrows, particularly in relation to the EU–UK exchange of PNR data.

[76] European Commission (2020) COM(2022) 731 final. The final text has been agreed but has not been formally adopted yet.

Nevertheless, it must be recalled that the arrangements in Part Three of the TCA can be suspended or even terminated if the UK does not remain in step with changes to EU data protection law (eg, if the UK were to significantly repeal the Data Protection Act 2018), or if the UK is found to have breached fundamental rights when handling personal data. This is reflected in the use of a sunset clause in the EU adequacy decision according to which the validity of the adequacy is limited to 27 June 2025.[77] Furthermore, it is clear that the loss of access to SIS is a gaping hole with a significant operational impact for both the EU and the UK. This is evidenced by the ongoing efforts to ensure mutual access to police databases for authorities in the EU and UK, but also beyond. Thus, Brexit has had a catalysing effect in reconfiguring the European security architecture. Importantly, the chapter demonstrated that the forthcoming reforms of the information exchange mechanisms, including through the implementation and expansion of the interoperability framework, will necessitate amendments to the TCA, with corresponding challenges about parliamentary scrutiny and the ability of the UK to significantly deviate from what its EU counterparts have already agreed at EU level (without its participation). Furthermore, initiatives such as interoperability of information exchange mechanisms, both centralised and decentralised, will create opportunities for EUMS on which the UK will miss out.

[77] European Commission Implementing Decision (EU) 2021/1773 of 28 June 2021 pursuant to Directive (EU) 2016/680 of the European Parliament and of the Council on the adequate protection of personal data by the United Kingdom [2021] OJ L360/69, Art 4.

# 9

# Cross-border Policing Cooperation under UK–EU Agreements: Policing the Post-Brexit Irish Border

VICKY CONWAY, SHELLEY DEANE AND KATY HAYWARD*

## I. Introduction

Cross-border police cooperation is challenging in and of itself,[1] with a particular set of complex 'logistic, legal, institutional, cultural and political problems'.[2] Rules followed by the police services on either side of the border can vary significantly, for example around surveillance, electronic communications, exclusionary rules and when disclosure occurs. Differences can also exist in police roles and competencies in each jurisdiction. More broadly, state priorities and resources can also differ, leading to a mismatch in what can be committed to a cross-border policing investigation. Limitations encountered in sharing information and data between jurisdictions can mean that even the scale of a cross-border criminal operation may not be known.

Such complexities are all the greater in the case of a border that is both physically and politically at the core of historical contestation between two states. The 499km/310-mile border on the island of Ireland became a security frontier during the 'Troubles' for the last three decades of the twentieth century, with military and police forces seeking to monitor and control movement across it. The dismantling of the military watchtowers and checkpoints along the border, and the reopening of small roads that traversed it were seen as signs of the success of the 1998 Good Friday/Belfast Agreement that brought the Troubles to an end.[3] When added to the ever-closer integration between

* Dr Vicky Conway tragically died before this chapter was completed. Her research on policing provides the spine of the essay and we are deeply grateful to the Conway family for permission to use – as Vicky had intended – some of her unpublished work in this chapter. Suaimhneas síoraí dá hanam.

[1] Seven interviews with PSNI and AGS officers were conducted as background research for this chapter. For reasons of confidentiality, we only refer to them by a letter (A–G) and do not quote from them directly but paraphrase their points, in accordance with the permission they granted us.

[2] L Block, 'EU joint investigation teams: Political ambitions and police practices' in S Hufnagel, S Bronit and C Harfield (eds), *Cross-Border Law Enforcement: Regional Law Enforcement Cooperation–European, Australian and Asia-Pacific Perspectives* (Routledge, 2012) 87.

[3] K Hayward, *What do we know and what should we do about … The Irish border* (Sage, 2021).

the United Kingdom (UK) and Ireland through common European Union (EU) single market membership, there was a sense that the Irish border was fading in significance. However, this rapidly changed with the UK Government's decision to leave the EU following the 2016 referendum.

The 'unique circumstances on the island of Ireland' that centre on the border were recognised by both the EU and the UK at the early stages of the Brexit process.[4] The shared objective of 'avoiding a hard border' on the island translated from a core priority in the UK–EU withdrawal negotiations into a dedicated Protocol on Ireland/Northern Ireland in the Withdrawal Agreement (2019).[5] As reflected in the subsequent controversy around it, the Protocol saw the EU's external border for goods effectively move from the UK/Ireland land border to the Irish Sea. This avoided the need for additional border management mechanisms on the island, which had been seen as a potential security risk and target for paramilitary activity.[6] However, it did not automatically provide for continuing the type of cooperation that had made the regions around the border as integrated as they had become under EU membership. Policing the Irish border after Brexit is largely conditioned by two things: the scope of the security dimensions of the Trade and Cooperation Agreement (and related decisions, eg on data adequacy); and the joint experience and practices for policing cooperation on the island built over time.[7] This chapter considers the case of the post-Brexit Irish border in order to reveal the achievements and vulnerabilities of cooperation between the two police services on either side of the border. The challenges have been acute: some are the same as faced pre-Brexit (eg, operationally, resourcing disparities) but others are new, forged in part by renewed criminal exploitation of the 'blind spots' of the border and also by the uncertainty that comes from being subject to the outcome of high-level EU–UK negotiations far-removed from policing on the ground.

## II. Police Cooperation on the Island before Brexit

There are two police services on the island of Ireland: An Garda Síochána (AGS) ('The Guardians of the Peace') for Ireland and the Police Service of Northern Ireland (PSNI), which was formed after the 1998 Agreement and the subsequent Patten Review of Policing in 1999. Both services have a shared history, emanating as they did in the 1920s from the one police force (the Royal Irish Constabulary). Today, the governance frameworks for policing differ between Ireland and Northern Ireland. The Irish

[4] K Hayward, 'The Pivotal Position of the Irish Border in the UK's Withdrawal from the European Union' (2018) 22(2) *Space and Polity* 238.

[5] K Hayward, 'The New Trading 'Relationship' between Great Britain and Northern Ireland: Why, What and How' (2021) 92(2) *The Political Quarterly* 360. Agreement on the withdrawal of the United Kingdom of Great Britain and Northern Ireland from the European Union and the European Atomic Energy Community [2019] OJ C384I/01.

[6] V Conway, 'Policing in a United Ireland: The Intractable Questions of Governance, Oversight and Accountability' (2022) 33(2) *Irish Studies in International Affairs* 71, 92.

[7] ibid. Trade and Cooperation Agreement between the European Union and the European Atomic Energy Community, of the one part, and the United Kingdom of Great Britain and Northern Ireland, of the other part [2020] OJ L149/10.

Government has the final say in appointing and removing the Garda Commissioner, whereas in Northern Ireland the Chief Constable is accountable to the Northern Ireland Policing Board, its policing body. The Policing Board in Northern Ireland has greater functions and is differently composed, with political appointments accounting for 53 per cent of members. The PSNI and AGS also differ in the means of accountability mechanisms. Levels of accountability are different in each jurisdiction, and expectations of what can and ought to be done in both jurisdictions can differ greatly.[8] The Police Ombudsman in Northern Ireland conducts all complaints investigations independently, while the head of the AGS security services is accountable to the minister.

Another key point of distinction is that in contrast to AGS, and unlike its Royal Ulster Constabulary (RUC) predecessor, the PSNI does not hold the national security portfolio for dealing with terrorist threats. Ireland's national security agency is AGS, whereas the PSNI is supported by UK agencies such as MI5 and the National Crime Agency. This is a significant difference for police services whose cooperation has been made all the more necessary by the common difficulty of so-called 'home-grown terrorism'. The 'back-to-back' existence of Northern Ireland and the Republic of Ireland for the first 50 years of the partition of Ireland was reflected in the lack of police cooperation too. Indeed, cross-border cooperation between the AGS and RUC was not formalised in any way until the 1980s, when the exigencies of the Troubles demanded it. During the 1970s and 1980s, security management of the border saw routine police and army checks on those crossing the border. At the height of the conflict, 10 per cent of AGS officers were stationed on the border, dealing both with the border itself and heightened terrorist activity in the area:[9] the AGS were supported by the Irish Army; the RUC was also intensely present, supported by the British Army. With terrorists exploiting the border in the Troubles, as a means both of escape and of criminal profiteering, it became increasingly fortified.[10] Security force efforts to restrict movement across the border – for example by blocking or destroying border roads – were deeply resented and at times physically resisted by locals.[11]

The exigencies of the Troubles, combined with a culture of mistrust of security and police forces, made the maintenance of police standards and accountability all the more difficult.[12] It is no coincidence that many policing scandals and concerns that have arisen in Ireland have related to policing along the border. The Morris Tribunal addressed the extent of police corruption in Donegal, which included, among other things, planting 'fake IRA bomb finds' for reputational gain.[13] The Smithwick Tribunal (2013) looked at the 1989 killing of two members of the RUC who had travelled to

[8] Interview D, May 2023.

[9] A Mulcahy, 'The Impact of the Northern 'Troubles' on Criminal Justice in the Irish Republic' in P O'Mahony (ed), *Criminal Justice in Ireland* (Institute of Public Administration, 2008, 275).

[10] H Patterson, *Ireland's Violent Frontier: The Border and Anglo-Irish Relations During the Troubles* (Palgrave, 2013).

[11] P Mulroe, *Bombs, Bullets and the Border. Policing Ireland's Frontier: Irish Security Policy, 1969–1978.* Dublin: Irish Academic Press, 2017).

[12] This is a universal experience, see L Boon-Kuo, 'Visible Policing Subjects and Low Visibility Policing: Migration and Race in Australia' in M Bosworth, A Parmar and Y Vázquez (eds), *Race, Criminal Justice, and Migration Control: Enforcing the Boundaries of Belonging* (Oxford University Press, 2018, 93).

[13] V Conway, *The Blue Wall of Silence: The Morris Tribunal and Police Accountability in Ireland* (Irish Academic Press, 2010).

Dundalk for a meeting with Gardaí.[14] The two men were killed by the Provisional IRA, but the Tribunal found there had been collusion between Gardaí and the IRA. And in 2014, whistleblower Maurice McCabe spoke out about poor standards in the Cavan-Monaghan division of the border counties.[15] North of the border, the infamous Glennane group of loyalist terrorists and some rogue RUC officers operated along the border, engaging in sectarian shooting and bombing attacks on Catholics. A number of officers were caught by RUC colleagues, prosecuted and served long sentences for criminal offences, including murder.[16] Such conditions within police divisions on both sides of the border undermined confidence in relations between AGS and the RUC/PSNI, impacting both personal and organisational relationships. Notwithstanding the temporary erosion of relationships in light of the Morris and Smithwick tribunal revelations, individuals in the PSNI and AGS worked to restore personal contacts between them, knowing it was essential for effective security delivery.[17] Such contact is particularly important in the areas, such as those around the border, in which they work with deliberately low visibility, rendering them unsuitable for high-profile joint cooperative initiatives. Sustaining relations of trust between the police forces on either side of the border, as individual police officers, key to such contact, are promoted or retire, has been one challenge; so too has establishing good communication between those located in the border region and those in the respective headquarters in Dublin and Belfast.

Practical difficulties in policing cooperation across a sensitive security border can easily become political difficulties too. Historically, the Anglo-Irish Agreement of 1985 addressed issues of extradition, cross-border trials and evidence-taking; it also established a regular work programme between the two police forces (AGS and the then RUC) and an Intergovernmental Conference, to include the Ministers for Justice, the RUC Chief Constable and the Garda Commissioner. Later, its successor agreement, the 1998 Good Friday/Belfast Agreement, contained sections dedicated to policing and justice. The 175 recommendations of the subsequent report of the Independent Commission on Policing for Northern Ireland, 'A New Beginning: Policing in Northern Ireland', chaired by Chris Patten, recognised the need for cross-border police cooperation. It noted the existence of some excellent informal relations but very limited structured arrangements. To address this, Patten sought written protocols on all aspects of cooperation, working groups, long-term personnel exchanges, a liaison system, structured cooperation in training, effective communications supported by the necessary ICT infrastructure, and joint databases on cross-border issues as well as joint major incident teams. Described as a blueprint for democratic policing, the Commission heralded a new policing order in Northern Ireland and encouraged the Irish state to ensure that AGS were equally committed to human rights as the PSNI was intended to be.[18]

In 2002, the Intergovernmental Agreement on Police Cooperation was signed. It did not address several gaps in formal cooperation and coordination between AGS

[14] Report of the Smithwick Tribunal of Inquiry (2013) available at www.rte.ie/documents/news/smithwick-tribunal-final.pdf (last accessed 24 October 2024).

[15] M Clifford, *A Force For Change: The Maurice McCabe Story* (Hachette Books Ireland, 2017).

[16] Interview B, May 2023.

[17] Interview G, August 2023.

[18] G Ellison and J Smyth, *The Crowned Harp: Policing Northern Ireland* (Pluto Press, 2000).

and the PSNI, such as hot pursuit across the border, surveillance and evidence/intelligence transfer. Notably, such areas of cross-border policing are increasingly challenging since Brexit.[19] However, it did make several commitments and initiatives that remain important today in sustaining bilateral cooperation. This included regular rank-based meetings, occasional joint training initiatives, secondments, forensic service cooperation, and the development of protocols on sex offenders, disaster planning and sharing DNA evidence.[20] Three cross-border police strategies have since been issued (in 2006, 2010 and 2016), but they are sets of intentions rather than clear strategies with measurable outputs. Nevertheless, they provide for a Joint Tasking and Coordination Group, Memoranda of Understanding (MOUs) on relevant issues, and a joint manual of guidance for cross-border investigations.[21] In addition to these, there is an Annual Cross Border Organised Crime Seminar, and cross-border organised crime threat assessments are conducted and published on an annual basis.

The updated Cross Border Policing Strategy was published in 2016.[22] It contained some imaginative recommendations, which reflected some of the unique opportunities to come from multilevel cooperation across a border. For instance, it urged a 'twin town' approach to address crime and security issues in neighbouring border urban areas alongside cooperation with local and regional government policing committees and local non-governmental organisations. Joint EU membership facilitated PSNI and AGS cross-border liaison in suburbs in areas like Muff[23] and Killea, located on the border between County Donegal and County Londonderry. In more conventional ways, it also pointed to the importance of information and technology – two factors that continue to be returned to as essential in effective cross-border policing. For example, it encouraged AGS and the PSNI to identify ways to maximise the effectiveness of their information-sharing agreement relating to sex offenders. And it also recommended further means of enabling the use of automatic number plate recognition (ANPR) in the border region for detections and information sharing. In concrete terms, the Cross Border Policing Strategy led to the creation of the Joint Agency Task Force, which includes representatives from police, Customs and Revenue, the Criminal Assets Bureau in Ireland and the National Crime Agency in Northern Ireland. The Joint Agency Task Force has an Oversight Group and an Operations Coordination Group, and holds biannual meetings. The capacity of this Task Force, however, has been limited by the lack of a fully functioning legislative Assembly and Executive in Northern Ireland from February 2017–January 2020 and February 2022–February 2024.[24]

[19] Interview C, May 2023.

[20] 'Agreement between the Government of Ireland and the Government of the United Kingdom of Great Britain and Northern Ireland on Police Co-operation' (29 April 2002) available at www.dfa.ie/media/dfa/alldfawebsitemedia/treatyseries/uploads/documents/treaties/docs/200202.pdf (last accessed 24 October 2024).

[21] Neither the manual, nor the MOUs are published.

[22] AGS and PSNI, *Cross Border Policing Strategy* (2016) available at www.justice-ni.gov.uk/sites/default/files/publications/justice/cross-border-policing-strategy-2016.pdf (last accessed 24 October 2024).

[23] Muff in East Donegal was one of several predominantly Protestant villages destined to be transferred to Northern Ireland had the recommendations of the post-partition Boundary Commission of 1925 been fulfilled.

[24] G Davies, 'Criminal Justice Cooperation Between the UK and Ireland After Brexit' (2021) 85 *The Journal of Criminal Law* 73, doi.org/10.1177/0022018320977529. The dysfunctionality of the Assembly and Executive reflects the vulnerability of the governing arrangements in Northern Ireland to exogenous shocks and internal party tensions.

Despite such developments and reports, the state of police cooperation between AGS and the PSNI has never been subjected to substantial external scrutiny. Walsh conducted the primary review examining practice, methods and regulation of cross-border cooperation in 2011.[25] This concluded that cooperation has been built, survived and flourished due to individuals and relationships, rather than on agreements and arrangements. There is no doubt that interpersonal, informal cross-border relationships are strong and essential.[26] However, while informalism may be necessary for trust and engagement, good relationships do not permit the sharing of information if the law does not allow it. Moreover, as Walsh noted, informalism tends towards a lack of transparency, accountability, oversight and, thereby, legitimacy.[27] This serves to underscore the importance of cooperation as it was enabled by common EU membership, which necessarily included formal structures and common legal standards (eg, around the General Data Protection Regulation).[28] There were concerns that these would be severely undermined by Brexit.

## III. The Challenges of Border-Related Criminal Activity

The primary concerns about the impact of Brexit on post-border policing related to two things: (i) increased opportunities for border-related criminal activity, exploiting the border to avoid detection, and differing operational procedures and investigative solutions across two jurisdictions (this section); and (ii) the diminution of the means of cooperation between UK police forces and their EU counterparts (see section IV). We will consider each of these in turn.

First, even after the 1998 Agreement and the decommissioning of terrorist weapons, the border remained a particular challenge for security, law and order on the island. The porous nature of the border enables criminals to evade detection and creates new opportunities for serious organised crime such as drug trafficking, human trafficking and smuggling, which finance the criminal activity of dissident terrorist groups and increasingly mobile organised crime gangs (MOCGs). Differences in currency and taxation on either side of the border are exploited as a means of financing paramilitary activity, for example through diesel laundering (removing the dye from lower-tax fuel intended for agricultural use only, then sold on at a profit) and contraband excise goods. A report by the British-Irish Parliamentary Assembly (BIPA) in 2015 found

[25] DPJ Walsh, 'Policing Cooperation across the Irish Border: Familiarity Breeding Contempt for Transparency and Accountability' (2011) 38 *Journal of Law and Society* 301.

[26] The Commissioner of AGS, Drew Harris, was former Deputy Chief Constable of the PSNI before his appointment in 2018. At the time of writing, in 2023, three members of the Policing Authority, the oversight body for AGS, are based in Northern Ireland. And prior to his appointment to the Garda Síochána Ombudsman Commission in 2021, Hugh Hume served in the PSNI for over 30 years.

[27] Walsh (n 25).

[28] Regulation (EU) 2016/679 on the protection of natural persons with regard to the processing of personal data and on the free movement of such data, and repealing Directive 95/46/EC (Data Protection Directive) [2016] OJ L119/01.

that some €350m were potentially lost to the two economies annually through fuel fraud.[29] There was subsequently a targeted, coordinated effort between AGS and the PSNI to address this issue, and in 2016 it was reported that 'a blitz on ex-IRA gangs and border criminals' had 'virtually wiped out' the illegal activity.[30] However, within a few years, police raids along the Irish border were uncovering multi-million fuel-laundering plants.[31]

Similarly, other criminal gangs exploit the relative remoteness of some parts of the border region for illegal waste disposal or the selling of counterfeit goods (see Farrand, chapter 19). Recognising that remote border areas are 'very difficult environments to police', the BIPA report commended the value of the Joint AGS–PSNI Task Forces such as the Fuel Fraud Enforcement Group and the Tobacco Enforcement Group, and good customs cooperation.[32] Coordinated police responses are also essential to counter sophisticated criminal enterprises affiliated with dissident (ie anti-1998 Peace Agreement) paramilitary groups initially engaged in counterfeit cigarette- and alcohol-smuggling operation networks. These extended to Britain and continental Europe, and progressed later to paving the way for the subsequent distribution of cocaine and illegal narcotics. In and of itself, this shows the significance of the criminal exploitation of the excise border between Ireland and the UK, even when they were both in the EU.

After the UK's EU exit, the first thing that made the difference was the unanticipated pandemic-related travel restrictions, which saw an increase in reporting of organised crime. During the pandemic, detection rates for burglary in Northern Ireland improved by 50 per cent on 2019, up from 10.6 per cent to 15.9 per cent.[33] This was in part because travel restrictions imposed during lockdown hindered the activities of the MOCGs. In their absence, local thieves became more active, including targeting the vulnerable and elderly. Such criminals are more susceptible to effective traditional policing practices (eg, witness line ups, and forensics) than those in MOCGs, and more likely to be detected. Indeed, the noted increase in detection rates reflects the level of crime for which MOCGs are responsible, and the ability of the PSNI to solve burglaries when MOCGs are excluded.[34] As such, the PSNI identifies and includes MOCG burglaries in the Service's priority area of serious organised acquisitive crime.[35] The gangs are

[29] Committee A British–Irish Parliamentary Assembly, *Cross-border Police Cooperation and Illicit Trade* (2015) available at www.britishirish.org/assets/CommitteeAFINAL.pdf (last accessed 24 October 2024).

[30] 'Ireland has virtually wiped out illegal fuel laundering' *The News Letter* (13 October 2016) available at www.newsletter.co.uk/news/ireland-has-virtually-wiped-out-illegal-fuel-laundering-1190851 (last accessed 24 October 2024).

[31] For example, 'Suspected "multi-million pound" fuel laundering raid in Newry' *BBC News* (11 January 2019) available at www.bbc.com/news/uk-northern-ireland-46844898 (last accessed 24 October 2024).

[32] BIPA (n 29) 7.

[33] PSNI, *Police Recorded Crime in Northern Ireland: Update to 31 March 2022* (12 May 2022) available at www.psni.police.uk/sites/default/files/2022-08/crime-bulletin-mar-_22.pdf (last accessed 24 October 2024).

[34] Interview A, May 2023. In Ireland, MOCGs have benefitted from an improved road infrastructure in the past decade, in part funded with EU support, but the advanced motorway network had the effect of increasing burglary rates in some Irish rural areas.

[35] National Crime Agency, *The National Strategic Assessment for Serious and Organised Crime* (2023) available at www.nationalcrimeagency.gov.uk/nsa-organised-acquisitive-crime (last accessed 24 October 2024).

mobile and transient; their activity across the border and in the border region adds a previously unknown level of complexity to the challenge of cross-border policing. MOCGs are also escalating their activity and sophistication.[36] The 2018 Cross Border Organised Crime Threat Assessment by AGS and the PSNI stated:

> The UK leaving the European Union has the potential to increase cross-border criminality. A number of Northern Ireland based MOCGs have the expertise to adapt and change, both to avoid detection by law enforcement partners and to exploit changes in profitability (including potential changes to trade agreements, etc). It is likely that they will attempt to profit from any of these changes.[37]

The prospect of hardening the border through Brexit brought its own, more direct concerns. The Cross Border Organised Crime Threat Assessment of 2018 identified specific risks relating to organised crime and drugs, human trafficking, criminal finances, agricultural crime, immigration crime, financial fraud (tobacco, fuel and alcohol) and firearms. Even though the Withdrawal Agreement meant that the Irish border remained open, and it is not a hard border for the movement of goods, it has become more profitable post-Brexit for criminal exploitation. This includes through smuggling (which can be affected by currency fluctuations) and through crime related to trafficking of migrants and exploitation.

The security context was also later complicated by the fact that loyalist paramilitaries responded to the unique arrangements for Northern Ireland under the Withdrawal Agreement (Protocol) by threatening to breach their ceasefires.[38] In early 2021, the Loyalist Communities Council – on behalf of a number of loyalist paramilitary groups – said that they were temporarily withdrawing their support for the 1998 Agreement in protest at the Protocol.[39] Loyalist paramilitary involvement in some scattered riots and organised protests at the Protocol continued into 2022 and 2023, with some political support. Their threats of unrest have been made in an attempt to bolster and prolong the Democratic Unionist Party's opposition to the Protocol.[40] Although most violent activity and displays of force exercised by loyalist paramilitary groups in recent years have remained intra-community, 'new life' has been breathed into loyalist paramilitary structures by fears that Northern Ireland's place in the UK union is weakened by its unique post-Brexit arrangements.[41]

[36] Interview F, August 2023.

[37] AGS and PSNI, *Cross Border Organised Crime: Threat Assessment 2018* (November 2018) available at www.justice-ni.gov.uk/sites/default/files/publications/justice/cross-border-organised-crime-assessment-2018.PDF (last accessed 24 October 2024).

[38] UK Parliament Intelligence and Security Committee, *Report on Northern Ireland Related Terrorism* (5 October 2020) available at https://isc.independent.gov.uk/wp-content/uploads/2021/01/20201005_NIRT_Press_Notice.pdf (last accessed 24 October 2024).

[39] 'Loyalist group withdraws support for Good Friday Agreement' *BBC News* (4 March 2021) available at www.bbc.co.uk/news/uk-northern-ireland-56276653 (last accessed 24 October 2024).

[40] 'Loyalist Communities Council chairman: If DUP goes soft on Northern Ireland Protocol it will stir unrest in UVF/UDA ranks' *The News Letter* (18 February 2023) available at www.newsletter.co.uk/news/politics/loyalist-communities-council-chairman-if-dup-goes-soft-on-northern-ireland-protocol-it-will-stir-unrest-in-uvfuda-ranks-4032399 (last accessed 24 October 2024).

[41] R Black, 'More loyalist paramilitaries in NI today than 30 years ago, academic tells MPs' *Belfast Telegraph* (18 October 2023) available at www.belfasttelegraph.co.uk/news/northern-ireland/more-loyalist-paramilitaries-in-ni-today-than-30-years-ago-academic-tells-mps/a1754611766.html (last accessed 24 October 2024).

## IV. The Effects of Brexit on Cooperation

The second concern around the impact of Brexit on cross-border policing came in relation to new difficulties for UK–EU policing cooperation. Davies noted the numerous bilateral police cooperation arrangements established between AGS and the PSNI (as set out in Section II) but that much of the cooperation relied, pre-Brexit, on EU processes and institutions.[42] Both police forces have acknowledged that these arrangements improved their ability to respond to crime and criminality, particularly in tackling organised criminal gangs. The 2018 Cross Border Organised Crime Threat Assessment warned that the absence of UK access to the Schengen Information System (SIS) and the European Arrest Warrant (EAW),[43] plus slower access to Joint Investigation Teams (JITs), could be seen by some organised criminals as creating opportunities to exploit, in the belief that their crimes would be less likely to be detected.

Furthermore, the context of EU membership enabled better police cooperation across borders as an EU-wide concern. The expansion of the EU and the Schengen borderless area increased the need for criminal justice cooperation and the sharing of personal data between Member States. In addition, the entry into force of the Lisbon Treaty in 2009 gave the EU greater power to adopt police and criminal justice measures.[44] The Hague Programme[45] on law enforcement information exchange introduced the concept of availability as the guiding principle for exchanging law enforcement information – a hallmark of EU police and criminal justice measures. The UK had benefited from a bespoke arrangement that allowed it to opt in on a case-by-case basis after adoption based on the final text. And thus, as an EU member after 2014, the UK opted in to over a hundred EU measures aimed at increasing security and criminal justice cooperation, such as the EAW.[46] Shared access to EU Justice and Home Affairs databases was essential to effective transnational policing cooperation. After Brexit, the UK lost full access to many of these mechanisms (eg, only observer status in Europol and no access to the EAW). From September 2018 to August 2019, the PSNI issued 38 EAWs, 26 of which related to the Republic of Ireland and 12 to all other EU states. Ireland was the primary country of EAW traffic for the North. In part this is due to the nature of the Irish border, which makes it very easy for someone to run to the other side. With the post-Brexit reversion to extradition, there is greater risk of a political dimension to the decision making. It is easy to imagine, in the Irish context, that this could be problematic, especially as it relates to national security. In practice, nevertheless, the EAW was never a simple flawless process, and the present arrangements appear to be working.[47]

[42] Davies (n 24).

[43] 'The European Arrest Warrant (EAW) was never a simple flawless process and the present arrangements appear to be working' (Interview G, August 2023). Council Framework Decision of 13 June 2002 on the European arrest warrant and the surrender procedures between Member States [2002] OJ C584/JHA.

[44] Treaty of Lisbon amending the Treaty on European Union and the Treaty establishing the European Community [2007] OJ C306/01.

[45] 'The Hague Programme: Strengthening Freedom, Security and Justice in the European Union' (2005/C 53/01).

[46] For a full list of JHA (Title V) opt-in and Schengen opt-out decisions taken by the UK between December 2009 and October 2015, as cited in House of Lords European Union Committee, 'Brexit: future UK–EU security and police cooperation' (7th Report of Session 2016–17, HL Paper 77) (16 December 2016) available at www.gov.uk/government/uploads/system/uploads/attachment_data/file/515125/2016-optin-webpage-update.pdf (last accessed 24 October 2024).

[47] Interview D, May 2023.

Post-Brexit, the UK still seeks access to a great deal of data for the purpose of criminal investigations. The 2021 decision of the EU on UK data adequacy saw the UK avoid the need to seek data adequacy decisions on a bilateral basis. While there is now greater uncertainty over access to crime and security databases for the UK, it seems that Ireland/Northern Ireland intelligence sharing has been quite unaffected by Brexit so far. For example, the exchange of Passenger Name Records (PNRs), biometric data, vehicle registration and dactyloscopic data functions well.[48] Furthermore, the UK's move from European Criminal Records Information Services (ECRIS) to UK-CRIS (United Kingdom Criminal Record Information System) appears to be facilitating the exchange of criminal record data. Interpol databases have also been utilised to mitigate loss of access to SIS.

While JITs are something Ireland has only recently engaged in, had Brexit not occurred it was foreseeable that these would increase in frequency, with benefits for both jurisdictions in criminal investigations. This opportunity is now limited post-Brexit as the UK cannot lead or initiate JITs and it is only be permitted to join as a third country. In other instances, both police services will have to revert to International Letters of Request (ILORs). This is bureaucratic, cumbersome and will unquestionably cause delays in cross-border investigations. This is frustrating for police, and upsetting for suspects, victims and witnesses.

As a consequence of the post-Brexit change towards asymmetry in access to information systems and measures for political cooperation, bilateral cooperation structures between UK and Irish crime agencies are becoming increasingly important. The many bilateral mechanisms previously noted continue to exist and function: the secondment of staff, the MOUs, the manual, the regular meetings, the Joint Agency Task Force. The live sharing of information between the PSNI and the Gardaí does not appear to be affected by the ending of the transition period. In July 2023, AGS shared intelligence about the PSNI data breach (when a police-issued laptop and documents identifying PSNI personnel were stolen from a car) with their counterparts in minutes when the data was found in dissident Irish republican hands.[49] However, for the work that these interactions ultimately focus on – investigations and prosecutions – legal underpinning and authority for actions is required, especially where they may infringe rights.

## V. Looking Ahead

The UK's withdrawal from the EU on policing cooperation on the island of Ireland after Brexit has proved to be less damaging than it could have been; this is in part because of the securing of the Withdrawal Agreement (2019) and Trade and Cooperation Agreement (2020), and in part because of the strength of cooperation that already existed across the Irish border. Information gathering, knowledge transfer

[48] 'Operational information continues to be shared on the basis of arrangements which were put in place when the UK were utilising SIS and Ireland had yet to engage. This situation is now reversed but the arrangements remain valid and viable.' Interview D, May 2023.

[49] Interview G, August 2023.

and intelligence sharing are essential to this cooperation.[50] This includes secondments, exchange of intelligence, and cooperation on criminal investigations, international investigation liaison and counter-terrorism. However, cultural and procedural differences between the and the PSNI remain challenging. Part of this comes from the failure of both services to reflect the make-up of the societies they serve. One interviewee argued that recruiting more female officers and officers from new communities to AGS and the PSNI to reflect diversity on the island would benefit policing across the border and beyond.[51] Related to this, we find that there is a 'perfect storm' impacting public confidence in policing on the border. Police morale is comparatively low in the PSNI, compounded by too few PSNI officers and budgetary limitations. A service gap between districts and senior management in both jurisdictions can hinder effective and timely policing, and reduce public confidence in the Service.

Recommendations from serving officers policing the border area and interviewed for this chapter align with the findings of more formal reviews of cross-border policing. Together these indicate that there are three main areas for further attention and potential for growth in cross-border policing cooperation. First, communication: contact on a personal level between police officers on either side of the border is key. There is a need to strengthen the processes and procedures around such contact, though, to ensure the integrity of these contacts and their sustainability beyond committed individual officers. The South Armagh Policing Review (2022) concentrated very much on the importance of frequent human contact and communication.[52] For example, it recommended that all operational officers should have access to and monitor shared radio networks as a matter of standard practice, that routine daily telephone briefings should take place between supervisors from both policing jurisdictions, and that weekly cross-border 'Pacesetter' meetings should take place, chaired at Inspector level or above. Overarching all this was the recommendation for a cross-border external communications plan to be jointly developed, 'focusing on daily policing activity and local community priorities'. The Review argued that such outward-facing communications should be 'proactively sought at operational, tactical and strategic level' in order to demonstrate joint working and thus enhance public awareness of and confidence in policing. The rationale for such proposed initiatives was to 'ensure working relationships are developed and information sharing/situational awareness is increased'.

Second, training: regular joint major-incident training opportunities and coordinated training using Interpol standards as a shared benchmark would forge stronger cross-border policing coordination. Support for greater East/West and international training opportunities and secondments would further enhance representation. To focus on a particular problem: MOCG operations offer insights and add a new level of complexity to policing border crime; they also offer an opportunity for mutual learning. In 2017, the Europol Threat Assessment classed MOCGs as a 'high threat'

[50] Interview F, July 2023.
[51] Interview D, May 2023.
[52] PSNI, *South Armagh Policing Review* (2022) available at www.psni.police.uk/sites/default/files/2022-08/police_service_of_northern_ireland_-_south_armagh_policing_review_-_findings_and_recommendations.pdf (last accessed 24 October 2024).

crime priority.[53] By this time, AGS had already launched Operation Thor – a multi-agency, integrated task force, with senior detectives from roads, policing and the Garda analyst service, the Criminal Assets Bureau and Forensic Science Ireland – to target known MOCG members and offenders. The Thor taskforce acknowledged the difference between opportunistic offenders and professional organised MOCGs. It sought to focus on crime prevention, crime control and protecting communities by means of diverse intelligence and community policing strategies.[54] This included visible focused patrols at specific times of day, targeting burglary 'hot-spots', high-visibility check points to prevent ease of movement, strong crime prevention communications and reassurance with communities. The gangs are adept at forensics and policing them requires adaptive investigative techniques, surveillance and specialist training (in pursuit, for example). Thus, MOCGs have generated opportunities for knowledge transfer as well as institutional learning across and between the PSNI and AGS. For example, the PSNI could engage in a fact-finding mission with AGS to determine how Operation Thor has achieved sustained results.[55]

Third, liaison: there is still a lot of room for more formal mechanisms for cross-bordering policing cooperation. The South Armagh Policing Review recommended that a bilateral policing agreement should be explored with the Northern Ireland Department of Justice and Irish Department of Justice and Equality, with the aim of facilitating joint rather than parallel policing operations by the PSNI and AGS. It is also proposed that this agreement should enable cross-border pursuit and advanced pursuit training between policing jurisdictions in defined circumstances, within a timescale of between three to five years. The report recommends increased cross-border communication and collaboration, the development of a 'command and control and pursuit prevention protocol' and the introduction of a cross-border accountability mechanism at local level between both forces. The last of these could focus on day-to-day operational demand and outcomes with potential alignment to Policing and Community Safety Partnerships (NI) and Joint Policing Committee structures (Ireland). Indeed, more broadly, officers recommend amalgamating the best of both policing worlds, working to the AGS historical tradition of community relations and the PSNI college's policing professionalism. Encouraging and, where necessary, financing working cross-border relationships is central to furthering effective and adaptive cross-border policing. Relationships need to be forged and maintained, with efforts to retain staff in border areas. Sustained relationships require building a framework for responsive rather than reactive policing. Ultimately, the intention should be to enable the police to deliver equality of experience so that people who live on the border are policed in the same way.[56]

There are some outstanding challenges, too. Some of these are in areas previously identified. The aforementioned Cross Border Policing Strategy of 2016, established to improve public safety, disrupt criminal activity and enhance policing capability of both

[53] Interview E, May 2023.

[54] K Bullock 'Community, intelligence-led policing and crime control' (2013) 23 *Policing and Society* 125.

[55] Interview C, May 2023; Interview A, May 2023. See also at www.garda.ie/en/about-us/our-departments/office-of-corporate-communications/press-releases/2022/september/an-garda-siochana-launch-the-winter-phase-2022-2023-of-operation-thor.html (last accessed 24 October 2024).

[56] Interview F, August 2023.

police services on the island, contains some recommendations that remain unrealised, for example the existence of border liaison officers and more frequent joint major-incident planning. The South Armagh Policing Review recommended as a minimum that a formal agreement should enable cross-border hot pursuits between policing jurisdictions in the interests of community safety and policing effectiveness. It also recommended that a cross-border accountability mechanism should be established at local level with bi-annual reporting by the PSNI and AGS on joint cross-border performance priorities. Again, these have not been realised. Other challenges could not have been envisaged a decade ago but have become much more pressing in the post-Brexit environment. For example, in human rights. Unilateral threats to withdraw from the European Convention on Human Rights by the UK Government could lead to further pressure on security frameworks and governance structures on either side of the border. The NI Human Rights Commission recommends that strong human rights protections be built into any bilateral agreement on policing, security and criminal justice, and that the highest standards of victims' rights and rights of accused persons be central to any future of cross-border cooperation.[57]

There is clearly a growing need to enhance and formalise routine cross-border policing collaboration on the island of Ireland. However, it is important to recognise that AGS and the PSNI have been able to navigate significant changes to the context in which they are working post-Brexit, in part as a result of the informal, personal relationships that have been built between them over time. The Irish border remains highly challenging to police and vulnerable to new forms of criminal exploitation. At the same time, it is an opportune space for innovative and close policing cooperation, even outside the common frameworks of the EU.

[57] Northern Ireland Humans Rights Commission, Submission to NI Affairs Committee Inquiry on Cross-border Cooperation on Policing, Security and Criminal Justice after Brexit (2020) available at https://nihrc.org/uploads/publications/NIHRC-NIAC_Brexit_and_Cross-Border_Cooperation-FINAL.PDF (last accessed 24 October 2024).

# 10

# The EUROPOL–National Crime Agency Cooperation

CLARA COTRONEO AND FABRIZIO COSTANTINO

## I. The EUROPOL–NCA Cooperation

Prior to exiting the European Union (EU), the United Kingdom (UK) had access to several mechanisms for police cooperation between Member States. To counterbalance its loss of full membership from mechanisms such as Europol, Eurojust and the European Arrest Warrant (EAW), as well as data exchange tools such as the SIS II[1] and ECRIS,[2] the UK Government and relevant agencies are likely to revert to bilateral/multilateral forms of cooperation with EU Member States.[3]

One of the main initiatives is the working and administrative arrangement (WAA) signed in September 2021 between the UK's National Crime Agency (NCA) and Europol. This arrangement implements and complements the provisions of the Trade and Cooperation Agreement (TCA),[4] by detailing the operational cooperation between the two entities. The objective of the arrangement is

> to support and strengthen the action by the Member States of the European Union and the United Kingdom, as well as their mutual cooperation in preventing and combating serious crime, terrorism, and forms of crime which affect a common interest covered by a Union policy …, in particular through the exchange of information.[5]

[1] The Schengen Information System (SIS) is the most widely used and largest information-sharing system for security and border management in Europe.

[2] The European Criminal Records Information System (ECRIS) was established as a decentralised IT database in order to improve the exchange of information on criminal records.

[3] Covington & Burling LLP, *Cross-Border Criminal Cooperation in a Post-Brexit World* (27 January 2021) available at www.lexology.com/library/detail.aspx?g=6a964051-a653-49af-ba9f-34f5c964df35 (last accessed 1 October 2024).

[4] European Union (30 April 2021), *Trade and Cooperation Agreement between the European Union and the European Atomic Energy Community, of the one part, and the United Kingdom of Great Britain and Northern Ireland, of the other part* [2021] OJ L149/10 available at https://eur-lex.europa.eu/legal-content/EN/TXT/?uri=uriserv%3AOJ.L_.2021.149.01.0010.01.ENG&toc=OJ%3AL%3A2021%3A149%3ATOC (last accessed 14 January 2024).

[5] Working and Administrative Arrangement establishing cooperative relations between the competent authorities of the UK and Europol (Article 1), available at www.europol.europa.eu/partners-collaboration/

The key components of this arrangement may be summarised as follows:

(a) organisation of regular meetings between Europol and representatives of the NCA to discuss cooperation-related issues and matters of common interest;
(b) secondment of UK/NCA liaison officer(s) to Europol headquarters and vice versa;
(c) establishment of rules for the exchange of personal data, as well as specific conditions for its collection, storage, processing and transfer (including onward transmission and assessment of the source of information);
(d) establishment of a secure communication line for the exchange of information;
(e) ability to participate in Europol analysis projects in order to take advantage of the agency's coordination and analytical capabilities.

## II. Strengths and Limitations of the Current Arrangements

Both the TCA and the WAA only came into force between the end of 2020 and 2021 and are currently in their third year of implementation. This timeline, combined with the fast-paced initiatives that EU and UK agencies are developing to step up international police cooperation, makes it difficult to fully assess how well the new arrangement is working. However, it is possible to identify a number of key strengths and challenges.

First, with the presence of 17 liaison officers (LOs) at Europol's headquarters, the UK has the second largest representation of LOs seconded for a third country after the United States (US).[6] Liaison officers support operational coordination and cooperation by facilitating the identification and exchange of crime-related data and criminal intelligence.[7] This physical presence also facilitates collaboration and communication, thus enhancing mutual trust between Europol and the NCA.

Second, concerning the exchange of personal data, the WAA establishes several guarantees, as well as specific conditions for its collection, storage, processing and transfer, including transmission to third parties and the assessment of the information's reliability. Article 14 of the WAA makes reference to a separate arrangement, to be signed between the Agencies, for the exchange of classified information.[8] The arrangement also foresees the establishment of a secure communication channel for the exchange of information.[9]

agreements/working-and-administrative-arrangement-establishing-cooperative-relations-between-competent-authorities-of-uk-and-europol#downloads (last accessed 1 October 2024).

[6] The US has the largest representation with 37 officers. See at www.europol.europa.eu/about-europol/statistics-data (last accessed 1 October 2024).

[7] Liaison officers cooperate with EUROPOL by identifying, requesting and transmitting data (including personal information and criminal data) relevant to ongoing criminal investigations.

[8] Specifically, it is mentioned that the exchange and protection of classified information will be possible only on condition that such separate cooperation arrangement is signed.

[9] Indeed, a framework for the protection of personal data was being implemented by the EU and the UK with regard to law enforcement. The EU's Law Enforcement Directive (LED) lays out the guidelines for data processing by the police and other agencies when conducting criminal investigations, alongside its more well-known cousin, the General Data Protection Regulation (GDPR). In this sense, two adequacy decisions for

Third, with respect to analytical intelligence, the WAA preserves the NCA's ability to contribute to Europol's strategic analysis products,[10] contributing to the Agency's operational planning and coordination. In this sense, the arrangement also foresees the participation of the NCA in analysis projects, taking advantage of the Agency's coordination and analytical capabilities.

However, although the WAA foresees several channels to discuss issues pertaining to the TCA in the field of internal and transnational security,[11] the UK no longer plays an official role in the governance and strategic direction of Europol. The UK's withdrawal from Europol makes it more difficult to align its national efforts to European strategies.[12] This is because the EU and UK crime priorities may not coincide, as there can be differences in emphasis and specific priorities based on specific circumstances, legal systems and policies. As a consequence, strategies for operational cooperation may need to be renegotiated.

Furthermore, channels such as Europol's Secure Information Exchange Network Application (SIENA), widely used by the NCA prior to Brexit to exchange sensitive and restricted information, can now only be accessed to a limited extent.[13] SIENA is used by EU and non-EU countries alike. The year before the WAA was signed (2021), a significant decrease (20 per cent) was registered in the number of SIENA messages that the UK had exchanged.[14] After Brexit, the NCA's access to SIENA has now changed from 'EU Confidential' to 'EU Restricted', meaning that the UK remains excluded from SIENA Confidential Information. Moreover, the NCA has also lost direct access to the Europol Information System (EIS), the Agency's central criminal information and exchange database.

the UK have been approved by the Commission, one for the LED and the other for the GDPR. The adequacy rulings also facilitate the implementation of the provisions concerning the sharing of personal information in the TCA and the WAA. See European Parliament and Council of the European Union (4 May 2016), Directive (EU) 2016/680 of the European Parliament and of the Council of 27 April 2016 on the protection of natural persons with regard to the processing of personal data by competent authorities for the purposes of the prevention, investigation, detection or prosecution of criminal offences or the execution of criminal penalties, and on the free movement of such data, and repealing Council Framework Decision 2008/977/JHA [2016] OJ L119/89; and Regulation (EU) 2016/679 of the European Parliament and of the Council of 27 April 2016 on the protection of natural persons with regard to the processing of personal data and on the free movement of such data, and repealing Directive 95/46/EC (General Data Protection Regulation) [2016] OJ L119/1 (last accessed 14 January 2024).

[10] These include the Serious and Organised Crime Threat Assessment (SOCTA), the Internet Organised Crime Threat Assessment (IOCTA) and the EU Terrorism Situation and Trend Report (TE-SAT), as well as early-warning notifications.

[11] See footnote 5, Art 4(1) and (2).

[12] The European Multidisciplinary Platform Against Criminal Threats (EMPACT) introduces the integrated approach to EU internal security. It is the key instrument through which the EU identifies and sets the priority crime threats in the EU. See at www.europol.europa.eu/crime-areas-and-statistics/empact. Before Brexit, the UK lead two EMPACT priorities, Trafficking in Human Beings and Excise Fraud and co-lead four other priorities. Through its leading role, the UK brought leadership experience in tackling these crime areas.

[13] R Dickson and A Kramer, 'The Changing Landscape of UK–EU Policing and Justice Cooperation' (2020) 1 *European Papers – A Journal on Law and Integration* 479.

[14] The definition of EU Classified Information (EUCI) is provided for in Art 2 of the Council Decision of 23 September 2013 on the security rules for protecting EU classified information (2013/488/EU), while Table 3.2.5 "Security" of the TCA restricts the UK from accessing EU Confidential information. See Council of the European Union (23 September 2013), Council Decision of 23 September 2013 on the security rules for protecting EU classified information [2013] OJ L274/1 available at https://eur-lex.europa.eu/eli/dec/2013/488/oj/eng (last accessed 14 January 2024). See also footnote 4.

## III. Short- to Mid-term Prospect

Although the working and administrative agreements between Europol and the NCA relieved some of the worries regarding the depth, effectiveness and efficiency of UK–EU cross-border policing and investigations, considerable obstacles to cooperation between the NCA and Europol still exist due to the loss of access to key systems and the lack of reliable replacements. Manual processes, bilateral relations and the development of alternative capabilities are currently filling many of the capability gaps caused by the loss of such mechanisms and technologies. One example is the I-LEAP programme[15] to strengthen the UK's access to the Interpol database. The ability of this arrangement to somehow mitigate the consequences of the UK's disconnection from SIS II, however, rests on the goodwill of EU officers to double-key information on EU as well as the Interpol databases.

Indeed, Brexit has led to a general increase in bureaucracy between UK and the EU, affecting the speed and effectiveness of police cooperation.[16] The loss of access to SIS II, EAW and EIO has further exacerbated this. As suggested by Shellaker et al, these issues can be solved by developing a 'nodal police cooperation model' to ensure that police officers in the UK and EU Member States can strengthen interconnectivity and share information in a more effective way, at the same time providing investigators with relevant materials.[17]

[15] UK Home Office (6 December 2024), *International Law Enforcement Alerts Platform (I-LEAP) Programme Accounting Officer Assessment* available at www.gov.uk/government/publications/home-office-major-programmes-accounting-officer-assessments/international-law-enforcement-alerts-platform-i-leap-programme. (last accessed 14 January 2024).

[16] M Shellaker, S Tong and P Swallow, 'UK–EU law enforcement cooperation post-Brexit: A UK law enforcement practitioner perspective' (2023) 24(1) *Criminology & Criminal Justice* 841. See also P Swallow and S Tong, 'The impact of Brexit on European police cooperation for British policing agencies', Paper presented at the 22nd Annual Conference of the European Society of Criminology, 21–24 September 2022, Malaga, Spain.

[17] Shellaker et al (n 16).

# 11

# The Impact of Brexit on UK Policing – A Practitioner's View

CHRISTOPHER THOMSON

The creation of the International Crime Coordination Centre (ICCC) in March 2019 was intended to mitigate the impact of Brexit for policing in the United Kingdom (UK) by identifying those international policing tools to which the UK might lose access, together with a contingency or alternative system for each of them, and to raise awareness of and assist forces to access and use the tools that remained. The unit was staffed with a mix of seconded police officers, former officers with specialist experience, officers of the National Crime Agency (NCA) and contacts from Immigration Enforcement and the Crown Prosecution Service (CPS).

The ICCC included liaison officers corresponding to the 10 Regional Organised Crime Units (ROCUs) in England and Wales, with a slightly different arrangement for Police Scotland and the Police Service of Northern Ireland. These acted as 'single points of contact' (SPOCs) for forces working closely with intelligence bureaux, training departments and ROCUs.

The ICCC provided a 24/7 helpline, which has been maintained by the Joint International Crime Centre (JICC), and both SPOCs and officers on the specialist desks have provided advice in relation to thousands of operational inquiries to UK forces on a wide variety of international matters.

Prior to Brexit, most forces convened 'gold' groups, often including the relevant ICCC SPOC. Communications material was disseminated, and key messages were publicised by a variety of means to raise awareness of the systems available to check international subjects and conduct international inquiries.

Training was delivered to key staff in intelligence, specialist investigation, control-room and custody functions to increase the numbers of staff licensed to use the Interpol I-24/7 system – identified as the replacement for Schengen Information System II (SIS II) and used to conduct checks on foreign nationals and circulate relevant intelligence. Training was targeted more selectively at force intelligence officers and ROCU staff to increase numbers licensed to use the Europol SIENA application.

Staff were provided with a 'checklist' of basic inquiries to make when dealing with foreign nationals, and force custody suites received inputs and materials to try to ensure that these basic checks were done on all foreign nationals arrested or attending voluntarily. These included checks with Immigration Enforcement, a Criminal Records Office (ACRO) conviction check, a SIS II and I-24/7 check before Brexit, and an I-24/7 thereafter.

The ICCC developed an app for frontline officers providing simple guidance when faced with any situation with an international dimension, and SPOCs worked with individual forces to have this added to force mobile telephones and handheld devices, and to publicise it.

These measures were designed to ensure that any known risk relating to an individual had the best chance of being identified and effectively managed. Most forces were able to make significant improvements in the percentages of those checked, though relatively few were able to consistently demonstrate 100 per cent compliance.

The most foolproof methods involved some sort of automated function within the custody booking-in program, one it was impossible to bypass or 'skip'. However, with 43 different forces, each using different versions of different systems, some relatively old, different financial pressures after 10 years of austerity and with different priorities for IT upgrades across all their computer functionalities, this was not really possible.

Communication campaigns were effective but required regular repetition to become firmly embedded in practice and compete with a myriad of other 'key messages' to which forces are obliged to subject their staff. This 'priority and information overload' was another difficult barrier to overcome completely.

Taken nationally, the awareness and compliance of forces in this area is in a much better place than in 2018. Many forces created roles for 'International Liaison Officers' (ILOs) as in-house contacts and advisors. Sometimes a single officer, sometimes two or three or occasionally in a small unit, these officers also worked closely with ICCC staff to improve awareness and performance in their organisation.

The ICCC developed an international module, 'The Essentials for Senior Investigating Officers', which was accredited by the College of Policing for inclusion in the national Senior Investigating Officer (SIO) 'PIP 3' course. This was delivered to every new SIO course from 2020, and staff have targeted SIOs trained before the introduction of the module to ensure they have had the opportunity to complete it. Similar inputs have been delivered to a wide variety of officers in specialist investigative roles. These inputs were delivered face to face or online during lockdown, and most SIOs are much better equipped now to deal with any crime or incident with international aspects.

The creation of the National Extradition Unit within the ICCC, since absorbed into the JICC, is another significant addition to the capability of policing in England and Wales, providing advice and support to forces, risk assessing all incoming requests, liaising with foreign law enforcement, and undertaking removals from and collections to England and Wales. Prior to this, experience and expertise were patchy and did not always guarantee consistency.

Establishing the Unit, occasionally supplanting officers in some forces, was not always easy and mechanisms to capture local knowledge of high-risk areas in which to carry out arrests had to be acquired, but the high level of commitment by officers in the Unit and in most forces ensured a positive outcome generally.

In the same way that policing needs to build familiarity, expertise and confidence in international inquiries, the CPS was probably in a similar situation, despite individual pockets of excellence. A relatively inexperienced prosecutor, approached by an officer to request the preparation of an international instrument, might express reluctance or advise the officer to try informal channels instead. Sometimes this might be the right advice, but certainly in the early days of the ICCC this was a fairly common gripe of front-line officers. Similarly, prosecutors might complain that officers did not understand the criteria before certain applications could be made, nor the proportionality in some cases.

We worked to improve mutual understanding of organisational needs. The CPS proved a willing partner, and in most regions, regular meetings were instituted involving CPS regional international leads or heads of special casework, ICCC SPOCs, force international and ROCU leads.

These meetings resolved problems, identified and arranged mutual training opportunities and agreed action needed. In northeast England, the CPS was very helpful in assisting in the preparation of outstanding European Arrest Warrants (EAWs) before the Brexit deadline, helping to jointly map and monitor current international applications of various kinds, and helping overcome live-time issues with operations or trials.

Initial fears had been articulated in terms of whether the UK would be 'less safe' after Brexit due to the loss of access to European Union (EU) systems and databases. International policing, however, involves much more than protecting UK citizens from 'bad people' travelling here from the EU. Threats come from all countries and take many forms, including from individuals previously unknown to any law enforcement agency anywhere in the world.

International policing can involve tracing and safeguarding vulnerable people who are missing, or who may have been trafficked across borders and who should be seen as victims and treated accordingly; it can involve liaising in relation to UK citizens who have been killed, seriously injured or have died abroad; it can involve tracing and bringing to justice suspects (including UK citizens) who have fled abroad and who themselves present risk to the countries to which they flee. It can involve circulation of DNA or fingerprints across jurisdictions to identify suspects or unidentified bodies, or investigating online criminality, such as fraud or the sexual exploitation of children, not only in terms of the online criminality but in trying to safeguard a child who may have been harmed on the other side of the world.

Serious and organised crime involving foreign nationals in the UK continue to present significant challenges. Much of this criminality is hidden, with intelligence being harder to obtain because of difficulties in language and culture, many victims being reluctant to speak and those involved being periodically moved on to other countries as part of the operating business model. Strategic and tactical assessments need to continue to improve, as do the efforts to embed improvements in practice and through improved technological applications in systems.

Brexit did impact the ability of UK policing to exchange information with the EU, most significantly through the loss of SIS II, the EAW and the European Investigation Order (EIO). The loss of SIS II remains the most significant, with the loss of both the EAW and EIO being largely mitigated by other processes contained in the UK–EU Trade and Cooperation Agreement.

The work of the ICCC, developing and delivering training, building relationships with partner agencies, increasing the use of international tools, basic custody checks, and the creation and provision of a 24/7 helpline, can be seen as 'profit' on the international balance sheet. In April 2023 it was announced that the JICC had been created by combining elements of the ICCC with the NCA UK International Crime Bureau (UKICB) to consolidate what had been developed since 2019 and ensure a firm financial footing for the future. In terms of UK policing's capability vis-à-vis countries outside the EU, no losses were experienced, and the situation must be seen as improved.

Risk can never be eliminated, and it is difficult to ascribe values to concepts like public safety, but given the state of international capability in the UK prior to 2019, policing is generally better placed now.

# PART III

# Judicial Cooperation and Fundamental Rights under the Trade and Cooperation Agreement

# 12

# Judicial Cooperation between the UK and the EU in Criminal Matters Post-Brexit

MARIANNE L. WADE

## I. Introduction

As Brexit negotiations between the United Kingdom (UK) Government and the European Union (EU) proved far tougher than the UK Leave campaign had indicated they could possibly be,[1] the former remained adamant that a deal would be struck, citing the common interest in continuing security cooperation.[2] Although this had been a policy area in which the UK (as a Member State) had strongly voiced disagreement[3] with EU developments[4] it was neither the subject of much debate during the run up to the UK referendum nor did it draw much attention as the UK prepared to leave the EU. Nevertheless, anyone familiar with the nuts and bolts of security cooperation will not have been surprised by the considerable provision made for criminal justice mechanisms in the Trade and Cooperation Agreement (TCA)[5] regulating the relationship between the EU and UK post-Brexit. Unsurprisingly, because Continental European criminal justice systems are predominantly led by prosecutors, the TCA dedicates significant space to providing for judicial cooperation as part of security cooperation and ensuring a continuing basis for this area of work in the post-Brexit era.

[1] E Casalicchio, '15 things Vote Leave promised on Brexit' *Politico* (24 December 2020) available at www.politico.eu/article/15-things-uk-vote-leave-promised-on-brexit-and-what-it-got/ (last accessed 16 April 2024).

[2] ibid.

[3] See, eg, S Cras, 'The Directive on the right of access to a lawyer in criminal proceedings and in European arrest warrant proceedings' (2004) 1 *Eucrim* 32, 37.

[4] Evidenced, eg, by the UK's longstanding objections to the inclusion of provisions relating to defence rights in this policy area, beginning with the 2004 proposed Framework Decision on Defence Rights in Criminal Proceedings through to the sceptical stance adopted during negotiations for the measures of the Stockholm Programme.

[5] Trade and Cooperation Agreement between the European Union and the European Atomic Energy Community, of the one part, and the United Kingdom of Great Britain and Northern Ireland, of the other part, [2021] OJ L149/10.

Section II of this chapter sets out the relevant provisions of the TCA relating to judicial cooperation. The articles – at first glance – evoke an impression of business continuing as usual. Detailed provision is made to ensure that the 'good' of EU developments remains available. Section III reveals that the judicial cooperation provisions are framed strongly by how the UK might define this 'good', with no attention paid to mechanisms such as those produced under the Stockholm Programme and other developments one might view as signalling the direction of travel of the EU.[6] It further reveals that even these mechanisms are often provided for in a 'slimmed-down' version. The context of these provisions is then examined to facilitate deeper comprehension of what the TCA means in reality, surveying also what is not included and the 'good' lost in this new, cooperative relationship.[7] This analysis is augmented by a brief examination of the information available as to on-going work within this relationship. Above all, there appears to be an identifiable trend of UK practitioners working hard to maintain as much of the criminal justice 'good' of EU membership as possible. A clear consensus that there are enormous practical benefits worth salvaging is apparent. Just how far such efforts at the coalface of cross-border criminal justice can durably succeed is, however, thrown into question in section IV of this chapter. The gaps noted in the TCA appear to reveal a refusal to acknowledge the reality of the EU's becoming a criminal justice governance level in its own right. Because the TCA appears to ignore such developments, the question of whether it forms a basis for durable EU–UK cooperation presents itself.

## II. Judicial Cooperation as Foreseen by the TCA

In relation to judicial cooperation, the UK's time in the EU was marked by the twin characteristics of principled opposition to integration beyond multilateral cooperation[8] and strong support of, and participation in, institutions created within that framework.[9] So, on the one hand the UK was a vocal critic of any attempt to drive integration along what it considered to be federalist lines. The UK was fundamentally opposed to any move that would allow the EU to become a criminal justice actor in its own right.[10] Instead, the UK vision featured the EU as a forum implementing, modifying, supporting and

[6] Such as, eg, the European Public Prosecutor's Office (EPPO) or the recent appointment of an Anti-Racism Commissioner: see commission.europa.eu/strategy-and-policy/policies/justice-and-fundamental-rights/combatting-discrimination/racism-and-xenophobia/commissions-coordinator-combating-racism_en.

[7] From the UK perspective, eg, the loss of access to the Schengen Information System is a very significant one.

[8] European Union Committee, *The European Union's Policy on Criminal Procedure* (30th Report of Session 2011–12, HL 20) available at https://publications.parliament.uk/pa/ld201012/ldselect/ldeucom/288/28802.htm (last accessed 16 April 2024).

[9] Eurojust Annual Reports, eg, attest to the UK desk's consistently being one of the busiest, and UK authorities were keen users of Joint Investigation Teams: see eg, Eurojust, *Annual Report 2011*, 70, 75 and 76; Eurojust *Annual Report 2016*, 10, 16, 19.

[10] Perhaps best exemplified by the UK's extraordinary opposition to the EPPO. Note that the European Union Act of 2011 effectively altered the UK constitution to ensure that UK participation in this institution (viewed as a federal EU development) became practically impossible, with sch 1 making participation dependent on an affirming referendum.

augmenting Member State criminal justice mechanisms; a vehicle but never a driver.[11] On the other hand, however, UK practitioners were active within institutions and keen users of mechanisms of cooperation provided by the EU (see chapter 2).

Given the strong 'euro-sceptic' stance of the UK, observers might reasonably have been surprised to find the UK so actively engaged in pan-European criminal justice activities and judicial cooperation in particular. The first President of the College of Eurojust (which has now become the European Union Agency for Criminal Justice Cooperation and is – undoubtedly – the heart of judicial cooperation within the EU) was a British prosecutor, and for many of the early years the UK was the national desk with the biggest caseload. United Kingdom practitioners used relevant mechanisms with enthusiasm. They did so with full support from the UK Government precisely because Eurojust, until 2019, was not an EU agency; it was an institution supporting judicial cooperation within the EU. Legally and structurally, however, this institution could be described as a mutation of transnational law/'next-level' multi-lateral cooperation. All national members of Eurojust remained practitioners within their own, national criminal justice systems, with powers explicitly provided to them by their domestic governments.[12] Nevertheless, one could not walk the halls of Eurojust and fail to notice that this was a house of European cooperation,[13] one powered by the willingness of the Member States (and the practitioners deployed by them) to make it so. From the UK perspective, however, Eurojust was decisively not a centralised European house but one built by its component countries.

It is this vision of judicial cooperation that can be found in the TCA. Judicial cooperation is presented in its component parts, harnessing the power of Eurojust, mutual legal assistance (MLA) and the portable version of the European Arrest Warrant (EAW). Part Three of the TCA appears very much to reflect the British understanding of judicial cooperation within the EU (of which it was an active Member State), and would have been palatable to the EU because it ensured the continued, smooth operation of what had become established European practice.

As anyone familiar with EU criminal justice activity would expect, police and judicial cooperation are addressed together in Part Three of the TCA. Provision is made, in concrete terms, relating to specific measures and particularly to the institutions that facilitate their practice. The overriding objective of both forms of cooperation is declared to be 'the prevention, investigation, detection and prosecution of criminal offences' (Article 522).

Provisions specifically recognised as judicial cooperation are to be found in Title VI of the Treaty, from Article 580 onwards. This section of the TCA identifies Eurojust as the heart of this cooperation and then details the legitimate substantive reach of judicial cooperation ('combating serious crimes as referred to in Article 582', which in turn states that 'cooperation … relates to the forms of serious crime

[11] Reflected clearly in the UK Government's position outlined in relation to the new Europol Regulation in 2013, see, eg, Written statement to Parliament, 18 July 2013, The European Commission's proposal for a Europol regulation, available at www.gov.uk/government/speeches/the-european-commissions-proposal-for-a-europol-regulation (last accessed 16 April 2024).

[12] ML Wade, 'A European public prosecutor: potential and pitfalls' (2013) 59 *Crime, Law and Social Change* 439, 454.

[13] ML Wade, *EuroNEEDs* (European Commission, 2011) 86.

within the competence of Eurojust, as listed in Annex 42, including related criminal offences'). With reference to detailed provision in Annex 42, Article 582 of the TCA sets out the forms of crime for which judicial cooperation is permitted. These include the classic transnational crimes (terrorism, trafficking drugs and human beings, etc[14]), very serious crimes, those featured in relevant historic EU legislation (racism and xenophobia, 'computer crimes') and crimes under international law (ie genocide). Article 582(2) ensures that 'wrap around' competences are available to deal with related offences.

The beating heart of practical judicial cooperation within the EU is revealed and provided with a lifeline to continue with the UK in what follows. Provision is immediately made for a UK contact point for Eurojust and one specific for cooperation relating to domestic terrorism (Article 584 (1) and (2)). The UK's history of having a busy national desk at Eurojust is reflected in the provision for a liaison magistrate with up to five assistants (Article 585(1) and (3)). Article 586 ensures reciprocity, allowing Eurojust to post a liaison magistrate to the UK.

Judicial cooperation between the UK and EU in the post-Brexit era profits significantly from the well-established practice of liaison magistrates working with and within Eurojust. From its inception, states that were and remain politically sceptical of – or divided over – stronger integration with the EU (such as Norway) have demonstrated a commitment to strong and effective, hands-on judicial cooperation via this mechanism (now also well-established with states from further afield[15]). Articles 587 and 588 of the TCA can thus fall back on modalities tried and tested at Eurojust, ensuring that a UK liaison magistrate can participate in meetings and non-personal data exchange. Although participation in operational meetings depends on the consent of the national members involved (Article 587(1)), this is unlikely to create any practical barriers, as Eurojust national members are well accustomed to working in this manner. The established institutional practice of cooperation within the EU means that legal norms representing highly pragmatic solutions reflect effective workable mechanism without requiring further, detailed provision.[16]

Articles 589 to 593 ensure that more sensitive data exchange is provided for in the manner one would expect in the EU and criminal justice context, whilst Articles 594 and 595 provide further indication of the TCA as slotting into a well-oiled machine in which trust is established. Details of working arrangements are simply made subject to agreements between Eurojust and the competent UK authority (Article 594), though all obligations placed upon Eurojust are – naturally – restricted to its existing competences (Article 595). Working Arrangements with the UK were signed in December 2021, setting out the practical and operational arrangements. The TCA emanates a sense of business as usual, being continued in this area with a clear sense of established trust and practices.

[14] See Art 83, Consolidated version of the Treaty on the Functioning of the European Union [2012] OJ C326/01.

[15] See at www.eurojust.europa.eu/states-and-partners/third-countries/liaison-prosecutors (last accessed 16 April 2024).

[16] Contrast this provision – which relates operational criminal justice (the very heart of national sovereignty being exercised) – with the reference made in Art 586 requiring that a detailed, separate working agreement be made for Eurojust in posting a liaison magistrate to the UK.

This tone also permeates the more detailed TCA provisions made to ensure the preservation – in as far as possible – of what is doubtlessly regarded as the main EU criminal justice advance. Title VII of the TCA is devoted to preserving the spirit of the EAW as a mechanism of cooperation with the UK, presenting the UK–EU relationship as a setting in which surrender (not extradition) continues to be the norm (see Arnell, chapter 13). The UK House of Lords has evaluated the result of the UK's access to the EAW having been replaced by extradition arrangements as 'largely mirror[ing] the surrender agreement agreed between the EU and Iceland and Norway'.[17] So, the TCA represents a step backwards but not a complete loss of the benefits EU membership had brought to the UK in this context.

Title VIII of the Agreement is devoted to MLA in a similar – though considerably less detailed – manner. Articles 633 to 642 are clearly intended to ensure MLA advances are not lost to either party, though there is no ignoring the omission of more recent EU mechanisms, such as the European Investigation Order.[18] Going forward, the Agreement seeks to ensure a robust foundation, to operate based on the 1959 Council of Europe Convention and protocols.[19] These are overtly regulated as the cornerstone of judicial cooperation within, and for the UK going forward, with the EU. Wherever possible, however, traditional MLA is seemingly enhanced (Article 633 (1)), and thus Article 642 determines that joint investigation teams (JITs) – another key EU innovation and mechanism of criminal justice (and often prosecutorial, thus judicial) cooperation – within the EU can be formed, governed by EU law.

Furthermore, the TCA ensures that the existing framework for key activities can continue post-Brexit. Title IX regulates the exchange of criminal record information, Title X focuses on anti-money laundering and counterterrorist financing, and Title XI is dedicated to freezing and confiscation in considerable detail. Again, this regulation mirrors established legislation and practice, which criminal justice practitioners in the EU have become accustomed to have at their fingertips. It has become necessary, of course, in part because Brexit has caused those practitioners to lose access to EU and Schengen databases. As is no doubt viewed as desirable by all parties, the TCA ensures that as much of these mechanisms as possible remains available for UK practitioners, even as Brexit becomes a reality. That the TCA makes no mention of the Schengen Information System (SIS) is, however, the sharp reminder that such accommodation only goes so far. The UK fought, unsuccessfully, to retain this EU privilege, but this reality reflects the loss of access to a prized mechanism from an investigatory perspective (see Pearson, chapter 6).[20] The SIS is resoundingly noticeable by its absence, and the TCA reflects the reality of the UK's future as a third state, making provision to ensure the continuation of the mechanisms available to a non-Member State only (see Vavoula, chapter 8).[21]

[17] European Union Committee, *Beyond Brexit: policing, law enforcement and security* (25th Report of Session 2019–21, HL 36) available at https://lordslibrary.parliament.uk/beyond-brexit-policing-law-enforcement-and-security/ (last accessed 16 April 2024).

[18] See L Bachmeier-Winter, 'European investigation order for obtaining evidence in the criminal proceedings' *Zeitschrift für Internationale Strafrechtsdogmatik* 9/2010, 580.

[19] European Convention on Mutual Assistance in Criminal Matters 1959 (ETS No 30).

[20] European Union Committee (n 17) 3.

[21] Such as Eucaris. As the UK is not a Schengen Member State, exiting the EU places it informationally in a worse position than third states that are.

Overall, the TCA can be seen as a concerted effort to sustain judicial cooperation to the greatest extent possible, despite the changes in the political landscape. It is clear that no party involved has any appetite for a reduction in security as a result of Brexit. Nevertheless, the difference between EU membership and third-country status will be clear to any reader of the Agreement familiar with mechanisms not mentioned. The EU has become a forum adept at extending the reach of both national criminal justice systems and their practitioners – not least via access to common databases. Whilst the TCA clearly demonstrates both parties to the Agreement seeking to preserve advances, in as far as the circumstances permit, those circumstances do have some very clear limits.

In relation to criminal justice cooperation more broadly, it is furthermore key to remember that it is institutional development within the EU that breathes (effective) life into the mechanisms the TCA does mention. The successes attributed to the EU have not been made on the pages of treaties alone. The latter constitute an essential basis, but it is the institutional framework of the EU that makes them the valued tools they are.[22] Indeed, as is reflected in the text of the TCA, legislation often formalises the solutions developed by practice. Many key EU advances resulted from suggestions made by practitioners. Judicial cooperation would not have developed without the European Judicial Network,[23] just as Europol would not have come into being were it not for the Police Chiefs Operational Task Force.[24] Eurojust's organisational structure – the corridors along which prosecutors can take a short walk to ask a (like-minded) colleague to follow up on an EAW or an MLA request, and (in the vast majority of cases[25]) the willingness of those colleagues to throw their prosecutorial (judicial) authority behind an insistence that their Member State colleagues (working in their domestic criminal justice system) must give effect to those mechanisms – is what makes the EU a place of particularly strong functional judicial cooperation. Transnational law has numerous legislative instruments supporting judicial cooperation but features no other judicial cooperation forum equivalent to that of the EU. The EU is the setting for the next step in the evolutionary development of such law because of its institutional framework and the (European) spirit of cooperation that shapes those institutions' practice.[26]

The TCA can preserve some of the former by securing the UK's continued access to Eurojust in particular, and can capture in words the mechanisms of how this cooperation has worked thus far. What happens to the latter, post-Brexit, is another matter, however, and one that remains to be seen.

The TCA is distinctly marked by a vision of what the UK perceives to be the 'greatest hits' of EU criminal justice cooperation. The Agreement resoundingly fails to include

[22] EU criminal law mechanisms can be viewed as mutations of TCL mechanisms in the sense that they are an evolutionary step forward. See, eg, Boister's reference to these in N Boister, *Transnational Criminal Law*, 2nd edn (Oxford University Press, 2018).

[23] And note its apparent renewed importance for the post-Brexit era. See C Rhiele, 'European Judicial Network (EJN) Creates Dedicated Brexit Area' *Eucrim* (2021) available at https://eucrim.eu/news/european-judicial-network-ejn-creates-dedicated-brexit-area/ (last accessed 16 April 2024).

[24] S Peers, *EU Justice and Home Affairs Law*, 3rd edn (Oxford University Press, 2011) 541.

[25] See Wade (n 13) 86.

[26] ibid.

more recent developments, however, seemingly reflecting the status quo of criminal justice cooperation in the EU with which the UK was happy, and ignoring developments such as the EPPO. Development of this kind by the EU is, however, undeniably taking place under considerable pressure.[27] In the near future, it seems likely the TCA will be tested not in relation to the things it regulates, but rather in relation to those left on one side. It is understandable that an Agreement drawn up under such time pressure ignored such topics.[28] There is explosive material in the matters not mentioned.[29] The question remains, however, how durable an agreement the TCA will prove to be in light of these omissions.

## III. The TCA Vision in Context

Whilst a UK vision can influence the parameters of the TCA, the reality remains that the EPPO will increasingly feature in the reality of judicial cooperation across Europe. It may have been politically wise for the drafters of the TCA to (seemingly) ignore that fact in the short term; what it means for the medium and longer term is likely to become clear before all too long. Judicial cooperation should not and cannot be viewed devoid of political context (and direction of travel). Since the TCA was drafted, the EU has also, for example, appointed a Commission coordinator for anti-racism[30] and tried to negotiate uncomfortable conflicts on rule-of-law issues (some of the latter going to the heart of judicial practice).[31] The TCA makes light of such issues, seemingly clinging to a vision of the world in which the EU has but a minimal role in relation to them. The intricacies of the TCA primarily concern the aspects that the UK would have been eager to preserve. The EU accommodates these concerns to the extent possible, given that its negotiators would have been keenly aware that the benefits linked to EU membership should remain precisely as such.

That is not to say that the TCA is entirely silent on matters concerning the evolving nature of the EU (as a community of values). A keener eye will recognise that whilst overt emphasis was avoided, some drafters were clearly aware of the potential for conflict. The TCA requires the UK to remain a member of the European Convention on Human Rights (ECHR),[32] and the need to ensure non-discriminatory practice is, for example, also explicitly mentioned.[33] The TCA clearly appears to have been drawn

[27] The rule-of-law conflicts with some Member States, for example, mean that the EU itself, in turn, cannot be seen to be facilitating breaches.

[28] There was, eg, insufficient time for the UK delegation to develop a position on how the UK might interact with the EPPO.

[29] See Wade (n 12) for detail on the EPPO as a topic with which the then British Prime Minister tried to stave off Eurosceptic sentiment.

[30] See European Commission, 'The Commission's Coordinator in Combating Racism' (2021) available at https://commission.europa.eu/strategy-and-policy/policies/justice-and-fundamental-rights/combatting-discrimination/racism-and-xenophobia/commissions-coordinator-combating-racism_en (last accessed 16 April 2024).

[31] N Scicluna and S Auer, 'Europe's constitutional unsettlement: testing the political limits of legal integration' (2023) 99(2) *International Affairs* 769.

[32] See TCA Arts 692 and 693.

[33] In relation to Passenger Name Records, see Art 547.

up in a manner palatable to the UK Government, but it is not devoid of an indication of the broader political UK context, which is viewed as problematic from the EU's perspective. There is clear desire by all parties to continue the successes of intra-EU cooperation and ensure they are still available to UK criminal justice practitioners, but this desire is not entirely unconditional on the EU's part. Red lines – such as ECHR membership – are evident in the Agreement too (see Mallory, chapter 16).[34]

In some of the more detailed provisions of the TCA, the reality of the evolving EU is more subtly reflected, as the following example will demonstrate. United Kingdom practitioners expressed concern at losing access to EU mechanisms for good reason. Investigations and prosecutions are strongly aided by them because expertise has developed. But the institutional framing of this expertise within the EU (which strongly supported its development) is precisely what led to unease on the UK Government's part. Brexit was heralded by objections to the expansion of institutional powers[35] and an unwillingness to support the demands practitioners working, say, in Eurojust were making.[36]

Setting political arguments aside, it is important to consider why such calls emerged. The pragmatic and practice-driven demands that led to the creation, first, of the European Judicial Network and then Eurojust were assertions that criminal justice practitioners were disadvantaged in relation to criminals perpetrating offences utilising the four freedoms provided by the EU.[37] Given that both Europol and Eurojust developed as demands grew for centralised processing of information and support in ensuring that criminal justice practitioners could prevent offender abuse of the four freedoms, it seems plausible that those institutions, in turn, developed a view of offender activity that enabled better understanding of any cross-border dimension to criminal activity. An overview not as readily available to practitioners working in national authorities. Once those EU-level practitioners – and others in equivalent positions – gained that overview, it seems reasonable that they would wish criminal justice practitioners 'on the ground' to be provided with – and respond to – that knowledge.[38]

In that scenario, of course, conflicts concerning sovereignty and subsidiarity are to be found.[39] As it relates to criminal justice systems, this matter strikes at the

[34] Note also the detailed regulation of data protection (Art 555). Purpose is expressly restricted to 'further security': Art 559.

[35] See, eg, Written statement to Parliament (n 10).

[36] ibid. Institutional reforms immediately preceding Brexit were marked (for both Europol and Eurojust) by a demand for these bodies to be given greater factual power. Key provisions for both related to an obligation's being placed upon national authorities to share data and a duty to heed suggestions to initiate investigations by the European bodies. The responding UK Government made very clear it viewed this as fundamentally and unacceptably changing the nature of the relationship between the EU institution and Member States.

[37] Council of the European Union, Presidency Conclusions, Tampere European Council (15–16 October 1999) para 5, available at www.europarl.europa.eu/summits/tam_en.htm (last accessed 16 April 2024).

[38] And this reality was given priority by the reformed legislation, see eg, Art 21 of the Regulation of the European Parliament and of the Council on the European Union Agency for Criminal Justice Cooperation, replacing and repealing Council Decision 2002/187/JHA, [2018] OJ L 295, 138.

[39] Reflected, for instance, in the responses of the Member States to a proposal to further expand Europol's powers to initiate investigations, recorded in N Vavoula and V Mitsilegas, *Strengthening Europol's mandate – A legal assessment of the Commission's proposal to amend the Europol Regulation*, European Parliament, Policy Department for Citizens' Rights and Constitutional Affairs Directorate-General for Internal Policies, PE 694.200 (Brussels, 2021) 60 available at www.europarl.europa.eu/RegData/etudes/STUD/2021/694200/IPOL_STU(2021)694200_EN.pdf (last accessed 16 April 2024).

core of national sovereignty as fervently portrayed by UK governments over the past decade. That is the background of Brexit.[40] The needs of practitioners, which the UK Government was always keen to develop pragmatic solutions to meet, including at the EU level,[41] triggered a development (demanding greater, centralised power) raising sensitive substantive issues of the highest order further down the line.

Given that it is the UK's choice to prioritise principles – such as national sovereignty – over the advantages of EU membership, it is particularly interesting to note that even the TCA is – on occasion – deferential to the expertise developed at the EU level. Thus, it also features specialist provisions, such as that in Article 546 (relating to Passenger Name Records). That article prescribes a specific relationship between EU agencies and UK authorities when it comes to terrorism and serious crime, and it includes an obligation to comply with Europol and Eurojust requests. The TCA thus lends EU agencies authority – in limited cases – to direct UK criminal justice personnel. When addressing terrorism and serious crime, any alternative approach would likely make a principled mountain of a molehill: UK practitioners would likely assert that if counterparts within Europol or Eurojust submit a request for them to take actions aimed at combating terrorism or organised crime, it would be counter-intuitive (and indeed contrary to UK security interests) for them to disregard such a request. Such is the established trust in these EU mechanisms relating to these offences. The inclusion of such provisions in the TCA presumably also demonstrates a very pragmatic belief on the UK side that its criminal justice practitioners would always cooperate with such requests. Otherwise, surely the UK Government would not enter into an obligation of this kind? It is EU competence precisely of the sort it is seeking to escape.

Provisions of this kind can also be viewed as indicating that the strongly espoused principles of Brexit are not being upheld in practice and in the face of overriding interests. They are perhaps also indications of the reality of power relationships and expertise in the EU–UK relationship. Undoubtedly, they also hold the potential for conflicts, considering the circumstances that necessitated the creation of the TCA.[42] Details of the TCA, however, reveal nuances, highlighting that ongoing UK involvement in EU criminal justice mechanisms is subject to conditions. As will be discussed in what follows, those appear likely to evolve.

## IV. The Reality(ies) of Judicial Cooperation Post-Brexit

An examination of judicial cooperation post-Brexit at this point reveals that the UK approach appears to be bearing fruit. Business as usual is continuing. Practitioners

[40] For a critical review of the UK Government's understanding of sovereignty and its effect, see R Niblett, *Britain, the EU and the Sovereignty Myth* (Chatham House, 2016).

[41] Note the confirmation of the value attached to Europol 'as established' in 2013, in the Ministerial Position cited in Written statement to Parliament (n 10).

[42] Recognised in provisions such as Art 552.

have adapted and made every effort to ensure that they continue to utilise the mechanisms and practices they valued and the functioning of which they very much want to preserve.

The Eurojust website indicates that the EU–UK judicial cooperation is working in an effective fashion. The UK is naturally listed as a country that has a liaison magistrate rather than a national desk, but the statistics demonstrate that work is plentiful. While its caseload does not match the business of the early years (during which the UK was one of the few astonishingly active national desks, with the majority of other Member States very significantly less active[43]), it is not nearly as far below that level as one might expect for a country exiting such mechanisms (see Table 12.1).

**Table 12.1** Casework of the UK liaison magistrate to Eurojust

| | 2017 | 2018 | 2019 | 2020 | 2021 |
|---|---|---|---|---|---|
| **New cases (total)** | 372 | 444 | 520 | 481 | 395 |
| – of which initiating | 82 | 98 | 69 | 47 | 71 |
| – of which participating | 290 | 346 | 451 | 434 | 324 |
| Coordination meetings (initiating and/or participating) | 82 | 77 | 96 | 64 | 64 |
| Coordination centres (organising and/or participating) | 2 | – | 8 | 2 | 5 |
| Joint investigation teams (newly signed and/or ongoing) | 65 | 72 | 75 | 65 | 49 |

*Source*: www.eurojust.europa.eu/united-kingdom.

This look at UK–EU judicial cooperation confirms the situation reflected in the TCA, that is, that the practice of judicial cooperation very much requires the advances made within the EU to continue to apply to judicial cooperation with the UK going forward.

The latest Eurojust annual report conveys a clear picture of the UK as a key player in European judicial cooperation. Although the statistics indicate that 2021 was marked by a clear decrease in the number of new cases, coordination centres and JITs the UK in which is participating, the UK is recorded as initiating more coordination meetings than in the previous year.[44] The UK is furthermore documented as having the highest participation in cases initiated by other desks (at 268 with 712 ongoing cases), alongside the most frequent participation in coordination meetings, JITs and action days (joint highest).[45] The UK has 47 new cases initiated by a national desk, with a majority of those (41) being bilateral cases; it may be, then, that EU mechanisms are being utilised to create partnerships with specific Member States. Not surprisingly, perhaps, the UK's

[43] See, eg, Eurojust, *Annual Report 2009* (The Hague) 54 and 55; and Eurojust, *Annual Report 2008* (The Hague) 14 and 15.

[44] Eurojust, *Annual Report 2022* (The Hague) 59. The UK is participating in more cases in 2021 than it did in 2017, perhaps reflecting just how hard practitioners are working to secure the benefits of EU mechanisms post-Brexit.

[45] ibid 60.

liaison magistrate has the highest participation in Eurojust cases of any liaison magistrate for 2021[46] and 2022.[47]

The decline in the use of JITs is a topic that likely warrants examination. The UK was notably enthusiastic in employing JITs, and reportedly gained substantial benefits, as the EU funded the involvement of units in criminal justice systems that otherwise might not have had the financial means to take part in such investigations.[48] It is not straightforward, however, to gain an overview of JIT use. The latest report by Eurojust and by the Network of National Experts on JITs only mentions that there are reports of delays in setting up JITs, due to uncertainties caused by Brexit.[49]

How trends in practice emerge is doubtlessly a matter that will be of great interest to all observers. It is clear that the TCA facilitates the continuation of work being done previously, albeit sometimes via less efficient means. The UK presence at Eurojust, however, is doubtlessly a crucial one: UK judicial cooperation with the EU remains very considerable indeed.

## V. Future Prospects

The TCA can perhaps be viewed as reflecting the history of judicial cooperation in the EU. This was always marked by British desire for multilateral (as opposed to supranational) mechanisms; an approach characterising the evolution of the EAW and Eurojust's College structure for instance.[50] Judicial cooperation within the EU is now, however, a strongly evolving beast, and its trajectory is part of the Brexit story that, in the end, necessitated the TCA. Consequently, examination of the broader context of judicial cooperation in and with the EU is important, in order to understand the TCA and reflect on how it may fare.

As indicated in section III, the EU currently finds itself at a number of decisive junctures. For a long time, discussions on criminal justice cooperation in the EU centred on its imbalanced nature and the need to provide appropriately for defence rights as police and prosecutorial judicial mechanisms evolved.[51] With the end of the Stockholm Programme,[52] demands were subdued (arguments over the demands being made on Member States' budgets, and indeed principled/political conflicts spearheaded by the

[46] Eurojust, *Annual Report 2021: 20 years of criminal justice across borders* (The Hague) 75.

[47] Eurojust, *Annual Report 2022* (The Hague) 31.

[48] Crown Prosecution Service, *Joint Investigation Teams Legal Guidance* (2023) available at www.cps.gov.uk/legal-guidance/international (last accessed 16 April 2024).

[49] Eurojust, *Fourth JITS Evaluation Report* (The Hague, 2023) 10.

[50] V Mitsilegas, 'Mutual recognition in criminal matters' (2006) 43 *Common Market Law Review* 1277, 1278.

[51] See, eg, B Schünemann, 'Grundzüge eines Alternativ-Entwurfs zur europäischen Strafverfolgung' (2004) 116 *Zeitschrift fur die gesamte Strafrechtswissenschaft* 376; B Schünemann (ed), *Ein Gesamtkonzept für die Euroäische Strafrechtspflege* (Carl Heymanns Verlag, 2006); V Costa Ramos, M Luchtman and G Munteanu, 'Improving Defence Rights Including Available Remedies in and (or as a Consequence of) Cross-Border Criminal Proceedings' (2020) 3 *Eucrim* 230.

[52] European Council, 'The Stockholm Programme – An open and secure Europe serving and protecting citizens' 2010/C 115/01 (Brussels, 2010); European Commission, Communication from the Commission to the European Parliament, The European Council, the Council, the European Economic and Social Committee and the Committee of the Regions, 'The EU Justice Agenda for 2020 – Strengthening Trust, Mobility and Growth within the Union' COM(2014) 144 final.

UK, had meant negotiations around the Stockholm Programme rights were draining), with a period of consolidation being foreseen.[53] Nevertheless, issues that might have been addressed as part of a more robust defence rights discussion reared their head.

The EU now features a Commission coordinator for anti-racism,[54] and discrimination within criminal justice has been a key concern in discussions[55] surrounding the EU Anti-Racism Action Plan.[56] Conflicts surrounding rule-of- law issues[57] have dominated discussions around the European judiciary. The invasion of Ukraine immediately raised questions for the EU, including ones relating to the role judicial institutions and mechanisms should play regarding any response. On all of these fronts, the EU has been forced to decide what kind of Union it wants to be. For the purposes of this chapter, it appears reasonable to suggest that these discussions involve various efforts to shape the EU into the type of Union that the UK declined to be a part of. Assertions of a 'Europe of values' indicate a governance level with constitutional features, shifting relationships relating to sovereignty and the meaning of subsidiarity.

Brexit resulted, inter alia, from political opposition to impulses deepening and changing the nature of European integration. The UK Government tried first to redirect then to halt these.[58] Whilst many British commentators, academics and practitioners doubtlessly felt, for example, that the EAW required counterbalancing defence rights provision (or that calls for Eurojust to be lent genuine powers were justified), those espousing principled objections to such developments (and what they represented more broadly) secured the backing of (a slim majority of) the UK electorate.[59] Hence, the necessity for the TCA arose.

The context of judicial cooperation in – and therefore to some extent with – the EU remains the same, however. No longer working with the UK as an opposing Member State, judicial cooperation is evolving at pace. Eurojust is considerably enhanced, having gained the status of an EU agency.[60] Its powers and profile are likely to be further enhanced by activities responding to crimes (under international law) committed in Ukraine and through working with the EPPO.

[53] European Commission, 'Communication on the EU Security Union Strategy' COM(2020) 605 final.

[54] See European Commission (n 28).

[55] See, eg, European Parliament, Parliament condemns all forms of racism, hate and violence and calls for action', Press Release of 19 June 2020 available at www.europarl.europa.eu/news/en/press-room/20200615IPR81223/parliament-condemns-all-forms-of-racism-hate-and-violence-and-calls-for-action (last accessed 16 April 2024).

[56] European Commission Communication, 'A Union of equality: EU anti-racism action plan 2020–2025' COM(2020) 565 final.

[57] See Scicluna and Auer (n 29).

[58] Beginning with the steer towards mutual recognition (and away from harmonisation) at Tampere, demonstrated by the concerted effort made to ensure Eurojust was successful as a cooperative forum through to the principled opposition to defence rights legislation and Europol reform as described.

[59] Though, as previously noted, this is a largely technical discussion that was not specifically referenced in the high-profile efforts of the Leave campaign.

[60] Via Art 1 of the Regulation on the European Union Agency for Criminal Justice Cooperation (n 38) in 2019. This, of course, occurred during the period that saw Brexit being negotiated, and it is notable that the UK opted in to this Regulation. Given that nothing had changed regarding the principled opposition of the UK Government to such a direction of travel, it seems reasonable to speculate that this was a pragmatic decision to ensure that the UK could continue to work with, and within, Eurojust as closely and effectively as possible on a practical level, in full knowledge that the UK would not long be bound (as a Member State) by the new nature of Eurojust.

The declared nightmare of Brexiteers, the EPPO, now exists and is taking a muscular approach to its role in EU criminal justice.[61] It is also empowered to join JITs.[62] Its remit is currently confined to protecting the financial interests of the EU, but it is a player in judicial cooperation and a developing model of how things may work in the EU. As a third country, the UK is, of course, not subject to the rules of these agencies, but the question remains how it will fare in cooperation with institutions that have evolved in a direction the UK fundamentally opposed. The extent of UK-initiated activity within Eurojust may also be an indicator of the need for UK practitioners to work harder because of the advantages lost. Should that be the case, the provisions of the TCA may come to be viewed critically by those practitioners and anyone valuing their work (as law-and-order-oriented politicians, for example, are likely to) and come under considerable pressure fairly quickly.

It is important to recall that developments in criminal justice, including at the EU level, are also driven by incidents. A proposal for a counterterrorism EPPO was tabled in 2018[63] and (similarly to the EAW in September 2001) may, unfortunately, become of great relevance if events so determine. The question is how arguments insisting that the TCA must do[64] will hold up in the face of any argument that, for example, more effective counterterrorism could be achieved via the EU's integrative model. Any such position would be strengthened inordinately should British practitioners attest to the losses of Brexit as being in any way considerable. Only time will tell.

Criminal justice issues are also a powerful force. Western democracies are populated by citizens (taxpayers) willing to 'invest' above all in security and criminal justice, whilst demanding that the state leave them be on most other fronts.[65] The four freedoms carry inherent risks (as illicit markets thrive alongside the legal economy), creating a need for a governance framework that aims to tackle these challenges effectively. The UK Government itself also has a significant history of seeking to harness the power of the EU in relation to terrorism, trafficking human beings, etc.[66] The vision of the UK Government could be summarised as an 'enhanced form of transnational law'. However, the TCA became a necessity because the UK Government could not convince enough fellow Member States that this iteration of the EU held more appeal than the distinct model (centred around harmonisation and intensified integration) that the EU embodies.

Other countries without the historical luxury of defendable, stable borders are seemingly less concerned with matters of principle when the prospect of more efficient

[61] Exemplified by the approach taken in a conflict with Ireland, see EPPO, 'European Chief Prosecutor addresses letter to the Commission on Ireland's refusal to cooperate with the EPPO' *News* (2022) 23 November, available at www.eppo.europa.eu/en/news/european-chief-prosecutor-addresses-letter-commission-irelands-refusal-cooperate-eppo (last accessed 16 April 2024).

[62] Eurojust, *Fourth JITS Evaluation Report* (2023) 44.

[63] European Commission, Communication on the EU Security Union Strategy, 'A Europe that protects: an initiative to extend the competences of the European Public Prosecutor's Office to cross-border terrorist crimes' COM(2018) 641 final.

[64] This must be the position of those who advocated for Brexit – an insistence that the UK is better off out of the EU, even if it comes at the expense of SIS access.

[65] Z Bauman, *Globalisation: The Human Consequences* (Columbia University Press, 1998).

[66] See, eg, UK Presidency of the Council, *Presidency Priorities* (July-December 2005) available at www.asser.nl/upload/eel-webroot/www/documents/UKEUPresidency2005.pdf (last accessed 16 April 2024).

security arrangements beckons. As described in section III, if Eurojust is, for example, enabled to gain an informational advantage, arguments against giving it authority to use that advantage become ever harder to justify. The EU is on a journey that features an organic integration of judicial cooperation and its evolution into something else. There are institutional (and human) pulls and pushes too – of course – but there is a linear development to be discerned in EU development, now also clearly visible in relation to judicial cooperation. The facts and figures demonstrate the UK as being centrally involved in the latter. It is difficult to imagine the demand for this abating, and so the provisions of the TCA look set to be tested. Thus far, UK practitioners have seemingly continued to validate their reputation for making things work in practice. How successful they can be in the longer term will likely be determined by the priority lent by other criminal justice systems to relations with the UK as a third state. And how the TCA fares will be subject to comparison with mechanisms evolving within the EU.

The UK is an island nation. Its history of judicial cooperation within the EU demonstrates a keenly felt need to build bridges to ensure that its criminal justice practitioners are not confined to their island. The TCA offers a landscape that attempts to maintain those bridges with older materials. As the structures on the European mainland – to which those bridges lead – change, it will certainly be interesting to see how those materials fare.[67] The judicial landscape in the EU is already being shaped by actors not featured in the TCA – such as the EPPO – and that fact alone may be reason to doubt the Agreement's durability.

[67] There is no reason to believe practitioners will not voice any frustration at advantages lost through Brexit. If the UK can be viewed as suffering security disadvantages because of the post-Brexit scenario, this will likely generate pressure to improve mechanisms once again. The voices of practitioners fighting crimes such as terrorism and trafficking human beings tend to have currency with politicians.

# 13

# Extradition/Surrender under the Trade and Cooperation Agreement – The Shifting Cooperative–Protective Balance

PAUL ARNELL*

## I. Introduction

Extradition between the United Kingdom (UK) and European Union (EU) Member States is now governed by Title VII of Part Three of the Trade and Cooperation Agreement 2020 (TCA).[1] The TCA replaced the Framework Decision on the European Arrest Warrant 2002.[2] The latter created a unique system of extradition with heightened cooperation well beyond orthodox treaty regimes, including the European Convention on Extradition 1957. The Framework Decision did so through reliance upon the principles of mutual trust and recognition.[3] Following Brexit and the conclusion of the TCA, the important question for the UK and EU Member states is whether the new rules will function as effectively and efficiently. For accused and convicted persons subject to extradition, on the other hand, the most important question is whether the process will be fair and just, and pay due regard to their human rights. The answers to these questions are arguably mutually exclusive. This is because extradition has two competing purposes, the facilitation of criminal cooperation between jurisdictions and the protection of requested persons.[4] States, with their desire for effective and efficient

*This chapter considers provisions of the Trade and Cooperation Agreement 2020 specific to surrender and notably distinct from the Framework Decision on the European Arrest Warrant 2002. It does not discuss more general changes affecting or possibly affecting the process, such as the jurisdiction of the Court of Justice of the European Union and dispute settlement and the loss of access to the Schengen Information System II (SIS II). These are covered elsewhere in this volume.

[1] Trade and Cooperation Agreement between the European Union and the European Atomic Energy Community and the United Kingdom of Great Britain and Northern Ireland [2012] OJ L149/10.

[2] Council Framework Decision on 13 June 2002 on the European arrest warrant and surrender procedures between Member States [2002] OJ L190/1 ('the Framework Decision').

[3] The Recital to the Framework Decision refers, inter alia, to the principle of mutual recognition of criminal decisions and the high level of confidence between Member States.

[4] Warbrick refers to the cooperative and protective purposes of extradition in C Warbrick, 'Recent Developments in Extradition Law' (2007) 56(1) *International and Comparative Law Quarterly* 199.

transnational criminal justice, generally favour the cooperative purpose. Requested persons align with the protective function. The challenge facing any system of extradition is to properly balance the two. Whilst quite similar, the rules under the TCA are notably less cooperative than those under the Framework Decision. In the context of the historical oscillations in the purposes of extradition, the TCA moves the pendulum towards the protection of requested persons at the expense of transnational criminal cooperation.[5]

## II. Extradition and Surrender

Extradition is the formal process of transferring an accused or a convicted person from one jurisdiction to another. 'Extradition' and 'surrender' are related but not synonymous. Extradition is the orthodox term for the process, said to have first found its place in law in the French *décret-loi* of 19 February 1791.[6] It has naturally evolved and developed over the centuries.[7] A feature of this has been the variation in emphasis of the contradictory goals of enhanced cooperation and increased protection for requested persons. Without doubt, the most advanced example of a cooperative international system is that created by the Framework Decision. It is rightly termed a system of surrender, rather than extradition. 'Surrender' denotes a streamlined form of extradition that, inter alia, eschews judicial scrutiny of evidence and provides fewer protections to requested persons, being based on a high degree of trust between the parties.[8] Illuminatively, the word 'surrender' is employed in the TCA. Whilst not inaccurate, it belies the fact that the process under the TCA is distinctly less cooperative than that under the Framework Decision.[9]

## III. The Framework Decision on the EAW

To trace and appreciate the changes to the system of surrender with adoption of the TCA, the core features of the Framework Decision must be noted. Applying throughout the EU from 1 January 2004, it introduced a system of surrender.[10] It was designed to

[5] Lord Mustill noted that the history of the political offence exception in extradition 'discloses a series of oscillations', in *T v Secretary of State* [1996] AC 742, 761. It is clear that extradition itself has swung back and forth in its purposes.

[6] CL Blakesley, 'The Practice of Extradition from Antiquity to Modern France and the United States: A Brief History' (1981) 39 *Boston College International & Comparative Law Review* 40.

[7] Outlining the history in UK law is the report of the Baker Review of UK extradition, S Baker, D Perry and A Doobay, 'A Review of the United Kingdom's Extradition Arrangements' (2011) available at https://assets.publishing.service.gov.uk/government/uploads/system/uploads/attachment_data/file/117673/extradition-review.pdf (last accessed 16 April 2024).

[8] The UK introduced a prima facie evidence requirement into its law by s 10 of the Extradition Act 1870. It does not apply where a person is sought to serve a sentence rather than stand trial. Civil law states generally did not require such evidence, with an arrest warrant setting out the nature of the charge deemed sufficient evidence of guilt to justify extradition: Baker Review, ibid 258.

[9] Noting the demise of the principles with the conclusion of the TCA is McCloskey LJ in *Kilgasts v Latvia* [2022] NIQB 60, para 14, where he said 'the principle of mutual trust and confidence … has evaporated'.

[10] Case C-303/05 *Advocaten Vor de Wereld VZW v Leden Van de Ministerrad* [2001] ECR 1-3633, para 49 (per AG Colomer).

make the transfer of accused and convicted persons more efficient and effective. The Framework Decision implemented the principles of mutual trust and mutual recognition of judicial decisions in criminal matters. This entailed the acceptance of a warrant without an inquiry into the facts or circumstances giving rise to it.[11] Executive decision making was removed from the surrender process. The Framework Decision supplemented the traditional double-criminality requirement, that the act be criminal in the requested as well as the requesting territories, with a Framework List of offences. This obviated double criminality where the possible punishment in an accusation case was at least three years or where, in a conviction case, a sentence of at least four months had been imposed.[12] Further, the Framework Decision did not admit the possibility of a Member State's refusing to surrender its own nationals – a significant development for several civil law states.

Further significant features of the Framework Decision exist by virtue of their absence. No provision is made for them. These are a political offence exception and a proportionality and human rights bar. As regards the first, in the stead of an orthodox exception, political motivation and bias are mentioned in recital 12, which, inter alia, provides that nothing in the Framework Decision 'may be interpreted as prohibiting refusal to surrender … when there are reasons to believe, on the basis of objective elements, that the said arrest warrant has been issued for the purpose of prosecuting or punishing a person on the grounds of his … political opinions'. This is not a political offence exception. Such a bar prevents extradition for offences of a political character. Also of relevance in this vein is the fact that the Framework List of offences includes sabotage and terrorism – offences that can have, or indeed necessarily have, a political element.

There is no principle of proportionality in the Framework Decision, which has been the focus of criticism.[13] The third Commission Report on the EAW, dated 13 April 2011, noted that confidence in the application of EAWs had been undermined by their systematic use for the surrender of persons sought in respect of minor offences. It stated that there was general agreement among Member States that a proportionality requirement was necessary to prevent the issuing of warrants for offences that were not serious enough to justify the issuance and execution of an EAW.[14] Bringing this issue to the fore was the practice of certain Member States to seek surrender for relatively minor offences, with Poland being notable here in doing so.[15] To date, the terms of the Framework Decision have not been amended in this regard.

[11] Baker Review (n 7) 100.

[12] Criticism in the UK of the Framework List system was addressed, in part, by the Extradition Act 2003, requiring surrender for such an offence to be conditional on the fact that none of it occurred within the UK. This addressed the possibility that an individual could be surrendered for an offence that was not criminal in the UK for acts committed within the country: see Baker Review (n 7) 188.

[13] See Human Rights Joint Committee, *The Human Rights Implications of UK Extradition Policy*, 15th Report, June 2011, paras 143 et seq, available at https://publications.parliament.uk/pa/jt201012/jtselect/jtrights/156/15602.htm (last accessed 16 April 2024).

[14] Baker Review (n 7) 106–07. The EU Commission's *Handbook on How to Issue and Execute a European Arrest Warrant* (2017/C 335/01) advised issuing judicial authorities (at 14) to consider whether issuing an EAW is justified in a particular case with reference to factors including the seriousness of the offence, the likely penalty imposed if the individual is found guilty and the interests of victims, available at https://eur-lex.europa.eu/legal-content/EN/TXT/PDF/?uri=CELEX:52017XC1006(02)&from=SL (last accessed 16 April 2024).

[15] This follows its adherence to the principle of legality, where prosecutors are obliged to prosecute all crime.

In line with the principles of mutual trust and recognition, there is no place for human rights as a ground for refusal of a surrender request within the text of the Framework Decision. They are mentioned in recitals 6(1) and 6(3). The EU Commission, in its first report on the operation of the EAW, stated 'the Council did not intend to make the general condition of respect for fundamental human rights an explicit ground for refusal in event of infringement'.[16] Notably, the Court of Justice of the European Union (CJEU) has come to accept the applicability of human rights in the execution of an EAW in certain limited circumstances. In *Criminal Proceedings against Aranyosi*,[17] the Grand Chamber held that the execution of an EAW must be deferred where there is a real risk of inhuman or degrading treatment for the individual concerned because of conditions in the issuing state. If, after considering further information, including that provided by the issuing state, the risk could not be discounted, the executing authority must decide whether the surrender procedure should end.

Overall, it is clear that the Framework Decision created the most streamlined and administrative system of transfer of accused and convicted persons between states ever devised. A former Member of the European Parliament said that it had 'delivered big improvements in the speed of extradition through the free movement of judicial decisions in place of traditional inter-governmental relations. This is important for the public interest in bringing criminals to justice and it is also important for victims.'[18] On the other side of the coin, there have been criticisms about the lack of protections for requested persons. The important surrender-related questions during the Brexit negotiations were whether there would be an agreement (or instead a reversion by default to the European Convention on Extradition) and, if so, where on the cooperation–protection continuum that agreement would fall.

## IV. Title VII of Part Three of the Trade and Cooperation Agreement 2020 – Surrender

The TCA was signed on 30 December 2020. It applied provisionally as of 1 January 2021 and entered into force on 1 May 2021. Persons arrested under an arrest warrant (AW) after 31 December 2021 are covered by the rules therein. Those rules are found in Title VII of Part Three of the TCA, 'Law Enforcement and Judicial Cooperation in Criminal Matters'. They govern the surrender relations between the UK and EU Member States. The Agreement sought to 'create a hybrid of the EAW and United Kingdom recent practice'.[19] The Political Declaration setting out the Framework for the Future

[16] Report from the Commission based on art 34 of the Council Framework Decision of 13 June 2002 on the European arrest warrant and the surrender procedures between Member States (revised version), European Commission, 24 January 2006, COM (2006) 8 and SEC (2006) 79.

[17] *Criminal Proceedings against Aranyosi* [2016] QB 921.

[18] Baroness Ludford, in evidence to the House of Lords Select Committee on Extradition Law, February 2015, at para 322, available at https://publications.parliament.uk/pa/ld201415/ldselect/ldextradition/126/12602.htm (last accessed 16 April 2024).

[19] E Grange, B Keith and S Kerridge 'Extradition under the EU-UK Trade and Cooperation Agreement' (2021) 12(2) *New Journal of European Criminal Law* 214.

Relationship between the European Union and the United Kingdom of 19 October 2019 stated that the parties should agree 'effective arrangements based on streamlined procedures and time limits enabling the United Kingdom and Member States to surrender suspected and convicted persons efficiently and expeditiously'.[20] The surrender-related provisions of the TCA, then, were written 'to provide a level of continuity' between the EU and UK.[21]

## A. Similarities with the EAW

There are considerable similarities between the surrender rules in the TCA and those in the Framework Decision. Article 596 of the TCA provides that the objective of Title VII is to ensure that extradition between the UK and EU Member States 'is based on a mechanism of surrender'. As noted, that entails a streamlined form of extradition, which, inter alia, eschews political involvement and judicial scrutiny of evidence against the accused in the requested state.[22] The TCA retains these aspects of the process in the sense that no provision is made for them – they are notable by way of their continued absence. As such, the arrest warrant system retains core features of the process intrinsic to its cooperative nature. A consequence of this is that the relatively short time limits that operated under the Framework Decision can be, and are, followed in the TCA. These are that, where the individual consents, surrender is to take place within 10 days, and in other cases the final decision should generally take place within a period of 60 days following the individual's arrest.[23]

Illustrating the degree of similarity between Title VII of Part Three and the Framework Decision from a practical perspective is that the required content of a warrant under each is very similar. Article 8 of the Framework Decision and Article 606(1)(a)–(g) of the TCA are largely the same. Both require, in general terms, the identity and nationality of the requested person, details of the issuing authority, an arrest warrant, details of the nature and circumstances of the offence, the penalty imposed if a conviction warrant, and (if possible) other consequences of the offence. Annex 43 to the TCA contains the form required to be used by issuing authorities; again, this is akin to the form in the Annex to the Framework Decision. In this operational sense there is very little difference between the two warrants.

There is also a high degree of similarity between the mandatory and optional grounds for refusal of a surrender request in both the TCA and the Framework Decision. The mandatory grounds are identical, including an amnesty and *non bis in idem*. The optional grounds for refusal are also the same, although they have been consolidated

[20] At para 87, available at https://assets.publishing.service.gov.uk/government/uploads/system/uploads/attachment_data/file/840656/Political_Declaration_setting_out_the_framework_for_the_future_relationship_between_the_European_Union_and_the_United_Kingdom.pdf (last accessed 16 April 2024). Note the Declaration signposted changes as to double criminality, the nationality bar and the political offence exemption, as discussed in sections IV.B.ii–iv.

[21] Grange, Keith and Kerridge (n 19) 217.

[22] The Baker Review (n 7) 122, opined that a surrender process effected almost wholly through judicial authorities was an entirely positive development.

[23] Art 615 of the TCA. Art 621 provides that surrender should take place no longer than 10 days after the final decision.

in Article 601 of the TCA, having been found in different articles of the Framework Decision. Somewhat similarly, the general protections provided to requested persons are largely the same in both instruments, being found in Article 11 of the Framework Decision and Article 609 of the TCA. Amongst them are the right to be informed of the contents of the warrant and the provision of an interpreter. Note, though, that the TCA contains two additional protections – the right to consular services and the right to a lawyer in the issuing state. These are facets of the additional protection offered to requested persons under the TCA.[24] They sit alongside other substantive protections that *in toto* mark a clear line between the Framework Decision and the TCA in the balance between cooperation and protection.

## B. Differences from the EAW

### *i. An Explicit Proportionality Provision*

The TCA contains a provision expressly referring to the principle of proportionality, in Article 597.[25] It provides:

> Cooperation through the arrest warrant shall be necessary and proportionate, taking into account the rights of the requested person and the interests of the victims, and having regard to the seriousness of the act, the likely penalty that would be imposed and the possibility of a State taking measures less coercive than the surrender of the requested person particularly with a view to avoiding unnecessarily long periods of pre-trial detention.[26]

In practice, proportionality can be considered at both the point of issuing an arrest warrant and at the point of its execution. Article 613, entitled 'Surrender decision', provides in paragraph (1) that the executing judicial authority shall decide whether the person is to be surrendered, inter alia, in accordance with the principle. Notably, Article 613(2) requires the executing authority to request further information from the issuing state where that provided to it is insufficient to allow it to decide on surrender.[27] In other words, the executing state can ask the issuing state for information justifying the

[24] The right to a lawyer in both the executing and issuing states reflects the right within Art 10 of Directive (EU) 2013/48/EU, on the right of access to a lawyer in criminal proceedings and in European arrest warrant proceedings [2013] OJ L294/01. It applies to both accusation and conviction cases. The UK chose not to opt in to the Directive.

[25] The only other surrender agreement the EU has entered into with third countries (with Iceland and Norway) does not contain such a provision. It is found at https://eur-lex.europa.eu/legal-content/EN/TXT/?uri=CELEX%3A22006A1021%2801%29. In many other ways that agreement mirrors the relevant terms of the TCA.

[26] In *Badea v Romania* [2022] EWHC 1025 (Admin), the English High Court rejected arguments that proportionality in Art 597 of the TCA required a distinctive evaluation of 'seriousness of the act', and one broader than that required in an balance-sheet evaluation under Art 8 of the European Convention on Human Rights, ETS No 005, 1950 (ECHR). In other words, the terms of the TCA did not affect existing UK extradition law on proportionality.

[27] In addition to proportionality, the article requires the executing authority to seek information where required in addressing the mandatory and non-mandatory grounds of refusal, the political offence exception, a possible life sentence and human rights, and the content and form of the arrest warrant itself, under Arts 600–620, 604 and 606 respectively. Giving guidance on the operation of Art 613 is *Kilgasts v Latvia* (n 9) para 50.

proportionality of the arrest warrant. Therefore, whilst there is not an explicit requirement upon the issuing state to undertake a proportionality assessment, Article 613(2) can act in that manner on an *ex post facto* basis.[28] The inclusion of proportionality in the TCA formalises the Commission's *Handbook* on the point and appears to provide greater protection to individuals subject to the process from disproportionate surrenders as between the UK and EU Member States. Note, though, in *Bancia v Romania* the English High Court held that the proportionality principle in Article 597 did not prescribe anything that the Article 8 ECHR balancing exercise would not deliver.[29] In *Dujka v Czech Republic*, however, it was held that an extradition judge now has to consider how concern with proportionality in extradition has been enhanced following Brexit.[30] Clearly, the position remains unsettled.

### *ii. Reintroduction of Nationality Bar by Certain Member States*

Arguably the most significant change to the system of surrender under the TCA is that it admits the possibility of the reintroduction of a nationality bar. Article 603(1) provides that the execution of an arrest warrant may not be refused on the grounds that the requested person is a national of the executing state. Article 603(2) then provides, however, that the UK and the EU on the behalf of any Member State may notify the Specialised Committee on Law Enforcement and Judicial Cooperation ('Specialised Committee') that the state's nationals will not be surrendered, or will be surrendered only under certain conditions. Where a state refuses to surrender an individual on the basis of her nationality then Article 603(3) provides that that country should consider instituting proceedings against the person. This is in line with the principle of extradite or prosecute, or *aut dedere aut judicare*. Nine Member States have notified the Specialised Committee that they will not extradite their nationals.[31] Thirteen Member States have notified that the surrender of their nationals will take place only under certain conditions, mainly reciprocity or consent. Four Member States have intimated that they will not make a notification under Article 603(2). Accordingly, from a UK perspective, it will not be possible to secure individuals from some of the states that were its main partners under the Framework Decision, including Germany and France.[32] As regards requests

[28] The UK and EU's Joint Political Declaration on Title VII [Surrender] of Part Three provides, inter alia, that '[t]he principle of proportionality is relevant throughout the process leading to the surrender decision': available at https://assets.publishing.service.gov.uk/government/uploads/system/uploads/attachment_data/file/948105/EU-UK_Declarations_24.12.2020.pdf (last accessed 16 April 2024).

[29] *Bancia v Romania* [2023] EWHC 405 (Admin) [42].

[30] *Dujka v Czech Republic* [2023] EWHC 1842 (Admin) [22].

[31] Notification must be renewed every five years in order to remain applicable. Such renewal also applies to the other exemptions limiting surrender.

[32] In the calendar year 2021, the Member States where the greatest number of persons were arrested following UK requests were Spain (31), Romania (30), Ireland (24), Germany (12), Italy (12 and France (10). Of these, Germany and France have fully invoked the exception, Romania has done so conditionally, and Spain, Ireland and Italy have indicated that they do not intend to invoke the exception. See Notifications Made by the European Union to the UK under Part Three of the UK–EU Trade and Cooperation Agreement, at 12, available at https://assets.publishing.service.gov.uk/government/uploads/system/uploads/attachment_data/file/1061828/2022-02-11_EU_Notifications_to_the_UK_-_FINAL_VERSION.pdf (last accessed 16 April 2024) (hereinafter 'Notifications'). And for statistics, see www.nationalcrimeagency.gov.uk/what-we-do/how-we-work/providing-specialist-capabilities-for-law-enforcement/

from EU Member States, the UK has not notified the Specialised Committee that it will not institute a nationality bar. This is in line with the UK's traditional position of not considering nationality as germane in deciding upon extradition.[33] There is no mention of reciprocity in Article 603. The UK will, assuming there are no other obstacles, surrender its nationals under the TCA to all Member States, including those who refuse to do so in converse circumstances.[34]

The difficulties arising from the nationality bar may be magnified in two ways. These are an expansive conception of who is considered a national for the purposes of the exception and the EU rules on discrimination based on nationality. As to the former, the Netherlands, for example, provided in its declaration under the Iceland/Norway agreement that the nationality bar can extend to third-country nationals within it who are in possession of a valid unlimited residence permit.[35] Whilst no Member State to date has taken such an approach in its notification to the Specialised Committee, this may happen in future. As to the latter, in *Criminal Proceedings against Petruhhin*,[36] the Grand Chamber of the CJEU held that the operation of the nationality bar as regards third states fell within the scope of non-discrimination on the grounds of nationality and the rules on free movement. This in essence meant that where a requested person was a national of one Member State and within another Member State that operated a nationality bar, that individual had to be offered to her state of nationality for prosecution prior to surrender.[37] This has the possibility of extending the nationality bar to all EU nationals within the territory of those states who apply it. Even discounting these avenues for extending the nationality bar, there is no doubt that its reintroduction, as against the UK, provides protection from possible surrender to the UK to many millions of persons within the EU.

### *iii. Reintroduction of Political Offence Exception*

Article 602 of the TCA introduces a political offence exception into UK–EU surrender, albeit in a roundabout way. An orthodox political offence exception permits requested states to refuse to extradite individuals they consider to be sought for offences of a

fugitives-and-international-crime/extradition-arrangements-with-eu-countries (last accessed 16 April 2024) (hereinafter ''Statistics'). Note that Poland originally notified the Specialised Committee that it would not extradite its nationals in an circumstances, however, on 26 July 2023 it partially withdrew that notification (2023/C 263/02) available at https://eur-lex.europa.eu/legal-content/EN/TXT/PDF/?uri=CELEX:22023X0726(01) (last accessed 16 April 2024). Poland will now extradite its nationals, inter alia, where the act referred to in the arrest warrant was committed outside the territory of Poland.

[33] A slight inroad to this has been the introduction of a forum bar to extradition into UK law. One of the matters to be considered by a judge in considering forum are the connections between the requested person and the UK. See P Arnell and G Davies, 'The Forum Bar in UK Extradition Law – An Unnecessary Failure' (2020) 84(2) *The Journal of Criminal Law* 142.

[34] The numbers are likely to be quite small. In 2020, 49 UK nationals were extradited or surrendered from the UK to a third country – see Statistics (n 33).

[35] As noted in R Davidson, 'Everything is Different but Nothing has Changed: the New post-Brexit Extradition Arrangements between the UK and the EU' (2021) 6 *Criminal Law Review* 437.

[36] *Criminal Proceedings against Petruhhin* [2017] QB 299.

[37] See M Bose, 'Mutual Recognition, Extradition to Third Countries and Union Citizenship: Petruhhin' (2017) 54(6) *Common Market Law Review* 1781. The rule was extended to EEA nationals by *Criminal Proceedings against IN* [2020] 1 WLR 4564, and to requests to serve a sentence (as opposed to be tried) in *Proceedings Relating to Raugevicius* [2019]2 CMLR 3.

political character. In this vein, Article 602(1) first provides that a warrant may not be refused on the grounds that the executing state regards the offence as a political offence, an offence connected to one or an offence inspired by political motives. Article 602(2), however, provides that the UK, or the EU acting on behalf of any of its Member States, may notify the Specialised Committee that the scope of this provision is limited to offences listed in Articles 1 and 2 of the European Convention on the Suppression of Terrorism 1977,[38] offences of conspiracy or association to commit one of those offences and terrorism as defined in Annex 45 to the TCA. Twelve Member States have limited the scope of the exception in this way.[39] They may, therefore, reinstitute a limited political offence exception in their surrender relations with the UK. The UK itself has not made such a notification. Article 603(3), however, provides that where an issuing party has made a notification under Article 602, the executing party may apply reciprocity. In other words where, say, Italy makes a request to the UK, it would be entitled to refuse surrender on the basis of it considering the offence as political but not falling under the definition of terrorism. In practice, Article 602 may provide protection from surrender in only a limited number of cases. Whilst Spain has not made a notification under Article 602, if it had, then the UK might well have been justified under the terms of the TCA to refuse to surrender Clara Ponsati, who was accused of sedition following her role in the referendum held in Catalonia in 2017.

### *iv. Reintroduction of Double/Dual Criminality*

The TCA adopts an approach to double criminality akin to that under the Framework Decision List.[40] Nevertheless, it requires notification to the Specialised Committee in order to be engaged. Double criminality applies, under Article 599(2), unless the UK and the EU on behalf of any of its Member States give notification that it will not. As of November 2022, 16 Member States and the UK had given such notification.[41] Significantly, from a UK perspective, section 64(5) of the Extradition Act 2003, giving effect to the European Framework List, was repealed, and a similar provision referring to the Trade and Cooperation List has not been introduced in its stead. As UK law stands, then, double criminality has been reintroduced as between it and all EU Member States.[42] It will need to be proved in every case that the conduct constituting the offence within the issuing state would also constitute an offence within one of the UK's jurisdictions had it occurred there. Whilst a significant change in principle, it is doubtful that this will make much difference in practice.[43] This is because the substantive criminal law in the UK and EU Member States is such that only very rarely would an individual be sought for something not criminal in the executing state. That noted, the UK's failure to reintroduce a list system in its domestic law gives a degree

[38] ETS No 090.

[39] Notifications (n 33) 11.

[40] The only difference being the addition of bribery as coming under corruption, in Art 599(5).

[41] Notifications (n 33) 11.

[42] As regards outgoing UK Extradition Arrest Warrants, s 142 of the Extradition Act 2003 has been amended to allow UK courts to certify a request that the conduct falls within the list within Art 599 of the TCA. This allows EU Member States to waive double criminality if they so wish.

[43] See JR Spencer, 'The Sunny Uplands?' (2021) 1 *Arch Rev* 10.

of protection in exceptional cases to requested persons in the form of an orthodox double-criminality rule. It also appears set to increase challenges to extradition on the lack of double criminality, which will in turn lengthen the judicial process.

## v. *Enhanced Position of Human Rights*

The TCA provides a greater degree of human rights protection to requested persons than the Framework Decision. There are two aspects to this enhanced protection, general and specific. Generally, Article 524 of the TCA provides, inter alia, that the cooperation governed under Part Three is based on the respect for the protection of fundamental human rights as set out in the ECHR and on the importance of giving effect to the rights and freedoms in that Convention domestically. Human rights are again referred to in Article 763(1), which provides, inter alia, '[t]he Parties shall continue to uphold the shared values and principles of democracy, the rule of law, and respect for human rights … [t]he Parties reaffirm their respect for the Universal Declaration of Human Rights and the international human rights treaties to which they are parties'. By Article 771, human rights are one of the essential elements of the UK–EU arrangement, and a serious and substantial failure to fulfil Article 763(1) entitles either party to terminate or suspend the TCA or any part of it, under Article 772.[44] These general references to human rights, in a sense, fill the gap left by the absence of explicit provision on the principles of mutual trust and recognition.

Specifically, Article 604(c) makes express provision for the use of diplomatic assurances where there are substantial grounds for believing that there is a real risk to the fundamental rights of the requested person in the issuing state. This is the first time this elemental facet of extradition jurisprudence has been included in an extradition agreement.[45] The test has its origins in the seminal European Court of Human Rights (ECtHR) case of *Soering v UK*.[46] As noted in section III, the CJEU has adopted similar phraseology. A further assurance-related article with a human rights connection is Article 604(a). It concerns whole-life sentences and permits the executing state to require an assurance that, if imposed, such a punishment will be reviewed after 20 years or that the requesting state will encourage the application of measures of clemency. This relates to the vexed issue of the compatibility of whole-life sentences with Article 3 ECHR, something the ECtHR considered again in 2022 in *Sanchez-Sanchez v UK*.[47] Overall, as to human rights, there is no doubt that the TCA refers to and relies upon them to a materially greater extent than the Framework Decision. By adopting and

[44] Art 692(2) provides that Part Three shall cease to be in force upon the date that the UK or a Member State denounces the ECHR, or Protocols 1, 6 or 13 in the event of that happening.

[45] Grange (n 19) 221. In UK extradition practice, assurances are not uncommonly requested and relied upon.

[46] *Soering v UK* (1989) 11 EHRR 439. See generally as to human rights and extradition P Arnell, 'The European Human Rights Influence upon UK Extradition – Myth Debunked' (2013) 21 *European Journal of Crime, Criminal law and Criminal Justice* 317.

[47] *Sanchez-Sanchez v UK* App no 22852/20 (ECtHR, 3 November 2022) available at https://hudoc.echr.coe.int/eng?i=001-220484 (last accessed 16 April 2024). See P Arnell, 'Extradition and the Regrettable Influence of Politics Upon Law the ECtHR Decision in Sanchez-Sanchez v UK' *Verfassungsblog* (17 November 2022) available at https://verfassungsblog.de/extradition-and-the-regrettable-influence-of-politics-upon-law/ (last accessed 16 April 2024).

formalising the human rights jurisprudence and assurance-related practice that has developed over the past several decades, it has strengthened the protective aspect of the process from a human rights perspective.

### *vi. Little Change to the Extradition Act 2003*

The TCA surrender provisions are a compromise by the UK and EU that has accommodated the positions of both parties as far as possible.[48] This is natural. In this vein, it is notable that the TCA reflects two significant pre-existing provisions in the Extradition Act 2003, such that relatively little change to that legislation was required to accommodate its terms.[49] First, an explicit reference to human rights has been found in the Extradition Act 2003 since it was enacted. From 1 January 2004, a judge considering an extradition from the UK had to consider whether it was compatible with 'Convention Rights', under section 21 for intra-EU surrenders.[50] Illustrating the impact of Brexit upon the application of human rights is *Ziembinski v Poland*, where the uncertainty created by a person's immigration status was a matter to be considered in an Article 8 ECHR balancing exercise.[51] As to proportionality, the Extradition Act 2003 was amended in 2014 by the Anti-social Behaviour, Crime and Policing Act 2014 to include a proportionality bar. Section 21A obliges the extradition judge to decide whether the extradition would be disproportionate with reference to the seriousness of the conduct, the likely penalty imposed if the individual was convicted, and the possibility of the issuing authorities' taking less coercive measures.[52]

## V. Conclusion

A new era in criminal cooperation between the UK and the EU has begun. In the course of the Brexit negotiations, practitioners and commentators alike expressed concerns that the high level of partnership in matters of transnational criminal justice, including surrender, would be negatively affected. This has happened, but not to the degree that many feared. As regards surrender, what has happened has been a regression in degree of cooperation and, at the same time, an enhancement in the level of

[48] From the EU's perspective, the reintroduction of the nationality bar and the non-extension of the SIS II stand out as being non-negotiable.

[49] The primacy of the Extradition Act 2003 in governing extradition practice within the UK was emphasised in *Polakowski v Westminster Magistrates' Court* [2021] EWHC 53 (Admin) [16]–[18]. It was stated, inter alia, '[t]he Trade and Cooperation Agreement (TCA) … is not part of UK domestic law save to the limited extent it is specifically incorporated by statute … any legal question involving rights or obligations said to be derived from EU law should now be approached in the first instance through the lens of domestic law'.

[50] Now found in s 21A. The rights being those incorporated into UK law by the Human Rights Act 1998 as of 2 October 2000, mirroring those found in Arts 2–12 and 14 ECHR, Arts 1–3 of the First Protocol and Arts 1–2 of the Sixth Protocol. Note, as of June 2004, reference to the Sixth Protocol was replaced by reference to the Thirteenth Protocol.

[51] *Ziembinski v Poland* [2022] EWHC 693 (Admin). In *Jackson-Osumah v Spain* [2022] EWHC 3505 (Admin), the High Court held that the 'Brexit point', that the individual may be refused re-entry into the UK following his extradition, was not such to affect the balancing exercise that found against him.

[52] The list of considerations within the proportionality provision of the TCA, noted in section IV.B.i, is greater than that found in s 21A of the 2003 Act.

protection afforded to requested persons. This increased protection in the terms of the TCA is both real and reflective. It is real through the institution or reinstitution of protections, including the nationality bar, the political offence exception and an expanded proportionality bar. It is reflective in that proportionality and human rights were already present in UK extradition law prior to the conclusion of the TCA, and the CJEU had developed its jurisprudence to recognise, to an extent, the effect of human rights under the Framework Decision *per se*. The future of surrender practice under the TCA remains to be seen, but the terms of the Agreement itself should lead to a roughly equivalent level of cooperation, with the greatest single effect coming from the resurrected nationality bar. Of importance is the approach taken by the authorities and judiciaries in both parties. The early signs in this regard appear positive. In *Kilgasts v Latvia*, for example, the Northern Irish High Court considered several decisions of the CJEU in its reasoning, not out of compulsion but out of choice.[53] It is to be hoped that good will on the part of the judicial and prosecuting authorities in the UK and across the EU will be maintained, such that the previous high level of cooperation will be maintained and requested persons will be treated fairly and justly.

[53] *Kilgasts v Latvia* (n 9) para 62.

# 14

# Extradition between the UK and Ireland Post-Brexit

ANDREA RYAN

## I. Introduction

Extradition by Member States of the European Union (EU) has greatly improved since the implementation in 2004 of the European Arrest Warrant (EAW) system. This was particularly true between the United Kingdom (UK) and Ireland.[1] The departure of the UK from the EU naturally meant it could no longer enjoy the benefit of this valuable instrument. The EAW system has been replaced by a new system of surrender between the UK and EU Member States, under the provisions in Part Three, Title VII of the Trade and Cooperation Agreement (TCA). The TCA arrest warrant (TCAW) has attempted to create as seamless a transition as possible. However, it remains the case that there are now two systems of surrender operating in the EU, the EAW and the TCAW. Due to the need to cooperate closely with the UK, Ireland has had to quickly adapt to both.

Unsurprisingly, given the close historic and geographic connections between the jurisdictions, a large number of surrender requests arise between Ireland and the UK.[2] Currently, the UK remains the state with which Ireland has the greatest interaction. Under the EAW scheme, the largest number of requests to Ireland for surrender came

[1] For useful commentary on improvements brought to extradition between Ireland and the UK, see G Davies and P Arnell, 'Extradition Between the UK and Ireland After Brexit- Understanding the Past and Present to prepare for the Future' (2020) 85(2) *The Journal of Criminal Law* 98, https://doi.org/10.1177/0022018320977531.

[2] 'In 2017 the vast majority of European Arrest Warrants sent abroad were sent to the UK. As of 31 March 2019 the current arrangements, which are very efficient in securing the return of persons wanted for prosecution, will no longer operate. It is therefore crucial that an agreement is reached on an alternative system prior to that date. I know that the Department of Justice and Equality and the Government are acutely aware of the imperatives in this area. One hopes that a practical solution will be found so that mechanisms are put in place to enable us to seek the extradition of an accused or seek important evidence from that jurisdiction. This is particularly important having regard to the shared border with Northern Ireland, and the ongoing necessity for prosecutions in respect of dissident subversive activity.' Office of the Director of Public Prosecutions (DPP), *Annual Report* (2017) 5.

from the UK, and the same is true for surrender requests issued by Ireland.[3] There is no reason to suppose that this will change under the post-Brexit extradition process. This chapter will explore surrender in the unique context of the relationship between the UK and the Republic of Ireland. It will first examine the key differences between the EAW and TCAW schemes of surrender, highlighting the issue of proportionality and delay. The chapter will then turn to an analysis of the extradition/surrender practice between Ireland and the UK under the EAW and under the TCAW, discussing the issues of trial readiness, proportionality, fundamental rights and abuse of process. It will then examine how UK courts have approached requests for surrender to Ireland since the TCAW has been in force, and explore how the courts in Ireland have dealt with requests for surrender from the UK under the TCAW. Finally, the chapter will address some recent developments in Ireland, which are expected to have an impact on EAWs between Ireland and EU Member States. Given the UK and Ireland's shared common law culture, however, these impacts are not likely to be reflected in surrender processes between Ireland and the UK.

## II. Principal Differences between the EAW and TCAW Surrender Schemes

While much of the EAW scheme is mirrored in the TCAW, there are some differences. This has resulted in a disparity between the terms of the TCAW and Ireland's domestic legislation. Article 597 of the TCA provides for an overarching principle of proportionality. It reads:

> Cooperation through the arrest warrant shall be necessary and proportionate, taking into account the rights of the requested person and the interests of the victims, and having regard to the seriousness of the act, the likely penalty that would be imposed and the possibility of a State taking measures less coercive than the surrender of the requested person particularly with a view to avoiding unnecessarily long periods of pre-trial detention.

The inclusion of a proportionality requirement came at the insistence of the UK, which had inserted a proportionality requirement into the Extradition Act 2003 (section 21A) in 2014 because of criticisms that EAWs were being issued for very minor offences. The Act provides that a judge must decide whether the 'extradition is proportionate'. Ireland has not provided for an explicit proportionality bar in its domestic law. Proportionality was, however, included in the EAW Handbook, and therefore has been the focus of some case law of the Court of Justice of the European Union (CJEU).

There is one other area where UK and Irish extradition law do not match: delay. This is provided for in section 14 of the UK Extradition Act 2003, which states that surrender is barred 'by the passage of time if (and only if) it appears that it would be unjust or oppressive to extradite [a person] by reason of the passage of time'. There is

[3] A total of 262 warrants were received from the UK in 2020, and a total of 105 warrants were issued by Ireland to the UK. European Arrest Warrant (Amendment) Bill 2022: Second Stage, Seanad Debates, 25 October 2022.

no equivalent bar in the EAW Framework Decision, in the TCAW or in Irish legislation. Despite this, delay frequently features in the Irish cases by means of another route, namely, the common law doctrine of abuse of process.

Finally, there is one area where the UK and Ireland were both aligned but have recently diverged. The Irish original EAW Act and the UK's extradition legislation contain provisions often referred to as 'trial readiness', though this terminology does not appear in either the EAW Framework Decision or the TCAW. Section 12A of the UK's Extradition Act 2003 provides that surrender may be barred 'by reason of absence of prosecution decision if … the competent authorities [in the requesting state] have not made a decision to charge or have not made a decision to try'. The equivalent provision was found in section 21A of the Irish European Arrest Warrant (EAW) Act 2003, which provided for refusal of surrender if the decision has not been made to charge the person and try him or her. Ireland has now abolished the requirement that a decision must have been made to charge and to try the requested person before surrender can be made.[4] The legislation is in response to infringement proceedings taken against Ireland by the European Commission.[5]

## III. The Extradition/Surrender Practice between Ireland and the UK under the EAW and the TCAW

Irish law prepared for surrender with the UK through the European Union European Arrest Warrant Act 2003 Amendment Regulations 2021.[6] No major change has taken place as a result of implementing these Regulations; they simply add the words 'Trade and Cooperation arrest warrant' wherever the words 'European arrest warrant' appear in the EAW Act 2003. The rest of the Act remains as it was prior to Brexit.

In Ireland, the obligation to surrender and limited grounds for refusal are set out in the EAW Act 2003 and reflect the EAW Framework Decision. The provisions that have most frequently been raised in Irish courts when resisting a surrender on foot of an EAW are section 21A, which relates to trial readiness, and section 37, relating to the breach of the European Convention on Human Rights or the constitutional rights under section 37.1.b that would arise if surrender were ordered. Objections based on absence of correspondence (that the offence for which the surrender is sought does not correspond with an offence under Irish law) also frequently arise, but this generally does not succeed.[7] Finally, abuse of process, although not a ground for refusal under the 2003 Act, is frequently relied on and has been successful in the Irish jurisdiction.

[4] European Arrest Warrant (Amendment) Act 2024 s31.

[5] October Infringement decisions 30/10/2020 INF-29-1687 Non-Communication and Non-Conformity of National Measures transposing into National Law Council Framework Decision 2002/584/JHA (European Arrest Warrant). 'Ireland has failed to comply with the mandatory time limits to execute a European Arrest Warrant. Moreover, Ireland has provided additional grounds for refusal of a European Arrest Warrant, which affect judicial cross-border co-operation in criminal matters.'

[6] SI 150/2021, in force since March 2021. A transition law was created by statutory instrument, the European Arrest Warrant (Application to Third Countries) (United Kingdom) Order 2020 (SI 2020/720).

[7] Section 21A and s 37(1)(b) have recently been repealed (n 4). For a detailed explanation of how correspondence should be approached under the EAW Act 2003, see *MJELR v Saulius Ferenca* [2008] IESC 52.

This includes, as already noted, arguments relating to 'passage of time'. This is despite the ruling of the European Court of Justice (ECJ) in *Tupikas* that 'the execution of the European arrest warrant constitutes the rule and the refusal to execute is intended to be an exception which must be interpreted strictly'.[8]

## A. Absence of Prosecution Decision

Turning first to the issue of the absence of a prosecution decision or trial readiness. In the UK, section 12A(1) of the Extradition Act 2003 provides that extradition

> is barred by reason of absence of prosecution decision if (and only if)—
>
> (a) it appears to the appropriate judge there are reasonable grounds for believing that—
>
> (i) the competent authorities … have not made a decision to charge or have not made a decision to try (or have made neither of those decisions) …
>
> (ii) …; and
>
> (b) those representing the category 1 territory do not prove that—
>
> (i) the competent authorities … have made a decision to charge and a decision to try ….

The burden therefore rests with the requesting state to satisfy the court that such a decision has been made. Section 12A has been frequently litigated but is rarely successful. The courts have tended to read down the bar relying on a 'cosmopolitan approach'. In *Killoran v Investigative Judge*, in the Antwerp Court of First Instance, Belgium,[9] it was held sufficient to prove that a category 1 territory had decided to try a requested person with offences where the public prosecutor had signed a certificate stating that they had decided to try a requested person. This is despite the fact that this is not the person responsible for making a decision to try in Belgium. The court cited the case of *Re Ismail*[10] and held that it should afford 'a broad and generous interpretation so far as the text permit in order to facilitate extradition'.[11]

By contrast, in Ireland, section 21A of the EAW Act 2003 provided that 'where a European arrest warrant is issued in respect of a person who has not been convicted of an offence specified therein, the High Court shall refuse to surrender the person if it is satisfied that a decision has not been made to charge the person with, and try him or her for, that offence in the issuing state'. However, the section contained a rebuttable presumption that a decision has been made to charge and to try. The presumption must therefore be rebutted by the person resisting surrender. It has arisen in a very wide number of cases, and in many has resulted in refusal to surrender. The leading case is *Olsson*.[12] There, the Irish Supreme Court stressed that surrender should only be refused where the court is satisfied that no decision has been made to charge or try that person, and that would be so where there is no intention to try the requested person at the

[8] Case C-270/17 PPU *Openbaar Ministerie v Tadas Tupikas*, ECLI:EU:C:2017:628.

[9] *Killoran v Investigative Judge* [2021] EWHC 2290 (Admin).

[10] *Re Ismail* [1999] 1 AC 320, 327.

[11] *Killoran* (n 9) [42].

[12] *MJELR v Olsson* [2011] IESC 1.

time the warrant is issued. However, it then clarified that the concept of 'decision' in section 21A should be understood in light of the 'intention' referred to in section 10 of the 2003 Act, and the 'purpose' referred to in Article 1 of the EAW Framework Decision. Section 10 reads:

> Where a judicial authority in an issuing state duly issues a European arrest warrant in respect of a person—
>
> (a) against whom that state intends to bring proceedings for the offence to which the European arrest warrant relates ….

and Article 1 of the EAW Framework Decision provides that warrants are issued 'for the purposes of conducting a criminal prosecution or executing a sentence'. Section 21A should therefore be understood 'for the purposes of conducting a criminal prosecution'. However, this has not always been the case, which has significantly contributed to delays in the execution of warrants, thereby defeating the EAW's purpose of providing a timely and efficient extradition process. Once the requested person has produced his or her own evidence in the attempt to rebut the presumption, the court will generally seek further information from the issuing state. Section 21A arguments therefore take up a considerable amount of time, recurrently resulting in failure by Ireland to work within the strict deadlines set out in the EAW Framework Decision. While the Irish and UK courts insist on the ordering of surrender only where the intention to try the accused can be established – as opposed to surrender for the purpose of further investigation – that does not translate into a speedy trial following surrender. In Ireland, where a surrendered person is held in pre-trial detention, the trial will be held as soon as possible; defendants who are in custody take precedence. Nonetheless, the accused will generally wait for at least eight to 20 months before a trial commences.[13] The recent high-profile trial of Gerard Hutch is particularly illustrative of this type of delay. Although he was surrendered by the Spanish authorities to Ireland in September 2021 and charged with murder, the trial did not commence until October 2022, with Mr Hutch being acquitted in April 2023.[14]

## B. Proportionality

The objective of the TCAW, as set out in Article 596 of the TCA, is 'to ensure that the extradition system is based on the mechanism of surrender pursuant to an arrest warrant in accordance with the terms of this Title'. Article 613 then underlines that the decision to surrender shall involve a consideration of the principle of proportionality.

[13] Courts Service Annual Report 2020. There has been an increase in waiting times due to the backlogs created by the Covid pandemic. In domestic criminal trials, a person may have already waited for 3 to 6 months after arrest before the book of evidence is served. The book of evidence would be served sooner in the case of a person returned to Ireland on foot of an EAW (communication from Irish Extradition Unit to author).

[14] M Carolan, 'Gerard Hutch not guilty of the murder of David Byrne at Regency Hotel' *The Irish Times* (17 April 2023) available at www.irishtimes.com/crime-law/courts/2023/04/17/regency-hotel-trial-verdict-hutch/ (last accessed 16 April 2024); M Carolan, 'Prosecution approach in Gerard Hutch Regency attack case "mystifies" lawyers' *The Irish Times* (9 June 2023) available at www.irishtimes.com/crime-law/2023/06/10/prosecution-approach-in-gerard-hutch-regency-attack-case-mystifies-lawyers/ (last accessed 16 April 2024).

In the UK, proportionality is set out in section 21A of the 2003 Extradition Act. Where the judge is required to proceed, the judge must decide whether (i) the extradition would be compatible with Convention rights and (ii) the extradition would be disproportionate. Section 21A goes on to list all the specified matters that the judge should consider in relation to proportionality, including the seriousness of the offence, the likely penalty and the possibility of less coercive measures.[15] The proportionality assessment applies only to prosecution warrants – it does not cover 'persons at large', despite the fact that proportionality covers both accusation and conviction warrants in the TCAW.

In Ireland, where the issuing of a warrant is concerned, the High Court has stated that proportionality has to be assessed by the issuing state. In *In the Matter of an Application Pursuant to s 33(1) of the European Arrest Warrant Act 2003*, the Court stated that

> the purpose of the proportionality test is … to assess whether the issue of the European arrest warrant is a justified measure in all the circumstances. There is a public interest in the prosecution of crime even, and sometimes especially, when that requires cross-border cooperation. The use of international arrest warrants may not be justified where their effects on the requested person (and the requested state) are disproportionate to the end to be achieved.[16]

This was a pre-Brexit decision and did not refer to proportionality as found in the TCAW.

Regarding proportionality in the execution of a warrant, the leading Irish case is that of *Ostrowski*, relating to surrender sought by Poland.[17] The High Court found that surrender would represent a disproportionate interference with the respondent's fundamental rights, particularly his right to liberty. The High Court, nonetheless, submitted a question to the Supreme Court on whether proportionality was a matter solely for consideration by the issuing judicial authority when deciding whether to issue the warrant, or whether the High Court would also be entitled to take proportionality into account when it is considering whether to surrender the respondent. The Chief Justice responded that the High Court need not consider possible sentences that might be awarded in the issuing state, nor whether the sentence is proportionate. *Ostrowski* therefore confirms that there is no role for the High Court to assess proportionality at the executing stage of the EAW. There is, for the moment, no known Irish case that has considered proportionality in relation to the UK.

## C. Fundamental Rights

In relation to fundamental rights, in Ireland, a specific fundamental rights clause is contained in section 37 of the EAW Act 2003. In nearly all the cases where there is an objection to surrender, the section 37 rights have been pleaded. Objections have

[15] For a detailed consideration of how proportionality should be assessed, see *Lucian Florin Badea v Romanian Judicial Authority* [2022] EWHC 1025 (Admin).

[16] Proportionality was addressed in the only published decision in relation to the issuing of a warrant; such decisions are all *ex parte* so not normally published: *In the Matter of an Application Pursuant to s 33(1) of the European Arrest Warrant Act 2003* [2018] IEHC 586 [42].

[17] *MJELR v Ostrowski* [2013] IESC 24.

often relied on family rights, or on the applicant's medical conditions. The cases have also considered delay.[18] The detention conditions in the issuing state are also frequently raised, and there have been several cases regarding the rule of law, given the number of requests Ireland receives from Poland, where rule-of-law concerns have been rife.[19]

Usually, however, objections based on section 37 rights have proved to be unsuccessful. Section 4A of the 2003 Act provides that 'it shall be presumed that the issuing state will comply with the requirements of the Framework Decision unless the contrary is shown', and on that basis a person resisting surrender will have to satisfy the Court that the issuing state is in fact not complying with its requirements to respect fundamental rights in accordance with Article 1.3 of the Framework Decision. In *Rettinger*, the Supreme Court established that the burden rests on the respondent to adduce evidence that there are substantial grounds for believing that he or she would be at real risk of being exposed to a flagrant denial of justice. Therefore, it is the responsibility of the person resisting surrender to rebut the presumption.[20] As mentioned above, family rights are frequently raised, but often are unsuccessful as an argument to resist surrender. These rights are generally raised through reliance on the constitutional right under section 37(1)(b) of the 2003 Act (now repealed) and under Article 8 ECHR. The leading case is *JAT (No 2)*,[21] on tax fraud, where the person successfully resisted surrender on Article 8 grounds on the basis of his medical condition, in addition to being the sole caregiver to his son who had substantial needs. The objection was also based on the delays involved in the case, which were attributable to both the issuing state (UK) and the Irish authorities.[22] While the Supreme Court considered that health conditions and family circumstances 'would never, in themselves, be remotely a ground for refusing surrender', the avoidable delays and the knowledge on the part of both authorities of the health concerns made this case 'exceptional', although 'even then close to the margin'.

In *Vesartas*,[23] the Supreme Court dealt with the issue of breach of fundamental rights on grounds of delay. In this case, the person was a Lithuanian national who had been released on parole for conviction of various offences (a total of 43, committed when he was a juvenile under 18), and who had absconded to Ireland. The Supreme Court ordered the surrender, as it considered that 'unless truly exceptional or egregious, delay will not alter the public interest'. It also added that the family circumstances must be 'well outside the norm', such as would make an order for surrender incompatible with the State's obligations under Art 8 ECHR.

Finally, several Irish cases have related to the detention conditions that the person will face if surrendered. In support of his or her argument, the respondent would usually produce the evidence in the form of reports about that particular country, such as a Committee Against the Prevention of Torture report, and the Court will then follow up by seeking further information from the requesting state. Generally, these objections

[18] *MJELR v Pyzowski* [2020] IEHC 270.

[19] Case C-204/21 *Commission* v *Poland*, ECLI:EU:C:2021:593. Polish citizens makes up second largest population in Ireland, having overtaken UK citizens, as revealed in the 2016 Census.

[20] *MJELR v Rettinger* [2010] IESC 45.

[21] *MJE v JAT (No 2)* [2016] IESC 17.

[22] ibid.

[23] *MJE v Vesartas* [2020] IESC 12.

have been unsuccessful, as in the majority of cases, the Court has been satisfied that the situation has improved and has responded that the state in question measured up to ECHR standards of cell space.[24] This has been notwithstanding that other poor detention conditions continue to prevail, especially those relating to prisoner safety and violence within specific prisons. There have also been successful objections on the basis of detention conditions, as illustrated by the *Gheorghe* case.[25]

## D. Delay and Abuse of Process

In the UK Extradition Act 2003, under section 11 on bars to extradition, the judge must decide whether the person's extradition is barred by reason of the passage of time. It will be so barred 'if (and only if) it appears that it would be unjust or oppressive to extradite him by reason of the passage of time'.[26]

Unlike its UK counterpart, the Irish EAW Act 2003 contains no grounds for refusal on the basis of delay. Nonetheless, the latter frequently features in Irish cases by means of another route, namely, the shared common law doctrine of abuse of process. The doctrine is relied on as an objection to surrender most usually connected with either a delay in issuing the warrant or, as happened in *Bedzarnek*,[27] a retransmission of an arrest warrant, where a surrender order had been previously granted by the High Court but had not in fact been effected by the issuing state. In *Bedzarnek*, the EAWs were issued in 2007 and 2009 respectively, for the purpose of prosecution for fraud offences, though it was noted the offences were 'not at the most serious level of offending'. It was submitted by the defence that the surrender would amount to an abuse of process. The High Court had ordered the person's surrender in 2012, but no surrender took place. Following correspondence with the Polish authorities, the suspect was released from prison once it became clear that Poland were unable to complete the surrender on the dates indicated by Ireland. No further action took place until 2019, when the EAW was retransmitted to Ireland. Relying on the Supreme Court decision in *Vestartas*[28] regarding delay, the Court considered that the delay of seven years in effecting surrender 'could not be justified', and that there had been 'an abject failure on the part of both the issuing and executing authorities to follow up on the Order for surrender with any degree of alacrity or expedition'.[29] Relying on the CJEU case of *Vilkas*,[30] it was argued by the State that 'member states should persevere with attempts to surrender where the surrender was not effected due to circumstances beyond the control of the State, even where the

[24] Cell space and detention conditions were analysed in detail in *Muršić v Croatia* App no 7334/13, (ECtHR GC, 20 October 2016).

[25] *MJELR v Gheorghe* [2009] IESC 76.

[26] Extradition Act 2003, s 14; however, where a person is a 'fugitive', the s 14 bar cannot be invoked. *Gbajobi v High Court Republic of Ireland* [2020] EWHC 2892 (Admin).

[27] *MJE v Bednarczyk* [2021] IEHC 316.

[28] *MJE v Vestartas* [2020] IESC 12.

[29] See further A Ryan in 'Strengthening Trust in the European Criminal Justice Area through Mutual Recognition and the Streamlined Application of the European Arrest Warrant' (Stream). Stream Country Report Ireland. available at https://stream-eaw.eu/country-reports/ (last accessed 16 April 2024).

[30] *Bednarczyk* (n 27) [16]; Case C-640/15 *Reference for a preliminary ruling from Court of Appeal (Ireland) made on 2 December 2015 – Minister for Justice and Equality v Tomas Vilkas*, ECLI:EU:C:2017:39.

requested person had been released,' and that this was a retransmission as opposed to a fresh warrant. The Court concluded that the facts in the present case, taken cumulatively, were exceptional and constituted a rare case where surrender should be refused on grounds of abuse of process. The Court also doubted 'that *Vilkas* is authority for the proposition that the issuing state and/or the executing state may permit a prolonged and inexcusable delay in effecting surrender to occur so that some 7 years later, the executing judicial authority is obliged in all circumstances to order surrender'. The Court therefore refused the application for surrender. A similar failure to complete a surrender order, granted in 2009, resulted in a refusal of surrender under a new warrant on grounds of abuse of process in *Lach*.[31]

The argument of abuse of process on grounds of delay is often linked with arguments relating to medical conditions of the requested person, or his or her position as carer. It was successful in the *JAT* and the *Bailey* cases[32] on such combination of grounds, although, at the same time, the courts have also highlighted, as they did in *Siklosi*, that abuse of process is not a ground for refusal listed in the Framework Decision.[33] Abuse of process has also appeared as an argument resisting surrender in an English case, *Cotton v HC of Ireland*.[34] Here, the Court looked at hardship and oppression, however the Court rejected the argument finding that it would be up to the Irish authorities to consider the abuse of process in relation to the delay at the time of the trial.

## IV. How have UK Courts Dealt with Requests for Surrender to Ireland Since the TCAW has been in Force?

### A. How have UK Courts Dealt with Requests for Surrender to Ireland?

To date, there has been paucity of contested cases, with many of those coming through still being proceeded on EAWs, as opposed to the TCAWs. Nevertheless, the cases that have emerged under TCAWs indicate a confidence in the Irish courts and justice system.

In *Bullman*,[35] the Court considered that 'the Irish courts are more than capable of dealing with any proper concerns raised with regard to the fairness of proceeding' and found there was 'no basis to conclude that the care that would be afforded to Mr Bullman in an Irish prison would be any worse than the care he would receive while on remand at Wandsworth prison'. The Court was confident that 'even allowing for the cumulative effect … the Republic of Ireland would be willing and able to provide

[31] *MJE v Lach* [2021] IEHC 632; the offences were also on the lower end of the seriousness spectrum.

[32] *JAT* (n 21); *Bailey (No 2)* [2017] IEHC 482; *Bailey (No 3)* [2020] IEHC 528. For a detailed discussion of *Bailey*, see A Ryan, 'The Malfunctioning of the European Arrest Warrant in Ireland' in L Heffernan (ed), *Criminal Law and Justice in the European Union* (Clarus Press, 2022) 71.

[33] *MJE v Siklosi* [2021] IECA 210.

[34] *Coton v HC of Ireland* [2012] EWHC 3874 (Admin).

[35] *Bullman v HC in Dublin* [2022] EWHC 194 (Admin) [31].

appropriate medical care in these conditions'.[36] In the case of *Jess*, surrender was resisted on the basis that extradition would be oppressive or unjust by reason of the Appellant's health. Rejecting the argument, the Court concluded that there was no evidence that the Appellant would not receive appropriate medical care in prison in Ireland.[37] In *Duffy*,[38] the issuance of a surrender warrant seeking the return of Mr Duffy to Northern Ireland for breach of parole conditions was unsuccessfully challenged as amounting to an abuse of process, based on the delay of 10 years in bringing the application.

All these requests for surrender were granted. The case of *BM*[39] constitutes an exception, characterised by a list of hardships that were set out, not dissimilar to that in the Irish case of *JAT*. In *BM*, the District Judge had granted the surrender but the High Court in England overturned the order, finding it was 'one of those very rare cases' in which, all things balanced, the surrender should be refused and the applicant discharged. A noteworthy feature of the UK case law is the level of trust placed in the courts of Ireland to administer justice. In a pre-TCA case, it was noted that 'apart from the fact of the Republic of Ireland is a member of the European Union and an adherent to the European Convention on Human Rights, this court places a very high degree of trust in the competence and the sense of justice which operates in the Irish judiciary'.[40]

## B. Surrender from Ireland to the UK under TCAWs

Initially, surrender to the UK was resisted on the basis that the Withdrawal Agreement was not binding on Ireland since it had not exercised its opt in under Protocol 21 to the Lisbon Treaty.[41] The question went to the ECJ, which confirmed that both the Withdrawal Agreement and the TCA were binding on Ireland given their legal basis in the Lisbon Treaty.[42] There is again a very small number of reported cases since the TCAW entered into force.[43] The contested cases that have emerged to date have

[36] Ibid [39].

[37] *Jess v HC Ireland* [2020] EWHC 3134 (Admin), para 16. See also *Clarke v HC of Ireland* [2020] EWHC 1772 (Admin), where an argument based on interference with family rights under Art 8 ECHR was rejected; *O'Donnell v HC of Ireland* [2022] EWHC 458 (Admin), which also rejected the argument based on Art 8 ECHR rights and an argument based on s 25 of the Extradition Act 2003, finding (at [22]) that 'the evidence in this case falls short – and by a substantial measure – of the high threshold of section 25 oppression (or injustice) by reason of mental health (and/or health) condition'.

[38] *Duffy v Judge Conner & Secretary of State for Northern Ireland* [2022] NIQB 47. The Court rejected the argument that the District Judge should have made further inquiry relating to the delay, particularly whether the applicant was still considered a risk; the Court concluded that it is not the function of the District Judge to make any assessment of risk, and that all statutory criteria had been fulfilled ([49[–[51]).

[39] *BM v Republic of Ireland* [2020] EWHC 442 (Admin).

[40] *Coton* (n 34).

[41] *Saqlain v Governor of Cloverhill Prison* [2021] IESC 45.

[42] 'The Withdrawal Agreement and the TCA were not concluded on the basis of that title, [Title V] but on the basis of Article 50(2) TEU and Article 217 TFEU respectively.' Case C-479/21 PPU *Reference for a preliminary ruling from Supreme Court (Ireland) made on 3 August 2021 – Minister for Justice and Equality v SN, SD*, ECLI:EU:C:2021:929, para 46.

[43] The TCAAW entered into force on 31 December 2020. The *Annual Report of the DPP 2021* records 29 TCAAWs issued for 2021 with just two surrenders effected; it notes that the 'low number of persons surrendered is largely due to the fact that the majority of TCA Arrest Warrants issued in 2021 were issued in the second half of that year. There were also some delays in extradition hearings in the United Kingdom due to the Covid-19 pandemic.' ibid 39.

attempted to resist surrender, arguing lack of correspondence between offences sought under TCAWs and those contained under Irish law. In *Casey*, the court had no difficulty in establishing correspondence with the offence that was being sought under the TCAW, and similarly in *Hull*,[44] *Porter*[45] and *Harty*,[46] the surrenders were ordered. So far, there does not appear to be any difficulty in establishing correspondence in requests under the TCAAWs, and Ireland has ordered the surrender in all cases.

Two cases have been reported where surrender was objected to on the ground that it would breach fundamental rights. In *MJE v Knowles*, the objection to surrender was based on the medical condition of the respondent in that he was 'a vulnerable person who has been diagnosed with brain aneurysms which appear to be causing him profound cognitive issues'.[47] The High Court nonetheless ordered the surrender following receipt of further psychological reports that did not support the contentions of the respondent. In *MJE v Sean Walsh*,[48] surrender was ordered to Northern Ireland where the High Court found no basis for the grounds of objection alleging systematic or generalised deficiencies in the prison system of Northern Ireland relating to surveillance of his legal consultations. The Northern Irish Court of Appeal had found that legislation that would apply to the respondent if convicted was incompatible with Article 7 ECHR. The High Court, however, stressed that despite the departure of the UK from the EU, it still remained a member of the ECHR and, despite the finding of incompatibility, the legislation remained in force and the Northern Irish courts were permitted to apply it until it was amended, just as would be the case in the Republic. By contrast, in *Sharples*, the High Court initially refused surrender to Scotland, finding that there were valid concerns that Mr Sharples would face a 'real and substantial risk of inhuman or degrading treatment' due to his mental health; however, the surrender was later ordered following assurances given by the Scottish authorities that he would receive adequate health care.[49]

## V. Recent Developments in Ireland

Infringement proceedings were commenced against Ireland by the European Commission in 2020 on the basis that Ireland had failed to comply with the mandatory time limits set out in the EAW Framework Decision, and that it had 'provided additional grounds for refusal of the European arrest warrant which affect judicial cross-border cooperation in criminal matters'.[50]

[44] *MJE v Hull* [2022] IEHC 159.

[45] In *MJE v Porter* [2022] IEHC 162, para 32, the Court reiterated that 'correspondence will not be established by looking at the name of the offence itself under the law of the issuing state. Rather, the description of the facts for the offence is the key consideration.' See also *MJE v Harty* [2022] IEHC 635.

[46] *MJE v Harty* (n 45).

[47] *MJE v Knowles* [2022] IEHC 636.

[48] *MJE v Sean Walsh* [2022] IEHC 633.

[49] *In the matter of the European Arrest Warrant Act 2003 (as amended) between Minister for Justice & Equality and Richard Sharples* [2024] IEHC 282.

[50] European Commission, 30 October 2020, Brussels October infringements package. The letter of formal notice issued in October 2020 followed by a reasoned opinion.

The European Arrest Warrant (Amendment) Act 2024 was finally enacted in response to the infringement proceedings. Section 31 of the Amendment Act repeals a number of sections, targeting those under which Ireland had been refusing surrender, specifically section 21A of the EAW Act 2003, relating to the decision to charge and to try, and section 37(1)(b), relating to breach of constitutional rights. It leaves intact the ground for refusal based on breach of Convention rights under section 37(1)(a). Section 11 of the Act also inserts a new section (section 16A) into the 2003 Act to provide that failure to comply with the time periods shall not constitute grounds to refuse surrender.

Since the Act has come into force, therefore, the trial readiness argument has become unavailable, as has any possible argument relating to a potential breach of constitutional rights that the surrender would entail. Given the insertion of a clause clarifying that non-compliance with the time limits will not provide a ground for refusal of surrender, that may also foreclose any argument of abuse of process, since the latter argument has been for the most part connected with a delay factor in the case. Overall, the available grounds for persons resisting surrender from Ireland appear to be considerably reduced. Whereas under the EAW, persons sought would be subject to one and the same law, regardless of the Member State seeking them, there will be a different symmetry between the EU and the UK. Requests from Ireland to the UK will depend on the UK judge's assessment of proportionality, and consideration of passage of time, whereas in requests from the UK to Ireland, the Irish court will no longer have to consider those issues. Ireland would also have to satisfy the UK that the Irish authorities have made a decision to charge and to try. That argument will not be available to a person trying to resist surrender to the UK, however, because the amending Act abolishes it, and no differentiation is made in the Act for the case of TCAAWs; the same applies to the delay amending provision.

Furthermore, the EAW scheme does not operate in a vacuum. The effectiveness of extradition between Ireland and the UK may also depend on the arrangements in relation to the sharing of information. Ireland has the benefit of the EU intelligence-sharing mechanisms, that is, ECRIS, Prüm, the Schengen alert system and Europol. Ireland has also signalled its intention to participate in the new proposal for a common platform, which will achieve interoperability of all these systems. Law enforcement authorities across the EU will have instant and easy access to the information, shared across all the Member States of the EU simultaneously. The SIS has been used extensively by the UK, but following withdrawal from the EU, the UK no longer has access to SIS II. In its place, the UK now needs to fall back on the Interpol system, which is not directly integrated with the UK's police national computer, nor with those of EU Member States. It remains to be seen what effect this will have on the number of surrenders between Ireland and England.

## VI. Conclusion

It is in the mutual interest of Ireland and of the UK to have a system of extradition that works efficiently. This is particularly important having regard to the shared border with Northern Ireland, 'the ongoing necessity for prosecutions in respect of dissident subversive activity',[51] and organised crime involving participants from both sides of the border. Since the departure of the UK from the EU, Ireland remains the only Member State that operates a criminal process based on the common law tradition, unlike the other EU Member States, which adhere to a civil law system.[52] When it comes to mutual assistance in cross-border crime, the shared legal tradition and culture that has always existed between the UK and Ireland may assist in the post-Brexit arrangements. It is clear that there is a strong mutual trust, as expressed by the English authorities referred to in section IV.

Given our shared legal tradition, difficulties that have arisen in EAW cases involving Irish and UK jurisdictions with their civil law counterparts in the EU should not arise. There have been numerous cases in Ireland where time is taken up through exercising the option under Article 15 of the EAW Framework Decision (seeking further information), in attempts by the Irish judiciary to gain an understanding of the criminal procedural process of these civil law systems, to reach a decision on surrender. Not only do the judges need to grapple with an understanding of the procedural processes at work, but they also invariably do this through reliance on translated materials, which are not always accurate.[53] Whether the extradition process between Ireland and UK in the new post-Brexit landscape develops seamlessly remains to be seen. A clear advantage lies in our common heritage, both linguistic and legal.[54]

[51] DPP (n 2).

[52] L Heffernan, (2021) 'Irish Criminal Trials and European Legal Culture: A Backdrop to Brexit'. (2021) 85(2) *The Journal of Criminal Law* 114, doi.org/10.1177/0022018320977530.

[53] For a detailed discussion of this point, see Ryan (n 32).

[54] *Bullman v HC in Dublin* [2022] EWHC 194 (Admin) [48]: 'As Lord Brown pointed out in *Gomes* at [35], states which are parties to the European Convention on Human Rights can generally be assumed to be capable of protecting accused persons against an unjust trial. That applies with particular force to Ireland, which has a common law-based judicial system similar to our own. Mr Costello's evidence shows that the abuse of process jurisdiction in Ireland operates in a similar way to the jurisdiction in England and Wales.'

# 15

# Prisoner Transfer between the UK and EU27: A 'Striking' Omission from the Trade and Cooperation Agreement?

TIM J WILSON

## I. Introduction

In 2020 the United Kingdom (UK) failed to achieve the following objective, that is,

> effective and reciprocal arrangements to transfer prisoners between the UK and EU Member States, enabling prisoners to be moved closer to home and be rehabilitated in the community to which they will be released. These should build and improve on arrangements provided by the 1983 Council of Europe Convention on the Transfer of Sentenced Persons and its Protocols, and could include time limited processes.[1]

Governments in the UK appear to have always thought that international prisoner transfer (IPT) should be part of any negotiated post-Brexit cooperation agreement between the European Union (EU) and the UK. Losing access to the EU Prisoner Transfer Framework Decision (PTFD)[2] was identified by Ministers at the beginning of 2019 as an adverse consequence of leaving the EU 'without a "deal"'. 'Falling back on the older Council of Europe [Prisoner Transfer] Convention' (PTC[3]) would be 'a less effective mechanism' equated with a foreseeable decline in transfers.[4]

[1] HM Government, *The Future Relationship with the EU: The UK's Approach to Negotiations* (CP 211, 2020) para 53, available at https://assets.publishing.service.gov.uk/media/5e579695e90e07110306a2f5/The_Future_Relationship_with_the_EU.pdf (last accessed 16 April 2024).

[2] Council Framework Decision on Mutual Recognition of Custodial Sentences 2008/909/JHA [2008] OJ L32/27.

[3] The Convention on the Transfer of Sentenced Persons (ETS 112) (Strasbourg, 21 March.1983), and additional protocols of 1997 (ETS 167) and 2017 (CTES 222).

[4] See, eg, HC Deb 5 February 2019, vol 654, col 155; and HC Written Answers UIN 220146-7 (18 February 2019).

The omission of IPT from the Trade and Cooperation Agreement (TCA) was noted immediately as 'striking'.[5] Two (at the time of writing) changes of UK government later post-TCA, there is still the impression that the PTC is viewed as second best. Despite the desire for transfer arrangements that could be the 'strongest and most effective' alternative to the PTFD, the pattern of long-delayed UK transpositions of PTC protocols continues.[6]

Such views do not acknowledge the complexity – analysed in this chapter – of including IPT within the scope of TCA criminal justice cooperation. In 2020 there was insufficient time. Five years on, the obstacle of EU 'Brexit fatigue' to 'exploiting' or 'expanding' the TCA makes it harder to envisage additional cooperation measures soon.[7] In addition, two 2023 UK TCA extradition failures[8] demonstrated how deteriorating UK prison conditions might restrict judicial cooperation more than was probably anticipated when the TCA was signed. The same legal considerations could also block IPT-facilitated transfers to the UK and from the UK to Member States where prison conditions are at least as bad, if not worse.[9]

Development of IPT policy requires the management of tensions between the political economy of national criminal justice systems and the original rehabilitative aims of such arrangements. The academic literature on this subject suggests that generally the former has proved stronger. The weight of evidence and opinions highlighted in this chapter is consistent with that view. Nevertheless, the thrust of the argument in this chapter is that a new EU–UK prisoner transfer cooperation arrangement could introduce a more balanced outcome. This is premised on a radical change of approach: using common international obligations (the Bangkok Rules) so that such transfer arrangements would be part of a suite of anti-discriminatory and rehabilitative measures.

This chapter includes analysis of the distinctive legal and penological nature of IPT (section II); what (and why) the UK Government was seeking to achieve in 2020 (section III); the potential scope for common ground in any future negotiations about IPT (section IV); and the challenges that the EU and the UK would need to overcome (section V).

[5] W Schomburg and A Oehmichen'Brexit: First observations on the EU–UK Trade and Cooperation Agreement in criminal law' (2021) 12 *New Journal of European Criminal Law* 193, 200. (Please note that the Trade and Cooperation Agreement between The European Union and The European Atomic Energy Community, of the One Part, and The United Kingdom of Great Britain and Northern Ireland, of The Other Part [2020] OJ L444/1 has been replaced ab initio by 22021A0430(01) eur-lex.europa.eu/legal-content/EN/TXT/PDF/?uri=CELEX:22020A1231(01) OJ L444 14.).

[6] Protocol Amending the Additional Protocol on the Convention on the Transfer of Sentenced Persons, (CPC 762, 2022). This 1997 Protocol permitting non-consensual transfers where the prisoner would be deported and a further 2017 (CETS 222) amendment that removed the earlier link between the use of deportation and the actual sentence to be served on transfer were not ratified until, respectively, 2009 and 2022.

[7] This reflects the TCA revision/expansion models and obstacles to progress identified in J Reland and J Wachowiak, *Reviewing the Trade and Cooperation Agreement: Potential Paths*, available at https://ukandeu.ac.uk/reports/reviewing-the-trade-and-cooperation-agreement/ (last accessed 15 January 2025).

[8] See J Goldsmith, 'A new blow for our justice system' *Law Gazette* (21 August 2023) available at www.lawgazette.co.uk/commentary-and-opinion/a-new-blow-for-our-justice-system/5117009.article (last accessed 16 April 2024); and T Ross, 'When did Scotland become a rogue nation?' *Scottish Legal News* (5 July 2023) available at www.scottishlegal.com/articles/thomas-ross-kc-when-did-scotland-become-a-rogue-nation (last accessed 16 April 2024).

[9] See TJ Wilson, 'Prisoner Transfer Within the Irish-UK Common Travel Area (CTA) After Brexit: Human Rights Between Politics and Penal Reform' (2021) 85(2) *The Journal of Criminal Law* 121.

## II. International Prisoner Transfer

International prisoner transfer is a distinct category of international cooperation distinguishable from extradition or surrender because the purpose is not chiefly to prevent impunity from trial or punishment. The stated primary purpose of the PTFD and equivalent arrangements in the United States (US) is penological: social rehabilitation or reintegration.[10] The apparent simplicity of such terms in the legal instruments contrasts with the penological literature where their meaning is contested and variable.[11] Legal and official texts on IPT place a traditional penological emphasis on programmes or institutions in supporting rehabilitative change. For foreign prisoners, 'in practice, [social rehabilitation] can often be best achieved by transferring such individuals to their country of origin'.[12] This allows complementary secondary objectives to be added: even if social rehabilitation is unlikely, for example to quote from a United Nations (UN) source, 'it may be more humane for [prisoners] to serve their sentences in their home countries'.[13]

The power of the political economy of criminal justice to remodel IPT can be seen from the US precedent. International prisoner transter began in the late 1970s, when the US negotiated a series of bilateral treaties to repatriate US citizens serving sentences in poor or dangerous conditions. The US model today, however, is that of a wealthy sentencing state as a net exporter of prisoners to poorer executing states.[14] The influence of the political economy of criminal justice is more transparent in other sentenced prisoner repatriation methods and temporary transfers. With the purchase of prison places in another jurisdiction to reduce prison overcrowding in the sentencing state, European countries are again following a US precedent ('rent a cell principle').[15] Such bilateral arrangements differ legally and penologically from IPT because the transfer destination is not necessarily the country of nationality, residence or release, and such movements may simply be temporary reallocations from the sentencing state.[16] The power of the political economy over repatriation policy is transparent, with 'tough' sentencing UK governments trading earlier release with

[10] See, eg, PTFD, Art 4 (3) and (4); and, more descriptively, 'Detention and transfer of prisoners' available at https://commission.europa.eu/law/cross-border-cases/judicial-cooperation/types-judicial-cooperation/detention-and-transfer-prisoners_en (last accessed 16 April 2024) and 'International Prisoner Transfer' available at www.justice.gov/criminal/criminal-oia/iptu (last accessed 16 April 2024).

[11] See, generally, R Canton, N Flynn and J Woods *Social Rehabilitation Through the Prison Gate* (De Montfort University, 2016).

[12] UNODC, *Handbook on the International Transfer of Sentenced Persons* (United Nations, 2012) 11; for an approach that aligns IPT reform to prisoner autonomy, see Wilson (n 9) 121, 136–42.

[13] UNODC (n 12): 11.

[14] See, esp, S Royce'International Prisoner Transfer' (2009) 21 *Federal Sentencing Reporter* 186.

[15] See, generally, LK Minke and AS Vanhouche 'Renting cells abroad: Understanding contemporary policy responses to prison overcrowding' (2023) 24(1) *Nordic Journal of Criminology* 1. More recently, the Sunak Conservative Government sought powers to detain prisoners from England and Wales in foreign prisons (cls 25–27, as introduced, of the Criminal Justice Bill 2023-24). This Bill had reached the HC report stage when Parliament was dissolved on 30 May 2024.

[16] A Liebling et al, 'Where Two "Exceptional" Prison Cultures Meet: Negotiating Order in a Transnational Prison' (2021) 61(1) *British Journal of Criminology* 41.

voluntary repatriation under their Early Release Scheme (ERS).[17] These UK governments use ERS to boast about being a net exporter of foreign prisoners (382 outward repatriations versus 102 inward in 2017/18),[18] thus externalising economic migration and border-control failures.

A focus on political economy loses sight of an important instrumental distinction between IPT and other forms of repatriation: IPT is structured – through timely and detailed information sharing[19] – to have a public protection dimension at the destination, such as inclusion on a sexual offenders register, or to protect a prisoner from a risk of serious harm in the sentencing state[20] or for wider purposes, especially in international cooperation against corruption and organised crime. Prisoners who travel abroad to commit crime may be eager to be repatriated as early and unobtrusively as possible. Some may then return illicitly to the sentencing state at a time of their choosing,[21] sometimes to participate in organised cross-border crime.[22] It is unclear whether ERS is underpinned by any bilateral information exchanges. Even if that were the case, however, it would fall far short of the European-wide criminal justice and intelligence sharing that has been a major UK policy objective both before and after Brexit.

Legally, the PTFD complements the European Arrest Warrant (EAW), so that a sentence can be served without a transfer back to the sentencing state or when surrender for the execution of a sentence has been refused.[23] An additional political dimension for Ireland and the UK is its importance since the Good Friday Agreement negotiations for cross-border and intra-community relationships.[24]

## III. What the UK Government was Seeking to Achieve in 2020 and Why

In one respect it is perhaps surprising that UK governments have been so enthusiastic about the PTFD compared with the PTC: consistent with EU law generally and

[17] The Nationality and Borders Act 2022, s 47 increased to a year the reduction in such circumstances applicable to most fixed-term sentences, after serving half of the sentence in custody. Previously the maximum ERS reduction had been nine months.

[18] HC Written Answers UIN 220146-7 (n 4).

[19] UNODC (n 12) 13–14.

[20] D Raleigh, 'Convicted murderer transferred to UK jail due to "security risks" in Irish prison system' *BreakingNews.ie.* (22 March 2023) available at www.breakingnews.ie/ireland/convicted-murder-transferred-to-uk-jail-due-to-security-risks-in-irish-prison-system-1451493.html (last accessed 16 April 2024).

[21] L Williamson, 'Albanian prisoners paid by UK government to return home' *BBC News* (17 May 2023) available at www.bbc.co.uk/news/world-europe-65533198 (last accessed 16 April 2024).

[22] R Mulgrew, 'The role of oversight in foreign-national only prisons: counteracting the disapplication of rehabilitation' (2018) 70 *Crime Law Social Change* 77, 86.

[23] W van Ballegooij and IK Krišto, *European arrest warrant: Framework for analysis and preliminary findings on its implementation* (European Parliamentary Research Service, 2020) 17.

[24] Wilson (n 9) 131.

precursor Schengen rules,[25] residency may trump nationality.[26] This appears to have been outweighed by the prospect (indicated in the quotation at the start of this chapter) of quicker repatriation through mutual legal recognition (MLR). The PTFD also offers less legally ambiguous arrangements. The 'limited grounds' to refuse repatriation[27] (including a simpler approach to double criminality[28]) was specifically cited in 2019 as a major advantage.[29] There is less scope to alter custodial terms.[30] Although the two states may, on a case-by-case basis, negotiate how to adapt a custodial term for part of the sentence to be served in the executing state, this may not result in a more severe penalty.[31] Under the PTC, on the other hand, if the sentence is 'by its nature or duration incompatible with the law of the administering state, or its law so requires', the term may be altered judicially in the executing state to correspond to its own custodial tariffs. Under the Convention, the nature or duration of the sanction cannot exceed, as with the Framework Decision, the maximum equivalent sentence in the executing state, but significantly it cannot be bound by executing-state minima.[32] Also, unlike the PTC, which is silent on matters such as conditional release, the executing state has sole discretion about how the sentence is to be served, including specifically the grounds for early or conditional release, although transposition may provide for taking into account the national law of the sentencing state when making such decisions.[33]

Finalised a little later than the weakening of the consensual principle (more accurately, 'tripartite consent': both states and the potential transferee[34]), under the Convention (1997 onwards) the non-consensual approach of the PTFD was described at the time as 'contrary to the philosophy of reintegration' and an indication that its purpose was to increase the number of repatriations.[35] More recently, it has been argued that the non-consensual approach of PTFD and the related instrument for the supervision of probation measures and alternative sanction were 'two steps back from their point of origin, the Council of Europe conventions'.[36] The non-consensual principle, however, prevented potential discord between the Government and ultra-Brexiters at Westminster in 2020 over seeking to continue EU arrangements.[37] Such an unequivocable right-wing

[25] T Vander Beken and G Vermeulen, 'The transfer of sentenced persons in Europe: Much ado about reintegration' (2009) 11 *Punishment and Society* 111.

[26] PTFD Art 4.

[27] ibid Art 9.

[28] ibid Art 7.

[29] HC Deb 19 February 2019, vol 654, col 526WH.

[30] PTFD Art 8.

[31] ibid Art 10.

[32] PTC Arts 10.2. and 11.1.d.

[33] PTFD Art 17.

[34] I Wieczorek and A Weyembergh, 'Transfer of Prisoners and Extradition Cases Between Europe and Japan' in S Matsuzawa, A Weyembergh and I Wieczorek (eds), *Europe and Japan Cooperation in the Fight against Cross-border Crime* (Routledge, 2022) 1, 5.

[35] Vander Beken and Vermeulen (n 25) 124.

[36] P Feraldo-Cabana, 'One step forward, two steps back? Social rehabilitation of foreign offenders under Framework Decisions 2008/909/JHA and 2008/947/JHA' (2019) 10 *New Journal of European Criminal Law* 151.

[37] HC Deb 5 February 2019 (n 4) (As is clear from exchanges during the previous year.).

consensus might help to neutralise or weaken criticism at Westminster of any future EU–UK IPT arrangement.

There was a marked decline in foreign prisoner repatriations to all countries from the UK at the height of the Covid-19 pandemic. Figure 15.1[38] indicates that total repatriations in 2022 were 40 per cent lower than pre-pandemic levels (3,079, compared with 5,128 in 2019); however, the trend established in 2014 for the repatriation of EU citizens to exceed non-EU repatriations continued.

**Figure 15.1** Foreign national 'repatriations' from the UK (including ERS and entry refusals), 2013 to 2022

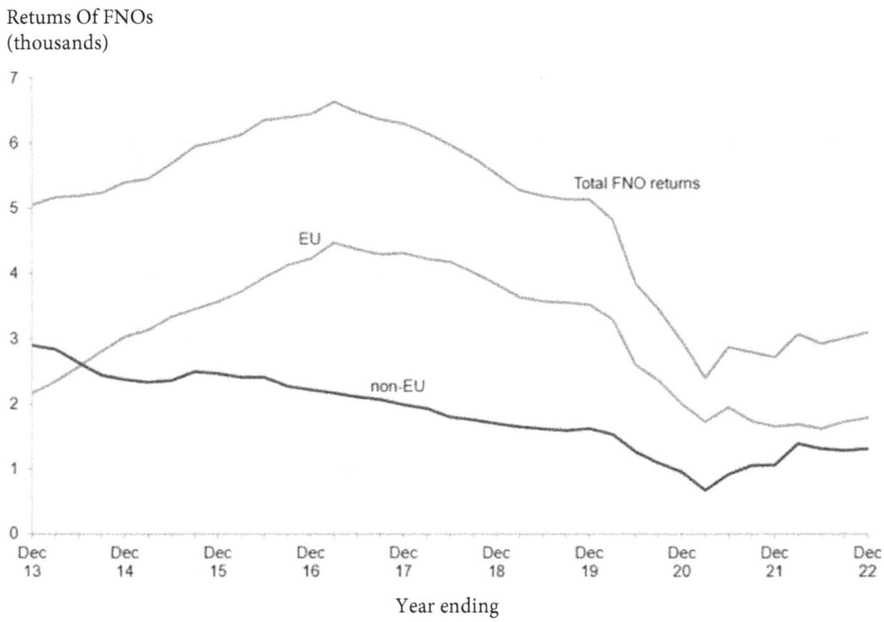


Three points about the data in Figure 15.1 contextualises the UK's Government's anxiety about the impact of any fall in EU repatriations and its dependence on European destinations for maintaining its record of prisoner/ex-prisoner expulsions:

1. Prisoner repatriation statistics chiefly reflect voluntary early custodial-term removals and deportations not PTFD/PTC prisoner transfers.[39] In 2017/18, only 382 transfers (mainly to EU countries) were recorded compared with over 2,000 ERS repatriations (all countries).[40]

[38] Home Office *How many people are detained or returned?* (2023) available at www.gov.uk/government/statistics/immigration-system-statistics-year-ending-june-2024/how-many-people-are-detained-or-returned (last accessed 16 April 2024).

[39] 'UK and Albania agree groundbreaking new arrangement on prisoner transfers' MOJ Press Release (24 May 2023) available at www.gov.uk; and L Williamson 'Albanian prisoners paid by UK government to return home' *BBC News* (17 May 2023) available at www.bbc.co.uk/news/world-europe-65533198 (last accessed 16 April 2024).

[40] HC Written Answers (n 4).

2. Post-Brexit changes in deportation rules extended the default deportation regime to EU citizens.[41] This was the culmination of a decrease in the threshold of seriousness of crimes that could trigger the deportation of an EU citizen that began in 2009 (when Labour was in power).[42]
3. Four of the nationalities (Irish, Jamaican, Pakistani and Somalian) that make up over half of the foreign national population in English prisons[43] are not matched by comparable repatriation rates.[44]

The cost of repatriation is estimated to be outweighed by savings made on the cost of holding a foreign offender[45] or adding additional prison places (costed in 2023 at £0.5 million per place).[46] During the PTFD transposition period, the National Audit Office (NAO) had questioned whether the transfer rate assumptions for such estimates (calculated at an average of 440 repatriations a year) were over-optimistic.[47] The assumptions, however, appear to have been justified by the 357 EU transfers in 2017/18 even before PTFD transposition ended.[48] Foreign prisoners certainly experience longer cumulative and, therefore, more expensive detention (remand, sentence, denial of open conditions and immigration detention while awaiting deportation) than their UK counterparts,[49] though this may have been reduced to some extent since 2014 because appeals against deportation are no longer suspensive.[50]

Political scrutiny of the NAO report identified a potentially more substantial question: whether the time limits[51] that distinguish PTFD from the PTC are achievable?[52] There is some evidence of at least initial problems with document translation, interpreting the sentence and information exchange with agencies involved in physical transfer arrangements.[53] There appears to be no information about whether these issues have

[41] The Immigration, Nationality and Asylum (EU Exit) Regulations 2019 (SI 2019/745) aligned the deportation threshold (with a presumption in favour of deportation) for non-EEA and EEA nationals with that for any foreign national sentenced to 12 months' imprisonment or longer, irrespective of the length or nature of their residence in the UK.

[42] PW Walsh, Deportation and voluntary departure from the UK. Migration Observatory briefing (COMPAS, 2022).

[43] M Halliday, *Bromley Briefings Prison Factfile January 23* (Prison Reform Trust, 2023) 37.

[44] Walsh (n 42), Figure 8.

[45] CP 762 (n 6) paras 7.3– 7.4.

[46] HC Deb 16 October 2023, vol 738 col 59 (Oral statement to Parliament by The Lord Chancellor on The Government's approach to criminal justice).

[47] NAO, *Managing and removing foreign national offenders* (2014-15, HC 441) 34–35, paras 3.19–3.20.

[48] HC Written Answers (n 4).

[49] Halliday (n 43). In England and Wales, a lower proportion of foreign nationals are in prison for violent (27%) and sexual offences (14%), compared with the overall prison population (29% and 17%, respectively). They are more likely to be in prison for a drug offence or miscellaneous crimes against society (26% and 18%, respectively, compared with 10% and 4%).

[50] S Turnbull and I Hasselberg, 'From prison to detention: The carceral trajectories of foreign-national prisoners in the United Kingdom' (2017) 19(2) *Punishment & Society* 135.

[51] Under the PTFD, the executing state has 90 days to decide whether it will take over the enforcement of the sentence (Art 12), and after that the transfer should be completed with 30 days of the final decision (Art 15).

[52] Public Accounts Committee, *Managing and removing foreign national offenders* (2014–15, HC 708) 14, para 18.

[53] V Elliott, *Resource Book on the Transfer of Sentenced Prisoners under EU Framework Decision 909* (The European Organisation of Prison and Correctional Services, 2017) 9.

been resolved, but they may well be comparatively easier to deal with (thereby less costly) than unblocking the causes of indeterminate immigration detention after a prisoner's release date.[54]

## IV. Common Starting Points for Negotiation?

Global imprisonment rates are never constant, but significant national, sub-regional and regional trends and comparative characteristics have been relatively stable for decades.

The UK has high imprisonment rates for a long-established democratic European state. For example, this was estimated to be 130 per 100,000 of the national population in October 2021 compared with the EU mean of 90 (within a range of 50–190). At that date, only nine EU Member States had a higher rate: the three Baltic states, Malta, the Czech Republic, Hungary, Poland, Romania and Slovakia. (This data can be seen in perspective through a comparison with the figures for the US and the Russian Federation, of respectively, 629 and 326.[55])

This data suggests that politicians and officials from the EU and UK would initially approach IPT negotiations from a broadly similar place: overcrowded prisons, because of changes in sentencing law and practice that have increased minimum sentences and reduced judicial discretion over the type and duration of penalties. The latter trend reflects populist arguments that discretion excessively prioritises the offender's needs for rehabilitation as opposed to retributive and incapacity requirements.[56] Within the carceral systems that such policies have created, foreign national prisoners represent a significant cohort of the national prison population and have become a priority consideration for governments and prison administrations.[57]

There are significant variations, however, about how these issues play out among EU Member States. Lappi-Seppälä's sub-regional classifications (using 2016 data) root foreign prisoner incarceration generally in older Member States. Also, this analysis showed how the British Isles had a smaller foreign prisoner population than Southeast Europe and the three Baltic states.[58] Analysis (Table 15.1[59]) of more recent data indicates that foreign incarceration is still a wealthier country issue.

[54] Turnbull and Hasselberg (n 50) 135, 143.

[55] H Fair and R Walmsley, *World Prison Population List*, 13th edn (The Institute for Crime & Justice Policy Research, 2022).

[56] JL Díez-Ripollés, 'Analytical Approach, Rules and Practices' in PH van Kempen and M Jendly (eds), *Overuse in the Criminal Justice System* (Intersentia, 2019) 47.

[57] Mulgrew (n 22) 77.

[58] T Lappi-Seppälä, 'Statistical Analysis of Incarceration Rates across the World' in van Kempen and Jendly (eds) (n 56) 165, 182.

[59] Data as recorded on 20 September 2023 in the *World Prison Brief* (prisonstudies.org) and the *World Economic Outlook* (April 2023), GDP per capita, current prices (imf.org).

**Table 15.1** Proportion of foreign prisoners and degree of penal overcrowding among the wealthier European states

| | % foreign prisoners | % overcrowding | GDP per capita (000,000) |
|---|---|---|---|
| Luxembourg | 73.7% | 77.5% | $132.4 |
| Ireland | 23.3% | 102.5% | $114.6 |
| Norway | 27.0% | 80.7% | $101.1 |
| Denmark | 26.9% | 97.4% | $068.8 |
| Netherlands | 23.1% | 90.6% | $061.1 |
| Austria | 51.4% | 103.8% | $056.8 |
| Sweden | 22.1% | 105.0% | $055.4 |
| Finland | 16.3% | 94.9% | $054.4 |
| Germany | 27.0% | 77.6% | $051.38 |
| UK | 12.4% (England & Wales) | 111.1% (England & Wales) | $046.4 |
| France | 25.0% | 122.8% | $044.4 |
| Italy | 31.5% | 114.1% | $036.8 |

Conversely, poorer states are impacted disproportionately by post-repatriation burdens. Based on data for only England and Wales, within the global (all countries and forms of repatriation) total, outward prisoner repatriations in 2021 were predominantly of citizens of three EU countries, Romania (25 per cent), Poland (10 per cent) and Lithuania (10 per cent), and aspirant member, Albania.[60] Their citizens, together with Irish and Portuguese nationals, form a significant part of the overall foreign prisoner population.[61]

International rehabilitative/humanitarian obligations accepted by all EU Member States and the UK cut across such divisions. These stem from recognising how the disproportionate and discriminatory imprisonment of foreign prisoners has particularly serious consequences for foreign women prisoners (see Figure 15.2[62]).

**Figure 15.2** The imprisonment of women in England and Wales

Hibiscus Initiatives (Hibiscus) and the Prison Reform Trust (PRT) reported in 2018 that:

- The level of incarceration had declined since 2013 when foreign national women represented 17.5% of all women received into prison (over 23% of those remanded), but they still accounted for over 12% of all female receptions (nearly 19% of those remanded).
- Support for foreign national women in prison, such as interpreting and immigration legal advice, was found to vary considerably and resettlement support was generally poor.

[60] Walsh (n 42) 12.
[61] Halliday (n 43) 37.
[62] Prison Reform Trust, *Still No Way Out: Foreign national women and trafficked women in the criminal justice system* (2018) available at https://prisonreformtrust.org.uk/wp-content/uploads/old_files/Documents/Still%20No%20Way%20Out%20full%20report.pdf (last accessed 16 April 2024).

- Foreign national women were rarely considered for open prison (on 31 December 2017 there were only two in open prisons) and release on temporary licence (ROTL).
- Hibiscus case work identified 45 women as victims or potential victims of trafficking from February 2013 to March 2017, potentially unlawfully detained in prison despite the disclosure of their exploitation.

More timely and possibly more extensive IPT arrangements – where individual circumstances make such action appropriate – as part of the response to this discriminatory treatment would be consistent with UN standards and recommendations (the Bangkok Rules) for the treatment of detained women and girls.[63] Rule 53.1 promotes the consideration of the transfer (subject to 'informed consent') of non-resident foreign national women prisoners to their home country, especially if they have children there, 'as early as possible during their imprisonment'. The Rules link IPT to complementary non-carceral penalties, diversionary and bail policy reforms – summarised in Figure 15.3 – that could be supported in the principal destination countries through UK financial support for which there are precedents.[64] The impact of such funding could be verifiable in cases where transfer is challenged and where successful transfers would increase the range of options available to UK courts in individual measures if PTFD were to be linked to the associated EU MLR financial penalties, probation and bail instruments.

**Figure 15.3** Bangkok Rules complementarity (i); policy reforms

The Bangkok Rules contain a commitment that UN Member States will implement a package of non-custodial measures for women prisoners, including:

- Providing gender specific diversionary measures, eg remand and sentencing alternatives to custody
- Requiring consideration of a woman's background when contemplating a decision that would separate her from her background and family ties
- Giving courts the power to consider mitigating factors such as lack of criminal history and relative non-severity and nature of the criminal conduct, in the light of women's caretaking responsibilities and typical backgrounds.

Rules 57–62.

The Bangkok Rules, in addition to requiring basic decency (including with security searches and how healthcare is delivered) also set minimum allocation and regime objectives, illustrated in Figure 15.4. Their comparative objectivity means that they would be directly justiciable, as can be seen from the (albeit limited) case law of the

[63] United Nations, *United Nation Rules for the Treatment of Women Prisoners and Non-Custodial Measures for Women Offenders* (21 December 2010) available at www.ohchr.org/en/instruments-mechanisms/instruments/united-nations-rules-treatment-women-prisoners-and-non-custodial (last accessed 16 April 2024).

[64] See, eg, HC Deb 19 February 2019 (n 29) col 524WH.

European Court of Human Rights (ECtHR)[65] that is also relevant to proceedings in the Court of Justice of the European Union (CJEU).[66]

**Figure 15.4** Bangkok Rules complementarity (ii); custodial facilities and regime reforms

> The Bangkok Rules also contain a commitment that UN Member States will implement custodial measures for women prisoners, including:
>
> - Allocation to a prison close to home; where this is not possible, practical measures shall be taken to counterbalance the resulting disadvantages.
> - Contact with children and families should be encouraged and facilitated.
> - Age/gender-specific programmes and services, including women's healthcare, should be accessible.
> - Staff employed in women's prisons should be trained to address the special social reintegration requirements of women prisoners and to manage safe and rehabilitative facilities.
>
> Rules 4 and 53(i); 26; 38; 29 and 40

It is surely inconceivable that the Bangkok Rules – adopted unanimously by the UN General Assembly in 2010 – would not contextualise, at least for women prisoners, the objectives for any future EU–UK IPT negotiations. An IPT agreement reflecting these rules would also result in economic benefits for both the sentence and destination locations. For example, diversion from custody would reduce costs earlier (see, for example, the discriminatory remand rates in Figure 15.2) in criminal proceedings, and thereby contribute to greater aggregate savings and have a modest impact on prison overcrowding. Discrimination against male foreign citizens, however, would also need to cease to maximise the potential benefits.

## V. Challenges if IPT Negotiations are Re-opened

The EU would be faced with at least three major issues in any attempt to add IPT to the scope of post-TCA criminal justice cooperation.

First, the highly disciplined and systematic EU approach to both Brexit treaty negotiations reflected how its negotiators succeeded in managing divergent Member State and EU institutional interests.[67] The next phase of Brexit readjustment process may be less manageable and predictable.[68] As noted in section IV, IPT cooperation would

[65] *Korneykova and Korneykov v Ukraine* App no 56660/12 (ECtHR, 24 June 2016).

[66] See, eg, Case C-897/19 PPU *Ruska Federacija v IN*, ECLI:EU:C:2020:262, referring to both UN proceedings and ECtHR case law.

[67] M Barnier, *My Secret Brexit Diary* (Polity, 2021).

[68] TJ Wilson, 'EU–UK criminal justice and security cooperation after Brexit: A perspective' (2021) 3 *Forensic Science International: Synergy* 100144.

place a disproportionate burden on Romania, Poland, Lithuania, Ireland and Portugal as executing states. Any negotiations would need significant funding assurances.

Second, IPT as an element of anti-discriminatory/rehabilitative measures – as far as can be seen – has had a disappointing implementation history within the EU. Four major problems were anticipated by the Commission in 2011: exceptionally poor physical conditions in some states; inadequate information (all parties); budget-driven decisions; and different early release or remission arrangements that could materially extend carceral time. These were substantially confirmed in academic research published in 2018, which added concerns about inadequate specialist legal assistance to prisoners and ineffective judicial oversight.[69] A little earlier, the EU Agency for Fundamental Rights (FRA) had identified significant differences in national transposition legislation about how the grounds for refusal might be interpreted and indications that quality of decision making would vary significantly.[70] All of this research, however, took place during the transposition period and also pre-dates the Lisbon Treaty infringement powers and full jurisdiction of the CJEU over the Area of Freedom, Security and Justice (AFSJ) acquis.

Third, the PTFD is part of what was intended to be a package of coherent and complementary legislation aimed at reducing discriminatory pre-trial detention, as well as facilitating the social rehabilitation of prisoners through cross-border cooperation based on mutual legal recognition. This includes bail (the European Supervision Order) and probation or other alternative (ie non-custodial) sanctions in the country of nationality or residence.[71] Logically, the objective behind the package – ensuring that the citizens and residents of other Member States are not treated more punitively than citizens and residents,[72] is also associated[73] with the Monetary Penalties Framework Decision.[74] The problems here are that (i) this rehabilitative/anti-discriminatory policy area has been developed within the EU legal order through ad hoc decisions in a piecemeal manner,[75] and (ii) the UK, as an EU Member State, had a record of 'ultimately random' cherry picking from the AFSJ acquis.[76] In 2020, the UK sought to prolong this behaviour by cherry picking only PTFD from the anti-discriminatory/rehabilitative package.[77] Such behaviour threatens the general development of the AFSJ acquis as 'a coherent system with weights and counterweights'.[78] Hence, the potential significance

[69] Summarised in Wilson (n 9) 121, 132.

[70] FRA, Criminal detention and alternatives: fundamental rights aspects in EU cross-border transfers (Vienna, 2016) 43–47.

[71] Report from The Commission to The European Parliament and The Council on the implementation by the Member States of the Framework Decisions 2008/909/JHA, 2008/947/JHA and 2009/829/JHA on the mutual recognition of judicial decisions on custodial sentences or measures involving deprivation of liberty, on probation decisions and alternative sanctions and on supervision measures as an alternative to provisional detention (COM(2014) 57 final), 4–7.

[72] ibid 4.

[73] van Ballegooij and Krišto (n 23) 11–12.

[74] Framework Decision on the mutual recognition of financial penalties 2005/214/JHA [2005] OJ L81/24.

[75] See, eg, S Montaldo, 'Intersections among EU judicial cooperation instruments and the quest for an advanced and consistent European judicial space: The case of the transfer and surrender of convicts in the EU' (2022) 13 *New Journal of European Criminal Law* 252.

[76] A Weyembergh, 'Consequences of Brexit for European Union criminal law' (2017) 8 *New Journal of European Criminal Law* 284, 289.

[77] See, eg, CP 211 (n 1) 24–27.

[78] Weyembergh (n 76) 284, 290.

of the Bangkok Rules for helping to resolve both problems, by helpfully refocusing the EU side and blocking UK cherry picking in order to ensure that any IPT cooperation measures are part of a coherent and complementary anti-discriminatory and rehabilitative package that integrates EU and UK legal procedures and thereby complies with international obligations already accepted by all the parties from outside the EU legal order.

The UK would probably need to come to the negotiating table with solutions to four problems. First, under three (at the time of writing) Conservative Governments – and this could continue under a Brexit-timid Labour Administration – there have been repeated tensions between the continuation of high-priority criminal justice cooperation measures and the conditionality contained in the TCA through UK human rights compliance and data adequacy. Despite criticism of the European Convention on Human Rights (ECHR) and ECtHR, the Johnson Government in November 2022 fell back disingenuously on Articles 3 and 8 ECHR as domestically enforceable safeguards against erroneous repatriation decisions.[79] This, however, did not acknowledge a Bill it had introduced earlier to weaken such protection, chiefly by limiting the interpretation of rights to a literal reading of the Convention text and requiring 'a greater willingness by the domestic courts to decline to follow Strasbourg jurisprudence'.[80]

Second, since Brexit, as already noted, the UK has fully extended to EU citizens foreign prisoner treatment that sidesteps rehabilitative efforts, denies 'second chances' and seeks to achieve permanent exclusion through bans on re-entry.[81] The PTFD, however, recognises both residency and nationality as the grounds within the EU legal order for determining the permissibility of repatriation and destination.[82] Consistent with this dual test, the Commission argued in 2014 that acceptance or refusal of a transfer should be based on a case-by-case approach, with careful consideration of a potential transferee's objections, and ultimately refusal should normally reflect a decision that transfer would 'not be in the interest of the sentenced person'.[83] Similarly, in 2021, Advocate General Bobek urged a strict reading of the PTFD to secure that any transfers maximise the prisoner's chances of social rehabilitation, and that it should be particularly strict for a proposed non-consensual transfer. (Unfortunately, the request for a preliminary ruling was withdrawn before a ruling could be issued.[84])

Third, the general challenge of ensuring that the PTFD operates, as originally envisaged as part of a coherent and complementary package of anti-discriminatory and

[79] CP 762 (n 6) para 8.1.

[80] UK Government, *Bill of Rights: European Convention on Human Rights Memorandum – Summary of the Bill HRmemo* (2022) available at https://publications.parliament.uk/pa/bills/cbill/58-03/0117/HRmemo.pdf (last accessed 16 April 2024); see also Bill of Rights Bill (as introduced, 22 June 2022), cls 3–8.

[81] Turnbull and Hasselberg (n 50) 135.

[82] Council Framework Decision on Mutual Recognition of Custodial Sentences (n 2) Arts 1.7(a)–(b) and recitals (7), (8) and (17).

[83] European Commission (n 71) 10. See also Directive 2004/38/EC on the right of citizens of the Union and their family members to move and reside freely within the territory of the Member State, where Art 28 provides that EU citizens can only be deported from another Member State for reasons of public policy or public security.

[84] Opinion of AG Bobek, Case C-919/19 *Generálna prokuratura Slovenskej republiky v XY*, ECLI:EU:C:2021:454. See, also Montaldo (n 75).

rehabilitative measures, would require the UK to reverse some previous Member State and TCA opt-outs, principally: (i) access to assistance and legal aid when a potential transferee is consulted about repatriation, so that judicial scrutiny of contested repatriation can be as effective as possible; and (ii) by agreeing to IPT as part of a MLR package with pre-trial bail, monetary penalties and non-custodial disposals.

Fourth, the English High Court has clarified that the starting point for any analysis of the TCA is the relevant domestic legislation and not any unincorporated international agreement that was not part of UK domestic law. Hence, any IPT agreement and the UK transposition legislation would need to provide for how legal problems in individual cases could be resolved without bringing cooperation to a standstill. For example, a UK interpretation of 'proportionate' or 'unnecessarily long periods of pre-trial detention' that differs substantially from that applied by the CJEU or courts in EU Member States could ultimately undermine the effectiveness of the TCA extradition/surrender arrangements.[85]

Potential tensions over IPT can be seen from *IZ*,[86] in which the CJEU ruled that whether measures other than carceral detention (eg, electronic tagging with a curfew) should count towards custody time served in the requesting state for EAW purposes should be determined by the law of the issuing state. This or very similar questions may easily arise when calculating release dates following repatriation. This problem is therefore a live issue, and its potential effect can be gauged from problems that arose from different conditional release arrangements in Ireland and the UK. After PTC enabled cooperation for almost two decades, three Irish cases arising from IPT interpretation issues between 2014 and 2016 stalled all inward transfers from the UK. This created immediate public-safety and security concerns following the immediate release of prisoners transferred to Ireland to serve lengthy sentences, including for plotting a bombing campaign (the 'Slovak three', arrested after a MI5 arms sting in Slovakia).[87]

The problems were resolved and the PTFD was transposed under new legislation,[88] enacted some seven years after cooperation had stalled and two years after it had originally been introduced into the Oireachtas. As Irish politicians came to recognise, IPT can give rise to complex adaptation and interpretation issues:

> There are no straightforward solutions to these difficulties, and the possibility of further legal challenge will, of course, arise. Legislation cannot account for every possible sentencing structure which might be in place in another state now and in the future. Accordingly, what the Bill sets out is a flexible mechanism to ensure that both the courts and the Minister have appropriate powers to deal with a range of scenarios.[89]

For the UK governments seeking to return to what they have regularly indicated is an 'effective' IPT model, the lesson from Ireland is that any EU–UK IPT arrangements need to provide for judicial flexibility and cross-jurisdictional dialogue. To make such a measure work, the UK domestic interpretation of the relevant legal principles would need to keep in step with the evolving EU legal order.

[85] The author wishes to acknowledge advice from G Davies and I Wieczorek on this point.
[86] Case C-294/16 PPU *JZ v Prokuratura Rejonowa Łódź – Śródmieście*, ECLI:EU:C:2016:610.
[87] See Wilson (n 9) 121, 130–31.
[88] The Criminal Justice (Mutual Recognition of Custodial Sentences) Act 2023.
[89] James Browne, Minister of State, Justice Dept, Seanad Éireann debate, Wednesday, 15 February 2023, vol 292 no 1.

Such a significant political recalibration by the UK is conceivable in the future because it would reduce the instability of all criminal justice and security cooperation under the current TCA arrangements that hinge so abruptly at present on conditionality over ECHR compliance and data-adequacy decisions. It would also give the UK a place at a table where discussions might begin about cross-European reforms that, inter alia, could reduce the risk of failure of cross-jurisdictional detainee transfers because of poor prison conditions.

## VI. Conclusion

The IPT omission from the TCA is not so striking after all. The analysis in this chapter suggests that TCA arrangements are unlikely to be quickly and easily extended to include an IPT measure. The initial omission is linked to cherry picking from the AFSJ acquis. It is unclear whether the UK is now willing to break this habit and seek closer and more comprehensive engagement with the development of MLR-facilitated cooperation. On the other hand, the UK ambition to negotiate a post-Brexit IPT arrangement is a matter of record, and the economic and penal management calculations that at least partly account for this are also clear.

Anything written about the eventual evolution of TCA cooperation only a few years on is bound to be speculative. The analysis in this chapter starts, however, with the identification of common ground between EU institutions, Member States and the UK over the scope for and desirability of IPT cooperation. It ends by suggesting how success over IPT might be achieved through an innovative change of approach inspired by the Bangkok Rules. Such an approach would foreground rehabilitative and humanitarian considerations. It would also – because of the multi-dimensional nature of IPT arrangements outlined at the beginning of this chapter – have significant economic, public safety and security benefits, while modestly reducing the risks to key elements – notably TCA extradition/EAW surrender – of MLR-based criminal justice cooperation that arise from abject prison conditions. Perhaps not achievable by the formal TCA review date of 2026, but what is suggested here is clearly something that would contribute significantly to a Labour 'reset' of UK–EU cooperation while being unequivocally consistent with the concerns and aspirations of their Conservative predecessors.

# 16

# Protection of Human Rights and Fundamental Freedoms

CONALL MALLORY*

## I. Introduction

The United Kingdom's (UK's) exit from the European Union (EU) did not occur in a political vacuum. It was not an isolated event insulated from the surrounding political climate but rather the culmination of a lengthy process of antipathy from a section of the political class and public towards external influence within the British order. That hostility, particularly towards European authority, initiated the momentum towards a referendum and subsequently saw the 'Leave' vote over the line in June 2016. Drinking from the same pool of antipathy towards European influence has been a long-standing hostility amongst some, particularly in the Conservative Party, towards the European Convention on Human Rights 1950 (ECHR).[1] It was thus unsurprising that in the aftermath of the EU referendum, the British Government set out to minimise binding international commitments during the negotiations which would form the Trade and Cooperation Agreement (TCA) with the EU.[2] Continuing the mantra of 'take back control' would not be fulfilled if the UK initiated new pledges, binding itself ever deeper into international obligations.[3]

* My thanks go to the editors for their encouragement and many helpful comments. My thanks also to Colin Murray (Newcastle University) for his comments on a draft version of the chapter. Any errors remain my own.

[1] Convention for the Protection of Human Rights and Fundamental Freedoms (adopted 4 November 1950, entered into force 3 September 1953) 213 UNTS 222 (ECHR).

[2] Trade and Cooperation Agreement between the European Union and the European Atomic Energy Community and the United Kingdom of Great Britain and Northern Ireland (adopted 30 December 2020, entered into force 1 May 2021) [2021] OJ L149/10.

[3] Although note that the non-binding political declaration of October 2019 recognised that any future agreement would include the UK's 'continued commitment to respect the framework of the European Convention on Human Rights (ECHR)'. HM Government, *Political Declaration setting out the framework for the future relationship between the European Union and the United Kingdom* (19 October 2019) 7, available at https://assets.publishing.service.gov.uk/media/5daaaba040f0b6598f806460/Political_Declaration_setting_out_the_framework_for_the_future_relationship_between_the_European_Union_and_the_United_Kingdom.pdf (last accessed 16 April 2024).

During TCA negotiations, the British side sought generic aspirational commitments instead of directly binding provisions that could impact the overall agreement if not fulfilled. Specifically, the UK sought to circumvent reference to how human rights would be operationalised domestically,[4] and any specific grounds 'for invoking any suspension or termination mechanism'.[5] For its part, the EU's negotiating mandate had sought an ongoing commitment to the ECHR as an essential element of the Agreement.[6] Negotiators for the EU also sought to secure a provision on automatic termination on matters concerning law enforcement and judicial cooperation if the UK were to denounce the ECHR, and automatic suspension were it 'to abrogate domestic law giving effect to the ECHR, thus making it impossible for individuals to invoke the rights under the ECHR before [British] courts'.[7]

This chapter maps the end point of these negotiations with a particular focus on Part Three of the TCA and the developments that have taken place over the initial operation of the Law Enforcement and Judicial Cooperation (LEJC) provisions. Section II sets out the legal provisions of the TCA that address the protection of human rights and fundamental freedoms. These provisions link both parties to their ongoing commitment to shared values of democracy, the rule of law and human rights. However, the real crux of the legal provisions boils down to the ability for either party to trigger a fast-track suspension or termination of the LEJC, were the other party to end their membership of the ECHR. Section III then charts the potential for breach on these grounds by focusing on the possibility of a UK Brexit from the ECHR. This section outlines how, despite the extensive anti-ECHR rhetoric in British political discourse, there have yet to be steps towards a formal exit from the Strasbourg-based system. Nonetheless, the chapter identifies how over the initial period of the LEJC's operation, a fertile political space for ECHR exit has been cultivated. Section IV concludes by taking stock of the provisions in the LEJC against the backdrop of ongoing British rancour with the ECHR. It addresses the likely catalysts for further anti-ECHR sentiment, before drawing out the rhetorical power of the Part Three commitments in respect of the ongoing challenges.

## II. Human Rights in the Trade and Cooperation Agreement

The commitment to the protection of human rights and fundamental freedoms is threaded throughout the TCA. This section fleshes out the power of this commitment within (A) the TCA as a whole, and (B) Part Three provisions regarding LEJC.

[4] HM Government, *The Future Relationship with the EU The UK's Approach to Negotiations* (CP No 211, February 2020) 31. available at https://assets.publishing.service.gov.uk/media/5e579695e90e07110306a2f5/The_Future_Relationship_with_the_EU.pdf (last accessed 16 April 2024).

[5] ibid 33.

[6] Council of the European Union, *ANNEX to COUNCIL DECISION authorising the opening of negotiations with the United Kingdom of Great Britain and Northern Ireland for a new partnership agreement* (5870/20, 25 February 2020) 12.

[7] ibid 118.

## A. Human Rights in the Wider Agreement

Democracy, the rule of law and human rights protection are recognised in both the Preamble to the Treaty and Article 763 as the basis for cooperation within the TCA as a whole.[8] There is a commitment to uphold these shared values, including reaffirming respect for the Universal Declaration of Human Rights and the international human rights treaties to which the parties are already members,[9] and also a pledge to 'promote such shared values and principles in international forums'.[10] As the text does not directly stipulate ongoing membership of any particular human rights treaty (eg, the ECHR or the International Covenant on Civil and Political Rights 1966), the clause has an aspirational tone to it. And yet Article 771 identifies the commitment to democracy, the rule of law and human rights as an essential element of the entire Agreement.[11]

Designation as an 'essential element' provides legal teeth to the commitment. It allows for a party to terminate or suspend the Agreement in whole or in part if the other party is in breach. The standards for such a sanction are high. First, the failure in respect of the essential element must be 'serious or substantial' in nature.[12] The parties define this as an occurrence whose 'gravity and nature would have to be of an exceptional sort that threatens peace and security or that has international repercussions'.[13] The implication of this is that domestic restrictions on rights, democracy and the rule of law – even of a pervasive nature – may not meet the threshold to trigger termination or suspension. A level of intervention that either destabilises the state or has an international dynamic appears to be required. Second, the sanction must be both proportionate and of a nature that 'least disturb[s] the functioning of [the] Agreement', suggesting that where breaches occur, priority will be given to options that suspend the Agreement.[14] Given the breadth of the areas covered in the TCA, this is clearly a pragmatic way to ring-fence ongoing collaboration. Third, the process invoking the termination or suspension procedure begins with a request to the Partnership Council to meet with a view to the negotiation of a timely and mutually agreeable solution. Only after 30 days from the request to convene the Partnership Council, can the application for further action be triggered.[15]

The result is an aspiration clause with bite. One that leans heavily towards protecting ongoing cooperation between the parties to the Agreement, but from which departure or suspension remain possible ramifications for breach. One would be hard pressed to think of an example of a situation where either the UK or the EU would seek to enforce

[8] Along with the 'Fight against climate change' (Art 764); 'Countering weapons of mass destruction' (Art 765); 'Small arms and light weapons and other conventional weapons' (Art 766); 'The most serious crimes to the international community' (Art 767); 'Counter-terrorism' (Art 768); 'Personal data-sharing' (Art 769); 'Global cooperation on issues of shared economic, environmental and social interest' (Art 770).

[9] Art 763(1).

[10] Art 763(2); R Smith, C Mallory and S Molloy, 'Brexiting Human Rights Diplomacy' (2019) 24(4) *International Journal of Human Rights* 414.

[11] Notably alongside the 'Fight against climate change' (Art 764) and 'Countering weapons of mass destruction (Art 765), but not the other shared values underpinning the Agreement.

[12] Art 772(1).

[13] Art 772(4).

[14] Art 772(3).

[15] Art 772(2).

this aspect, and yet there remains considerable importance in embedding these shared values within the overall Agreement.

Beyond this overarching commitment, human rights standards are integrated into several specific provisions within the wider TCA.[16] In respect of services and investment, parties are required to reject benefits to states that deny human rights protections.[17] Particular business and human rights commitments are recognised in respect of trade and supply-chain management.[18] Personal data obligations include provisions concerning the transfer of information that has been obtained in violation of human rights, or where it could be used 'to request, hand down or execute a death penalty or any form of cruel or inhuman treatment'.[19] Where fast-track extradition is requested, the executing judicial authority may require additional guarantees regarding the treatment of the individual where there is deemed to be a real risk that executing the request would give rise to a violation of fundamental rights.[20] Similarly, where there is a request to freeze and confiscate assets, 'the requested State shall, before it decides on the execution of the freezing or confiscation order, consult the requesting State and may require any necessary information to be provided'.[21] Both of the last two provisions would not cease extradition or asset freezing respectively, but would impose on the state a communicative obligation to mitigate concerns of a fundamental rights violation. Beyond these measures, the real bulwark of human rights protection within the TCA lies in Part Three.

## B. Human Rights in Part Three of the Trade and Cooperation Agreement

Like the wider Agreement, Part Three commences with a clause recognising the underlying shared values for cooperation. In this respect, law enforcement and judicial cooperation in criminal matters are premised in Article 524 on the parties' 'respect for democracy, the rule of law and the protection of fundamental rights and freedoms of individuals'. However, on this occasion, the text goes beyond merely generically stating that commitment pertains to 'international human rights treaties' to which they are party. Instead, it directly identifies the 'European Convention on Human Rights, and … the importance of giving effect to the rights and freedoms in that Convention domestically'.[22]

The bite to this provision lies later in Article 692, which provides the process for termination of Part Three. It states that general termination can be notified at any time by either party and will take effect 'on the first day of the ninth month following the date of notification'.[23] And yet were the UK or a Member State to denounce the ECHR

[16] For further analysis, see S Peers, 'Analysis 3 of the Brexit deal: Human Rights and EU/UK Trade and Cooperation Agreement' *EU Law Analysis* (4 January 2021) available at https://eulawanalysis.blogspot.com/2021/01/analysis-3-of-brexit-deal-human-rights.html (last accessed 16 April 2024).

[17] Art 125.

[18] Art 406(2)(b).

[19] Art 570.

[20] Art 604(c).

[21] Art 671.

[22] Art 524.

[23] Art 692(1).

or Protocols 1 (relating to the right to property, education and free elections), 6 or 13 (both relating to the abolition of the death penalty) then a fast-track termination of Part Three could be operationalised.[24] Part Three would cease to have effect from the date the denunciation of the ECHR became effective. Under the provisions of the ECHR, a party's denunciation is effective six months after its notification to the Secretary General of the Council of Europe.[25] To date, Greece is the only Contracting Party to exit the Convention in this manner, when it terminated its membership of the Council of Europe following a military coup d'état in 1967. The circumstances surrounding the coup, and subsequent draconian measures during military rule, were the subject of a complaint by a host of European states to the (now defunct) European Commission on Human Rights.[26] In December 1969, following the leak of the Commission report that would find several violations and admonish the military rule, the Greek Foreign Ministry announced its withdrawal from the Council and thereby termination of its membership of the Convention.[27]

The six-month time period would appear to be the same for expulsion from the Council of Europe. Again, there is only one example of these circumstances in action, this time pertaining to the aggressive Russian invasion of Ukraine in February 2022.[28] On 16 March 2022, the Committee of Ministers of the Council of Europe adopted a resolution terminating Russian membership of the organisation.[29] A week later, the Committee passed a separate resolution in respect of Russian legal and financial obligations, in which it confirmed that Russian membership of the ECHR would cease on 16 September 2022.[30] The implications of this are that, whether by denunciation or expulsion, the exit of the UK or a Member State from the ECHR could result in a simultaneous termination of the LEJC agreement.[31] On notification of termination, a scramble would thereafter ensue through the Specialised Committee on Law Enforcement and Judicial Cooperation to decide how best to conclude cooperation with respect to the measures that had been in operation.[32]

[24] Consensus suggests that the EU would trigger this provision were the UK to denounce the ECHR. See, for instance, L O'Carroll, 'Brexit trade treaty 'could be terminated' if UK quits ECHR over small boat crossings'. *The Guardian* (8 March 2023) available at www.theguardian.com/uk-news/2023/mar/08/eu-could-terminate-police-and-security-agreement-if-uk-quits-echr (last accessed 16 April 2024).

[25] Art 58 ECHR.

[26] *Denmark v Greece* App no 3321/67 (ECommHR, 20 September 1967); *Norway v Greece* App no 3322/67 (ECommHR, 20 September 1967); *Sweden v Greece* App no 3323/67 (ECommHR, 20 September 1967); *Netherlands v Greece App* no 3344/67 (ECommHR, 27 September 1967).

[27] I Risini, 'Parting Paths – Russia's Inevitable Exit From the Council of Europe' *Volkerrechtsblog* (12 March 2022) available at https://voelkerrechtsblog.org/parting-paths-russias-inevitable-exit-from-the-council-of-europe/ (last accessed 16 April 2024).

[28] The annexation of Crimea gave rise to sanctions against the Russian regime that included suspension from several Council of Europe bodies. For further information, see K Dzehtsiarou and D Coffey 'Suspension and Expulsion of Members of the Council of Europe: Difficult Decisions in Troubled Times' (2019) 68(2) *International and Comparative Law Quarterly*. 443.

[29] Council of Europe, *Resolution CM/Res(2022)2 on the cessation of the membership of the Russian Federation to the Council of Europe* (16 March 2022, Committee of Ministers).

[30] Council of Europe, *Resolution CM/Res(2022)3 on legal and financial consequences of the cessation of membership of the Russian Federation in the Council of Europe* (23 March 2022, Committee of Ministers) 7.

[31] If the notification of termination is made after that date, then termination would take effect on the 15th day following such notification.

[32] Art 692(3).

Beyond the nuclear approach of termination, there is one further tether linking the parties to the Agreement to human rights standards. Article 693 of the TCA stipulates the grounds upon which a party can seek to have the Agreement suspended, whether in whole or in relation to isolated titles. Similar to the standards outlined above in respect of the TCA as a whole, the standard of circumstances required for suspension is high. It requires 'serious and systemic deficiencies within one Party as regards the protection of fundamental rights or the principle of the rule of law'.[33] The nomenclature is distinct from the standard of 'gross and systematic' violations, which is more regularly adopted by United Nations bodies.[34] The deployment of the word 'serious' indicates that a certain order of magnitude will be required for the violation, and that minor breaches and infringements will not suffice.[35] 'Systematic' will require the deficiencies to be deployed in an organised and deliberate way.[36] Over time, the term 'systematic' has grown to refer to violations of rights that the international community see as being fundamental.[37] Karimova has noted that when considering whether a practice is systematic, 'the volume or scale of the violation seems to be relevant'.[38] The use of the conjunctive 'and', instead of the disjunctive 'or', further elevates the standard by requiring that the presence of both deficiencies (serious and systematic) is at play.

In the event of such deficiencies, the party alleging the breach would be required to specify the circumstances on which the suspension is based. The significance and scale of the violation required to reach the level for potential suspension of Part Three make its operation less likely. It may be more foreseeable that partial suspension is triggered in respect of serious human rights concerns in one discrete area. More interesting, and perhaps plausible, would be an instance where one party took decisive action against the ECHR not by withdrawing, but through a total failure to implement judgments of the ECtHR in a specific area.

In sum, both the wider TCA and Part Three include sweeping general obligations towards human rights. Yet, due to the high threshold for infringement, the significance of these clauses lies more in their discursive value than in any legal enforceability. On the other hand, the direct tether that Part Three creates between membership of the ECHR and the ongoing collaboration in LEJC provides a sharp focus, with the possibility of immediate material ramifications for breach. The prescience of including this in the Agreement has been demonstrated on numerous occasions throughout the TCA's early implementation.

[33] Art 693(1).

[34] eg UN Human Rights Council General Assembly Resolution 60/251 of 3 April 2006, 3; Human Rights Council Resolution 5/1, Institution-building of the United Nations Human Rights Council, Annex; The Vienna Declaration and Programme of Action, World Conference on Human Rights, 1993, 30.

[35] International Law Commission Draft Articles on State Responsibility for Internationally Wrongful Acts 2001, with Commentaries, Official Records of the General Assembly, Fifty-sixth Session, Supp No 10, UN Doc A/56/10, Art 40, comments, 7.

[36] ibid 8.

[37] Geneva Academy, 'What amounts to 'a serious violation of international human rights law?' Academy Briefing no 6 (August 2014) available at www.geneva-academy.ch/joomlatools-files/docman-files/Publications/Academy%20Briefings/Briefing%206%20What%20is%20a%20serious%20violation%20of%20human%20rights%20law_Academy%20Briefing%20No%206.pdf (last accessed 16 April 2024).

[38] ibid 17.

## III. The United Kingdom, ECHR and the TCA: Legally Committed but Politically Conflicted

Since coming into force, the principal threat to the ongoing operation of Part Three of the TCA has been the risk that the UK would give notice to leave the ECHR, pushing the EU to invoke Article 692 and terminate the ongoing operation of the LEJC agreement. It is perhaps odd, for a treaty that has been so recently agreed, that the most pressing question is whether one party is likely to seek termination or suspension on account of the other party's breach of such an unambiguous component of it. Odder still that, in the party most likely to commit the breach, it would be the same political leadership that negotiated, drafted and signed the Agreement, to invoke that breach.[39] And yet such is the nature of the UK's inconsistent and sometimes paradoxical contemporary relationship with both European and international human-rights monitoring, and in particular with the European Court of Human Rights in Strasbourg.

In this section I contend that while the UK is likely to remain legally committed to the ECHR, particularly with the return of the Labour Party to power, a political space has now been firmly established that could see the UK exit the Convention system, thereby endangering the ongoing operation of Part Three of the TCA.

### A. Brexit from the ECHR

Rather than being a recent development, antipathy from the UK towards the ECHR and its organs has been a regular feature since the Convention's inception in 1950.[40] The relationship has often been characterised by a dissonant belligerence on the British part. The UK played a significant role in drafting the treaty that enshrines the largely civil and political rights, and yet it was initially reticent to become a signatory, and would not accept the relevant protocol allowing for individual petitions until 1966.[41] After losing a series of cases in the 1980s, the UK threatened to leave the system.[42] This threat would re-emerge in the early 1990s after the Grand Chamber had found the UK in violation of the right to life when SAS agents killed IRA operatives in Gibraltar.[43] Nonetheless, not only would the UK remain part of the Convention system, the New Labour constitutional reforms post-1997 saw most Convention rights brought within the domestic legal order with the enactment of the Human Rights Act (HRA) 1998.

The dominant theme, since the HRA 1998 was brought into force in October 2000, has been one of constitutional psychosis: official government policy has been fully supportive of membership of the ECHR, and yet politicians – from the backbenches

[39] The UK's Conservative Party.

[40] See E Wicks and L Hodson, 'The UK and European Human Rights: A Strained Relationship?' in K Ziegler, E Wicks and L Hodson (eds), *The UK and European Human Rights: A Strained Relationship?* (Hart Publishing, 2015) 3.

[41] Lord Lester of Herne Hill, 'UK Acceptance of the Strasbourg Jurisdiction: What Really Went on in Whitehall in 1965' (PL 237, 1997).

[42] E Bates *The Evolution of the European Convention on Human Rights, From its Inception to the Creation of a Permanent Court of Human Rights* (Oxford University Press, 2010) 87.

[43] *McCann v UK* (1996) 21 EHRR 97.

to the office of the Prime Minister – have regularly raised the possibility, and often need, for the UK to leave the Convention system. While official government policy has therefore ensured ongoing membership of the ECHR, the discourse of political leaders has increasingly fortified a political space that pits the nation against the Convention system, often suggesting that it is only one step removed from exiting.

These dynamics have largely been driven from the British Conservative Party, but it is worth noting that the Labour Government that enacted the HRA 1998 did not always remain a steadfast supporter of it, nor of the UK's membership of the Convention. There were early robust criticisms from both Prime Minister Tony Blair[44] and Home Secretary David Blunkett.[45] By the end of their time in office, the Labour Party was already heralding a supplementary British Bill of Rights and Responsibilities.[46] As Hélène Tyrrell notes:

> Although Labour never actually altered the HRA or the relationship with the ECHR, the party's internal incoherence on the subject of human rights had set in motion a narrative that would gradually undermine public confidence in their legislative achievement and the rights that it protects.[47]

When the Conservative and Liberal Democrats entered into Coalition Government in 2010, reform of the HRA 1998 and membership of the Convention were firmly on the political agenda, and yet the official government policy remained unflinching in its support for the ECHR.[48] A Commission on a UK Bill of Rights was launched in March 2011, with a remit to 'investigate the creation of a UK Bill of Rights that incorporates and builds on all our obligations under the European Convention on Human Rights'.[49] As Attorney-General, Dominic Grieve was a strong supporter of membership of the ECHR, warning that the UK would risk being seen as a 'pariah state' were it to leave the Convention system.[50] As Deputy Prime Minister, Nick Clegg made it clear that there would be no exit from the ECHR while he was in government.[51]

The Conservative Government of 2015 was elected on a manifesto that pledged continuing commitment to the ECHR.[52] And yet, as Prime Minister during the

[44] N Temko and J Doward, 'Revealed: Blair Attack on Human Rights Law' *The Observer* (14 May 2006) available at www.theguardian.com/politics/2006/may/14/humanrights.ukcrime (last accessed 16 April 2024).

[45] A Travis, 'Human Rights Act Under Pressure' *The Guardian* (25 September 2001) available at www.theguardian.com/politics/2001/sep/25/uk.september111 (last accessed 16 April 2024).

[46] Ministry of Justice, *Rights and Responsibilities: Developing our Constitutional Framework* (Cmd 7577, 2009) 10. Note, however, that the envisioned Bill of Rights would build on and not replace the Convention.

[47] H Tyrrell, 'The Human Rights Act 1998: Two Decades Swimming Upstream' in M Gordon and A Tucker (eds), *The New Labour Constitution: Twenty Years On* (Hart Publishing, 2011) 43, 46.

[48] HC Deb 8 November 2011, vol 535, col 158 (Ken Clarke MP).

[49] 'Commission on a UK Bill of Rights Released' *HM Gov* (18 March 2011) available at www.gov.uk/government/news/commission-on-a-uk-bill-of-rights-launched (last accessed 16 April 2024).

[50] H Watt, 'Britain could become Belarus if it abandons human rights legislation', warns Attorney General', *The Daily Telegraph* (9 October 2012) available at www.telegraph.co.uk/news/politics/9596949/Britain-could-become-Belarus-if-it-abandons-human-rights-legislation-warns-Attorney-General.html (last accessed 16 April 2024).

[51] 'Nick Clegg: Tories are like a "broken shopping trolley"' *Channel 4 News* (10 March 2013) available at www.channel4.com/news/nick-clegg-liberal-democrat-speech-conference-conservatives (last accessed 16 April 2024).

[52] Conservative Party, *The Conservative Party Manifesto* (2015) 73.

prisoner-voting scandal in 2015, David Cameron ratcheted up the tensions, indicating that he was committed to 'breaking the link' between British courts and the ECtHR.[53] The inconsistency continued with the next Conservative leadership. In advance of the Brexit referendum in 2016, then Home Secretary Theresa May argued that the UK should be leaving the ECHR and not the EU,[54] but as Prime Minister her party's manifesto in a snap election of 2017 pledged again to 'remain signatories to the European Convention on Human Rights for the duration of the next parliament'.[55]

The Brexit-induced necessity for attention elsewhere provided a brief respite from Conservative criticism of the Strasbourg system, and no mention was made of the ECHR in the 2019 manifesto. The Government instead focused on a programme of 'updating the Human Rights Act 1998'.[56] This wording was generously read by then Justice Minister, Dominic Raab, to mean the repeal of the HRA 1998 in its entirety and its replacement with a British Bill of Rights. Despite the constitutional upheaval this legislative change would have brought about, there remained official continuity around the position of the Convention. The reform was instigated with an Independent Review into the Human Rights Act in December 2020, premised on the UK remaining 'a signatory to the Convention'.[57] This position was echoed in the report findings,[58] and although it was largely side-lined by the Government in its consideration of further steps towards a British Bill of Rights, official policy continued to be that the UK would remain a member of the Convention. Under parliamentary questioning in both the House of Commons and the House of Lords, this position endured unchanged.[59]

And yet simultaneously, the political discourse concerning ECHR membership became more febrile, particularly in the wake of the ECtHR's interim order halting a flagship government policy of sending asylum seekers to Rwanda in June 2022.[60] Representatives of then Prime Minister Boris Johnson responded by briefing that the Government was considering withdrawal from the ECHR.[61] After he was deposed by his Cabinet, candidates to replace him as Prime Minister took to platforms giving similar indications towards an exit.[62] One of the Convention's most prominent critics, Suella

[53] N Watt and R Masonm 'Cameron "committed to breaking link with European court of human rights"' *The Guardian* (1 June 2015) available at www.theguardian.com/law/2015/jun/01/david-cameron-european-court-of-human-rights (last accessed 16 April 2024).

[54] A Asthana and R Mason, 'UK must leave European convention on human rights, says Theresa May' *The Guardian* (25 April 2016) available at www.theguardian.com/politics/2016/apr/25/uk-must-leave-european-convention-on-human-rights-theresa-may-eu-referendum (last accessed 16 April 2024).

[55] Conservative Party, *Forward Together: The Conservative and Unionist Party Manifesto* (2017) 37.

[56] Conservative Party, *Get Brexit Done: The Conservative and Unionist Party Manifesto 2019* (2019) 48.

[57] Sir Peter Gross, Independent Human Rights Act Review Call for Evidence (December 2020) available at https://assets.publishing.service.gov.uk/government/uploads/system/uploads/attachment_data/file/962423/Call-for-Evidence.pdf (last accessed 16 April 2024) 5.

[58] Sir Peter Gross, Independent Human Rights Act (CP 586, December 2021) available at https://assets.publishing.service.gov.uk/government/uploads/system/uploads/attachment_data/file/1040525/ihrar-final-report.pdf (last accessed 16 April 2024): 2.

[59] HL Deb 18 July 2022, vol 823, col 1751; HC Deb 21 February 2023, vol 728, col 109.

[60] *NSK v the United Kingdom* App no 28774/22 (ECtHR, 14 June 2022).

[61] A Woodcock, '"All options on the table": Downing street confirms Boris Johnson considering withdrawal from human rights treaty' *The Independent* (15 June 2022) available at www.independent.co.uk/news/uk/politics/boris-johnson-rwanda-echr-rights-b2101658.html (last accessed 16 April 2024).

[62] A Forrest, 'Liz Truss Prepared to Withdraw the UK from European Convention on Human Rights' *The Independent* 13 July 2022) available at www.independent.co.uk/news/uk/politics/liz-truss-uk-human-rights-convention-b2122084.html (last accessed 16 April 2024).

Braverman, ran on an anti-ECHR agenda, and would continue to make threats to leave when (re)appointed as Home Secretary, railing that the ECHR was at-odds with 'British values'.[63] Dominic Raab was similarly antagonistic towards the Convention system, stating on multiple occasions that 'we rule nothing out' in respect of a UK exit,[64] and yet also suggesting that there was no possibility of a UK exit in the short to medium term.[65] Similar discontinuity in messaging came from the Prime Minister Rishi Sunak, whose office appeared to brief the *Sunday Times* that it was considering leaving the Convention, and yet within weeks he would make a parliamentary statement that the 'UK is and will remain a member of the ECHR'.[66]

Dominic Raab's resignation from office in the spring of 2023 heralded the demise of the Conservative Government's plans to revamp domestic human rights legislation with a new British Bill of Rights. By the summer, the new Justice Minister, Alex Chalk, confirmed that the Bill had been pulled from the legislative agenda.[67] This did not, however, quell the attacks on the ECHR, with further briefings relating to UK withdrawal continuing until the Conservative Party lost the General Election of 2024.[68]

The incoherence and discontinuity of the UK's position towards remaining in the ECHR is but a mere glimpse of the puzzle of its wider relationship with the Strasbourg organs. Alice Donald has charted how, despite years of complaints of victimisation by British politicians, the UK is one of the best-performing states at the Court. Indeed, she gave evidence to the Joint Committee on Human Rights that between 1999 and 2017, 'the UK "lost" fewer than one in 50 cases brought against it'.[69] Given this reality, as well as the consistency of *official* government policy in favour of remaining party to the Convention, one might ask whether all the threats, briefings and criticism have any impact at all?

While the persistent anti-ECHR discourse has not yet led anywhere materially in terms of official policy, it would be overly complacent to consider it mere rhetoric, or to consider ECHR exit entirely off the table with a Labour Government in charge. The discourse of recent years has shaped a political space that makes Convention exit more than a distant possibility. As Ed Bates aptly notes, a 'BrECHRit' from the ECHR may have moved from a taboo to tenable.[70] The more often that critics complain of the interference and illegitimacy of the ECHR, the more fertile an exit policy has become amongst the wider public. Through decades of misrepresentation of ECtHR judgments,

[63] 'European court at odds with British values, says Suella Braverman' *BBC News* (10 March 2023) available at www.bbc.co.uk/news/uk-politics-64907772 (last accessed 16 April 2024).

[64] Joint Committee on Human Rights, Oral evidence: Legislative scrutiny: Bill of Rights Bill (HC 611, 14 December 2022) 14; HC Deb 21 February 2023, vol 728, col 109.

[65] Justice and Home Affairs Committee, Uncorrected oral evidence: The Deputy Prime Minister, Lord Chancellor and Secretary of State for Justice (15 March 2023) 3.

[66] HC Deb 27 February 2023, vol 728, col 594.

[67] HC Deb, 27 June 2023, vol 735, col 145.

[68] N Eardley, 'Tories could campaign to leave European human rights treaty if Rwanda flights blocked' *BBC News* (9 August 2023) available at www.bbc.co.uk/news/uk-politics-66438422 (last accessed 16 April 2024).

[69] A Donald, Written evidence to the Joint Committee on Human Rights inquiry (HRA0021) (2018) available at http://data.parliament.uk/writtenevidence/committeeevidence.svc/evidencedocument/humanrights-committee/twenty-years-of-the-human-rights-act/written/89787.html (last accessed 16 April 2024).

[70] E Bates, (2024) 'UK Withdrawal From the ECHR ("BrECHRit"): From Taboo to Tenable?' (2024) 5(1) *European Convention on Human Rights Law Review* 24.

confusion over its institutional position and the relationship with British courts, a space now exists where an exit policy could be a valuable manifesto pledge at a general election.[71] It is not so many years since it was the EU that was being accused of making illegitimate inroads into UK sovereign decision making. At present, as with earlier periods in the UK–ECHR's protracted history, exit seems to be a step further than a British government would want to go. Nonetheless, should the political winds change, even slightly, the foundations for exit have been laid.

## IV. Taking Stock: A Belligerent Future?

So what, then, of the future relations, and the implications for Part Three of the TCA? Instead of exiting the ECHR, it looks more likely that the UK will remain a Member State for the foreseeable future, and yet that its relationship may intermittently relapse to echo the tensions that existed prior to the creation of the HRA 1998. While these tensions normally lie dormant, they are invoked on the occasions when the ECtHR holds the UK in violation of an aspect of the Convention. Given the raft of rights restricting legislation passed in recent years, the scene is set for a series of showdowns that could ratchet up that tension. For instance, the Overseas Operations Act 2021 and the Northern Ireland Troubles (Legacy and Reconciliation) Act 2023 both have highly dubious rights credentials and were directly criticised by the Council of Europe's Commissioner for Human Rights.[72] The compliance of actions relying on these texts with Articles 2 (right to life), 3 (freedom from torture) and 6 (right to a fair trial) of the ECHR is questionable. Elsewhere, there are questions over the compatibility of provisions within the Public Order Act 2023 and Articles 9 (freedom of conscience and religion), 10 (freedom of expression) and 11 (freedom of assembly) of the ECHR. It is entirely possible that cases arising from the application of such legislation could form the basis of a complaint to the ECtHR in the coming years.

Some collisions between the UK and Strasbourg Court have, however, been avoided in the wake of the Labour Party's electorial success in 2024, not least the impact of the Illegal Migration Act (IMA) 2023. This Act, explicitly designed by the Conservative Government to deal with small-boat crossings in the English Channel, had included provisions that tested the boundaries of the UK's compliance with the ECHR. Indeed,

[71] A Hall, 'Threatening to Leave the ECHR would be the perfect terrain for next conservative election campaign' *Byline Times* (8 March 2023) available at https://bylinetimes.com/2023/03/08/threatening-to-leave-the-echr-would-be-the-perfect-terrain-for-next-conservative-election-campaign/ (last accessed 16 April 2024).

[72] 'UK: Flawed Northern Ireland 'Troubles' Bill flagrantly contravenes rights obligations, says UN experts'. *UN News* (15 December 2022) available at www.ohchr.org/en/press-releases/2022/12/uk-flawed-northern-ireland-troubles-bill-flagrantly-contravenes-rights (last accessed 16 April 2024); Commissioner for Human Rights, 'Proposed United Kingdom legislation on the legacy of the Troubles in Northern Ireland raises human rights concerns' (Council of Europe, 13 August 2022) available at www.coe.int/en/web/commissioner/-/proposed-united-kingdom-legislation-on-the-legacy-of-the-troubles-in-northern-ireland-raises-human-rights-concerns (last accessed 16 April 2024); Commissioner for Human Rights 'UK lawmakers should reject provisions of the Overseas Operations Bill undermining the fight against impunity for serious human rights violations' (Council of Europe, 3 November 2021) available at www.coe.int/en/web/commissioner/-/uk-lawmakers-should-reject-provisions-of-the-overseas-operations-bill-undermining-the-fight-against-impunity-for-serious-human-rights-violations (last accessed 16 April 2024).

when the Bill was laid before Parliament, it did not carry the customary statement under section 19 of the HRA 1998 indicating the Government's opinion that it was compatible with the Convention.[73] It further included a provision that disapplied the section 3 interpretive obligation that judges are under from the HRA 1998, to read legislation in a manner that is compatible with the ECHR.[74] It is section 3 that has served as a bulwark behind which domestic judges have sought to interpret British legislation in a Convention-compliant manner, thus negating the need for many applicants to bring cases to the ECtHR. There was then something of an inevitability in the IMA 2023's not being read in a Convention-compliant manner, resulting in a greater number of complaints being brought to the ECtHR. And on reaching the Court, the IMA 2023 went further still, in containing a provision empowering government ministers to ignore interim-measure decisions from the ECtHR when certain criteria were met.[75] As interim measures are binding on contracting parties to the ECHR, ministerial action under this provision would almost certainly have given rise to a breach of the Convention.[76] On coming to power, the Labour Government swiftly passed Regulations amending the IMA 2023;[77] and yet by not repealing the Act entirely, there remains a possibility that it may be resurrected by a future government.

Collectively, the legacy of of rights-dubious legislation passed in recent parliaments may pave the way towards a more fractious relationship between the UK and the ECHR system. While recent measures are unlikely to meet the definition of 'serious and systematic deficiencies' required to trigger the suspension provision under Part Three of the TCA, they present the likelihood that the UK will find itself embroiled in more frequent litigation at the ECtHR. In the instances where the UK loses, the criticism of the Strasbourg body will increase, continuing to fortify further the anti-ECHR political space that has been growing in recent years. As the cycle continues, the prospect of a UK exit, and subsequently an EU-led termination of Part Three of the TCA, may become more real.

## V. Conclusion

The commitments under Part Three of the TCA are not the first international agreements to bind the UK Government to the ongoing protection of the ECHR. The Good Friday Agreement, an international treaty between the British and Irish Governments, cemented the position of the ECHR as both a safeguard and a starting basis for rights protection within Northern Ireland.[78] In particular, the British Government committed to providing direct access to the courts for those seeking to enforce their Convention rights.[79] Similar to the Good Friday Agreement, the measures that can be triggered

[73] s 19(1)(b) Human Rights Act 1998.
[74] s 1(5) Illegal Migration Act 2023.
[75] s 55 Illegal Migration Act 2023; criteria detailed in s 55(5).
[76] Rule 39, European Court of Human Rights Rules of Court (March 2024) Practice directions 6.
[77] Illegal Migration Act (2023) (Amendment) Regulations 2024 (SI 2024/815).
[78] The Belfast Agreement, *An Agreement at the Multi-party Talks on Northern Ireland* (CM 3883, 1998) Strand 1 [5] (B) and (c); [26] (a).
[79] ibid, Rights, Safeguards and Equality of Opportunity [2].

through application of Article 692 serve as a powerful tool for those who are interested in differentiating political criticism from a material threat. Political criticism is certainly not harmless. It has the capacity to build a space wherein further agitation can ultimately lead to major political change. Criticism can normalise an otherwise controversial outcome. Where a policy is repeated uncritically, it may even seem inevitable that the harbingers of doom will be proved correct at some point. Nonetheless, political criticism is not material action, and what the commitments around the ECHR in Part Three do is weed out the rhetoric from the reality. Where a politician, whether from the backbenches or the Cabinet, suggests exit from the ECHR, the clear response is to ask them whether they are prepared to forgo the benefits the UK obtains from cooperation with the EU in respect of LEJC.

# PART IV

# The Impact of the TCA Implementation on Crime and Insecurity

# 17

# Two Steps Forward, One Step Back? Fighting Terrorism under the Trade and Cooperation Agreement

ALEX MacKENZIE AND CHRISTIAN KAUNERT

## I. Introduction

The security concerns of Western states have changed significantly in the 20-plus years since 9/11. Al Qaeda-inspired terrorism was widely viewed as the foremost threat for much of the first decade of the twenty-first century, with Islamic State (IS) splitting from and eclipsing its parent group in the second decade. Both organisations are now shadows of what they were, and the United States (US) has lost interest in leading a 'war on terror', the long-term consequences of which have been globally disastrous. Today, the security agenda is more crowded given the recent Covid-19 pandemic, Russia's ongoing war with Ukraine and destabilising activities abroad, economic and energy concerns, environmental challenges, China's growing global role and friction with the US, and, most recently, a new crisis in the Middle East. Thus, terrorism is now merely one of several challenges facing states, with all the problems of competition for attention and resource allocation that follow.

Terrorist threats have evolved too. Twenty years ago, Western states were concerned about transnational jihadi groups, their affiliate and 'freelancers',[1] whereas today there is most emphasis on individual or small-group radicalisation of various forms not limited to jihadism through the Internet and peer networks.[2] The shift towards occasional attacks by individuals or small cells only sometimes known to security services suggests that many states have been relatively successful in combating jihadi terrorism. Yet such plots remain difficult to detect and prevent, as well as often being serious, rendering their neglect inadvisable.[3]

[1] P Errera, 'Three Circles of Threat' (2005) 47(1) *Survival* 71.

[2] J Kenyon, C Baker-Beall, and J Binder, 'Lone-Actor Terrorism – a Systematic Literature Review' (2023) 46(10) *Studies in Conflict and Terrorism* 2038.

[3] N Turner, S Chermak and J Freilich, 'An Empirical Examination of the Severity of Lone-Actor Terrorism Attacks' (2023) 69(5) *Crime and Delinquency* 915.

As a Member State of the European Union (EU) from 1973, the UK was frequently torn between European cooperation and concerns about sovereignty, despite terrorism often being high on its list of security priorities.[4] Consequently, British governments swayed between these positions – leading at times, lagging or resisting at others. The period after 9/11 under Labour Prime Minister Tony Blair saw the UK play an active role in the EU, whereas David Cameron's Conservative Party was noticeably more Eurosceptic and combative after 2010. By 2016, the UK had carved out a unique position in the EU, having arguably secured much of what it wanted, while avoiding several aspects deemed undesirable through its various opt ins and opt outs. What changed when the UK left the EU and the Trade and Cooperation Agreement (TCA) came into force?[5]

To date, Brexit and the TCA do not obviously seem to have seriously affected either side's ability to combat terrorism, yet neither actor would publicly admit to new vulnerabilities in any case. The security components of the TCA are not insubstantial, but they are a significant downgrade for the UK compared to what it possessed as a Member State. Future developments will hinge on terrorist threats, British Euroscepticism and the UK's ability to influence the EU. First, the threat landscape and whether perceptions of terrorism are shared between London and other European capitals is a significant issue. Without such alignment, there will likely be little impetus for enhancing cooperation, never mind tackling terrorism through similar means. Second, at the time of writing, the Conservative Government of Prime Minister Rishi Sunak, although noticeably less belligerent towards the EU than those of his two predecessors, includes many Brexiteers. Thus, on the British side, it is possible that any of political unwillingness, constitutional issues, regulatory divergence and loss of trust could obstruct the possibility of upgrading the EU–UK relationship in the future and may even lead to further downgrading.[6] Future governments could navigate these issues and avert many problems, though. Third, the EU has moved on since the UK left the Union. Beyond recognising and engaging with the UK as an important – and generally aligned – regional power on its doorstep, there appears to be little appetite in Brussels for much deeper engagement. It remains to be seen whether the UK can persuade the EU both to re-engage and to make any changes palatable to all stakeholders.

We structure our discussion in three sections: the changing security landscape (section II); European counter-terrorism cooperation up to the TCA (section III); and how terrorism will be fought under the Agreement, especially given possible future developments (section IV).

[4] S Wolff, A Piquet and H Carrapico, 'UK's Withdrawal From Justice and Home Affairs'(2022) 20 *Comparative European Politics* 609.

[5] United Kingdom and European Union, Trade and Co-operation Agreement Between the United Kingdom of Great Britain and Northern Ireland, of the one part, and the European Union and the European Atomic Energy Community, of the other part (30 December 2020) available at https://assets.publishing.service.gov.uk/media/608ae0c0d3bf7f0136332887/TS_8.2021_UK_EU_EAEC_Trade_and_Cooperation_Agreement.pdf (last accessed 8 January 2025).

[6] V Mitsilegas and E Guild, 'Police and Criminal Justice After Brexit' (2023) 30(11) *Journal of European Public Policy* 2519.

## II. The Changing Threat Landscape: Terrorism is More Diverse and One Challenge Among Many

Few European states have had a range of experiences of terrorism comparable to the UK, making tackling its many forms a long-term priority for the country. The British public have long regarded terrorism as a serious concern – more so than most other European states.[7] By way of example, in 2018, 65 per cent of Britons feared a terrorist attack that year, whereas Italians polled at only 32 per cent and Poles at 20 per cent.[8] While for the past two decades or more, jihadism has been the terrorist threat on which the EU has focused (including the UK as a Member State), we appear today to be facing myriad smaller challenges.[9] Terrorism is also increasingly competing with other threats – far from its high agenda status back in 2001. Yet, for now at least, British and EU terrorist threat perceptions seem mostly aligned, although differences are possible in due course.

Terrorism is still considered high up the list of the UK's security concerns. As can be seen in the 2021 Integrated Security Review, it ranks second beneath traditional military challenges.[10] At the time of writing, the UK was undergoing a review of its counter-terrorism strategy (CONTEST), with Matt Jukes, the Head of Counter-Terrorism Policing, claiming that 'today's threat is dominated by increasingly fragmented ideologies, self-initiated terrorism, and the reach of hateful online ideologies into the lives of young people'.[11] Britain's security apparatus remains focused on jihadism above all, but the far right is viewed as the fastest growing threat. Between 2017 and 2021, MI5, the UK's internal security service, claims to have thwarted 31 late-stage plots. Most of these were jihadist in nature, but a 'growing number' were planned by far-right terrorists.[12] At the same time, in a recent review of the UK's counter-extremism strategy, Prevent, there was a call for stronger emphasis on jihadism and less on the far right, although this is likely to do with disagreements in and around the then ruling Conservative Party about what are legitimate right-wing views.[13]

[7] V Bove, G Efthyvoulou and H Pickard, 'Did Terrorism Affect Voting in the Brexit Referendum?' (2021) 52(3) *British Journal of Political Science* 1133.

[8] M Bulman, 'UK More Concerned About Terror Than any Other Country, Finds Study' *The Independent* (8 January 2018) available at www.independent.co.uk/news/uk/home-news/uk-terror-concerns-higher-other-countries-isis-terrorism-attacks-study-ipsos-mori-britain-a8147691.html (last accessed 29 March 2023).

[9] J O'Neill and N Glynn, 'Northern Ireland Terrorism Threat Level Rises' *BBC News* (23 March 2023) available at www.bbc.co.uk/news/uk-northern-ireland-65096493 (last accessed 29 March 2023).

[10] Cabinet Office, *Global Britain in a Competitive Age: The Integrated Review of Security, Defence, Development, and Foreign Policy* (2021) available at www.gov.uk/government/publications/global-britain-in-a-competitive-age-the-integrated-review-of-security-defence-development-and-foreign-policy (last accessed 29 March 2023).

[11] Home Office, *Review of Government Counter-Terror Strategy to Tackle Threats* (30 October 2022) available at www.gov.uk/government/news/review-of-government-counter-terror-strategy-to-tackle-threats (last accessed 6 December 2022).

[12] L Turner, 'MI5: 31 Late-Stage Terror Plots Foiled in Four Years in UK' *BBC News* (10 September 2021) available at www.bbc.co.uk/news/uk-58512901 (last accessed 6 December 2022).

[13] R Syal and V Dodd, 'Review of Prevent Strategy to Call for More Focus on Islamist Terrorism' *The Guardian* (7 February 2023) available at www.theguardian.com/uk-news/2023/feb/07/review-of-uk-prevent-strategy-to-call-for-more-focus-on-islamist-terrorism (last accessed 31 March 2023).

In the EU's most recent major strategy document, the 2016 *Global Strategy*, terrorism was considered the second priority for external action.[14] Yet with 27 Member States, there are unsurprising national differences. Even so, what concerns about terrorism exist at present appear to align with the UK's assessments, going by the 2023 *Terrorism Situation and Trend Report* (TE-SAT), which is compiled and produced by Europol on an annual basis. Catherine De Bolle, the current Executive Director of Europol, asserts that Member States 'continue to view jihadist terrorism as the prominent terrorist threat', although there is concern about other forms, as well as radicalisation through the Internet. Furthermore, the *Report* documents 28 completed, failed or foiled attacks in the EU during 2022, with many types represented.[15]

Despite the fact that the threat landscape has been evolving and becoming more crowded since 2001, both the EU and UK have similar perceptions of terrorism today. Even so, the latter likely considers it higher up the list of priorities than is the case for many EU Member States. It is also possible that the UK worked hard to keep terrorism high on the agenda when it was an EU Member State. Consequently, the impetus for enhancing counterterrorism cooperation between the UK and EU seems lower than would have been the case several years ago. It is also entirely possible that the gap between the EU and UK will end up growing over time, which would render cooperation more difficult. There may be signs of dealignment already, even if only in terms of geographical focus. The EU is becoming more concerned about terrorism in the Sahel region of Africa – possibly indicating French influence.[16] Shifting towards foreseeable future challenges that could affect one or both actors, Russia may be tempted to use proxies in Europe due to its poor performance in its war with Ukraine. Moscow has built ties with disruptive actors, noticeably those on the far right, over the last two decades.[17] There have also been some concerning incidents in Northern Ireland in recent years, yet there are few signs of serious deterioration.[18] Most recently, Hamas' attack on Israel in October 2023 and the responses taken could contribute to terrorism in Europe. Finally, we cannot rule out a major shock in the future, as occurred on 9/11.

## III. European Counterterrorism Cooperation: From Trevi to the TCA

European intergovernmental cooperation on terrorism has existed since at least the formation of the Trevi Group in the 1970s, at which time there were several serious

[14] European Union, *Shared Vision, Common Action: A Stronger Europe: A Global Strategy for the European Union's Foreign and Security Policy* (June 2016) available at www.eeas.europa.eu/sites/default/files/eugs_review_web_0.pdf (last accessed 31 March 2023).

[15] Europol, *European Union Terrorism Situation and Trend Report 2023* (26 October 2023) available at www.europol.europa.eu/publication-events/main-reports/european-union-terrorism-situation-and-trend-report-2023-te-sat (last accessed 31 March 2023).

[16] J Borrell, 'The Terrorist Threat is Expanding in the Sahel' *European Union External Action Service* (19 August 2022) available at www.eeas.europa.eu/eeas/terrorist-threat-expanding-sahel_en (last accessed 31 March 2023).

[17] A Shekhovtsov, *Russia and the Western Far Right* (Routledge, 2017).

[18] R Carroll, 'Northern Ireland Republican Dissidents Lurk in the Shadows Hoping to be Noticed' *The Guardian* (23 February 2023) available at www.theguardian.com/politics/2023/feb/23/republican-dissidents-lurk-in-the-shadows-hoping-to-be-noticed (last accessed 2 October 2023).

outbreaks of terrorism across Europe.[19] For example, the 'Troubles' and sectarian violence in Northern Ireland during the 1970s, and Italy's 'Years of Lead' involving extremists of different kinds between the 1960s and 1980s. The UK is believed to have played a leading role in the creation of the Trevi Group, with then Foreign Secretary, James Callaghan, proposing in 1975 – and others agreeing to – the setting up of a special working group on terrorism.[20] In the 1990s, however, as leftist groups disappeared after the end of the Cold War and Northern Ireland calmed significantly, opening the way for talks that culminated in the 1998 Good Friday Agreement, there appeared to be little impetus for enhancing European counterterrorism cooperation. But 9/11 provided a massive external shock that initiated a quest to enhance counterterrorism cooperation in Europe and beyond. Jihadi terrorism transformed the EU, with the introduction of several measures previously thought impossible, following major terrorist attacks.[21] Significantly, this has meant that the EU's value in internal security has grown markedly since 9/11, given that many responses to terrorism have utility for combating other challenges too, including organised crime.

At this point, it is important to broadly summarise what the UK possessed as a full EU Member State. This helps show what was lost with Brexit, as well as what the UK managed to maintain access to in the TCA that is pertinent to counterterrorism. First, there are the rights of all Member States, including full roles in the decision-making apparatus of the EU, as well as the agencies Europol and Eurojust. Member States often attempt to upload their problems and solutions to the EU level, and the UK was no exception.[22] Second, some Member States negotiated various opt ins and opt outs. Particularly relevant here for the UK was that it had an opt in to Justice and Home Affairs (JHA) and an opt out from the Schengen Area. So, it had the ability to choose on a case-by-case basis the JHA measures in which it wanted to participate, which it obtained in the negotiations for the Treaty of Amsterdam in 1997.[23] This is how it was previously able to influence the trajectory of the EU from within, select the measures in which it participated and was the only Member State not involved in the Schengen Area to have partial access to the accompanying database from 2015 (the Schengen Information System or SIS II). By 2016, the UK had carved out a unique position in the EU, accessing a lot of what it wanted from European integration, while avoiding a fair amount of that which it did not want.[24] We now show how it got there, starting with 9/11.

After 9/11, the UK could be seen regularly pushing for more work at the European level. It was significant in the creation of the European Arrest Warrant (EAW);[25] the EU's counterterrorism strategy was agreed on during the UK's Presidency in the second

[19] O Bures, 'EU Counter-Terrorism Policy: A Paper Tiger?' (2006) 18(1) *Terrorism and Political Violence* 57.

[20] T Bunyan, 'Trevi, Europol, and the European State' *Statewatch* (1993) available at www.statewatch.org/media/documents/news/handbook-trevi.pdf (last accessed 29 March 2023).

[21] J Argomaniz, 'Post-9/11 Institutionalisation of European Union Counter-Terrorism: Emergence, Acceleration, and Inertia' (2009) 18(2) *European Security* 151.

[22] A MacKenzie, 'Conspicuous by their absence? the member states in European Union counter-terrorism' (2023) 46(2) *Journal of European Integration* 155, doi:10.1080/07036337.2023.2255729, 1.

[23] European Union, Treaty of Amsterdam Amending the Treaty on European Union, the Treaties Establishing the European Communities and Certain Related Acts (10 November 1997) [1997] OJ C340/01.

[24] See Davies and Carrapico, ch 2.

[25] European Union, Council Framework Decision of 13 June 2002 on the European Arrest Warrant on the European Arrest Warrant and the Surrender Procedures Between Member States (2002/584/JHA) [2002] OJ L190/1; C Mortera-Martinez, 'The European Arrest Warrant: A British Affair' *Centre for European*

half of 2005 and resembled that country's;[26] it led on several measures, from the Data Retention Directive (2006) to the EU Passenger Name Record Directive (EU PNR (2016);[27] and is considered to have reformed Europol under Rob Wainwright (Director from 2009 to 2018), among other contributions.[28] Still, during David Cameron's Conservative–Liberal Democrat Coalition (2010–15), the UK started to withdraw from JHA, primarily due to sovereignty concerns in the Conservative Party, exiting 130 JHA instruments and measures before rejoining 35 in 2014.[29] Many of the measures that the UK opted back into were relevant to counterterrorism, including the EAW; the establishment of Europol and Eurojust and their databases, such as the European Criminal Records Information System (ECRIS); data protection when processing for police and judicial cooperation; and the establishment and use of SIS II.[30]

After the shock of the vote to leave in June 2016, there were many discussions in the UK as to what its objectives should be in negotiations with the EU. Ultimately, the UK under Prime Minister Boris Johnson opted for a more distant Brexit than his predecessor Theresa May had attempted to obtain, necessitating a significant reduction in cooperation. There is little, if anything, in the TCA that could be thought of as specifically designed for combating terrorism, beyond where financing of it is mentioned. Still, the relevant parts of the Agreement, for our purposes, can be found in Part Three, Titles I to XII. Cooperation that has been maintained includes exchanges of DNA, fingerprints and vehicle registration data (Prüm Convention);[31] PNR data; operational data; cooperation with Europol; cooperation with Eurojust; surrender and arrest warrants; mutual assistance on criminal matters; exchange of criminal record information; and anti-money laundering and counter-terrorist financing.[32] While the list may sound impressive, the UK experienced significant losses, including access to SIS II; full participation in Eurojust and Europol, such as access to their databases and decisions on future direction; the ability to shape policy and threat perceptions from within, and more.

*Reform* (7 November 2014) available at www.cer.eu/insights/european-arrest-warrant-british-affair (last accessed 6 December 2022).

[26] C Baker-Beall and G Mott, 'The New Counter-Terrorism Agenda: Pre-emptive Security Through the Anticipation of Terrorist Events' (2021) 7(5) *Global Affairs* 711.

[27] Directive 2006/24/EC of the European Parliament and of the Council of 15 March 2006 on the retention of data generated or processed in connection with the provision of publicly available electronic communications services or of public communications networks and amending Directive 2002/58/EC [2006] OJ L105/54; Directive (EU) 2016/681 of the European Parliament and of the Council of 27 April 2016 on the use of passenger name record (PNR) data for the prevention, detection, investigation and prosecution of terrorist offences and serious crime [2016] OJ L119/132 MacKenzie (n 22) 1; A Ripoll Servent, *Institutional and Policy Change in the European Parliament – Deciding on Freedom, Security, and Justice* (Palgrave Macmillan, 2015).

[28] HM Government 'The UK's Co-operation With the EU on Justice and Home Affairs, and on Foreign Policy and Security Issues' (9 May 2016) available at https://assets.publishing.service.gov.uk/government/uploads/system/uploads/attachment_data/file/521926/The_UK_s_cooperation_with_the_EU_on_justice_and_home_affairs__and_on_foreign_policy_and_security_issues.pdf (last accessed 6 December 2022).

[29] Mortera-Martinez (n 25).

[30] HM Government 'Decision Pursuant to Article 10(5) of Protocol 36 to the Treaty on the Functioning of the European Union' (July 2014) available at https://assets.publishing.service.gov.uk/government/uploads/system/uploads/attachment_data/file/326698/41670_Cm_8897_Accessible.pdf (last accessed 29 March 2023).

[31] Council Decision 2008/615/JHA of 23 June 2008 on the stepping up of cross-border co-operation, particularly in combating terrorism and cross-border crime [2008] OJ L210/1.

[32] United Kingdom and European Union (n 5).

To summarise, the UK has swayed between European cooperation, on the one hand, and concerns about national sovereignty, on the other, for decades. Even so, fairly consistently for the past 50 years at least, London has attempted to find ways to cooperate more deeply on counterterrorism with other European states as an issue of particular concern to it, albeit within certain parameters. 9/11 and subsequent attacks, combined with the pro-European Labour Government of Tony Blair, pushed the UK to become more active in the EU. By contrast, the Conservative Party after 2010 was strongly Eurosceptic in composition and reduced its involvement in EU JHA to a handpicked set of measures. Still, the UK had negotiated a unique – and perhaps even desirable – position for itself in the EU by 2016. In comparison, we can see that the TCA was a substantial downgrade as regards security cooperation in general and counter-terrorism in particular. Nevertheless, given the red lines on both sides, the result 'arguably represents the best result that could have been achieved in the circumstances', noticeably due to the UK's insistence on the exclusion of the Court of Justice of the European Union.[33]

## IV. Fighting Terrorism under the TCA and Beyond

This final section further investigates the TCA and its consequences, especially how the UK is planning to address the adverse effects of Brexit in the future. Furthermore, it considers the likelihood of enhancement of existing cooperation amidst foreseeable obstacles. It seems probable that Boris Johnson's Government negotiated whatever could be done in the time available, believing that it would always be possible to build from this platform in the future. Rishi Sunak's Government was mostly pro-Brexit, although more conciliatory towards the EU than those that preceded it. Indeed, the negotiation of the Windsor Framework in relation to Northern Ireland in February 2023 signalled a thaw in EU–UK relations.[34] Several commentators have attempted to propose ways in which the UK might improve on the TCA, whether through a new 'affiliate' EU membership, an incremental approach or even the UK's unilaterally adjusting to make existing mechanisms work better.[35] However, some of these proposals look like 'cakeism', meaning that the EU would surely reject them were they to become official British objectives.[36] Moreover, whereas the Northern Ireland Protocol impacted on an EU Member State (the Republic of Ireland), there is now far less appetite in Brussels to engage with the UK given that any talks will be mainly about improving the latter's terms. The trade deal continues to be advantageous to the EU, and since the vote to leave in 2016, the UK has not always looked like a trustworthy partner but more like a country that adopted hardball tactics that did not reflect its inferior and now further-diminished status.[37] We

[33] P Arnell et al, 'Police Cooperation and Exchange of Information Under the EU-UK Trade and Co-operation Agreement' (2021) 12(2) *New Journal of European Criminal Law* 267.

[34] HM Government, *The Windsor Framework: A New Way Forward* (CP 806, 2023).

[35] J Rutter, 'The UK Can't Improve its Brexit Deal Without EU Agreement' *Institute for Government* (21 December 2022) available at www.instituteforgovernment.org.uk/comment/uk-brexit-deal-eu-agreement (last accessed 31 March 2023).

[36] A Glencross, 'The Origins of "Cakeism": The British Think Tank Debate Over Repatriating Sovereignty and its Impact on the UK's Brexit Strategy' (2023) 30(6) *Journal of European Public Policy* 995.

[37] B Martill and U Staiger, 'Negotiating Brexit: The Cultural Sources of British Hard Bargaining' (2021) 59(2) *Journal of Common Market Studies* 2611.

have already seen the UK attempting to cooperate with EU Member States bilaterally, and over 20 declarations have now been signed.[38] However, such efforts will likely prove time-consuming and complicated. A further possibility is the creation of new fora for cooperation involving many Member States, as well as the EU, in the years to come.

The House of Lords Select Committee on the European Union appears to believe that there is only one way in which the TCA could – in a minor way – improve on what the UK possessed prior to Brexit. London spent the best part of a decade attempting to push other Member States to adopt an EU PNR instrument, albeit primarily because it agreed not to collect what was then intra-EU data until there was a European measure. In terms of importance, continued access to PNR data after Brexit was considered almost on par with SIS II.[39] With the TCA, the UK is now a third state and might even have opportunities for extension of the uses of PNR data.[40] Yet other problems complicate this, such as loss of interest in several Member States since agreement on EU PNR in 2016,[41] the need for the UK to maintain data protection legislation that is considered 'adequate' by the EU, and the future issues of changing standards and agreements with other states where UK data might be shared.

Other aspects of cooperation have remained similar, such as those related to the Prüm Convention. This allows continued access to the DNA, fingerprint and vehicle registration data of the parties. However, the UK is sensitive to change here, in that it may not be able to influence in the ways that were possible previously.[42]

In most other areas, the UK has been downgraded. The greatest loss has long been considered SIS II, which allows real-time access to sensitive information.[43] The access given to the UK in 2015 was viewed as a 'game-changer' by law enforcement authorities in the UK, granting them 66 million records with which to work.[44] Yet the UK illegally made copies of the database in the years after 2016, much to the frustration of other EU actors.[45] The need to obtain capabilities similar to SIS II in a future agreement was frequently stated by the British Government during 2020.[46] After failing to do so in the TCA, London opted for use of Interpol's I-24/7 system, although this 'falls a long way short of the benefits provided by SIS II'.[47] At the same time, the system is considered 'sufficient' and at least provides a 'platform'.[48] Two problems have especially been

[38] Ministry of Defence, 'UK and Poland Strengthen Foreign Policy, Security, and Defence Co-operation' *gov.uk* (5 July 2023) available at www.gov.uk/government/news/uk-and-poland-strengthen-foreign-policy-security-and-defence-cooperation (last accessed 2 October 2023).

[39] T May, 'Home Secretary's Speech on the UK, EU, and Our Place in the World' *gov.uk* (25 April 2016) available at www.gov.uk/government/speeches/home-secretarys-speech-on-the-uk-eu-and-our-place-in-the-world (last accessed 31 March 2023).

[40] House of Lords, 'Chapter 3: Future UK-EU Sharing of Law Enforcement and Criminal Justice Data' *Parliament.uk* (26 March 2021) available at https://publications.parliament.uk/pa/ld5801/ldselect/ldeucom/250/25006.htm#_idTextAnchor055 (last accessed 31 March 2023).

[41] N Nielsen 'EU States Losing Interest in Anti-Terror Law'. *Euobserver* (7 September 2018) available at https://euobserver.com/rule-of-law/142767 (last accessed 1 April 2023).

[42] House of Lords (n 40).

[43] See Pearson, ch 6.

[44] ibid.

[45] N Nielsen, 'UK Taking "Steps" After Illegal Copying of EU Schengen Data' *Euobserver* (25 July 2019) available at https://euobserver.com/rule-of-law/145530 (last accessed 31 March 2023).

[46] House of Lords (n 40).

[47] Ibid.

[48] ibid.

emphasised by authorities here: first, dependence on EU Member States' 'double keying' records and data (ie once into SIS II and a second time into the I-24/7 system) and efforts to persuade them to do so; and, second, ensuring prompt availability of the data, which was not possible in real time but could be done in hours and perhaps be accelerated in the future.[49] Building on this, the UK is in discussions with the EU about setting up an International Law Enforcement Alerts Platform (I-LEAP), with the objective of achieving reciprocal data exchange for law enforcement authorities. The UK hopes to be able to access EU systems by 2027 or 2028.[50] Yet how the UK will attempt to persuade the EU to grant these permissions is unclear. A Commission proposal on the issue is expected at some point in the future, although this does not appear to have materialised by the time of writing.[51] A similar story applies to ECRIS, where the UK has had to rebuild its infrastructure from the ground to share criminal records data, which was originally called 'UKRIS'. Here, police authorities have experienced some complications that did not exist prior to the TCA.[52]

Cooperation with EU agencies, Europol and Eurojust, and the new extradition or 'surrender' provisions are also noticeably inferior than was the case prior to Brexit. When it comes to the agencies, the UK has secured arrangements comparable to other third states, such as the US and Canada, but there is the possibility for these relationships to develop further in the future. A major loss here is no longer being on the management boards of Europol and Eurojust, meaning that the UK will have great difficulty in influencing strategic decisions.[53] On the issue of the new surrender arrangements, there seems to have been some replication of EAW arrangements, yet many EU Member States have invoked constitutional rules not to extradite their citizens to the UK, rendering agreement here imbalanced.[54]

Before moving on to foreseeable obstacles, it is worth addressing counter-terrorism financing. Given that this is a shared goal and that the UK was previously vocal in support of such measures, one might expect this to be relatively uncontroversial. Yet there are problems here, too, given that the UK exited an established framework and also the Brexiteer desire for innovation in the financial sector.[55] London's divergence could be seen as beginning in 2018, when it chose to opt out of the EU's sixth Anti-Money

[49] ibid.

[50] Home Office, 'International Law Enforcement Alerts Platform (I-LEAP) Programme' *gov.uk* (12 May 2023) available at www.gov.uk/government/publications/home-office-major-programmes-accounting-officer-assessments/international-law-enforcement-alerts-platform-i-leap-programme (last accessed 31 March 2023).

[51] R Syal, 'UK Police and Border Force to Remain Locked Out of EU Database on Criminals' *The Guardian* (1 March 2023) available at www.theguardian.com/politics/2023/mar/01/uk-police-and-border-force-to-remain-locked-out-of-eu-database-of-criminals (last accessed 31 March 2023).

[52] House of Lords (n 40).

[53] House of Lords, 'Chapter 4: Future UK Involvement in EU Law Enforcement and Criminal Justice Agencies'. *Parliament.uk* (26 March 2021) available at https://publications.parliament.uk/pa/ld5801/ldselect/ldeucom/250/25007.htm#_idTextAnchor074 (last accessed 1 April 2023).

[54] House of Lords, 'Chapter 5: The Extradition Provisions'. *Parliament.uk* (26 March 2021) available at https://publications.parliament.uk/pa/ld5801/ldselect/ldeucom/250/25008.htm#_idTextAnchor082 (last accessed 1 April 2023).

[55] T Keatinge, 'Financial Crime and Brexit: Can We Agree on Nothing?' *Royal United Services Institute* (11 June 2020) available at https://rusi.org/explore-our-research/publications/commentary/financial-crime-and-brexit-can-we-agree-nothing (last accessed 31 March 2023).

Laundering and Countering the Financing of Terrorism (AML/CFT) Directive not because of substantive disagreement, but due to the British Government's belief that it had already gone further.[56] Crucial in EU AML/CFT efforts is data sharing between Member State Financial Intelligence Units (FIUs), and plans are afoot to enhance such ties.[57] With Brexit, the relationships between the UK FIU and those of the EU Member States have changed because of the different regulatory environments. Although the TCA commits both sides to cooperation on AML/CFT, it says nothing about how information will continue to be shared. Clearly, the UK has now lost access to EU channels, such as the FIU.net network. So this means that new, untested mechanisms will need to be established or less formal cooperation will have to be relied on. There are some fallback options, such as the Warsaw Convention on Laundering, Seizure and Confiscation of the Proceeds from Crime and on the Financing of Terrorism and the Egmont Group, but these are as described – fallbacks.[58] The UK's lack of input into the EU and divergence between the two partners will almost inevitably lead to new gaps in the years to come, but will also complicate in other ways, including what constitutes admissible evidence, investigations and more.[59]

Mitsilegas and Guild posit constitutional issues, regulatory divergence and mutual trust, and benchmarks for collaboration as the current challenges facing British participation in police and criminal justice cooperation after Brexit.[60] To this, we will add political will on both sides, which will change with governments. Historically, many Brexiteers were concerned about how British membership of the EU would affect the UK's constitution, meaning that any new arrangements will inevitably face scrutiny of this kind in Westminster. We have also seen how being outside the EU limits what is possible when it comes to extradition or the new 'surrender' arrangements; after all, some states will not extradite their citizens to non-EU states.

Moving on to divergence, some in the UK are keen to take advantage of what are supposedly new-found post-Brexit freedoms, such as regarding artificial intelligence, but maintenance of data protection legislation deemed 'adequate' by Brussels remains necessary. If the UK fails in this, the EU could terminate data sharing for security purposes and more, which would be disastrous for the UK. On occasion, legislation will need updating. Indeed, the EU's 1995 Data Protection Directive was viewed as being out of date given technological change and so was replaced by the General Data Protection Regulation in 2016.[61] In this way, the UK could end up being a rule-taker.

[56] Directive 2018/1673 of the European Parliament and of the Council of 23 October 2018 on combating money laundering by criminal law [2018] OJ L284/22; A Grignon and C Ascione Le Dréau, 'Anti-Money Laundering and Counter Terrorist Financing Under the EU-UK Trade and Co-operation Agreement' (2021) 12(2) *New Journal of European Criminal Law* 284.

[57] F Mouzakiti, 'Cooperation between Financial Intelligence Units in the European Union: Stuck in the Middle Between the General Data Protection Regulation and the Police Data Protection Directive' (2020) 11(3) *New Journal of European Criminal Law* 351.

[58] Council of Europe, Convention on Laundering, Search, Seizure and Confiscation of the Proceeds from Crime and on the Financing of Terrorism, No 198.

[59] Grignon and Ascione Le Dréau (n 56) 288-9.

[60] Mitsilegas and Guild (n 6) 2519.

[61] Directive 95/46/EC of the European Parliament and of the Council of 24 October 1995 on the protection of individuals with regard to the processing of personal data and on the free movement of such data [1995] OJ L281/31; Regulation (EU) of the European Parliament and of the Council of 27 April 2016 on the protection of natural persons with regard to the processing of personal data and on the free movement of such data, and repealing Directive 95/46/EC (General Data Protection Regulation) [2016] OJ L119/1.

Dealing now with mutual trust and benchmarks, the UK's Human Rights Act 1998 gives effect to the European Convention on Human Rights (ECHR).[62] This has long been criticised by a wing of the Conservative Party. May even advocated leaving the ECHR in the run up to the UK's EU referendum.[63] Such a move in the future, however, would place the UK in a difficult position given that the TCA is undergirded by continued participation in the ECHR.[64] Thus, any efforts in this direction would provide yet another reason for the EU to terminate security cooperation with the UK. The Illegal Migration Act 2023 raised the prospect of the UK's leaving the ECHR, and Home Secretary Suella Braverman refused to state whether it is compatible with the Convention.[65] In the end, the UK looks bound to the EU if it wants cooperation to continue, never mind improve.

Finally, only by building on the positive momentum stemming from the recent Windsor Framework can a better relationship with the EU be forged in the future. This moves us on to political will. The British population appears to be slowly turning against Brexit; and in any event, there was never the hostility in the general population that some Brexiteers showed towards the EU. Consequently, we are likely to see more diplomatic politicians come to the fore in the UK in the short term. That probably bodes well for a desire to improve EU-UK relations. However, why should the EU adjust this asymmetrical deal? Although Brexit was painful and regrettable for many in Brussels, renegotiating the TCA is not currently a priority for the EU.[66] It is keen to move on and face up to other serious global challenges, such as working with a cooperative US, facing down Russia and tackling climate change.

## V. Conclusion – Two Steps Forward, One Step Back?

Terrorism has probably figured more highly on the UK's security agenda than that of most other European states over the last five or more decades. Historically, the UK was often at the forefront of efforts to strengthen European counterterrorism cooperation. However, the EU was not seriously involved in the issue until the aftermath of 9/11 – an event that led to rapid and serious changes. Over the years, the EU's abilities have been enhanced further, to the point that the Union is now a major component of not only European counterterrorism cooperation but internal security more generally. Despite the advantageous position that the UK held in the organisation, membership of the EU was a divisive issue in British society that ended up trumping other interests.

The TCA maintains a fair amount of EU–UK cooperation relevant to terrorism, although the UK's access to the EU's security ecosystem has overall been downgraded. Given the consistency of the UK's commitment to combating terrorism with partners

[62] Council of Europe, European Convention on Human Rights (2 October 2013) available at www.echr.coe.int/documents/d/echr/convention_eng (last accessed 9 January 2025).

[63] May (n 39).

[64] See Mallory, ch 16.

[65] B Quinn, 'What are the Legal Obstacles Faced by the UK's Illegal Migration Bill' *The Guardian* (8 March 2023) available at www.theguardian.com/uk-news/2023/mar/08/what-are-the-legal-obstacles-faced-by-the-uks-migration-bill-suella-braverman (last accessed 1 April 2023).

[66] J Rutter, 'It Takes Two to Renegotiate a Trade Deal – as Keir Starmer Will Discover With the EU' *Institute for Government* (21 September 2023) available at www.instituteforgovernment.org.uk/comment/renegotiate-brexit-keir-starmer (last accessed 3 November 2023).

and the need to provide security for citizens, what can be done to address Brexit-related losses? As we show in this chapter, at present, London appears to be trying to compensate in different ways. It may be possible to partly address some vulnerabilities through new domestic measures, yet these cannot overcome major external obstacles. The UK thus needs to: first, sustain the improvement in ties across the Channel initiated by the Windsor Framework, above all with a focus on rebuilding trust given the damage done by Rishi Sunak's predecessors; second, ensure that it has a way of keeping terrorism on the EU's radar and maintain some kind of alignment on threats and solutions; and, third, ensure that it can improve on its current situation of slower access to less European data than it enjoyed previously. The optimal way to strengthen ties, enhance UK strategic and other influence, and build trust would appear to be to establish a new EU–UK forum that meets regularly, yet something similar was rebuffed by London in mid-2023 for fear of seeming too cosy with Brussels.[67] This decision looked petty and based on concerns mainly within the Conservative Party, although nothing is preventing future governments from creating bodies to support stronger EU–UK cooperation. The UK might also want to try to find ways to obtain more influence in the EU agencies, although there are no precedents here. Clearly, there are already efforts afoot by the UK to set up new data-sharing platforms, which will be necessary, yet tough negotiations, imagination, persuasion and reciprocal benefits will be needed. These will never be allowed to confer on the UK the same benefits enjoyed by the Member States either. Finally, the UK will have to be cautious, transparent and communicative as to how it diverges from the EU in the future in several areas. Some Brexiteers hoped to leave the ECHR and have a 'bonfire' of regulations. Many of these objectives will likely never be realised because doing so would jeopardise the TCA. Yet, ultimately, what we are involved in here is finding ways to repair EU–UK relations as far as possible after Brexit. Without genuine attempts to do so, citizens on both sides will be the main losers. Short of a UK move to rejoin the EU, cooperation seems likely to improve only marginally in the foreseeable future, but what can the UK offer to persuade the EU even to engage, never mind to devote time and resources primarily for the benefit of the former? What will be the quid pro quo of any such negotiations? There is much for London to ponder.

[67] P Foster, G Parker and A Bounds, 'UK Rebuffs EU Offer for Strategic Dialogue' *Financial Times* (27 July 2023) available at www.ft.com/content/1147fc63-59f9-45c3-aee2-a15ee570bb84 (last accessed 3 November 2023).

# 18

# Fighting Organised Crime under the Trade and Cooperation Agreement

DANIELA IRRERA

## I. Introduction

This chapter maps the evolving nature of the security landscape across Europe, and thus the need for the European Union (EU) and the United Kingdom (UK) to adapt their cooperation accordingly in the fight against organised crime. Although the Trade and Cooperation Agreement (TCA)[1] represents a significant step in externalising the EU's police and judicial cooperation framework, it lacks a clear framework for effectively addressing the multifaceted global and regional security challenges the UK and EU face from organised crime.

The chapter is divided into three main sections. Section II considers the development of organised crime policy as a matter of internal concern for the EU. Section III provides an overview of the key provisions relating to cross-border cooperation in the TCA, and demonstrates how this internalisation of organised crime policy has resulted in provisions that focus on police and judicial cooperation but are thin on policy coordination in the field of organised crime. Section IV assesses the main security threats, including organised crime, terrorism, insurgency and radicalisation. The interconnections between these threats and the extent to which organised crime can fund or support other security challenges are investigated. This highlights the need for much greater UK–EU cooperation than currently provided for. In section V, the chapter concludes by exploring the need for a broader policy framework to enhance cooperation in addressing these security threats. In particular, it is suggested that the existing provisions in the TCA may need to be amended or expanded to accommodate a more comprehensive approach to security, involving foreign and defence policies. This could involve creating new mechanisms for intelligence sharing, joint security operations and collaborative efforts to combat cross-border threats effectively.

[1] Trade and Cooperation Agreement between the European Union and the European Atomic Energy Community, on the one part and the United Kingdom of Great Britain and Northern Ireland, on the other part [2020] OJ L444/14, available at https://eur-lex.europa.eu/legal-content/EN/TXT/PDF/?uri=CELEX:22020A1231(01).

## II. The Development of EU Policy on Organised Crime

### A. Organised Crime as a Global Security Threat

Organised crime poses a multifaceted threat to security on various levels, encompassing local, national and even global scales. The Westphalian nation-state has historically held a dominant position in the global political landscape. For centuries, it served as the primary actor, shaping foreign policy and influencing global decision making. This dominance persisted through the tumultuous periods between the two World Wars and into the Cold War era.[2] However, the dynamics of international relations began to shift notably in the 1960s and 1970s. During this time, states began to acknowledge the emergence of new and diverse actors on the international stage. These actors, with their distinct requirements and demands, asserted themselves and sought inclusion in global affairs. The processes of globalisation played a significant role in fuelling the rise of these non-state actors. As the world became increasingly interconnected and interdependent, collective approaches to addressing global challenges became imperative. The traditional paradigm of state-centric decision making gave way to a more inclusive model that recognised the importance of involving various stakeholders in problem resolution. The globalisation of issues and problems presents a significant challenge to the traditional sovereignty of nation-states. In response, some states may find themselves compelled to retreat, either partially or substantially, from their sovereignty in favour of collaboration with non-state actors. This shift can facilitate the achievement of major goals and promote democratic principles and pluralism, particularly when working with positive non-state actors.

Positive non-state actors, such as non-governmental organisations, civil society organisations and advocacy groups, often contribute valuable expertise, resources and perspectives to address global challenges. Their involvement can enrich decision-making processes and enhance the effectiveness of initiatives aimed at promoting peace, development and human rights. However, the dynamics change when dealing with subversive non-state actors, such as criminal organisations, terrorist groups or paramilitaries. Unlike positive actors, these groups operate outside the bounds of law and morality. They may have territorial bases within states but transcend national borders, wielding significant influence on the global stage. Their actions, driven by illegal or subversive motives, pose serious threats to security, stability and the rule of law. Engaging with such non-state actors presents a complex dilemma. While dialogue and cooperation may be necessary to address underlying grievances and mitigate conflict, legitimising their activities risks undermining the integrity of national institutions and legal frameworks. The autonomy and clandestine nature of these groups make them inherently difficult to control or regulate through traditional means. In navigating this challenge, effective governance and

[2] D Roberts, 'War and the historical formation of States' in M Banks and M Shaw (eds), *State and Society in International Relations* (Wheatsheaf Publishing, 1991) 143.

international cooperation are vital in countering the negative influence of uncivil actors while fostering a conducive environment for constructive dialogue and collective action.[3]

One notable shift is the blurring of boundaries between internal and external threats. Traditional state-based conflicts have given way to complex civil conflicts that transcend national borders and involve a myriad of actors, including non-state groups, insurgent movements and criminal organisations. These conflicts are often fuelled by underlying grievances related to governance, economic inequality and identity politics, rather than conventional territorial disputes. The concept of security extends beyond the traditional military realm to encompass a broader range of threats, including terrorism, cyber attacks, transnational crime and environmental degradation. These non-traditional security challenges pose significant risks to global stability and require multifaceted responses that go beyond military solutions. Weak, collapsed or failed states have emerged as focal points of insecurity, serving as breeding grounds for extremism, organised crime and humanitarian crises. Institutional fragility, lack of rule of law, and economic underdevelopment exacerbate internal tensions and contribute to the proliferation of wars characterised by asymmetrical violence and protracted conflicts.[4]

The intertwining of organised crime groups with armed conflict poses a significant challenge to security that extends far beyond the traditional military dimension. In conflict zones characterised by deprivation and institutional weakness, organised crime thrives, exploiting the power vacuum and profiting from illicit activities such as drug trafficking, human trafficking and arms smuggling. These criminal networks often forge alliances with fighters, whether they are rebel groups, terrorist organisations or local paramilitaries, in order to further their own interests and expand their influence. By operating in the 'grey zones' of conflict where governance is weak and law enforcement is ineffective, they can manipulate and exploit the situation to their advantage.

These considerations can be complemented by empirical data provided by the criminality score, measured within *The Global Organized Crime Index*. This data provides a quantitative measure of criminal markets and actors, offering insights into the varying degrees of this nexus across different geographical areas.[5] The definition of organised crime within the Index encompasses a range of illegal activities coordinated by groups or networks with the aim of obtaining financial or material benefits, either directly or indirectly. Organised crime can occur both within a single country's borders and across international boundaries, reflecting its transnational nature and the interconnectedness of criminal operations on a global scale (see Figure 18.1).

[3] JN Rosenau, *Turbulence in World Politics: A Theory of Change and Continuity* (Harvester Wheatsheaf, 1990).

[4] K Holsti, *The State, War, and the State of War* (Cambridge University Press, 1996).

[5] In *The Global Organized Crime Index*, criminal actors are mafia-style groups, criminal networks, state-embedded actors and foreign actors, whereas criminal markets are human trafficking, human smuggling, arms trafficking, flora and fauna crimes, non-renewable resource crimes, and the heroin, cocaine, cannabis and synthetic drug trade.

**Figure 18.1** The impact of criminality in various regions

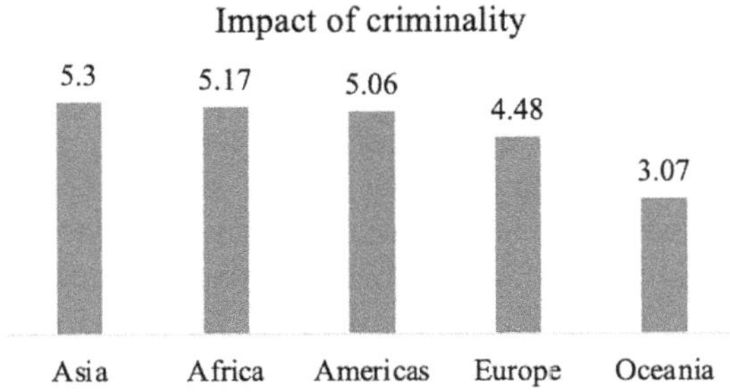


*Source: The Global Organized Crime Index 2021.*[6]

The high impact of non-state armed conflict in certain regions correlates with elevated levels of criminality, as evidenced by the findings of the Index. Specifically, Asia demonstrates the highest overall levels of criminality, with a score of 5.30 out of 10, closely followed by Africa (5.17) and the Americas (5.06). However, the data underscores also that criminality can affect consolidated democracies like European countries. This impact may manifest in various ways, including serving as a traditional base for criminal activities or as a significant transit area for criminal operations. The challenges posed by criminality extend to both national states and regional and international institutions, presenting a dual-level threat. On one hand, criminality undermines the state's capacity to ensure the security and safety of its citizens. On the other hand, it also hampers the ability of regional and international institutions to effectively manage and regulate cross-border flows of illicit activities.[7]

The consequences of this convergence between organised crime and armed conflict are profound. Not only does it fuel violence and instability, but it also undermines the efforts to establish peace and rebuild societies. Criminal groups undermine the rule of law, perpetuate corruption and erode trust in state institutions, making it difficult to achieve sustainable peace and development.

## B. Tackling Organised Crime within the EU Context

In 2000, the European Council of Santa Maria de Feira outlined several priorities for Justice and Home Affairs (JHA) cooperation, indicative of a comprehensive approach to addressing various challenges, both within and beyond the EU's borders. They included migration, terrorism, specific forms of crime and drug trafficking, as well as the development and consolidation of the rule of law in countries on the path to democracy. Justice and Home Affairs developed as a complex framework in which distinctive instruments are used to strengthen security across the EU. The development of cooperation mechanisms has sat alongside broader dialogue about the

[6] Global Initiative against Transnational Organized Crime, *The Global Organized Crime Index 2021*, available at https://globalinitiative.net/analysis/ocindex-2021/ (last accessed 30 April 2024).

[7] D Irrera, 'Criminality and Delinquency: The Impact on Regional and Global Security' in A Gruszczak and S Kaempf (eds), *Routledge Handbook of the Future of Warfare* (Routledge, 2024) 284.

significance of organised crime as a serious threat. Organised crime offered a paradigmatic example of how the internal and external dimensions of JHA intersected and at times conflicted. Research on the internal dimensions of security within the EU focused on how competences and resources are distributed within the EU's multi-level governance system, dealing with the allocation of responsibilities and the availability of resources.[8] Assessments of how well EU institutions function in addressing JHA concerns, including organised crime, are important for understanding the EU's effectiveness in tackling these challenges. The role of Member States in promoting and sustaining efficient cooperation in JHA has also been examined. Member States play a significant role in shaping EU policies and implementing measures, so their engagement is crucial for success. Studies have explained that the development of the JHA framework within the EU has been characterised as a slow and gradual process, due to the complexities of harmonising legal systems and policies across multiple Member States.[9] The balance between the supranational dimension (EU-level decision making) and the intergovernmental one (Member States' national sovereignty) has been a challenging aspect of JHA development. When it comes to the context of cooperation in criminal matters, measures relating to police and judicial cooperation, including those within the Schengen Agreement,[10] have been introduced to strengthen law enforcement and tackle cross-border crime.[11]

The compromise on JHA as an independent pillar within the EU was solidified by the signing of the Maastricht Treaty in 1992.[12] This marked a significant step in recognising the importance of addressing organised crime and other security threats as common interests for EU Member States. Its evolution towards the Area of Freedom, Security and Justice (AFSJ) and the recognition of organised crime as a serious threat reflects the ongoing commitment to ensuring the security and stability of the EU and its Member States. For example, the establishment of agencies like Europol and Eurojust, along with a formal definition of organised crime and a recognition of organised crime as a main priority during the completion of the Treaty of Amsterdam,[13] marked a crucial phase in the development of European anti-organised crime policies and the evolution of JHA.[14] Changes in the security landscape, due to the rise of globalisation and the interconnectedness of the global economy and society, have significantly influenced the JHA agenda, requiring better cooperation for tackling new security challenges, including transnational organised crime.

[8] M Smith, 'Toward a theory of EU foreign policy-making: multi-level governance, domestic politics, and national adaptation to Europe's common foreign and security policy' (2004) 11(4) *Journal of European Public Policy* 740.

[9] J Monar, 'Justice and Home Affairs' (2005) 43 *Journal of Common Market Studies* 131.

[10] The Schengen acquis – Convention implementing the Schengen Agreement of 14 June 1985 between the Governments of the States of the Benelux Economic Union, the Federal Republic of Germany and the French Republic on the gradual abolition of checks at their common borders [2000] OJ L239/19.

[11] W Rees, 'Transnational organized crime, security and the European Union' in F Allum and R Siebert (eds), *Organised Crime and the Challenge to Democracy* (Routledge, 2004) 100–11.

[12] Treaty of the European Union [1992] OJ C191/1.

[13] Treaty of Amsterdam amending the Treaty on European Union, the Treaties establishing the European Communities and certain related acts [1997] OJ C340/1.

[14] M Den Boer, 'The Fight against Organised Crime in Europe: A Comparative Perspective' (2001) 9 *European Journal on Criminal Policy and Research* 259.

Whereas migration and terrorism have been particular drivers of the EU's external dimension of JHA,[15] organised crime has been a key driver for developing the internal dimension.[16] The focus of organised crime policies within the EU was primarily to enhance cooperation among Member States, and to strengthen collaborative efforts to combat organised crime across EU borders, in relation to law enforcement agencies and the judicial system. In other words, such policies are designed and implemented with the primary goal of addressing organised crime within the EU and promoting internal security. They are not intended to be a set of norms or policies to be exported or applied outside the EU.[17]

Other studies, however, have illustrated how the internal and external dimensions of security cooperation can interact. These dimensions may coexist, coordinate or overlap, leading to diverse intersections that contribute to the complexity of security challenges and responses.[18] Research also indicates that certain policy domains, including asylum, terrorism and organised crime, affect both internal and external dimensions. This is because the EU is involved in internal coordination as well as external relations with non-EU countries regarding these matters.[19] This is particularly pertinent given that organised crime is often interconnected and intertwined with other security threats, such as terrorism, political violence and instability. The evolving nature of global security threats necessitates adapted tools and policies to address organised crime in a more comprehensive manner. While the Common Security and Defence Policy (CSDP) and the Common Foreign and Security Policy (CFSP) encompass elements of organised crime, these security issues were traditionally viewed as part of the JHA domain. The overlapping nature of various policies and practices reflects the current globalised landscape of security threats.[20] The fact that one of the primary challenges to the JHA agenda comes from internal security developments is consistent with the expansion of the global actorness of the EU and its role as a security provider. Factors within a country or region can present challenges to the JHA policies and initiatives. These may encompass domestic security concerns, shifts in political or social dynamics, or emerging threats within the EU or a particular country. The intersection of organised crime with other subversive actors, such as terrorist groups, suggests that organised crime and terrorism are not entirely distinct but may share common elements or objectives. Dealing with this intersection requires adjusting security practices and coordinating policies to address both organised crime and terrorism effectively. More recently, visible linkages between organised crime and militant Islamist cells throughout Europe and its

[15] S Hutchinson and P O'Malley, 'A crime–terror nexus? Thinking on some of the links between terrorism and criminality' (2007) 30(12) *Studies in Conflict and Terrorism* 1095; B Hoffman, 'Terrorism Trends and Prospects' in IO Lesser et al (eds), *Countering the New Terrorism* (RAND Corporation, 1999) 7.

[16] V Felbab-Brown, 'The crime-terror Nexus and its fallacies' in E Chenoweth (ed), *The Oxford Handbook of Terrorism* (Oxford University Press, 2019) 366.

[17] C Dishman, 'The leaderless nexus: When crime and terror converge' (2005) 28(3) *Studies in Conflict and Terrorism* 237.

[18] H Carrapico, D Irrera and B Tupman, 'Transnational organised crime and terrorism: different peas, same pod?' (2014) 15(3-4) *Global Crime* 213.

[19] A Alesina, S Piccolo and P Pinotti, 'Organized Crime, Violence, and Politics' (2019) 86(2) *The Review of Economic Studies* 457.

[20] S Sweeney and N Winn, 'Do or die? The UK, the EU, and internal/external security cooperation after Brexit' (2022) 21(2) *European Political Science* 237.

periphery have represented a growing concern for the internal and external dimensions of security. De-radicalisation policies, for example, deal with domestic contexts but also require cross-border coordination for tackling the sources and routes of the phenomenon that goes beyond the European territory.[21] The complex and interconnected nature of security challenges is, therefore, urgently creating the need to adapt policies, practices and norms. Fighting against organised crime, both at the domestic and European level, has turned into a more multilayered and cross-sectoral effort. As will be discussed in the following sections, the TCA has not taken this into account.

Prior to Brexit, the fight against organised crime was a shared priority among EU Member States, including the UK. The EU developed various mechanisms and initiatives to address organised crime, in which the UK actively participated. The cooperation focused on legislative measures, law enforcement cooperation, information sharing, financial measures and cross-border cooperation. While the UK's decision to leave the EU has led to changes in its relationship with EU law enforcement agencies and frameworks, efforts to combat organised crime remain a priority for both.

## III. Cooperation on Organised Crime within the TCA

The TCA has been conceived as a comprehensive and complex treaty that addresses various aspects of trade and cooperation between the EU and the UK, which prevented some of the more serious negative implications of the UK's exit from the EU. International agreements of significant magnitude often raise various legal issues and considerations. The TCA process of negotiating, drafting and implementing the Agreement has involved extensive legal work to address these issues. Legal experts, policymakers and diplomats have been committed to making the Agreement achieve the intended goals of ensuring a smooth departure, while respecting the legal and political realities of the parties involved.[22] The EU mandate for negotiating the TCA initially included not only law enforcement and criminal justice, but also foreign policy, security and defence.[23] In foreign policy and defence matters, joint efforts would require the EU and the UK to align their positions on various international issues, engage in diplomatic efforts together and strengthen security regarding shared security threats. Therefore, the EU's security mandate for the TCA negotiations aimed for a broad and multifaceted partnership with the UK going beyond just law enforcement and judicial cooperation. Legal scholars have observed how certain aspects of the TCA create and consolidate a parallel legal framework that is not necessarily connected to EU legislation but instead builds upon international conventions.[24] Cooperation in criminal matters, as set out in Part Three, is no exception. This framework is distinct from EU legislation and builds on

[21] Dishman (n 13).

[22] S Peers, 'So close, yet so far: the EU/UK trade and cooperation agreement' (2022) 59(1) *Common Market Law Review* 49.

[23] Sweeney and Winn (n 16).

[24] A Bennett and D Vines, 'The EU–UK trade and cooperation agreement: Lessons learnt' (2022) 38(1) *Oxford Review of Economic Policy* 68; C Eckes and P Leino-Sandberg, 'The 'EU-UK Trade and Cooperation Agreement'–exceptional circumstances or a new paradigm for EU external relations?' (2022) 85(1) *Modern Law Review* 164.

international conventions, making the legal landscape complex, with elements of international, EU and national law all coming into play.

For instance, extradition arrangements and asset freezing and confiscation procedures between the EU and the UK are regulated by the stipulations outlined in the TCA concerning mutual legal assistance and the sharing of criminal record data. However, it is essential to note that these provisions are not standalone but are rooted in the Council of Europe Conventions established by individual Member States. These Conventions, often ratified with reservations, are typically implemented through national legislation. The EU also adopted several Framework Decisions and Directives in the areas covered by these Conventions, and Member States approved the necessary national legislation giving effect to EU measures. This complex landscape of international, EU and national norms is now supplemented by the provisions of the TCA.[25]

The loss of access to mechanisms such as the European Investigation Order and databases such as the Schengen Information System may result in a reduced level of support for UK police detectives and prosecutors. As shown in other chapters, this may affect their ability to collaborate with their EU counterparts in fighting serious and organised crime. Investigators will need to work on rebuilding mutual trust and confidence within the new arrangements. This suggests that the UK will need to carefully navigate its law enforcement relationships with EU partners under the new post-Brexit framework. Whilst loss of key cooperation mechanisms has been covered elsewhere in this volume,[26] there are aspects of cooperation in the TCA that are particularly relevant for organised crime and worthy of discussion. The TCA does not deliver any significant changes in approach to Anti-Money Laundering (AML) and Counter Terrorism Financing (CTF) initiatives. The UK and EU states will continue to cooperate and coordinate on cross-border criminal investigations and proceedings relating to the freezing and confiscation of assets.[27] The Agreement sets out detailed procedural requirements and criteria, standard formats and methods of delivery for such requests, and deadlines for compliance, which in substance are not materially different from those already in place.[28]

The TCA sets out additional commitments or obligations in certain areas such as climate change, weapons of mass destruction (WMDs), small arms and light weapons, serious crime and counterterrorism. Within these commitments, the text specifies that only the provisions relating to human rights, climate change and WMDs are designated as 'essential elements' of the partnership established by this Agreement.[29] By so designating these issues, the Agreement emphasises their central role in the partnership and underscores the seriousness with which the parties view these matters. Defining certain issues within an agreement as 'essential elements' typically implies that they are subject

[25] Draft text of the Agreement on the New Partnership with the United Kingdom, available at https://commission.europa.eu/system/files/2020-03/200318-draft-agreement-gen.pdf (last accessed 14 April 2024); TCA (n 1).

[26] See Carrapico and Davies, ch 1; Marks, ch 5; Conway, Deane and Hayward, ch 9; and Pearson, ch 6.

[27] V Mitsilegas and E Guild, 'Police and criminal justice co-operation after Brexit' (2023) 30(11) *Journal of European Public Policy* 1.

[28] M Shellaker, S Tong and P Swallow, 'UK–EU law enforcement cooperation post-Brexit: A UK law enforcement practitioner perspective' (2023) 24(2) *Criminology & Criminal Justice* 1; Mitsilegas and Guild (n 24).

[29] Draft text of the Agreement (n 21); TCA (n 1).

to a special procedure or mechanism within the Agreement. This special procedure is put in place to ensure that these critical issues receive special attention, monitoring, enforcement and dispute resolution. The purpose of having a special procedure for essential elements is to ensure that these critical issues receive the necessary attention and resources to address them effectively. It helps prioritise and underscore the significance of these issues within the broader context of the Agreement, emphasising the commitment of the parties to addressing them comprehensively and with greater scrutiny. One significant consequence of designating an issue as an 'essential element' is that it can lead to fast-track termination or suspension of the entire Agreement or parts of it. This means that if any party to the Agreement fails to meet its commitments in relation to these essential elements, there may be expedited processes for acting.

Therefore, while there are various commitments in the Agreement, only a select few, designated as 'essential elements', have a special status with potentially more stringent consequences if they are not upheld by the parties involved in the Agreement. This is a common feature in international agreements and trade agreements to ensure that key issues are given heightened attention and enforcement mechanisms. The most relevant deficiency in the TCA is, therefore, the fact that the external dimension of security is not covered. Such a dimension, as already noted, is essential for tackling the globalisation of actions and alliances that organised crime groups can achieve, and for adapting quickly to changes in the security landscape: if no significant amendment is made to the Agreement in the long term, it will continue to represent a serious limitation on the TCA goals.

## IV. Facing a Complex Security Landscape

The increasing influence of non-state actors in the security environment is a significant and complex trend that has transformed the dynamics of global and regional security. The concept of 'New Wars' has been a valuable framework for understanding these shifts and trends, particularly in the context of conflicts and security challenges that do not neatly align with traditional state-centric models. The 'New Wars' paradigm acknowledges that contemporary conflicts often involve non-state actors as primary actors or major players. These conflicts are characterised by factors such as blurred boundaries, hybrid warfare tactics, and a focus on identity, ethnicity and ideology. They differ from traditional inter-state wars in terms of their causes, actors and dynamics. This paradigm emphasises that security challenges and violence are not solely or even primarily dependent on states. Non-state actors, ranging from rebel groups and militias to transnational criminal organisations and terrorist networks, play a significant role in contemporary conflicts and security issues. These actors may challenge or weaken the authority and capacity of states. Non-state actors have a diverse impact on security environments. Some non-state actors aim to establish their own states, while others seek to disrupt the functioning of existing states. They can also be involved in criminal activities, terrorism and insurgency. The impact of non-state actors can vary from localised violence to global threats, making them a complex and dynamic element in the security landscape. Non-state actors often operate in ambiguous environments with blurred boundaries. They may use both conventional and subversive methods, and employ hybrid tactics that combine elements of military, political and informational warfare. This ambiguity makes it challenging for states and international actors to respond effectively. Addressing the influence of non-state actors involves not only military responses but also political, economic and diplomatic efforts to address the root causes of conflicts and to build resilient societies and institutions.

Within these debates, organised crime emerges as an evolving security threat, subject to change but also able to rapidly adapt to new circumstances. The United Nations Convention Against Transnational Organised Crime provides an internationally accepted definition of an organised criminal group, which refers to an act committed for given a period of time, for producing one or more serious crimes or offences to obtain, directly or indirectly, financial or other material benefits.[30] This definition encompasses a broad range of criminal activities and actors, and it underscores the international community's commitment to combating transnational organised crime. This definition does not focus on distinctions like corporate crime, blue-collar crime or white-collar crime, as these classifications are often less relevant when analysing and addressing organised crime groups, which may engage in a variety of illegal activities for financial gain. Organised crime groups have also been investigated with respect to security threats. They may have a clandestine component but can also appear more legitimised and supported by local communities because of the tangible benefits they can provide. In so doing, they are deeply political in their activities, and benefit from the state's weakness and vulnerability. An analysis of their performance requires shifting the focus towards the use of violence and criminal tactics. The above-mentioned definitions have been employed for distinguishing terrorists from other non-state armed groups, such as paramilitary groups or private military companies employed by states for providing security services.[31]

Relations with terrorist groups have been investigated by scholars in the fields of criminology and international relations, in terms of the crime-terror nexus.[32] The tripartite conceptualisation of the crime-terror nexus proposed by Paoli and Fijnaut provides a framework for understanding the various ways in which organised crime and terrorism may interact.[33] This framework categorises these interactions into three types: interaction; transformation/imitation; and similarities, each with varying degrees of intensity. They argue that only the 'heavier' categories of the first type – regular collaboration, alliance formation and fusion – are rare and presuppose the simultaneous existence of organised crime and terrorist organisations in each place. Other types, such as transformation/imitation and similarities, may occur more frequently and can vary

[30] United Nations (2000) UN Convention against Transnational Organised Crime, A/RES/55/25, 15 November, available at www.unodc.org/documents/treaties/UNTOC/Publications/TOC%20Convention/TOCebook-e.pdf (last accessed 14 April 2024).

[31] Sullivan and Bunker (n 22); SG Jones and PB Johnston, 'The future of insurgency' (2013) 36(1) *Studies in Conflict & Terrorism* 1.

[32] C Oehme, 'Terrorists, Insurgents, and Criminal-Growing Nexus?' (2008) 31(1) *Studies in Conflict & Terrorism* 80; P Wang, 'The Crime-Terror Nexus: Transformation, Alliance, Convergence' (2010) 6(6) *Asian Social Science* 11.

[33] L Paoli and C Fijnaut, 'Conceptualizing the nexus between organized crime and terrorism' in L Paoli and C Fijnaut (eds), *The Nexus Between Organized Crime and Terrorism* (Edward Elgar Publishing, 2022) 48.

depending on factors such as the local context, the motivations of the groups involved and their respective performances. This conceptualisation offers a nuanced understanding of the diverse ways in which organised crime and terrorism may intersect, and emphasises that the nature of these interactions can vary significantly, from occasional cooperation to potential fusion.[34]

Other categorisation in the analysis of the crime-terror nexus introduces a more flexible and nuanced perspective by using the terms 'cooperation', 'coexistence' and 'convergence' to describe the different ways in which criminal and terrorist groups may interact. These categories recognise varying degrees and forms of interaction, making it a valuable framework for understanding the complex dynamics between these groups.[35] Cooperation refers to the establishment of formal or established alliances between terrorist and criminal groups. This level of interaction implies a clear and often ongoing collaboration between the two entities. Coexistence describes a condition in which criminal and terrorist groups operate in the same areas or sectors but maintain their distinct identities. They may choose to remain separate entities unless a rational and functional need arises for occasional or temporary connections. Convergence refers to a situation in which both criminal and terrorist groups utilise their respective techniques and methods for practical purposes without necessarily forming a formal alliance or direct cooperation. This categorisation acknowledges the multifaceted nature of the crime-terror nexus, recognising that interactions can vary from formal cooperation to more informal and opportunistic convergence. The choice of which form of interaction to engage in depends on the specific circumstances, objectives and needs of the groups involved.[36]

The intersection between organised criminal networks and terrorism is indeed a complex and evolving phenomenon. It involves various forms of collaboration, exploitation and adaptation to meet operational requirements. Several significant transformations have occurred in the global system that have influenced the behaviour of subversive actors and the dynamics between terrorism and organised crime.[37] Understanding these changes at the intersection of the two actors is vital for policymakers, law enforcement agencies and security experts. Effective counter-organised crime efforts need to be adaptive and comprehensive, recognising that these subversive actors may operate in more fluid and multifaceted ways in the contemporary global landscape. Additionally, regional context and the presence of other actors further complicate the analysis and response to these evolving security challenges.[38] In the field of organised crime studies, perspectives are quite unpredictable. Democratic and economically developed areas of the global system are not safe from the threat. Evidently, the EU has tried to adapt to such changes. The development of JHA and the building up of a

[34] ibid.

[35] D Irrera, 'The crime-terror-insurgency 'nexus': Implications on multilateral cooperation' in S Romaniuk (ed), *Insurgency and Counterinsurgency in Modern War* (CRC Press, 2016) 39.

[36] ibid.

[37] V Ruggiero, 'Hybrids: on the crime-terror nexus' (2017) 43(1) *International Journal of Comparative and Applied Criminal Justice* 49.

[38] T Makarenko, 'Criminal and Terrorist Networks: Gauging Interaction and the Resultant Impact on Counter-Terrorism' in E Brimmer (ed), *Five Dimensions of Homeland and International Security* (Centre for Transatlantic Relations: Johns Hopkins University, 2007) 57.

broader AFSJ have also intersected with foreign and defence policy, in a set of relations that have involved Member States and European institutions. The ongoing nature of this process within the EU complicates its translation into an agreement like the TCA, inevitably resulting in the loss of some important aspects.

## V. Conclusions: The Need for a Broader Policy Framework

According to the official declarations made by political parties at the European Parliament level, the EU and UK remain essential partners in fighting terrorism and organised crime, in working for a stronger NATO, and in ensuring tariff-free, quota-free trade in line with the Withdrawal Agreement and the Protocol on Ireland and Northern Ireland. The TCA is fair and balanced, protecting EU interests and respecting EU rules and high standards. After Brexit, it is a promising step forward.

In reality, as pointed out by legal scholars, there are several deficiencies in the procedures and practices that will become more evident in the future. Fighting against organised crime should be a key priority for both parties. The provisions outlined in the TCA have mitigated some concerns regarding the ongoing efficiency and effectiveness of cross-border policing and investigations. However, with the loss of access to key systems and agencies and the absence of suitable substitutes, significant challenges persist. Much of the capability gaps left by the loss of such tools will be filled by manual processes and bilateral relationships, at least in the short-term. In the long-term and in the absence of political will to re-join EU platforms, it is likely that governments will need to invest even more in personnel and systems to bridge these gaps. Significantly, the fact that the Agreement fails to address the global dimension of the organised crime threat is a major gap.

By using a non-state actor approach, organised crime has been investigated, in this chapter, as a global security threat that has a dynamic and multifaceted nature. Organised crime is highly adaptable. Groups can quickly adjust their tactics, strategies and operations to exploit vulnerabilities in legal and regulatory systems. This adaptability allows them to stay one step ahead of law enforcement and security agencies. Criminal operations have expanded across national borders, making organised crime a transnational or global phenomenon. These criminal networks engage in a wide range of illicit activities, including drug trafficking, human trafficking, cybercrime, money laundering and more. Their global reach poses a challenge for individual states to combat effectively. Organised crime is often interconnected with other global security threats, such as terrorism, insurgency and the illegal arms trade. These criminal networks can provide financial support, resources and logistical support to other violent and non-state actors, making them important players in the broader security landscape. In addition to law enforcement efforts, addressing the root causes of organised crime, such as poverty, lack of economic opportunities and weak governance, is crucial for preventing the expansion of these criminal networks. A limitation in the scope of the UK's post-Brexit relationship with the EU, particularly in areas related to foreign policy, external security and defence cooperation, was deliberate and clearly visible. This may have implications for how the two entities coordinate and respond to international challenges and crises in the future.

# 19

# Combating the Dissemination of Counterfeit Goods Post-Brexit: Intellectual Property, Information Sharing and Shared Insecurity

BENJAMIN FARRAND

## I. Introduction

Writing about a topic intimately connected to borders in the context of relations between the European Union (EU) and the United Kingdom (UK) is not unlike trying to hit a fast-moving, unpredictable target. While previous versions of this chapter had been written in the context of the conflicts over the Northern Ireland Protocol, the EU and UK have now agreed the 'Windsor Framework',[1] which serves as the basis of renewed cooperation in Northern Ireland. At this juncture, it can be seen as a positive step that may make security cooperation between the EU and UK easier to achieve, including in combating the sale and distribution of counterfeit goods, which is the focus of this chapter.

The sale of counterfeit goods, 'fake' goods seemingly identical (or at least indistinguishable) to those produced by legitimate commercial undertakings, is an ever-present problem for intellectual property right holders, and indeed the customs authorities tasked with identifying and seizing them at a border. The estimated value of the global supply of counterfeits has been calculated as approximately USD $464 billion annually as of 2019, or 2.5 per cent of world trade.[2] Increasingly, individual consignments of parcels or packages shipped to end users is becoming a key means of transport for counterfeits, presenting a significant challenge for customs and police authorities, as well as a greater risk of harm for individuals knowingly or unknowingly purchasing these items. Key to combating the trade of these goods, and thereby the security risks they present, is effective cooperation and data exchange. However, the level of cooperation provided

[1] Decision of the Withdrawal Agreement Joint Committee on laying down arrangements relating to the Windsor Framework, 24 March 2023.

[2] OECD/EUIPO, *Global Trade in Fakes: A Worrying Threat* (OECD, 2021) 8.

for under the Trade and Cooperation Agreement (TCA)[3] is relatively thin, and in no small way significantly impacted by the working (or failure to function) of the Northern Ireland Protocol.[4] With that in mind, how could better cooperation in this area, which intersects economic, national and personal security concerns, be achieved?

This chapter seeks to answer this question by considering the purpose of anti-counterfeiting initiatives and the extent to which they are covered by the existing EU–UK relationship. The chapter begins by providing an overview of what counterfeits are and the reason their dissemination constitutes a security threat. It examines the EU's current approach to controlling counterfeits, namely through effective information sharing, coordination and identifying best practices, all facilitated by the European Union Intellectual Property Office (EUIPO) and its EU IP Enforcement Portal. It then considers the implications of the UK's leaving the EU, and what provisions have been made for cooperation in this sector under the TCA. It goes on to discuss, however, that the key focus of anti-counterfeiting is based on border measures, which means that EU–UK cooperation is highly complicated by the Northern Ireland Protocol and conflicts over the security of this highly political border. It then concludes by considering what could be done to improve effective coordination, noting the positive first step that the provisional acceptance of the Windsor Framework represents. Should this effective partnership and 'enhanced coordination' on monitoring and enforcement at the border be implemented, this goes a significant way towards tackling the risks that individual packages of counterfeits will pass through Northern Ireland to the EU. However, the chapter will conclude by arguing that enhanced cooperation could be further facilitated by clearer rules on access to important tools such as the EUIPO's IP Enforcement Database, as a means of ensuring that UK authorities have up-to-date knowledge regarding trends, transit routes and best practices regarding the combating of counterfeit goods.

## II. Defining the Problem: What are Counterfeits, What Risks do they Present and How are they Tackled by the EU?

To understand the obligations concerning counterfeiting within the security-related part of the TCA, it is important to provide some brief context of its place in intellectual property law. In legal terms, counterfeiting concerns the direct infringement of trademarks. A trademark, the definition of which is harmonised through the World Trade Organization (WTO) Agreement on Trade Related Aspects of Intellectual Property Rights (TRIPS),[5] can be 'any sign, or any combination of signs, capable of distinguishing the goods or services of one undertaking from those of other undertakings',[6] which can

[3] Trade and Cooperation Agreement between the European Union and the European Atomic Energy Community, of the one part, and the United Kingdom of Great Britain and Northern Ireland, of the other part [2021] OJ L149/10.

[4] Consolidated text: Agreement on the withdrawal of the United Kingdom of Great Britain and Northern Ireland from the European Union and the European Atomic Energy Community, Protocol on Ireland/Northern Ireland [2020] OJ L29/7.

[5] Agreement on Trade-Related Aspects of Intellectual Property Rights 1994, 1869 UNTS 299.

[6] ibid Art 15(1).

include names, numbers, graphics and colours, or any combination of those elements. This infringement is one where there is an intentional imitation of goods marketed by a legitimate producer without their authorisation. The definition of counterfeit goods also comes from TRIPS, which states that the term refers to 'any goods, including packaging, bearing without authorisation a trademark which is identical to the trademark validly registered in respect of such goods, or which cannot be distinguished in its essential aspects from such a trademark'.[7]

The EU, as a WTO member, has implemented the TRIPS definition of a trademark by way of a Directive[8] and Regulation.[9] These instruments share a common definition, found in Articles 3 and 4 of the Directive and Regulation respectively, stating that trademarks consist of 'any signs, in particular words, including personal names, or designs, letters, numerals, colours, the shape of goods or of the packaging of goods, or sounds', going beyond the minimal protections afforded under TRIPS. The definition of counterfeiting has also been harmonised at the EU level through a separate Regulation,[10] which is broadly similar to that provided in TRIPS, aside from adding that goods will also be considered counterfeit where the trademark is not identical but is essentially indistinguishable in its essential aspects.[11] This will also apply to supplementary material such as packaging, labels, stickers, brochures, etc.[12] While there have been arguments that in certain luxury-good markets consumers are often aware that goods may be counterfeit (a Louis Vuitton bag being sold for €25 rather than €1,750, as a 'bargain' as opposed to a 'fake', is unlikely to fool any save the most credulous buyers),[13] in many product markets the basis for counterfeiting is misrepresentation and the intentional deception of the target audience for financial gain.[14]

The sale and distribution of counterfeit goods is a complex threat that presents numerous harms. The first and most obvious is the harm to the producers and sellers of legitimate goods, whose business reputation will suffer if the infringing goods are of poor quality,[15] and of course the economic harm caused to both right holders and purchasers of goods by parasitic trading (albeit with the proviso that the effective

[7] TRIPS (n 2) Art 51 at fn 14.

[8] The latest iteration of this legislation being Directive 2015/2436 to approximate the laws of the Member States relating to trademarks (recast) [2015] OJ L336/23 ('Trademark Directive').

[9] Regulation 2017/1001 on the European Union trademark [2017] OJ L154/1.

[10] Regulation 608/2013 concerning customs enforcement of intellectual property rights [2013] OJ L181/15.

[11] ibid Art 2(5)(a).

[12] ibid Art 2(5)(c).

[13] See, eg, E Penz and B Stöttinger, 'Original Brands and Counterfeit Brands – Do They Have Anything in Common?' (2008) 7 *Journal of Consumer Behaviour* 146; MJ Elsmore, 'Who's Deceiving Whom? The Curious Case of the "Counterfeitee"' (2010) 5 *Journal of Intellectual Property Law & Practice* 736; A Radon 'Counterfeit Luxury Goods Online: An Investigation of Consumer Perceptions' (2012) 4 *International Journal of Marketing Studies* 74.

[14] C Wadlow, '"Including Trade in Counterfeit Goods": The Origin of TRIPS as a GATT Anti-Counterfeiting Code' (2007) *Intellectual Property Quarterly* 350; M Blakeney, 'International Proposals for the Criminal Enforcement of Intellectual Property Rights: International Concern with Counterfeiting and Piracy' (2009) *Intellectual Property Quarterly*. 1.

[15] S Romani, G Gistri and S Pace, 'When Counterfeits Raise the Appeal of Luxury Brands' (2012) 23 *Marketing Letters* 807; T Li and B Seaton, 'Emerging Consumer Orientation, Ethical Perceptions, and Purchase Intention in the Counterfeit Smartphone Market in China' (2015) *Journal of International Consumer Marketing* 27; P Wingrove, 'Developing an In-House Trade Mark Enforcement Strategy Brand-Strategy Trade Mark Enforcement' (2018) 275 *Managing Intellectual Property* 39.

calculation of the scale of economic harm can often be very difficult to achieve).[16] However, the potential harms with counterfeits go beyond the economic. Many types of counterfeits present real threats to human life and health, from the more well-known examples of physical harm caused by unsafe and toxic toys, or defective electronics, to counterfeit prescription medicines and illegal drugs, counterfeit foods, alcohol, tobacco and automobile parts.[17] More recent evidence has also demonstrated the risk that counterfeit goods pose to the environment, such as through the use of damaging chemicals in the production process[18] or through sale as agrochemicals.[19] In terms of indirect harms, counterfeit goods are often sold or distributed by organised crime and terrorist organisations as a means of diversifying income streams[20] or financing other activities.[21] For this reason, counterfeit goods sit at a nexus of the EU's internal market and security policies, and anti-counterfeiting initiatives are pursued in the context of the Area of Freedom, Security and Justice (AFSJ).[22]

These policies, it must be stated, are premised on counterfeiting's being an issue of border control for the EU. This can be evidenced by the fact that the legal definition and control of counterfeits by the EU are provided in a Regulation on customs enforcement, as discussed above. Somewhat more concrete evidence can be found, however, in the reports produced by the OECD and EUIPO on counterfeiting trends. In 2019, according to the most recent data currently available, goods of Chinese provenance were responsible for approximately 55 per cent of seizures at the EU's borders and represented approximately 67 per cent of the total value of seized imports.[23] The vast majority of all counterfeits are produced outside the EU, and the organised crime groups involved in their production and distribution are predominantly based outside the EU, although the EUIPO and Europol note that this is changing to an extent as 'agromafia' becomes increasingly involved in food counterfeiting.[24] The proportion of counterfeit goods originating outside the EU, combined with the extreme difficulties in seizing and destroying counterfeit goods in free circulation once available in the single market, means that efforts at addressing their sale and distribution focus predominantly on ensuring the effectiveness of the EU's customs regime and the strength of its borders. This allows these goods to be seized and destroyed before they enter into free circulation.[25]

[16] See, eg, J Spink and Z Levente Fejes, 'A Review of the Economic Impact of Counterfeiting and Piracy Methodologies and Assessment of Currently Utilized Estimates' (2012) 36 *International Journal of Comparative and Applied Criminal Justice* 249.

[17] For more on these threats, see OECD/EUIPO, 'Dangerous Fakes: Trade in Counterfeit Goods That Pose Health, Safety and Environmental Risks' (OECD, 2022).

[18] DS Wall and J Large, 'Jailhouse Frocks: Locating the Public Interest in Policing Counterfeit Luxury Fashion Goods' (2010) 50 *The British Journal of Criminology* 1094.

[19] B Farrand, '"Alone We Can Do so Little; Together We Can Do so Much": The Essential Role of EU Agencies in Combatting the Sale of Counterfeit Goods' (2019) 28 *European Security* 22.

[20] GA Antonopoulos et al, 'Counterfeit Goods Fraud: An Account of Its Financial Management' (2020) 26 *European Journal on Criminal Policy and Research* 357.

[21] M Levi, 'Combating the Financing of Terrorism: A History and Assessment of the Control of "Threat Finance"' (2010) 50 *The British Journal of Criminology* 650.

[22] Farrand (n 16).

[23] OECD/EUIPO (n 1) 26.

[24] EUIPO/Europol, 'Intellectual Property Crime Threat Assessment 2022' (16 March 2022) 34–35.

[25] Farrand (n 16).

Furthermore, the increased use of the Internet to sell counterfeits has made it much easier to send counterfeit goods as individual consignments and small packages sent by air, rather than in large shipping containers, making identification and seizure harder.[26] Small packages have been identified by customs authorities as the most problematic, accounting for the majority of seizures.[27] While the value overall compared to large shipping containers is relatively small,[28] this does not mean that the personal risk to individual consumers presented by these potentially harmful items is negligible. This has meant that intelligence-led operations, identification of best practices, and data sharing regarding product trends and shipping routes for counterfeits have become essential for effectively countering these threats. Bodies such as the EUIPO and its Observatory on Intellectual Property Infringements and Europol's Intellectual Property Crime Coordinated Coalition (IPC3) have become focal points for this kind of information sharing.[29] Of particular importance are three databases run by the Observatory: the Anti-Counterfeiting Intelligence Support Tool (ACIST), which provides information on counterfeits detained at Member State borders; the Anti-Counterfeiting Rapid Intelligence System (ACRIS), which provides information for EU-based companies on infringements taking place in third countries; and the Enforcement Database, which collects trend information, such as the goods most likely to be counterfeited, indications of how to identify counterfeits from their packaging, as well as other logistical information, including known shipping routes. As of 2022, these three databases were integrated into a single platform, known as the IP Enforcement Portal.[30] Given that this is the approach to tackling counterfeits, then, what does this mean for continued UK–EU cooperation post-Brexit?

## III. Anti-Counterfeiting Efforts and the Trade and Cooperation Agreement

Continued cooperation between the UK and EU on combating counterfeit sales should be considered as having obvious mutual benefits. As one author stated regarding the implementation of the TRIPS Agreement's anti-counterfeiting provisions, 'like corruption, commercial counterfeiting has no apologists and no redeeming features'.[31] Anti-counterfeiting is not a wedge issue in the same way that issues such as (for example)

[26] J Treadwell, 'From the Car Boot to Booting It up? EBay, Online Counterfeit Crime and the Transformation of the Criminal Marketplace' (2012) 12 *Criminology and Criminal Justice* 175; A Lavorgna, 'The Online Trade in Counterfeit Pharmaceuticals: New Criminal Opportunities, Trends and Challenges' (2015) 12 *European Journal of Criminology* 226; B Farrand, 'Combatting Physical Threats Posed via Digital Means: The European Commission's Developing Approach to the Sale of Counterfeit Goods on the Internet' (2018) 19(3) *European Politics and Society* 338.

[27] OECD/EUIPO (n 1) 8.

[28] OECD/EUIPO, 'Misuse of Small Parcels for Trade in Counterfeit Goods: Facts and Trends' (11 December 2018) 39.

[29] Farrand (n 16).

[30] EUIPO, 'IP Enforcement Portal' (*EUIPO IP Enforcement Portal* (10 February 2023) available at https://euipo.europa.eu/ohimportal/en/web/observatory/ip-enforcement-portal-home-page (last accessed 24 February 2023).

[31] Wadlow (n 11) 350.

farming subsidies or social welfare may be. It benefits businesses, which are afforded some protection from parasitic trading and damage to reputation. It benefits consumers, who are not misled, and potentially harmed, by fake goods. And it benefits states, which do not lose taxation revenue from counterfeit sales or suffer the security impacts of the use of counterfeit sales to finance organised crime or terrorism. Cooperation on this issue would therefore seem to be of clear interest to both parties to the TCA.

However, comparatively little is said on the topic of counterfeits when compared to other security concerns. Articles 236–244 of the TCA deal with the civil dimensions of trademark protection, including the registration of marks, what type of marks should be protected, etc, which is relatively simple to achieve given the broadly equivalent protections between the Trademark Directive and the UK Trade Marks Act 1994.[32] Under the European Union (Withdrawal) Act 2018, there is a presumption that all EU law is retained unless specifically revoked under sections 2–7 of the legislation, and under the Retained EU Law (Revocation and Reform) Act 2023, no legislation pertaining to trademarks was subject to revocation under schedule 1. This is highly fortunate for continued cooperation, as under clause 1 of the originally proposed Retained EU Law Bill, all retained law would have been revoked unless a relevant national authority specifically specified retention (or assimilation, as referred to by clause 6) or implemented regulations to restate those laws before the end of 2023.[33] As of February 2023, the Intellectual Property Office had identified over 80 pieces of legislation that would have been impacted by this sunset clause, including 11 directly related to trademarks.[34] This would have resulted in significant divergences between EU and UK trademark law, which could have significant repercussions for continued cooperation, as will be discussed in section IV.

Regarding counterfeiting specifically, the only real reference in the TCA is contained as Article 271 on border measures, which states that the parties should adopt or maintain procedures under which right holders can have goods infringing their rights detained, which includes suspected counterfeits. Article 271(2) requires electronic systems to be put in place for the management by customs of the applications made and allows for right holders to receive information regarding the provenance of the goods if requested under Article 271(8). Article 271(13) provides for customs authorities to 'maintain a regular dialogue and promote cooperation with the relevant stakeholders and with others involved in the enforcement of intellectual property rights'; and under Article 271(14), the Parties are required, as far as possible, to 'share relevant information on trade in suspected goods affecting the other Party'.

Given the focus of anti-counterfeiting efforts on border measures,[35] it is essential to consider the issue of Northern Ireland's land border with the Republic of Ireland,

[32] For more on this in comprehensive detail, see P Johnson, *Intellectual Property, Free Trade Agreements and the United Kingdom: The Continuing Influence of European Union Law* (Edward Elgar Publishing, 2011) 111–34.

[33] Retained EU Law Bill, cl 12.

[34] Intellectual Property Office, 'Retained EU Law for Intellectual Property' *gov.uk* (22 February 2023) available at www.gov.uk/government/publications/intellectual-property-and-retained-european-union-law-the-facts/retained-eu-law-for-intellectual-property (last accessed 23 February 2023).

[35] Customs checks, as has been noted, are not only for ensuring any customs duties and tariffs are paid, but also to prevent the entry of counterfeit or other illegal goods into a market. On this, see K Hayward,

and the role of the Northern Ireland Protocol[36] on this issue. According to the revised Protocol, Northern Ireland remains part of the UK's customs territory, with the effect that any agreements concluded between the UK and third countries allow Northern Ireland-produced goods the same status as goods produced in the rest of the UK.[37] While no customs duties are to be payable on goods moved to Northern Ireland from another part of the UK, if those goods are considered 'at risk' of subsequently moving into the EU then customs duties will be payable.[38] Whether goods are likely to be at risk is to be determined by a Joint Committee.[39] Despite being part of the customs territory of the UK, Northern Ireland would nevertheless be subject to EU customs legislation,[40] defined in the EU Customs Code[41] as the Code itself and any supplementing and implementing legislation, the Common Customs Tariff, EU legislation on customs duty relief, and any relevant international agreements.[42] A list in Annex 2 to the Protocol makes it clear that intellectual property rights protection is included, with Regulation 608/2013 on customs enforcement of intellectual property rights appearing under the intellectual property section.

Article 5(3) of the Protocol exists as an apparent contradiction at its heart as, for the purpose of trade in goods, Northern Ireland is both inside and outside the EU.[43] Article 6(1) of the Protocol states that nothing it contains 'shall prevent the United Kingdom from ensuring unfettered access for goods moving from Northern Ireland to other parts of the United Kingdom's internal market'; and in Article 6(2) it is provided that as Northern Ireland is part of the UK's internal market, 'the Union and the United Kingdom shall use their best endeavours to facilitate the trade between Northern Ireland and other parts of the United Kingdom'. However, as the House of Lords noted in 2020, the Protocol ultimately requires a border between Great Britain and Northern Ireland, with adherence to the EU's Customs Code necessitating the filing of exit summary declarations for goods entering Northern Ireland,[44] and the Government's having confirmed to the European Union Committee that checks would be required on at least some goods moving between Great Brain and Northern Ireland,[45] with the end result that there appeared to be apparent incoherence between Article 5's requirements concerning the EU's Customs Code and the Article 6 guarantee of the integrity of the UK's internal market.[46] As we shall see in section IV, these inconsistencies have considerable impact upon the ability to control the movement of counterfeit goods.

M Campbell and R Murphy, 'The Irish Border as a Customs Frontier after Brexit' *CEPS* (11 July 2017) available at www.ceps.eu/ceps-publications/irish-border-customs-frontier-after-brexit/ (last accessed 4 November 2024).

[36] Northern Ireland Protocol (n 4).

[37] ibid Art 4.

[38] ibid Art 5(1).

[39] ibid Art 5(2).

[40] ibid Article 5(3).

[41] Regulation 952/2013 laying down the Union Customs Code [2013] OJ L269/1.

[42] ibid Art 5(2).

[43] N Moran, 'Customs and Movement of Goods' in F Fabbrini (ed), *The Law and Politics of Brexit*: vol IV, *The Protocol on Ireland / Northern Ireland* (Oxford University Press, 2022) 149.

[44] House of Lords European Union Committee, 'The Protocol on Ireland/Northern Ireland' (9th Report of Session 2019–2021, HL 66) paras 159–160.

[45] ibid para 148.

[46] ibid paras 172–173.

## IV. Moving Towards Cooperation? Post-Brexit UK–EU Relations, Anti-counterfeiting and Access to Information

The uneasy compromise the Northern Ireland Protocol represents was largely considered unsatisfactory by both the EU and the UK, and its internal contradictions create considerable tensions. For the EU, the Northern Ireland Protocol is highly unusual in its legal order and is not typical in how it engages with external actors.[47] This is due in no small part to the fact that the Protocol is a response to the EU's desire to ensure continued peace and stability, and respect for the Good Friday Agreement, by avoiding the establishment of a hard border between Northern Ireland and Ireland.[48] In economic terms, the Protocol is not necessarily to the EU's benefit, and necessitates considerable trust in the UK in order for it to have real effect. This trust has historically been in short supply.[49] For the UK, and in particular certain highly Eurosceptic elements in the Conservatives and the Democratic Unionist Party (DUP), the Northern Ireland Protocol constitutes a 'betrayal' of the promises of Brexit,[50] as well as a potential step toward Irish reunification and therefore a threat to the current structure of the UK.[51] For this reason, its continued operation has been subject to frequent interventions, from the British Government under Boris Johnson, making repeated threats to make use of Article 16's 'emergency clause' to allow it to unilaterally suspend the Protocol,[52] to the proposed Northern Ireland Protocol Bill,[53] which under clause 4 would see the UK unilaterally remove checks on 'qualifying movement of UK or non-EU destinated goods', which under clause 4(2) also disapplies Article 5(3) of and Annex 2 to the Protocol.

According to the House of Lords' explanatory notes, the Government's intention was that this would have allowed for the facilitation of its 'green channel/red channel' system, in which goods not intended for onward journey from Northern Ireland would move through a green channel without checks, whereas goods intended for onward travel into the EU would be in a red channel and subject to checks and payment of any customs duties required.[54] Considerable work was undertaken by the UK Government under Prime Minister Rishi Sunak and the European Commission on breaking the impasse over the Northern Ireland Protocol, which in part would address some of the issues identified here. On 27 February 2023, Sunak and Commission President Ursula von der Leyen gave a joint statement announcing the agreement of a 'Windsor Framework'[55] for

[47] K Hayward, '"Flexible and Imaginative": The EU's Accommodation of Northern Ireland in the UK–EU Withdrawal Agreement' (2021) 58 *International Studies* 201.

[48] B Melo Araujo, 'A Contextual Analysis of Article 16 of the Ireland–Northern Ireland Protocol' (2022) 71 *International & Comparative Law Quarterly* 531.

[49] B Farrand and H Carrapico, '"People like That Cannot Be Trusted": Populist and Technocratic Political Styles, Legitimacy, and Distrust in the Context of Brexit Negotiations' (2021) *Journal of Contemporary European Research* 17.

[50] MC Murphy, 'Northern Ireland and Brexit: Where Sovereignty and Stability Collide?' (2021) 29 *Journal of Contemporary European Studies* 405.

[51] N McEwen and MC Murphy, 'Brexit and the Union: Territorial Voice, Exit and Re-Entry Strategies in Scotland and Northern Ireland after EU Exit' (2022) 43 *International Political Science Review* 374.

[52] CJ Kelly and E Tannam, 'The Future of Northern Ireland: The Role of the Belfast/Good Friday Agreement Institutions' (2022) *The Political Quarterly* 1.

[53] Northern Ireland Protocol Bill (2022), HL 52.

[54] House of Lords, 'HL Bill 52 Explanatory Notes' (2022) 8.

[55] Windsor Framework (n 1).

interpretation and application of the Protocol, intended to alleviate concerns regarding its functioning held by both parties. As a sign of goodwill, Sunak announced that this would result in a termination of the proposed Northern Ireland Protocol Bill, while von der Leyen confirmed that this also meant the end of pending legal action against the UK for the alleged breach of international law.[56] Of direct relevance to the issues discussed in this chapter, the Framework establishes the UK's desired green channel (now called a green lane) for goods destined for Northern Ireland, with a red lane for goods intended to continue to the EU under Article 1, which modifies Article 6(2) of the Protocol. Similarly, Article 5 modifies Article 5(2) of the Protocol, stating new conditions for when goods would not be considered 'at risk' of continuing to the EU. This has resulted in certain goods now bearing stamps indicating the goods are 'NOT FOR EU', in light of the Windsor Framework reforms.

The UK Government had hoped that new 'smart' technologies could be used to facilitate speedy and frictionless checks of these goods, with mobile inspections and improved scanning technologies being used to identify illicit goods.[57] In 2021, news reports made clear that these technologies were far from ready to be implemented at the UK's borders[58] and, according to a leaked report from the Home Office, unlikely to be ready before 2030.[59] The Commission had already expressed concerns in 2022 that the customs checks taking place in the North Sea were not fit for purpose,[60] and as of October 2023, UK in a Changing Europe has indicated that concerns remain about how effectively a 'green lane–red lane' system can work,[61] particularly given worries regarding the effectiveness of UK-based customs checks and the UK Government's recent announcement of a fifth delay in implementing checks on goods entering from the EU.[62] Of course, even if these systems were in place and functioned, counterfeits are illicit goods that are subject to attempts to hide their provenance and destination, bringing into question the effectiveness of the green channel–red channel system. While there is some research into the use of technologies, including blockchain, for the purpose of verifying the authenticity of goods,[63] thereby reducing the risk that counterfeits will

[56] Prime Minister's Office, 'Windsor Framework Unveiled to Fix Problems of the Northern Ireland Protocol' *gov.uk* (27 February 2023) available at www.gov.uk/government/news/windsor-framework-unveiled-to-fix-problems-of-the-northern-ireland-protocol (last accessed 28 February 2023).

[57] HM Government, '2025 UK Border Strategy' (CP No 352, 2020) 21–22.

[58] G Noone, 'Technology Was Meant to Solve the Northern Irish Border by Now' *Tech Monitor* (9 April 2021) available at https://techmonitor.ai/policy/geopolitics/technology-meant-to-solve-northern-irish-border (last accessed 27 February 2023).

[59] B Kentish, 'Leaked Home Office Document Reveals High-Tech Solution to Avoid Hard Northern Ireland Border a "Decade Away"' *The Independent* (17 April 2019) available at www.independent.co.uk/news/uk/politics/brexit-northern-ireland-border-high-tech-solution-home-office-leak-backstop-a8875171.html (last accessed 27 February 2023).

[60] 'Brexit: Irish Sea Border Checks "Not Fit for Purpose"' *BBC News* (28 January 2022) available at www.bbc.com/news/uk-northern-ireland-60170761 (last accessed 19 October 2023).

[61] LC Whitten and D Phinnemore, 'Implementing the Windsor Framework' *UK in a Changing Europe* (3 October 2023) available at https://ukandeu.ac.uk/explainers/implementing-the-windsor-framework/ (last accessed 19 October 2023).

[62] L Fisher and P Foster, 'UK Government Announces Fifth Delay to Post-Brexit Border Controls for Food' *Financial Times* (29 August 2023) available at www.ft.com/content/7ae83ce4-69a5-4483-98d8-9b98ee01c39e (last accessed 19 October 2023).

[63] See, eg, H Lee and C Yeon, 'Research on How to Prevent Online Counterfeiting with Blockchain-Based Cross Border Data Sharing', 2020 International Conference on Information and Communication Technology Convergence., Jeju Island, 21–23 October 2020.

pass borders, such an approach is still in its infancy. It is not possible to determine at this stage whether the technology will be able to control counterfeit goods, meaning that border insecurity is not effectively addressed in the case of Ireland–Northern Ireland. This is proving highly problematic, with reports of attacks and threats of reprisals by loyalist paramilitaries on customs officials imposing checks at Northern Ireland ports,[64] as well as concerns that this border is becoming a key smuggling route for counterfeit goods destined for the EU.[65] Smuggling from Ireland to Northern Ireland and vice versa has traditionally been associated with the paramilitary groups operating along this border, reinforcing the association between counterfeit goods, organised crime and terror.[66]

So, what has changed with the Windsor Framework? Under Article 7, these 'not at risk' goods would constitute goods not intended for further processing in Northern Ireland, where they are brought into Northern Ireland by way of direct transport. They should not be subject to duty under the Common Customs Tariff,[67] where intended for sale or end use by Northern Ireland consumers,[68] or where sent in a parcel of a non-commercial nature by one private individual to another, or sent by a commercial operator for end use by a private individual.[69] Under Article 7(3), a 'package' is to be considered a consignment of goods with a weight of less than 31.5kg, or a single item good with a weight of no more than 100kg coming from a commercial transaction. As a means of countering potentially illegal or illicit conduct, Articles 12 and 13 lay down conditions for authorised carriers, which entail their being established in the UK, not having in the past three years committed any serious infringement or repeated infringements regarding their commercial operations, and having firm control of their operations. Furthermore, authorised carriers are tasked with taking responsibility for the goods transferred, maintaining systems to record and share data regarding goods transfers, and reporting any potentially suspicious activity. The UK has indicated its intention to monitor its green-lane activities effectively, perhaps aware of the potential opportunity such a system offers to smugglers of counterfeit goods, issuing a Unilateral Declaration on market surveillance and enforcement,[70] where it states that it will take measures to ensure 'robust enforcement to ensure traders are not abusing these new internal UK trade arrangements to move goods into the European Union'.[71]

[64] S Pogatchnik, 'Inspectors Pulled from Brexit Checks at Northern Ireland Ports over Threats' *POLITICO* (2 February 2021) available at www.politico.eu/article/inspectors-brexit-eu-uk-checks-northern-ireland-ports-threats/ (last accessed 27 February 2023).

[65] 'EU Claims Counterfeit Goods Are Smuggled into Single Market via Northern Ireland' *ITV News* (15 June 2022) available at www.itv.com/news/utv/2022-06-15/eu-claims-counterfeit-goods-are-smuggled-into-single-market-via-northern-ireland (last accessed 27 February 2023); D Young, 'Smugglers Trying to Move Counterfeit Goods into Single Market via Northern Ireland, Says EU' *The Irish News* (15 June 2022) available at www.irishnews.com/news/brexit/2022/06/15/news/smugglers-trying-to-move-counterfeit-goods-into-single-market-via-northern-ireland-says-eu-2744085/ (last accessed 27 February 2023).

[66] Organised Crime Task Force, 'Organised Crime Strategy Northern Ireland 2021–2025' (2020); Europol and EUIPO, 'IP Crime and Its Link to Other Serious Crimes: Focus on Poly-Criminality' (2020) 81–82.

[67] Decision (n 52) Art 7(1)(a)(i).

[68] ibid Art 7(1)(a)(ii).

[69] ibid Art 7(1)(a)(iii).

[70] Unilateral Declarations by the United Kingdom of Great Britain and Northern Ireland and the European Union in the Withdrawal Agreement Joint Committee on market surveillance and enforcement, 24 March 2023.

[71] ibid 1.

These measures will include building capability and capacity with relevant authorities; engaging in risk assessments and intelligence-led activities, including audits, inspections and spot-checks; using information and data gathering to identify emerging risks, including goods likely to move into the EU; and to share and receive information on the compliance of activities with market-surveillance and other competent authorities.[72] Unilateral Declarations were published with a Recommendation[73] that, under Article 1, provides for 'enhanced cooperation' between the EU and UK on market surveillance and enforcement. This could, according to the Recommendation, 'encompass knowledge-sharing, information exchange, work with operators and joint activity where appropriate … to tackle illegal activity and smuggling … and ensure enforcement and surveillance activity is prioritised based on risk and intelligence'. As discussed in section II, the key to effective anti-counterfeit strategy is information exchange, and so this is a highly positive development. In terms of existing mechanisms of cooperation and data exchange, the UK does have a Working Arrangement with Europol,[74] which under Article 566 of and Annex 41 to the TCA includes coordination on issues of counterfeiting and piracy. In comparison to the UK's previous membership of Europol, however, the level of cooperation afforded under Working Arrangements is relatively low[75] and does raise data protection concerns,[76] particularly given the UK Government's announcement that it intends to diverge from 'overcautious, unclear EU-derived rules on how they can use people's personal data'.[77] Significant divergence, meaning that UK data protection laws are no longer deemed adequate by the EU, could then have repercussions for cooperation under these Working Arrangements, and so an immediate recommendation would be for the UK to think very carefully about divergence in data protection rules and seek to maintain its current adequacy position.

Cooperation with the EUIPO is much more difficult to guarantee. The EUIPO does not have the same mechanisms for allowing cooperation with third countries,[78] and as a result of its withdrawal from the EU, the UK lost access to all the EUIPO databases.[79] Right holders based in the UK will only be able to access the IP Enforcement Portal in order to register their trademarked goods so that EU-based customs authorities may use this information for the purposes of preventing goods crossing into the EU, but this does not extend to access for UK customs authorities in order to prevent goods entering the UK. Indeed, the Regulation establishing the EUIPO and EU Trademark mentioned in

[72] ibid.

[73] Recommendation of the Withdrawal Joint Committee on market surveillance and enforcement, 24 March 2023.

[74] Working and Administrative Arrangement establishing cooperative relations between the competent authorities of the United Kingdom of Great Britain and Northern Ireland and the European Union Agency for Law Enforcement Cooperation, concluded in September 2021.

[75] F Coman-Kund, 'The International Dimension of the EU Agencies: Framing a Growing Legal-Institutional Phenomenon' (2018) 23 *European Foreign Affairs Review* 97.

[76] F Coman-Kund, 'Europol's International Exchanges of Data and Interoperability of AFSJ Databases' (2020) 26 *European Public Law* 181.

[77] Department for Digital, Culture, Media and Sport, 'Data: A New Direction – Government Response to Consultation' *gov.uk* (23 June 2022) available at www.gov.uk/government/consultations/data-a-new-direction/outcome/data-a-new-direction-government-response-to-consultation (last accessed 27 February 2023).

[78] Farrand (n 16).

[79] Communication No 2/20 of the Executive Director of the Office of 10 September 2020 on the impact of the United Kingdom's withdrawal from the European Union on certain aspects of the practice of the Office.

section II[80] makes no allowance for the EUIPO's cooperation with third countries, or for information exchange and access to the IP Enforcement Portal. Renewed and strengthened cooperation on this aspect of mutual security interest could be predicated on negotiations for a revised TCA, focusing on reforms to Regulation 2017/1001, to allow the EUIPO to have formal mechanisms of cooperation for IP enforcement, including data sharing on potential counterfeiting trends, routes and intelligence best practices. Allowing for this to occur would not only help protect the UK from goods potentially entering its market, but would also provide additional protection to the EU from illegal goods entering through Northern Ireland's border with the Republic of Ireland.

## V. Conclusions

The issue of counterfeiting is one that received little explicit attention in the TCA or the Withdrawal Agreement preceding it. Similarly, the somewhat incoherent substance of the Northern Ireland Protocol and the lack of effective cooperation arising from its contentious nature have served to make success of efforts aimed at preventing the spread of counterfeit goods difficult to achieve, rendered even more problematic given counterfeiting's historic links to organised crime and terror in Northern Ireland. Prior to the announcements regarding the proposal for the Windsor Framework, with relations appearing highly acrimonious, recommendations for reform were very much centred on how to restore trust and improve cooperation. With the adoption of the Framework, however, there is as a good starting point for developing the type of enhanced cooperation committed to in the UK's Unilateral Declaration on market surveillance and enforcement. However, enhanced cooperation in this field is only as effective as the information it is based upon – future reforms in this area should therefore focus on how best to facilitate that information sharing, and whether potential legal hurdles to the sharing of access to the EUIPO's knowledge can be overcome in order to provide mutual benefit to both parties.

[80] Regulation 2017/1001 (n 6).

# 20

# Post-Brexit Legal Challenges in the Cooperation against Migrant Smuggling

MATILDE VENTRELLA

## I. Introduction

This chapter focuses on the smuggling of migrants in the European Union (EU) and in the United Kingdom (UK), and on the possible cooperation in tackling this crime when perpetrated by sea, under the Trade and Cooperation Agreement (TCA).[1] Section II sets out the EU's policies and legislation on smuggling and migrants, and how these were implemented in the UK when it was a Member State. Section III then analyses the extremely thin measures in the TCA for cooperation on the smuggling of migrants, alongside the possibility for cooperation through other international treaties. Section IV analyses the British law on migration and the most recent developments adopted since 2022, including the now abandoned Rwanda deal and the case law of the European Court of Human Rights (ECtHR) and of the British courts on the deal. The same section focuses on UK laws post-Brexit, pertaining to the smuggling of migrants by boat. The chapter demonstrates how the recent increase in arrivals of undocumented migrants via small boats has led the UK to implement stringent migration laws, further solidifying the externalisation of migration. The chapter concludes that an agreement with the EU on migration and asylum, which as a minimum establishes safe and legal routes to the UK and sets out fair rules on redistribution, is essential.

## II. The EU's Legislation and Policy on the Smuggling of Migrants

The fight against the smuggling of migrants has reinforced policies on the externalisation of migration, which aim to keep migrants not only outside EU territory 'but also

[1] Trade and Cooperation Agreement between the European Union and the European Atomic Energy Community, of the one part, and the United Kingdom of Great Britain and Northern Ireland, of the other part [2021] OJ L149/10.

outside the material scope of European law'.[2] The Dublin Regulations have established rules on Member States' responsibility towards asylum applicants. Initially, the responsibility was established by the 1997 Dublin Convention.[3] The signatories of the Dublin Convention were the then 12 EU Member States. The Dublin Convention applied to the UK but not to the 'European territories for whose external relations the United Kingdom is responsible unless a declaration to the contrary is made by the United Kingdom'.[4] In 2003, the Dublin Convention was replaced by a Regulation (Dublin II),[5] which contributed to establishing the Common European Asylum System (CEAS)[6] based on the Tampere European Council 1999 objective, which was the establishment of a CEAS founded on respect for the principle of *non-refoulement*, in accordance with the 1951 Refugee Convention,[7] ensuring that no individuals are sent back to places where they may be persecuted.[8] The same provision stated that all Member States of the EU could be considered safe countries. The UK took part in the adoption and application of Dublin II.[9] This legislation established the criteria to determine the Member State responsible for examining asylum seekers' applications at the border.[10] The specific parameters for determining the Member State responsible were set out in chapter 3 of the Regulation. In the case of families, for example, the Member State responsible should be determined 'on the basis of the situation obtaining when the asylum seeker first lodged his application with a Member State'.[11] The family situation should be taken into consideration so that the Member State responsible should be the State where family members reside as refugees or, if the decision is pending, the State where the family member has lodged their application.[12] The impact was a transfer of responsibility from northern and western European Member States (the preferred destination for asylum seekers) to southern and eastern European Member States, which have less experience in dealing with high numbers of asylum seekers.[13] The European Court of Human Rights (ECtHR) found that Greece acted in violation of Article 13 of the European Convention on Human Rights (ECHR)[14] in conjunction with Article 3, because of deficiencies in the asylum procedures followed by the Greek authorities, with the consequent risk that the applicant would be transferred to Afghanistan without serious consideration of the

[2] T Spijkerboer, 'The Global Mobility Infrastructure: Reconceptualising the Externalisation of Migration (2018) 20 *European Journal of Migration and Law* 465.

[3] Convention determining the State responsible for examining applications for asylum lodged in one of the Member States of the European Communities – Dublin Convention [1997] OJ C254/1.

[4] ibid Art 19(4).

[5] Council Regulation (EC) No 343/2003 of 18 February 2003 establishing the criteria and mechanisms for determining the Member State responsible for examining an asylum application lodged in one of the Member States by a third-country national [2003] OJ L50/1.

[6] ibid recital (1) of the Preamble.

[7] Convention relating to the Status of Refugees (adopted 28 July 1951, entered into force 22 April 1954) 189 UNTS 137 ('Refugee Convention').

[8] Council Regulation (n 5) of the Preamble.

[9] Council Regulation (n 5) of the Preamble.

[10] Council Regulation (n 5) Art 1.

[11] Council Regulation (n 5) Art 5(2).

[12] Council Regulation (n 5) Arts 7 and 8.

[13] S Peers, 'The Dublin III Regulation' in S Peers e al (eds), *EU Immigration and Asylum Law. Text and Commentary: Second revised edition* (Brill Nijhoff, 2014) 346, 347.

[14] European Convention on Human Rights (1950), ETS 5.

merits of the asylum application or access to effective remedy.[15] At the same time, the ECtHR sanctioned Belgium because it sent the applicant to Greece and exposed him to detention and living conditions in breach of Articles 3 and 13 ECHR due to the deficiencies of the Greek asylum procedure.

Dublin II was replaced with another Regulation in 2013 (Dublin III).[16] The UK participated in the application and implementation of that Regulation.[17] Dublin III states that when it is not possible to designate the Member State responsible, 'the first Member State in which the application for international protection was lodged shall be responsible for examining it'.[18] In light of the ECtHR case law, the provision added that if there are systemic deficiencies in the asylum procedures of the responsible State, the determining Member State shall continue to examine the application and the applicants should not be sent to the responsible Member State. The determining Member State becomes the responsible Member State even when no applicants can be sent to any Member State.

The EU and its Member States have given high priority to the return of irregular migrants to their countries of origin or residence. However, for such returns to occur, the EU must enter into readmission agreements. Yet the European Court of Auditors has reported that very few agreements on this matter have been concluded with third countries.[19] The result is that, between 2015 and mid-2020, only one in three migrants ordered to leave the EU complied with the request, leading to a return rate of about 29 per cent.[20] What is the fate of smuggled people if readmission agreements cannot be concluded? Many of them live in a state of hiding in the countries of destination with no rights, 'barred from entering into contract relations'.[21] Many of them are 'accused of being "smugglers" themselves, and risk long periods of arbitrary detention, as well as exclusion from accessing asylum and other regularisation procedures'.[22] They are also subject 'to bullying practices of state authorities including dispersal policies, destruction of shelters, and the wilful destruction by state agents of tarpaulins and sleeping bags of migrants sleeping rough'.[23] In addition, the ECtHR has emphasised that many undocumented migrants are vulnerable to human trafficking.[24] The UK Government's Retained

[15] *MSS v Belgium and Greece* App no 30696/09 (ECtHR (GC), 21 January 2011).

[16] Regulation (EU) No 604/2013 of the European Parliament and of the Council of 26 June 2013 establishing the criteria and mechanisms for determining the Member State responsible for examining an application for international protection lodged in one of the Member States by a third-country national or a stateless person (recast) [2013] OJ L180/31.

[17] ibid recital (41) of the Preamble.

[18] ibid Art 3(2).

[19] Special Report 2021/17 EU readmission cooperation with third countries: relevant actions yielded limited results.

[20] ibid.

[21] Spijkerboer (n 1) 466.

[22] PICUM, 'Migrant Smuggling: Why we need a paradigm shift', Briefing Paper (July 2022) available at https://picum.org/wp-content/uploads/2022/07/Migrant-smuggling-why-we-need-a-paradigm-shift.pdf (last accessed 17 January 2025) 3.

[23] Special Report (n 16).

[24] See, eg, *Chowdury and Others v Greece* App no 21884/15 (ECtHR, 30 March 2017); and *VCL and AN v United Kingdom* App nos 77587/12 and 74603/12 (ECtHR, 16 February 2021). Human Trafficking is outside the scope of this chapter.

EU Law Dashboard does not list the Dublin Regulation among the EU legal measures that will be repealed or retained.[25]

## III. The EU–UK Trade and Cooperation Agreement and the Smuggling of Migrants

Before the UK left the EU, it chose to participate in both the Facilitation Directive and in the Framework Decision, which require states to impose criminal penalties on people who commit the crime of migrant smuggling.[26] The terms of the Directive and Framework Decision are not replicated in the TCA, although at the point of exit the UK retained the implementing legislation from both measures. The TCA, however, does not include any provision on cooperation between the UK and the EU on asylum and migration matters.[27] It is focused on police and judicial cooperation in criminal matters, following the Political Declaration set out by the UK and the EU in 2018 and amended in 2019.[28] The Declaration is based on Article 50(2) of the Treaty on European Union[29] and 'provides for … the arrangements for the withdrawal of a departing Member State, taking account of the framework for its future relationship with the Union'.[30] Future cooperation between the EU and the UK will be based on principles and values established by the ECHR, whilst the EU and its Member States will continue to be bound by the Charter of Fundamental Rights,[31] which reaffirms the rights protected by the ECHR.[32] The parties will cooperate to guarantee the safety of their respective citizens and for this purpose they 'should establish a broad, comprehensive and balanced security partnership'.[33] The partnership will also respect UK national sovereignty.[34] In order to preserve the reciprocal safety and security, the parties 'will provide for comprehensive, close, balanced and reciprocal law enforcement and judicial cooperation in criminal matters, with the view to delivering strong operational capabilities for the purposes of the prevention, investigation, detection and prosecution of criminal

[25] HM Government *Retained EU Law and Assimilated Law Dashboard* (2024) available at https://www.gov.uk/government/publications/retained-eu-law-dashboard (last accessed 17 January 2025).

[26] Council Directive 2002/90/EC of 28 November 2002 defining the facilitation of unauthorised entry, transit and residence [2002] OJ L328/17, para 7 (Facilitation Directive); Council Framework Decision of 28 November 2002 on the strengthening of the penal framework to prevent the facilitation of unauthorised entry, transit and residence [2002] OJ L328/1, para 7 (Framework Decision).

[27] House of Lords, *Beyond Brexit: policing, law enforcement and security*. European union Committee (25th Report of Session 2019–21, HL 250) para. 7.

[28] HM Government, Political Declaration setting out the framework for the future relationship between the European Union and the United Kingdom (19 October 2019) available at https://assets.publishing.service.gov.uk/media/5daaaba040f0b6598f806460/Political_Declaration_setting_out_the_framework_for_the_future_relationship_between_the_European_Union_and_the_United_Kingdom.pdf (last accessed 17 January 2025).

[29] Consolidated version of the Treaty on European Union [2012] OJ C326/13.

[30] Political Declaration (n 28) Section 1.

[31] Charter of Fundamental Rights of the European Union [2012] OJ C326/02.

[32] Political Declaration (n 28) Section 7.

[33] ibid Section 78.

[34] ibid.

offences'.[35] Operational cooperation between law enforcement authorities and judicial cooperation in criminal matters will be reinforced via Europol and Eurojust.[36]

In relation to irregular migration, the Declaration states that '[t]he Parties will cooperate to tackle illegal migration … whilst recognising the need to protect the most vulnerable'.[37] This provision is very important as, in the Declaration, the parties aim to address irregular migration using a holistic approach, which includes the fight against crime and the protection of vulnerable migrants. This holistic approach is also confirmed in the other provisions included in the same part of the Declaration, which state that cooperation against irregular migration will include 'operational cooperation with Europol to combat organised immigration crime', 'working with the European Border and Coastguard Agency to strengthen the Union's external border' and establishing a 'dialogue on shared objectives and cooperation, including in third countries and international fora, to tackle illegal migration upstream'.[38] Irregular migration and the smuggling of migrants should be addressed not only through criminal measures and cooperation in criminal matters, but also by taking into consideration the vulnerability of migrants by protecting their human rights. As Mitsilegas has emphasised, crimes committed against migrants should be considered crimes against humanity,[39] given that migrants' desperation to leave their countries of origin, combined with the absence of legal routes, results in individuals' becoming vulnerable. Research has shown that tough policies 'outsourced from EU areas (Croatia) to the EU neighbourhood put migrants, who become stranded in unknown transit terrains with little social connections, in a situation of violence and precarity'.[40] Nevertheless, migrants do not seem to enjoy any protection, and they are completely in the hands of smugglers whom they see as their only hope to leave their countries of origin. Research has shown that migrants are prepared to accept very dangerous jobs around borders in order to be able to pay the costs of their journey; and if caught by border authorities, they will are highly likely to experience various forms of violence.[41]

Despite the Political Declaration's proposal that the future UK–EU relationship should approach irregular migration and the crime of smuggling on the basis of a multi-faced approach, the TCA only contains provisions relating to cooperation on criminal matters. Article 599(5) specifically excludes the requirement of double criminality when the crimes of human trafficking and facilitation of unauthorised entry and residence have been committed.[42] This perspective emphasises that migrants are people who do not deserve protection from prosecution. However, such judgement can

[35] ibid Section 80.

[36] ibid Section 86.

[37] ibid Section 114.

[38] ibid.

[39] V Mitsilegas, 'The normative foundations of the criminalization of human smuggling: Exploring the fault lines between European and international law' (2019) 10(1) *New Journal of European Criminal Law* 74.

[40] K Augustova, H Carrapico and J Obradović-Wochnik, 'Becoming a Smuggler: Migration and Violence at EU External Borders'. (2021) 28(2) *Geopolitics* 619.

[41] ibid.

[42] Part Three of the TCA ('Law Enforcement and Judicial Cooperation in Criminal Matters'), Art 599(4) and (5).

only be established after an in-depth 'individual status determination process'.[43] Morris and Qureshi have suggested that in the UK, almost 70 per cent of people crossing the Channel by boat since 2018 would be granted asylum if their application were to be examined appropriately.[44] As regards the EU, the United Nations High Commissioner for Refugees (UNHCR) has confirmed that although, among those coming from Africa to Europe by boat, there are migrants travelling for economic reasons, the most common countries of origin are 'those affected by years of conflict and displacement, where human rights abuses are not uncommon, and some of the largest refugee and internal displacement crises due to conflict are in the East and Horn of Africa'.[45] Despite this situation, no agreements have been concluded by the EU and the UK on asylum and migration because there has been a reduction in mutual trust between the EU and the UK since Brexit.[46] It must be emphasised that in this area there had been UK disengagement even before Brexit, when, for example, the UK opted out from the recast of four asylum directives in 2011, because the Government was of the opinion that those directives did not give them any discretion in deciding the applicants who could be authorised to enter British territory, endangering the UK's ability to reduce the number of asylum seekers, detect false claimants and control its external borders.[47] Conversely, when it comes to cooperation against cross-border crimes, the UK has consistently played a crucial role[48] and intends to maintain its significant involvement. This is demonstrated by the agreements that the UK has concluded with EU agencies.[49] Before Brexit, an agreement between the EU and the UK that would include repressive measures against people smuggling was never considered as problematic. Since 2020, the principle of mutual

[43] J Carling, 'The phrase 'refugees and migrants' undermines analysis, policy and protection' (2023) 61(3) *International Migration* 399.

[44] M Morris and A Qureshi, 'Understanding the rise in Channell crossing' *IPPR* (26 October 2022) available at www.ippr.org/articles/understanding-the-rise-in-channel-crossings (last accessed 17 January 2025).

[45] UNHCR, 'No end in sight. Refugees and migrants moving irregularly to North Africa and Europe face unspeakable horrors along Mediterranean routes. The Mediterranean Situation. Yearly arrivals 2014–2021' available at https://storymaps.arcgis.com/stories/07502a24ce0646bb9703ce96630b15fa (last accessed on 17 January 2025).

[46] For a more in-depth analysis on this issue, see A Neidhardt, 'Post-Brexit EU–UK Cooperation on migration and asylum: How to live apart, together', European Policy Centre Discussion Paper, 2022) available at www.epc.eu/content/PDF/2022/EU-UK_post_Brexit_DP_v4.pdf (last accessed 17 January 2025).

[47] N El-Enanny, 'The Perils of Differentiated Integration in the Field of Asylum' in B De Witte, A Ott, and J Monnet (eds), *Between Flexibility and Disintegration: The Trajectory of Differentiation in EU Law* (Edward Elgar Publishing, 2017) 5; S Wolff, A Piquet and H Carrapico, 'UK's Withdrawal from Justice and Home Affairs: a historical institutionalist analysis of policy trajectory' (2022) 20 *Comparative European Politics* 604, 615.

[48] Wolff, Piquet and Carrapico (n 43) 607.

[49] National Crime Agency, 'NCA and EUROPOL sign up to a new working arrangement' (29 September 2021) available at www.nationalcrimeagency.gov.uk/news/nca-and-europol-sign-up-to-a-new-working-arrangement (last accessed 17 January 2025); Europol, Working and Administrative Arrangement establishing cooperative relations between the competent authorities of the UK and Europol (2023) available at www.europol.europa.eu/partners-collaboration/agreements/working-and-administrative-arrangement-establishing-cooperative-relations-between-competent-authorities-of-uk-and-europol (last accessed 17 January 2025); Eurojust, Working Arrangement between Eurojust and the Home Office, on behalf of the competent authorities of the United Kingdom of Great Britain and Northern Ireland implementing the Trade and Cooperation Agreement between the European Union and the European Atomic Energy Community and the United Kingdom of Great Britain and Northern Ireland (10 November 2021), available at https://www.eurojust.europa.eu/sites/default/files/assets/2021_11_10_eurojust_wa_final._rev.pdf (last accessed 17 January 2025); Working Arrangement Establishing Operational Cooperation between the European Border and Coastguard Agency and the Home Office of the United Kingdom of Great Britain and Northern Ireland (23 February) available at https://assets.

trust has gained significant importance. For the UK to participate in police and judicial cooperation with the EU, it must uphold high standards in the protection of human rights. The EU has always accorded very high importance to mutual trust, which has been confirmed by the ruling of the Court of Justice of European Union (CJEU) that, in the name of mutual trust, national Constitutions can be set aside as it can be assumed that all EU Member States respect human rights in the same way.[50] However, since the UK is no longer part of the Charter of Fundamental Rights, under Article 52(3) of which EU law is able to provide more extensive protection of human rights compared to the ECHR, the EU can no longer assume that the threshold for the protection of human rights will be high in the UK. Furthermore, the fact that the UK is adopting stringent laws on migration and asylum aggravates the situation, because lack of mutual trust may be caused by the fact that the UK may be proposing/ adopting laws incompatible with the ECHR and with the Charter. Lack of mutual trust caused by draconian legislation on asylum and migration can also endanger bilateral agreements, as EU Member States have to respect human rights as protected by the ECHR and by the Charter.

Recently, France and the UK have concluded a bilateral deal aimed at addressing small-boat crossings in the Channel that may be benefitting from the support of criminal organisations.[51] The deal was agreed on 14 November 2022, but it lacks provisions that could facilitate the relocation of migrants upon disembarkation.[52] The deal aims at preventing Channel crossings by focusing on smuggling. In the agreement, the Ministers of both countries 'acknowledge that efforts cannot stop here and are committed to maintaining regular dialogue on what other innovative steps can be taken to address illegal migration at all levels'.[53] However, they failed to take into consideration that a reduction in the number of legal routes tends to result in a higher number of migrants taking more dangerous journeys and 'a need for emergency humanitarian assistance'.[54] The UK also concluded a bilateral agreement with Greece in 2022.[55] Its

publishing.service.gov.uk/media/65d768b454f1e70011165897/Frontex-UK_WA_-_Final_version__2_.pdf (last accessed 17 January 2025).

[50] For example, Case C-399/11 *Melloni v Ministerio Fiscal*, ECLI:EU:C:2013:107, para 63, where the CJEU ruled that 'allowing a Member State to avail itself of Article 53 of the Charter to make the surrender of a person convicted *in absentia* conditional upon the conviction being open to review in the issuing Member State, a possibility not provided for under Framework Decision 2009/299, in order to avoid an adverse effect on the right to a fair trial and the rights of the defence guaranteed by the constitution of the executing Member State, by casting doubt on the uniformity of the standard of protection of fundamental rights as defined in that framework decision, would undermine the principles of mutual trust and recognition which that decision purports to uphold and would, therefore, compromise the efficacy of that Framework Decision'.

[51] 'UK and France in "final stage" of reaching deal on Channel crossing' *Financial Times* (7 November 2022) available at https://www.ft.com/content/9eac9c5c-45dc-4d44-9463-2c3b92cb6b96 (last accessed 17 January 2025).

[52] Home Office and UK Border Force, Policy paper: UK–France joint statement: enhancing cooperation against illegal migration (14 November 2022) available at www.gov.uk/government/publications/next-phase-in-partnership-to-tackle-illegal-migration-and-small-boat-arrivals/uk-france-joint-statement-enhancing-co-operation-against-illegal-migration (last accessed 17 January 2025).

[53] ibid.

[54] A Balch, 'UK–France migration deal: how does Brexit factor into the plan to stop small boats' *The Conversation* (18 November 2022) available at https://theconversation.com/uk-france-migration-deal-how-does-brexit-factor-into-the-plan-to-stop-small-boats-194763 (last accessed 17 January 2025).

[55] HM Government, 'Joint Action Plan by the UK and Greece on migration' *gov.uk* (27 September 2023) available at www.statewatch.org/media/3508/uk-gr-joint-action-plan-migration-4-20.pdf (last accessed 17 January 2025).

main purpose is the prevention of unlawful migration and the dismantling of migrant-smuggling networks. In terms of cooperation beyond criminal investigations, no further developments can be identified. The UK's departure from the EU has left a vacuum in the protection of asylum seekers as the UK is no longer part of the CEAS or Eurodac.[56] Eurodac is an information system that collects, transmits and compares fingerprints for the purpose of determining which EU Member State is responsible for examining an application for international protection lodged in a EU Member State by a third-country national or stateless person.[57] Dublin III and the Eurodac database aim to prevent what is usually labelled 'asylum shopping', which refers to asylum seekers applying for refugee status in different EU Member States, as well as 'refugees in orbit', where no State takes responsibility for asylum claims.[58] Through Dublin III and Eurodac, asylum seekers were distributed between EU Member States and the UK participated in the distribution. Now that the UK has left the CEAS, redistribution no longer takes place and the UK legislation has restricted access to legal routes. There is an emphasis in returning migrants to their countries of origin, rather than widening legal routes.

The EU and the UK should work together and try to find solutions by focusing on partnerships with third countries, opening legal routes, facilitating the return of migrants who have reached the UK unlawfully, seeking solutions that respect human rights, and at the same time improve the management of migration.[59]

## IV. Undocumented Migrants in the UK Post-Brexit and Cooperation with the EU

Access to the UK has become very difficult for third-country nationals seeking asylum. The UK enacted the Nationality and Borders Act 2022. Part 3 of this Act focuses on immigration controls and on the fight against the smuggling of migrants. Section 40 of the Act creates two new offences of arriving in the UK without a valid entry clearance or electronic travel authorisation (ETA) where required, in addition to the existing offence of entering without leave.[60] These offences cover all asylum claimants and refugees who arrive without the necessary entry clearance or ETA.[61] Section 41 amends the facilitation offences in sections 25 and 25A of the Immigration Act 1971, raising the maximum

[56] M Gower, *Brexit: The End of the Dublin Regulation III in the UK*, House of Commons Library (21 December 2020) available at https://researchbriefings.files.parliament.uk/documents/CBP-9031/CBP-9031.pdf (last accessed 17 January 2025).

[57] Regulation (EU) No 603/2013 of the European Parliament and of the Council of 26 June 2013 on the establishment of 'Eurodac' for the comparison of fingerprints for the effective application of Regulation (EU) No 604/2013 establishing the criteria and mechanisms for determining the Member State responsible for examining an application for international protection lodged in one of the Member States by a third-country national or a stateless person and on requests for the comparison with Eurodac data by Member States' law enforcement authorities and Europol for law enforcement purposes, and amending Regulation (EU) No 1077/2011 establishing a European Agency for the operational management of large-scale IT systems in the area of freedom, security and justice (recast) OJ L 180/1.

[58] ibid 6.

[59] ibid.

[60] Immigration Act 1971, s 24(1)(a).

[61] Immigration Act 1971, s 28LA(1), as amended by s.40 Nationality and Borders Act 2022, Explanatory Notes, para 399.

penalty from 14 years' to life imprisonment and removing the requirement of facilitation being 'for gain' in relation to section 25A. The Act distinguishes between legal and illegal migrants[62] and asylum seekers belong to the latter category.

Furthermore, the Immigration Act 1971, section 28LA(1), as amended by section 45 of the Nationality and Borders Act 2022, expands current maritime enforcement powers enabling maritime enforcement action to take place outside of UK waters in order to detect, prevent, investigate and prosecute the illegal entry of migrants as well as its facilitation. It includes powers to require migrant vessels to leave UK waters as well as powers intending to support the disembarkation of non-compliant passengers in a non-UK Ports.[63] An act is not considered to constitute assisting unlawful immigration if the act was done with the aim of assisting the migrant 'at any time between the time when the assisted individual was first in danger or distress at sea, and the time when the assisted individual was delivered to a place of safety on land'.[64] The vessels that can be subject to maritime enforcement actions are:

(a) a United Kingdom ship,
(b) a ship without nationality,
(c) a foreign ship,
(d) a ship registered under the law of a relevant territory ....[65]

and the enforcement powers can only be exercised 'for the purpose of preventing, detecting, investigating or prosecuting a relevant offence'.[66] This new offence was introduced because, since 2020, the assistance provided to unlawful migrants crossing the English Channel has increased.[67] Criminal organisations have become more sophisticated, with smugglers 'increasing the size of vessels used to facilitate illegal entry to the UK'.[68] Therefore, the 2022 Act has strengthened the maritime enforcement powers by authorising investigation of the crime extraterritorially.

The 2022 Act has reinforced the externalisation of migration by widening the power of immigration officers beyond territorial waters. Migrants may not even be given the opportunity to report their smugglers, if they have committed crimes against them during their journeys, as their expulsion will be automatic if it is ascertained that they are unlawful. In addition, people entitled to asylum may not have the opportunity to claim it in the UK.

The Nationality and Borders Act was passed at the same time the UK was negotiating the UK–Rwanda treaty.[69] This aimed to create a mechanism for relocating

[62] E Reyes, 'All at sea' *Law Gazette* (15 July 2022) available at www.lawgazette.co.uk/features/all-at-sea/5113152.article (last accessed 17 January 2025).

[63] Immigration Act 1971, s 28LA(1), as amended by the Nationality and Borders Act 2022, Explanatory Notes, para 453.

[64] Immigration Act 1971, s 28LA(1), as amended by the Nationality and Borders Act 2022, s 41(2).

[65] Immigration Act 1971, s 28LA(1), as amended by the Nationality and Borders Act 2022, sch 7.

[66] Immigration Act 1971, s 28LA(2)(a), as amended by the Nationality and Borders Act 2022, sch 7.

[67] Immigration Act 1971, s 28LA(1), as amended by the Nationality and Borders Act 2022, Explanatory Notes, para 454.

[68] Immigration Act 1971, s 28LA(1), as amended by the Nationality and Borders Act 2022, Explanatory Notes, para 455.

[69] Agreement between the Government of the United Kingdom of Great Britain and Northern Ireland and the Government of the Republic of Rwanda for the provision of an asylum partnership to strengthen shared international commitments on the protection of refugees and migrants. (published 5 December 2023).

asylum seekers whose claims were not to be heard in the UK to Rwanda.[70] Human Rights Watch described the deal between Rwanda and the UK as 'cruel' and added that 'Rwanda's appalling human rights record is well documented'.[71] The UNHCR criticised the UK–Rwanda deal, as the Refugee Agency is against shifting asylum responsibilities to third countries.[72] The UK–Rwanda deal has been described as 'nothing other than mass deportation'.[73] The ECtHR issued urgent interim relief in favour of an Iraqi national who travelled from Iraq to Turkey and then across Europe before reaching the UK by boat across the English Channel.[74] Subsequently, he made an asylum claim in the UK, which was considered inadmissible, and was set to be relocated to Rwanda. The High Court refused to grant him an interim relief, an appeal was dismissed and the UK Supreme Court refused permission for an appeal. The ECtHR took into consideration the UNHCR report stating that asylum seekers transferred to Rwanda 'will not have access to fair and efficient procedures for the determination of refugee status'.[75] It also considered the High Court's question, on whether Rwanda should be treated as a safe country, to be 'irrational or based on insufficient enquiry', and as giving 'rise to "serious triable issues"'.[76] Therefore, the ECtHR decided to grant an urgent interim relief on the basis of the fact that Rwanda could not guarantee and protect rights recognised by the ECHR, as Rwanda was not a State Party of the Convention and thus not legally bound by it. In addition, the interim relief was granted because of a mechanism allowing the return of the applicant to the UK 'in the event of a successful merits challenge before the domestic courts'.[77] Subsequently, the High Court dismissed the challenges against the UK Government but overturned the decision in each individual case, as asylum seekers were not given the opportunity to argue about the safety of Rwanda, were not permitted access to legal advice, and had only seven days to argue their case and five days to apply to the Court.[78] The Court of Appeal, on the other hand, ruled by majority that the UK policy on Rwanda was unlawful because Rwanda was not a safe country and there was the real risk that the principle of *non-refoulement* could be breached.[79] The Supreme Court agreed with the Court of Appeal, stating:

> [W]e conclude that the Court of Appeal was correct to reverse the decision of the Divisional Court, and was entitled to find that there are substantial grounds for believing that the

[70] Home Office, Statement concerning the Agreement between the Government of the United Kingdom of Great Britain and Northern Ireland and the Government of the Republic of Rwanda for the provision of an asylum partnership to strengthen shared international commitments on the protection of refugees and migrants (April 2024).

[71] Human Rights Watch, 'UK Plan to Ship Asylum Seekers to Rwanda is a cruelty' (14 April 2022) available at www.hrw.org/news/2022/04/14/uk-plan-ship-asylum-seekers-rwanda-cruelty-itself (last accessed 17 January 2025).

[72] UNHCR 'UN Refugee Agency opposes UK plan to export asylum', Press Release (14 April 2022) available at www.unhcr.org/uk/news/press/2022/4/62585e814/un-refugee-agency-opposes-uk-plan-export-asylum.html (last accessed 17 January 2025).

[73] 'Offshoring the asylum process: a dangerous move for health' *The Lancet* (30 April 2022) available at www.thelancet.com/journals/lancet/article/PIIS0140-6736(22)00772-3/fulltext (last accessed 17 January 2025).

[74] 'The European Court grants urgent interim measure in case concerning asylum seeker's imminent removal from the UK to Rwanda', Press Release (14 June 2022).

[75] ibid.

[76] ibid.

[77] ibid.

[78] *AAA & Ors v Secretary of State for the Home Department CO/2032/2022 & Or* [2022] EWHC 3230 (Admin) [414]–[426].

[79] *R (AAA) v Secretary of State for the Home Department* [2023] EWCA Civ 745 [492] et seq.

> removal of the claimants to Rwanda would expose them to a real risk of ill-treatment by reason of refoulement. It was accordingly correct to hold that the Secretary of State's policy is unlawful. The Secretary of State's appeal is therefore dismissed.[80]

Following the Supreme Court's ruling, the UK passed the Safety of Rwanda (Asylum and Immigration) Act 2024. The UK/Rwanda deal was replaced by a Treaty with the aim of preventing unlawful migration, as all migrants without the right to enter British territory were to be sent to Rwanda.[81] The Act indicated the steps to be taken to consider Rwanda a safe country. For this purpose, s 1(3) of the Act stated that the Republic of Rwanda had agreed:

(a) not to send any persons removed from the UK to another country;
(b) to relocate individuals and return them to the UK following a request from the British Government;
(c) to improve 'the system for the processing of protection claims by relocated individuals';
(d) to treat relocated individuals equally, irrespective of the status that they are granted in the Republic of Rwanda;
(e) to provide legal assistance to individuals' claims and appeals;
(f) to monitor independently that these provisions will be respected and 'subject to a form of binding dispute settlement'.

Section 1(6) stated that the UK would act in compliance with the major international Conventions, including, amongst others, the Refugee Convention and the ECHR. However, the UNCHR stated that despite improvements introduced by the Act in relation to the establishment of a Treaty between the UK and Rwanda, there remained issues, as the asylum system did 'not overcome continued procedural fairness and other protection gaps' that could only be addressed by 'long-term and fundamental engagement and changes in institutional culture'.[82]

Following the 2024 General Election, the Labour Government took the decision, in July, to cancel the Rwanda asylum scheme and repeal the 2024 Act, putting an end to any discussions on whether asylum seekers were to be sent there.[83] No migrants were ever forcibly relocated to Rwanda under the policy, but a small number did relocate voluntarily. Denmark's plan to transfer asylum seekers to Rwanda was also put on hold.[84] Italy often refuses to allow rescued migrants to disembark, in a lengthy saga with the EU and

[80] *R (AAA) v Secretary of State for the Home Department* [2023] UKSC 42 [149].

[81] Agreement between the Government of the United Kingdom of Great Britain and Northern Ireland and the Government of the Republic of Rwanda for the provision of an asylum partnership to strengthen shared international commitments on the protection of refugees and migrants (published 5 December 2023) available at www.gov.uk/government/publications/uk-rwanda-treaty-provision-of-an-asylum-partnership/uk-rwanda-treaty-provision-of-an-asylum-partnership-accessible (last accessed 17 January 2025).

[82] UNHCR, Analysis of the Legality and Appropriateness of the Transfer of Asylum-Seekers under the UK–Rwanda arrangement: an update (15 January 2024) available at www.refworld.org/legal/natlegcomments/unhcr/2024/en/147086 (last accessed 17 January 2025) para 20.

[83] S Francis, 'Starmer confirms Rwanda deportation plan dead' *BBC News* (6 July 2024) available at www.bbc.co.uk/news/articles/cz9dn8erg3zo (last accessed 16 January 2025).

[84] Bleona Restelica, 'Denmark Puts on Hold Plans to Transfer Asylum Seekers to Rwanda' (16 January 2025) https://schengen.news/denmark-puts-on-hold-plans-to-transfer-asylum-seekers-to-rwanda/#google_vignette <last accessed 17 January 2025>.

its Member States that began in 2019.[85] The Italian Government's actions appear to be in violation of the law as, under international law, once migrants have been rescued, they have the right to be disembarked in a safe country, which, in this case, would be the country that conducted the rescue.[86]

As states impose stricter restrictions, criminal organisations are more likely to exploit migrants who are willing to take risks in pursuit of a better life.[87] The UK is only targeting irregular migrants with restrictions. Parliament has also enacted the Illegal Immigration Act 2023, which establishes a duty for the Secretary of State to make arrangements to remove 'certain persons who enter or arrive in the United Kingdom in breach of immigration control as soon as is reasonably practicable after their entry or arrival'.[88] These restrictions have been adopted 'to deter unlawful migration'.[89] The title of the Act has negative connotations as it contributes to stereotyping all migrants who enter the UK irregularly, or who overstay, and presents them as deserving of punishment as criminals. However, further restricting access to British territory is likely to cause an increase in migrants trying to reach the UK irregularly, as it has been reported that increased maritime surveillance and the abolition of legal routes will not discourage people from trying to cross the Channel.[90] With a reduction in the number of available legal routes for asylum, more people will try to cross the border by embarking on more dangerous journeys.[91] Not only will they risk perishing along the way, they will also risk becoming victims of human trafficking. In September 2023, the Human Rights and Equalities Commission in Northern Ireland launched a legal challenge against the Act, as it neglects to protect the most vulnerable people, such as victims of human trafficking and children, and is therefore incompatible with the ECHR.[92] In May 2024, a judge at Northern Ireland's High Court ruled that parts of the Act should not apply in

[85] A Binley, 'Standoff as Italy stops male migrants from disembarking rescue ships' *BBC News* (6 November 2022) available at www.bbc.co.uk/news/world-europe-63533769 (last accessed 16 January 2025). See also ANSA, 'Salvini claims he acted 'his role' in Rackete defamation case' (13 June 2022) available at www.infomigrants.net/en/post/41132/salvini-claims-he-acted-his-role-in-rackete-defamation-case (last accessed 17 January 2025); J Barigazzi, 'Brussels steps in as Italy and France fight over migrant boats' (11 November 2022) available at www.politico.eu/article/eu-italy-france-fight-migrant-boat-ocean-viking-margaritis-schinas/ (last accessed 17 January 2025).

[86] International Convention on Maritime Search and Rescue (SAR), adopted 27 April 1979, entered into force 22 June 1985, 1405 UNTS 97; United Nations Convention on the Law of the Sea (UNCLOS), adopted 10 December 1982, entered into force 16 November 1994, 1833 UNTS 397; International Convention for the Safety of Life at Sea (SOLAS), adopted 1 November 1974, entered into force 25 May 1980, 1184 UNTS 278. The SOLAS Convention, for the safety of ships at sea, was adopted by the IMO and came into force on 25 May 1980 and was amended in 2004. See also the following ECtHR cases: *Hirsi Jamaa and Others v Italy* App no 27765/09 (ECtHR, 23 February 2012); and *Khlaifia and Others v Italy* App no. 16483/12 (ECtHR, 1 September 2015).

[87] UNODC, 'Smuggling of migrants: the harsh search for a better life' available at www.unodc.org/toc/en/crimes/migrant-smuggling.html (last accessed 17 January 2025).

[88] Illegal Immigration Act 2023, s 1(2)(a).

[89] Illegal Immigration Act 2023, s 1(1).

[90] Neidhardt (n 41).

[91] Balch (n 49).

[92] Northern Ireland Human Rights Commission, Northern Ireland Human Rights Commission begins a legal challenge of the Illegal Migration Act (3 October 2023) available at https://nihrc.org/news/detail/northern-ireland-human-rights-commission-begins-a-legal-challenge-of-the-illegal-migration-act (last accessed 17 January 2025).

Northern Ireland because they were incompatible with the European Convention on Human Rights[93] and caused a significant diminution of the rights enjoyed by asylum seekers residing in Northern Ireland under the terms of the Good Friday Agreement.[94] As part of the EU Withdrawal Agreement, the UK Government is required to ensure that there is no diminution of certain human rights and equality protections contained within the Belfast (Good Friday) Agreement.[95] Member States of the EU and the UK should cooperate to redistribute irregular migrants fairly and, where possible, give them the opportunity to legalise their status by granting them the right of residence if a claim can be made out.[96] All EU Member States are considered safe countries by the Dublin Regulations (see section II of this chapter). Therefore, the UK and the EU should reach an agreement in order to redistribute asylum seekers and other migrants. The Confederation of British Industry has recently revealed that three-quarters of British companies have been impacted by labour shortages, which are threatening their ability to operate at full capacity.[97] Lord Wolfson, a Conservative peer and a prominent Brexit advocate, affirmed that the Government should approach migration differently in order to attract more foreign workers into the UK to ease labour shortages.[98] Legal routes could give many migrants the opportunity to travel regularly, gain a working visa, become employed and escape from a situation of vulnerability. The smuggling of migrants could be defeated by facilitating such policies, and the EU and the UK need to cooperate to achieve this result.

## V. Conclusions

Migrant smuggling may only be defeated by effectively deterring migrants from reaching out to criminal organisations. Fighting the smuggling of migrants as a serious crime alone is currently not leading to its reduction. In fact, the adoption of a criminal justice approach simply means that smugglers are becoming ever more sophisticated. The Facilitation Directive and its implementation in the UK alongside the Dublin Regulations has created a hostile environment for migrants, which encourages undocumented migrants to seek out sophisticated networks to help them make their journeys.

[93] The court granted section 4 of the Human Rights Act 1999 declarations of incompatibility in respect of ss 2(1), 5(1), 6(3), 6(7) as they impose a duty to remove, ss (1), 5, 6 and 22 insofar as they relate to potential victims of modern slavery or human trafficking and ss 2(1), 5(1) and 6 relating to children.

[94] In the matter of an application by the Northern Ireland Human Rights Commission for Judicial Review in the matter of an application by JR295 for Judicial Review and in the Matter of the Illegal Migration Act 2023 [2024] NIKB 35.

[95] Northern Ireland Human Rights Commission, 'Call for Expression of Interest on Remedies and Windsor Framework Article 2' (July 2024) available at https://nihrc.org/assets/uploads/Call-for-Expression-of-Interest-on-Remedies-and-Windsor-Framework-Article-2-PDF.pdf (last accessed on 16 January 2025).

[96] KF Hinterberger, 'An EU Regularization Directive. An effective solution to the enforcement deficit in returning irregularly staying migrants' (2019) 26(6) *Maastricht Journal of European and Comparative Law* 740.

[97] Confederation of British Industry, 'Three-Quarters of UK Companies hit by Labour Shortages in Last 12 Months' (2022) available at www.cbi.org.uk/media-centre/articles/three-quarters-of-uk-companies-hit-by-labour-shortages-in-last-12-months-cbipertemps/ (last accessed on 17 January 2025).

[98] S Jack, 'Brexit-backing Next boss says UK needs more overseas workers' *BBC News* (10 November 2022) available at www.bbc.co.uk/news/business-63573988 (last accessed 17 January 2025).

Only the Residence Permit Directive[99] offers some protection to undocumented migrants and recognises their vulnerability. The EU has made return to country of origin a primary objective of its migration policies, as has the UK. However, the EU has only managed to conclude a small number of readmission agreements with third countries, which have had very limited success. In the five years leading up to Brexit, only one in three migrants ordered to leave the EU complied with the request, leading to a return rate from the EU to countries of origin of about 29 per cent. Problems in controlling migration and in the operation of the terms of the Dublin Agreement meant that the UK chose not to try to re-join the Dublin system post-Brexit. The TCA therefore contains no provisions on cooperation in asylum and immigration. There are only thin, non-binding commitments to ensure good management of migratory flows. One positive aspect of the TCA is that it has continued to facilitate cooperation with Europol and its European Migrant Smuggling Centre.

Post-Brexit, there are no longer safe and legal routes for asylum seekers, and the UK has experienced an unprecedented rise in arrivals by boat across the English Channel. Those wishing to be reunited with their families have no choice but to make the deadly journey. There is evidence that criminals have professionalised their activities. The UK and the EU need to work together to stamp out this practice. Post-Brexit there has a widening of the policy gap between the two. As the EU seeks to develop a new pact on migration and asylum aimed at addressing perceived imbalances in the Dublin Regulations, the UK has focused on creating a more hostile environment through the Nationality and Borders Act 2022 and the Illegal Migration Act 2023. Although the legislation is premised on there being safe and legal channels, '[t]here are no visa routes to enable people to claim asylum in the UK from overseas'.[100] The UK's agreement with Rwanda was heavily criticised as a breach of the UK's international obligations. Although argued to be the UK's answer to 'taking back control of its borders', it was deeply flawed, and there was no evidence that, even if it had become operational, it would have decreased the number of small-boat crossings.

The UK and the EU have deep economic, cultural, historical and political ties. The need for a comprehensive and balanced relationship has not diminished because of Brexit. Without an EU-wide agreement or bilateral agreements with neighbouring coastal states, the UK cannot remove individuals to EU Member States, leaving people in legal limbo and exposed to exploitation. Cooperation is in the interests of both the UK and EU, as both need to reduce the incentives to cross the English Channel on small boats. This cannot be done without creating safe and legal channels from the EU and a coherent policy on returns of third-country nationals. Such solutions will be much more stable if they respect the UK's international obligations, including its commitment to protect human rights.

A way to achieve this objective is not to consider the arrival of smuggled migrants in Europe as an emergency that should be tackled by emergency measures. Agreements with third countries should rather concentrate on long-term policies that aim to prevent people from leaving their countries of origin and residence in the first place.

[99] Council Directive 2004/81/EC of 29 April 2004 on the residence permit issued to third-country nationals who are victims of trafficking in human beings or who have been the subject of an action to facilitate illegal immigration, who cooperate with the competent authorities [2004] OJ L261/19.

[100] Home Office, 'Safe and Legal Routes' (20 July 2023) available at www.gov.uk/government/publications/illegal-migration-bill-factsheets/safe-and-legal-routes (last accessed 17 January 2025).

# 21

# Fighting Human Trafficking under the Trade and Cooperation Agreement

CHLOÉ BRIÈRE AND AMY WEATHERBURN*

## I. Introduction

Trafficking in human beings is a transnational crime, often committed with the involvement of criminal groups operating beyond the reach of one national jurisdiction. As a result, cooperation across borders is vital to assuring effective investigation and prosecution of human traffickers.[1] Yet, as highlighted by the Deputy Coordinator for Combating Human Trafficking of the Organization for Security and Cooperation in Europe, joint investigative efforts 'are a gold standard and are systematically underused by countries'.[2]

The European Union (EU) and its Member States appear, in contrast, rather proactive in ensuring a high level of cooperation in trafficking cases. The EU has over the years developed an 'ecosystem' favourable to cooperation that can support the attainment of the globally recognised 4P framework of prevention, prosecution, protection and partnership.[3] The Anti-Trafficking Coordinator embeds these objectives, defining the EU Strategy against trafficking.[4] Next to general instruments and mechanisms applicable to other crimes, the EU has also adopted specific mechanisms, such as the Directive approximating the definition of the offence and the level of sanctions, and defining minimum rules on prevention and protection of trafficking victims.[5] Trafficking in human beings has also always been among the priority areas identified

* With special thanks to Colin Wards and Darryl Dixon for contributing their practical expertise and insights into the topics addressed in this chapter.

[1] Anti-trafficking Monitoring Group, 'Brexit and the UK's fight against modern slavery' (July 2017) available at www.antislavery.org/wp-content/uploads/2017/07/ATMG-Brexit-paper.pdf (last accessed 6 November 2024); M Ventrella, 'Brexit and the fight against human trafficking: Actual situation and future uncertainty' (2018) 26 *Marmara Journal of European Studies* 119.

[2] Home Affairs Committee, *Human Trafficking Inquiry* (HC 2022–23, 1142) Q58.

[3] United Nations Global Plan of Action to Combat Trafficking in Persons. A/RES/64/293 (12 August 2010).

[4] European Commission Communication on the EU Strategy on Combating Trafficking in Human Beings 2021–2025. COM(2021) 171 final.

[5] Directive 2011/36/ EU of the European Parliament and of the Council of 5 April 2011 on preventing and combating trafficking in human beings and protecting its victims [2011] OJ L101/1.

for closer operational coordination since the launch of the EU policy cycle against serious and organised crime, also known as EMPACT.

Pre-Brexit, the United Kingdom (UK) had played a leading role in the development of the EU area of criminal justice,[6] and was particularly active in cooperating with other EU Member States in combating trafficking, gaining invaluable expertise in the matter.[7] With the UK's withdrawal from the EU and the resulting shift in status at regional and global levels in anti-trafficking developments, it is important to consider the impact Brexit may have on operational cooperation in countering human trafficking. The Trade and Cooperation Agreement (TCA),[8] combined with the Conventions developed within the Council of Europe, answered some concerns by maintaining certain highly appreciated mechanisms of cooperation. This is notably demonstrated by the UK's continuous involvement in Joint Investigation Teams (JITs),[9] pre-Brexit[10] and post-Brexit,[11] albeit on a different legal basis.[12] Yet, despite such extensive cooperation, trafficking in human beings was not identified in the TCA as a field envisaged for closer thematic cooperation.[13] Additionally, appraising the impact of Brexit and its consequences for operational cooperation in countering trafficking has not been particularly discussed in the literature,[14] which is a gap that it is hoped this chapter will fill.

Whilst the TCA is a point of departure, many aspects may influence the EU–UK police cooperation in countering human trafficking. The post-Brexit political climate in the UK has led to an increased risk of human trafficking and modified trafficking patterns, as we will discuss in section II, requiring expanding cooperation with new partners more distant geographically than EU Member States. This does not cast aside the challenges faced – to maintain EU–UK operational cooperation, and in section III, we highlight three consequences of Brexit on counter-trafficking cooperation. We conclude by stressing that, while Brexit may so far have had a limited impact on the EU–UK cooperation thanks to the close pre-existing ties and mitigating measures, its main consequence might be a displacement of the UK authorities' focus in favour of wider international cooperation, building upon their cooperation with the EU.

[6] V Mitsilegas (2017) 'EU Criminal Law after Brexit'. *Criminal Law Forum*. 28: 240; A. Weyembergh (2017) 'Consequences of Brexit for European Union Criminal Law' (2017) 8(3) *New Journal of European Criminal Law* 293; Davies and Carrapico, ch 4; McKenzie and Kaunert, ch 17.

[7] Anti-trafficking Monitoring Group (n 1); S Massey and G Rankin, *Exploiting People for Profit* (Palgrave Macmillan, 2020) 68; R Niblock, 'Cooperation with EU agencies and bodies under the EU–UK Trade and Cooperation Agreement: Eurojust, OLAF and the EPPO' (2021) 12(2) *New Journal of European Criminal Law* 277.

[8] Trade and Cooperation Agreement between the European Union and the European Atomic Energy Community, of the one part, and the United Kingdom of Great Britain and Northern Ireland, of the other part [2021] OJ L149/10.

[9] Niblock (n 7) 179; Anti-trafficking Monitoring Group (n 1) 9.

[10] Eurojust, *Report on Trafficking in Human Beings, Best practices and issues in judicial cooperation* (2021) 5 and 11.

[11] Eurojust, *Annual Report* (2022) 60.

[12] Eurojust, *Fourth JITs Evaluation Report* (2023) 10.

[13] TCA, Part Four, and the references to human trafficking in Art 599(5) and in Annexes 41 and 42.

[14] Ventrella (n 1) 119.

## II. The Impact of the Post-Brexit Hostile Environment on Human Trafficking

Post-Brexit Britain has been politically marked by an increased emphasis on the notion of regaining sovereignty and control of national borders, leading to legal changes that further perpetuate the hostile immigration environment that pre-dated the UK's departure from the EU.[15] In this section, after describing such an environment, two significant changes to immigration law that are directly attributable to Brexit are analysed: first, the withdrawal of freedom of movement and its consequences for EU citizens living in the UK; and, second, the introduction of a points-based system for third-country nationals, also applicable to EU citizens post-Brexit. These two aspects have a direct (adverse) impact on the prevalence of the phenomenon in the UK, its patterns and ultimately on counter-trafficking police cooperation.

### A. The Privileging of Immigration Enforcement Over Combating Human Trafficking

The pre-Brexit hostile immigration environment in the UK can be characterised by legislative measures requiring private actors, such as landlords and financial institutions, to carry out immigration 'enforcement' checks on third-country nationals.[16] Employers were criminalised for employing workers who they had reasonable cause to believe were not permitted to work,[17] and workers who were working without authorisation to do so faced the confiscation of their wages as proceeds of crime.[18] Whilst these measures were likely to (further) exacerbate the vulnerability of those who were dependent on unscrupulous employers (traffickers) not just for work but also for accommodation,[19] post-Brexit efforts to curb 'illegal' migration continue to take a toll on those who are the most in need of protection, and who, under international and regional law, are entitled to such support and assistance.

The hostile immigration environment has failed to reduce the unprecedented number of migrants seeking to enter the UK,[20] often via unsafe routes and tragically, in

[15] M Griffiths and C Yeo, 'The UK's hostile environment: Deputising immigration control' (2021) 41(4) *Critical Social Policy* 521.

[16] See Immigration Act 2014 and Immigration Act of 2016 for right-to-rent checks duties and offences on landlords and agencies.

[17] Employing an illegal worker had already been criminalised, but the mens rea was narrower, with an emphasis on knowingly employing an illegal worker.

[18] Immigration Act 2016, s 34.

[19] SN Hodkinson et al, 'Fighting or fuelling forced labour? The Modern Slavery Act 2015, irregular migrants and the vulnerabilising role of the UK's hostile environment' (2021) 41(1) *Critical Social Policy* 68.

[20] Home Office, 'Irregular Migration to the UK year ending December 2021' (24 February 2022) available at www.gov.uk/government/statistics/irregular-migration-to-the-uk-year-ending-december-2021/irregular-migration-to-the-uk-year-ending-december-2021 (last accessed 6 Novemebr 2024); Home Office, 'Irregular migration to the UK, year ending March 2023' (25 May 2023) available at www.gov.uk/government/statistics/irregular-migration-to-the-uk-year-ending-march-2023/irregular-migration-to-the-uk-year-ending-march-2023 (last accessed 6 Novemebr 2024).

some cases, leading to loss of life,[21] exposing them to recruitment by organised criminal groups that would exploit them upon arrival in the UK. A lack of access to safe and legal migration routes particularly affects low-skilled migrants, as their vulnerability and risk of labour exploitation are increased. This is particularly the case where there is a shift towards illegal working in sectors characterised by a high demand for labour that may be fuelled by criminal networks who facilitate access to the job market and to the territory. Additionally, delays and deficiencies in the asylum system expose migrants to increased vulnerability upon their arrival in the UK, making them ideal targets for traffickers.[22]

Victims of trafficking face the risk of secondary victimisation, as the National Referral Mechanism has received unprecedented numbers of referrals from first-responder organisations. This leads to significant delays in potential victims' receipt of conclusive grounds decisions and certainty as to the next steps in their recovery, rehabilitation and reintegration after their exploitation. Importantly, despite false claims in political discourse, the increased number of referrals is not due to abuse of the system, as demonstrated by acceptance rates above 80 per cent. However, assessment of victim status has been hampered by amendments introduced in January 2023 to the threshold for a 'reasonable grounds' decision, which has been followed by a reduction in referrals and an increase in negative reasonable grounds decisions.[23] Of more urgent concern is the denial of access to protection and specialised support and assistance services for potential victims of modern slavery (including human trafficking). New provisions, introduced by the Immigration Act 2023, require the Secretary of State to disapply modern slavery protections to recognised victims where they have been found to arrive in the UK irregularly, and to order detention and deportation.[24] The automatic disqualification of access to support and protection measures constitutes a violation of both the Council of Europe's Convention on Action Against Trafficking in Human Beings and the European Convention on Human Rights,[25] and represents significant backsliding as

[21] Ventrella, ch 20.

[22] UNHCR and British Red Cross, *At Risk: Exploitation and the UK Asylum System* (2022) available at file:///Users/kcpw6/Downloads/UNHCR%20and%20RED%20CROSS%20-%20Destitution%20study%20_FINAL.pdf (last accessed 6 November 2024) 43–44.

[23] Home Office, 'Modern Slavery: statutory guidance for England and Wales (under s 49 of the Modern Slavery Act 2015) and non-statutory guidance for Scotland and Northern Ireland' (last updated October 2023) available at https://assets.publishing.service.gov.uk/media/66ffde903b919067bb482c61/Modern+Slavery+Statutory+Guidance+_EW_+and+Non-Statutory+Guidance+_SNI_+v3.11.pdf (last accessed 6 November 2024) 132–39. See also A Smith, 'Modern Slavery Statutory Guidance Updates' *University of Hull Wilberforce Institute* (7 February 2023) available at www.hull.ac.uk/research/institutes/wilberforce/modern-slavery-statutory-guidance-updates (last accessed 6 November 2024); or K Roberts, 'Raising the threshold: recent government changes to the modern slavery system will significantly harm victims' *Focus on Labour Exploitation* (20 December 2022) available at https://labourexploitation.org/news/raising-the-threshold-recent-government-changes-to-the-modern-slavery-system-will-significantly-harm-victims/ (last accessed 6 November 2024).

[24] Immigration Act 2023, ss 22–29; see also Nationality and Borders Act 2022, s 63.

[25] Council of Europe Convention on Action against Trafficking in Human Beings, Warsaw, 16 May 2005; CETS 197 ('Anti-Trafficking Convention'); Council of Europe Convention for the Protection of Human Rights and Fundamental Freedoms, Rome, 4 November 1950, ETS 005.

OHCHR, 'United Kingdom Nationality and Borders Bill undermines rights of victims of trafficking and modern slavery, UN experts say', Press Release (14 January 2022) available at www.ohchr.org/en/press-releases/2022/01/united-kingdom-nationality-and-borders-bill-undermines-rights-victims (last accessed 6 November 2024); Council of Europe, 'UK's Illegal Migration Bill should be reviewed to ensure it complies

regards guaranteeing the access to support and assistance to which potential victims of exploitation are entitled.[26]

In that context, the legal implications of Brexit and the reality of trafficking in human beings in the UK is that the risk of exploitation and vulnerability to human trafficking, amongst European and third-country nationals alike, has undeniably been exacerbated by an increased precarity related to their migration status.

## B. The Withdrawal of Freedom of Movement for EU Citizens

Pre-Brexit, EU citizens could benefit from the freedom of movement enshrined in Article 20 of the Treaty on the Functioning of the European Union (TFEU).[27] It offered them legal access to the UK's territory, as well as the possibility to stay for 90 days without registration and then secure a right of residence under conditions defined by EU law.[28] It also guaranteed equal treatment of EU migrants working in the UK in relation to access to UK welfare benefits.[29] The withdrawal of freedom of movement was progressively introduced, with a transition period that ran until 31 December 2020.[30]

Accepting that there have always been limitations to social and political rights associated with free movement,[31] it is undeniable that the loss of rights protected under EU law greatly increases the insecurity and precarity of EU citizens who wish to remain in the UK post-Brexit. To date, the clearest example of this has been the way in which the application process for settled status and pre-settled status has been executed by the British authorities. Many EU citizens living in the UK had not completed the application process by the end of the transition period, leaving their long-term residence status uncertain, particularly affecting vulnerable persons.[32] Despite the scrutiny of

with the anti-trafficking convention, says GRETA' *Newsroom* (29 March 2023) available at www.coe.int/en/web/portal/-/-uk-s-illegal-migration-bill-should-be-reviewed-to-ensure-it-complies-with-the-anti-trafficking-convention-says-greta (last accessed 6 November 2024).

[26] M Jovanovic, 'Legal Analysis of the Human Rights Compatibility of the Modern Slavery Sections in the Illegal Migration Act (Sections 22–29)' (Modern Slavery and Human Rights Policy and Evidence Centre, 2023) available at https://modern-slavery.files.svdcdn.com/production/assets/downloads/Jovanovic-M.-Legal-Analysis-v.2.pdf?dm=1694424204 (last accessed 6 November 2024).

[27] Consolidated version of the Treaty on the Functioning of the European Union [2012] OJ C326/47.

[28] Directive 2004/38/EC of the European Parliament and of the Council of 29 April 2004 on the right of citizens of the Union and their family members to move and reside freely within the territory of the Member States [2004] OJ L158/77.

[29] Article 20(2)(a) TFEU. Access to the UK benefit system was subject to nationals of the European Economic Area (EEA) satisfying a habitual residence test and, since 2004, the right-to-reside requirement.

[30] Immigration and Social Security Coordination (EU Withdrawal) Act 2020, s 1; M Gower, CJ McKinney and G Sturge, 'The UK's new points-based immigration system', House of Commons Library, Research Briefing (27 September 2022) available at https://commonslibrary.parliament.uk/research-briefings/cbp-8911/ (last accessed 6 November 2024) 13–14.

[31] Massey and Rankin (n 7): 72; C Roos, 'Sectoral Views on Migration and Border Cooperation, Multiple Insecurities: Potential Implications of Terminating Freedom of Movement in the UK' in H Carrapico, A Niehuus and C Berthélémy (eds), *Brexit and Internal Security Political and Legal Concerns on the Future UK–EU Relationship* Palgrave Macmillan, 2019) 123, 124–28.

[32] Law Centres Network, *Vulnerability in the EU Settlement Scheme: looking back, going forward* (July 2021) available at https://the3million.org.uk/vulnerability-eu-settlement-scheme (last accessed 6 November 2024) 22.

non-governmental organisations and Parliament,[33] the backlog of cases still pending in 2023 has prolonged the uncertainty.[34]

With such uncertainty come many concerns related to increased vulnerability and EU citizens' likelihood of becoming involved in informal or illegal structures, leading to an increased prevalence of sexual and labour exploitation.[35] For example, EU migrant sex workers are left with no other option than to retreat further underground, given that a marked increase in arrests and deportations has been noted since the Brexit referendum in 2016.[36] Where such uncertainty leads to exploitation and formal recognition of their status as victims of human trafficking, EU and EEA nationals who are not recognised by the UK authorities as having settled or pre-settled status are now worse off, as they can no longer rely on the rights protected under EU law, such as social benefits and access to local authority housing.[37] With Brexit, an EEA national who is a victim of modern slavery but does not have settled or pre-settled status will now only be entitled to request discretionary leave to remain.[38]

## C. The Introduction of a Points-based System

The situation of EU citizens was further impacted by the revision of the Immigration Rules in relation to work and student migration towards the end of 2020.[39] Whilst it is contested that the revised work migration rules led to 'few substantive changes to the old rules',[40] the revision has certainly had a significant impact on EU citizens. The points-based immigration system is now extended to include EU citizens as third-country nationals; and to be eligible for a visa, they must accumulate 70 points to be able to work in the UK, mandatory conditions requiring an offer of employment, at the required skill level, and the ability to speak English to a required standard.[41]

In the first instance, the eligibility criterion of the points-based system prevents EU citizens from receiving a visa if they are low-skilled, as they are excluded from the system, a point of concern for some due to the 'increased risk of underpayment and

[33] See, eg, the inquiry on Citizens' Rights opened since 2021 by the House of Lords European Affairs Committee, or the letters and reports published by the organisation The 3 million advocating for EU citizens' rights.

[34] House of Lords, 'Lords Committee urges Home Secretary to address a range of significant problems regarding the post-Brexit rights of UK and EU Citizens' Press Release (25 May 2023) available at https://the3million.org.uk/sites/default/files/documents/PressRelease-EuropeanAffairsCommittee-letter-HomeSecretary-CitizensRights-25May2023.pdf (last accessed 6 November 2024).

[35] Roos (n 31) 127–28.

[36] L Connelly and The English Collective of Prostitutes, *EU-Migrant Sex Work in the UK Post-Referendum* (2021) available at https://prostitutescollective.net/wp-content/uploads/2021/05/Full-Report-EU-migrant-sex-work-in-the-UK-post-Referendum.pdf (last accessed 6 November 2024) 11–12.

[37] HL Deb (6 October 2020), vol 806, col 568.

[38] See ibid, cols 576–571, amendment 27, 'Grant of leave to remain for confirmed victims of modern slavery who are EEA nationals'.

[39] Home Office, *Statement of changes to the Immigration Rules* (HC 707, 10 September 2020) available at www.gov.uk/government/publications/statement-of-changes-to-the-immigration-rules-hc-707-10-september-2020 (last accessed 6 November 2024); Gower, McKinney and Sturge (n 30) 13.

[40] Gower, McKinney and Sturge (n 30).

[41] Home Office (n 39); Gower, McKinney and Sturge (n 30).

exploitation'.[42] Instead, the new Immigration Rules provide for concessions in only two sectors, namely, health and social care and agriculture. Outside of these sectors, EU citizens who may well satisfy two mandatory criteria of a job offer at a required skill level may face a further barrier if they do not speak English to a required level.[43] All the criteria now erect a significant barrier to accessing the UK labour market; and even where exceptions apply, it does not mean that the composition of the EU labour force has been retained.

This is demonstrated by a dramatic drop in the number of EU workers coming to the UK, which has contributed to labour market shortages in certain sectors, including agriculture and health and care work.[44] Recent trends indicate that sectors that would previously have had an EU workforce are now relying on third-country nationals from much further afield. For example, an increased number of construction workers now originate from Vietnam, whereas previously Romanian workers were prominent in this field.[45] The impact of this shift towards a pool of workers who travel a greater distance for work is a greater reliance on intermediaries as recruiting agents or providers of labour. Concerns have been raised by industry experts that this global reach will lead to increased recruitment scams, whereby overseas recruitment agencies make false promises and charge high fees to workers, leading to an increased risk of workers arriving in debt.[46]

Restrictive immigration rules can fuel the trafficking industry, as it responds to a demand for low-skilled workers, and they can also place persons whose migration status is uncertain in a position of vulnerability, increasing their risk of being recruited by criminals operating transnationally. The evolution of trafficking patterns to and within the UK, partly due to the hostile migration environment and the loss of free movement for EU citizens, does not alter the fact that traffickers continue to operate across jurisdictions to recruit, transport and exploit their victims in different countries, including EU Member States and outside the EU. Counter-trafficking responses must take into account the need for coordinated investigations on a large scale[47] and smooth police cooperation, which as result of Brexit, may present law enforcement authorities with some practical challenges.

[42] M Sumption, 'Shortages, high-demand occupations, and the post-Brexit UK immigration system' (2022) 38(1) *Oxford Review of Economic Policy* 97; M Fernandez Reino, 'Exploiting the Opportunity: Migrants in Low-skilled Work after Brexit' *Migration Observatory* (30 August 2018) available at https://migrationobservatory.ox.ac.uk/resources/reports/exploiting-the-opportunity-low-skilled-work-migration-after-brexit/ (last accessed 6 November 2024); Gower, McKinney and Sturge (n 30) 13–14.

[43] Massey and Rankin (n 7) 73.

[44] M Sumption et al, 'How is the End of Free Movement Affecting the Low-wage Labour Force in the UK?' *Migration Observatory* (15 August 2022) available at https://migrationobservatory.ox.ac.uk/resources/reports/how-is-the-end-of-free-movement-affecting-the-low-wage-labour-force-in-the-uk/ (last accessed 6 November 2024).

[45] Home Affairs Committee (n 2) Qs120–122.

[46] D Camp, *The impact of the new UK immigration system on human trafficking into the UK* (October 2020) available at https://www.fairrecruitmenthub.org/resources/impact-new-uk-immigration-system-human-trafficking-uk (last accessed 6 November 2024).

[47] Europol, '1426 potential victims identified in global operation against human trafficking', Press Release (1 June 2023), referring to Operation Global Chain involving the UK, Albania, the US, Vietnam or Nigeria, available at www.europol.europa.eu/media-press/newsroom/news/1-426-potential-victims-identified-in-global-operation-against-human-trafficking (last accessed 6 November 2024).

# III. The Practical Challenges Resulting from Brexit and their Mitigation

As the regime of police cooperation foreseen under the TCA, and its possible evolution, has already been commented upon in other contributions to this volume and in other publications,[48] this section focuses on the practical challenges specific to police cooperation in the field of counter-trafficking, especially with a view to the added difficulties that have emerged in the post-Brexit context, as outlined in section II. In what follows, the objective is to ascertain whether the UK's withdrawal from the EU and the resulting changes in the available modalities of police cooperation have had an impact on anti-trafficking efforts. We will discuss three points of attention: information exchange; legislative change; and informal cooperation.

## A. New Arrangements to Support the Exchange of Information

The exchange of information is at the core of police cooperation and is crucial for the prevention, detection and investigation of criminal offences, especially those susceptible to having a cross-border dimension, such as human trafficking. The latter may often happen in a domestic manner, and 44 per cent of registered victims in the EU in 2021 came from the reporting country.[49] Yet information exchange may help to detect victims transported from one country to another, or expose links with a perpetrator supervising and benefiting from their exploitation while living in a different country.

As noted at an early stage in the negotiations of the UK's withdrawal, the loss of access to the Schengen Information System (SIS) was a concern. The system has been praised by law enforcement across the EU as being a very effective and efficient method of sharing information and alerts with limited procedural steps. The database contains not only alerts on suspects involved in, or perpetrators convicted for, trafficking offences, but also alerts on persons who are at risk of being trafficked (minors, vulnerable persons), sought (missing persons) or able to assist investigations (witnesses). These alerts are crucial for trafficking cases, notably considering the abuse of free movement by criminal groups to avoid detection.[50] However, at the end of the transition period, the UK was 'unplugged' from SIS.

This did not mean that all methods and mechanisms to share information were lost, as the UK continues to have partial access to the Secure Information Exchange Network Application (SIENA), a protected communication platform open to law enforcement authorities within EU Member States and countries with which Europol has signed

[48] Davies and Carrapico, this volume, ch 4; Pearson, ch 6; H Carrapico et al, *Brexit and Internal Security – Political and Legal Concerns in the context of the Future UK–EU Relationship* (Palgrave, 2019).

[49] Eurostat, *Trafficking in human beings – statistics* (January 2023).

[50] Europol, *Serious and Organised Crime Threat Assessment (SOCTA 2013)*, available at www.europol.europa.eu/publications-events/main-reports/eu-serious-and-organised-crime-threat-assessment-socta-2013 (last accessed 6 November 2024).

agreements or working arrangements, and the UK remains one of the biggest users of the platform.[51]

British authorities rapidly identified recourse to Interpol databases as an alternative to SIS,[52] Despite assurances regarding the speed and efficiency of information exchange via Interpol, however, early reports and research demonstrate that it is a poor substitute. Interpol is reported as being slower, more clunky and as relying on more manual inputting than EU mechanisms. Law enforcement authorities located within the EU face more burdensome processing of the information as they have to place warrants and alerts on both SIS and Interpol databases.[53] This process, referred to as 'double keying', appears to be mostly followed by law enforcement authorities from EU Member States, at least for the time being.[54] In addition, the UK Government has been engaged in 'boosting' Interpol's capacities,[55] while the EU is negotiating a new cooperation agreement with the organisation, aiming notably at ensuring interoperability between some of the EU's and Interpol's databases, and opening access to Interpol's databases to EU agencies.[56] Yet the level and speed of exchange of information are not yet comparable to what was available before. The requirement for double keying may come with a pre-assessment of the potential cross-border dimension of the case,[57] which is particularly problematic in cases of trafficking suspected of being (or treated as) purely domestic or as unlikely to present a cross-border dimension.

The consequences of Brexit are less perceptible with regard to the Prüm framework, allowing exchanges of information 'through Member States granting each other access to their automated DNA analysis files, automated fingerprint identification systems and vehicle registration data'.[58] Pre-Brexit, the UK adopted reforms to comply with the Council's requests and obtained the right to join the Prüm framework.[59] The TCA provided for the continued participation of the UK,[60] allowing the EU and UK authorities to progress the connection of their respective databases. The added value of the UK's participation in Prüm has been confirmed by practitioners not only in connection to counterterrorism and high-level serious organised crime, but also as regards crimes on a lesser scale,[61] and participation in Prüm may be crucial in trafficking investigations, as DNA or fingerprints can constitute forensic evidence corroborating

[51] House of Lords European Union Committee, *Report Beyond Brexit: policing, law enforcement and security* (HL 2019–21, 250), available at https://lordslibrary.parliament.uk/beyond-brexit-policing-law-enforcement-and-security/ (last accessed 6 November 2024).

[52] Thomson, ch 11; Costantino and Cotroneo, ch 10.

[53] M Shellaker, S Tong and P Swallow,'UK–EU law enforcement cooperation post-Brexit: A UK law enforcement practitioner perspective' (2024) 4 *Criminology and Criminal Justice* 841.

[54] ibid.

[55] House of Lords, *Justice and Home Affairs Committee, Corrected oral evidence – Post-Brexit UK-EU security cooperation* (14 March 2023) Answer by Deputy Chief Constable Peter Ayling, available at https://committees.parliament.uk/event/17670/formal-meeting-oral-evidence-session/ (last accessed 6 November 2024).

[56] Council Decision (EU) 2021/1313 of 19 July 2021 authorizing the opening of negotiations for a cooperation agreement between the EU and Interpol [2021] OJ L287/6.

[57] House of Lords, *Oral evidence Post Brexit UK-EU security cooperation* (26 January 2021) Answer by Steve Rodhouse, available at https://committees.parliament.uk/event/3469/formal-meeting-oral-evidence-session/ (last accessed 6 November 2024).

[58] M Pencheva, *EU–UK Police and Judicial Cooperation in Criminal Matters.* Palgrave Macmillan, 2021) 83.

[59] ibid 84.

[60] TCA, Part Three, Title II, Arts 527–541.

[61] House of Lords (n 55) 6.

the victims' testimonies.[62] This is particularly important in the context of trafficking investigations that do not present a degree of seriousness requiring the mobilisation of advanced tools of cooperation. However, the EU is in the process of revising the Prüm framework, notably to update the technical operation of the system, integrate Europol as the holder of third-country-sourced biometric data, and add new categories of data, such as facial images.[63] While in November 2023 negotiations were approaching their end, this forthcoming evolution may require an amendment of the TCA's Title on Prüm (Article 541(1)) and reflects the ongoing evolution of the EU 'ecosystem', which may lead to a certain gap between the modalities of cooperation available to the UK and those applicable in the EU.

## B. The Evolution of Counter-trafficking Legislation

Police cooperation in countering human trafficking may further be impacted by the evolution of the legal framework applicable to that offence. The UK and the EU are currently engaged, although at different stages, in a process of evaluation and modernisation of their respective legal frameworks. In the EU, in December 2022, the Commission proposed revising Directive 2011/36/EU on trafficking in human beings.[64] Negotiations progressed quickly, as interinstitutional negotiations between the Council and the Parliament started in November 2023.[65] At the same time, the UK has also been engaged in a process aiming at taking stock of the implementation of the Modern Slavery Act 2015.[66] Such parallel processes may allow a certain level of convergence to be maintained between the applicable legislative frameworks, but they may also give rise to divergences.

First, the definitions of the purpose of exploitation, and the list of possible purposes identified by each legislator, present a similar evolution. The 2011 EU Directive had already expanded the list of the purposes of exploitation enshrined in previous EU instruments and international texts, and under Article 2(3) requires the Member States to criminalise these purposes as a minimum. Its evaluation pinpointed divergences among EU Member States,[67] and led to the proposition that forced marriage and illegal adoption should be included in the list.[68] The Council has supported such amendment, albeit with a slightly different formulation, and includes additional details in the

[62] UNODC, 'Evidential Issues in Trafficking in Persons Cases' (2017) available at www.unodc.org/documents/human-trafficking/2017/Case_Digest_Evidential_Issues_in_Trafficking.pdf (last accessed 6 November 2024) 47.

[63] European Commission, Proposal for a Regulation on automated data exchange for police cooperation ('Prüm II') COM(2021) 784 final.

[64] European Commission, Proposal for a Directive amending Directive 2011/36/EU, COM(2022) 732 final.

[65] European Parliament, 'Trafficking in human beings: MEPs ready to negotiate new EU rules', Press Release (18 October 2023) available at www.europarl.europa.eu/news/en/press-room/20231013IPR07128/trafficking-in-human-beings-meps-ready-to-negotiate-new-eu-rules (last accessed 6 November 2024).

[66] Home Affairs Committee, 'New inquiry examines human trafficking in the UK', Press Release (7 February 2023) available at https://committees.parliament.uk/work/7290/human-trafficking/news/ (last accessed 6 November 2024).

[67] European Commission, Impact Assessment accompanying the Proposal for a Directive revising Directive 2011/36, SWD(2022) 425 final, 16–17.

[68] European Commission (n 64), Art 1(1).

Preamble to circumscribe the scope of the offence,[69] while the Parliament has proposed several amendments further expanding the list to surrogacy for reproductive exploitation, exploitation of children in closed institutions, etc.[70] In the UK, the Modern Slavery Act 2015 follows the list of purposes of exploitation enshrined in the Council of Europe's Anti-Trafficking Convention and adds two other purposes, namely, securing services from children and securing services from vulnerable persons, that are sufficiently open to include all the purposes enshrined in the EU Directive.[71] Yet similar reflections on the need to explicitly mention new rising forms of exploitation in the national legislation were echoed by experts, stressing the 'value in considering the place of forced marriage and its intersection with trafficking and modern slavery'.[72]

Second, parallel evolutions can also be witnessed in relation to the criminalisation of clients buying services that are the object of exploitation with the knowledge that the person being exploited is a victim of trafficking. The EU Directive already mentioned this possibility but left a wide margin of discretionto the Member States, resulting in a very diverse legal landscape.[73] The transposition of this provision in the UK demonstrates how equally divisive this issue is, with a diversity of legal regimes currently applicable in England and Wales, Northern Ireland and Scotland.[74] The European Commission proposed a revision of the Directive's provision, establishing an obligation for the Member States to criminalise such use of services.[75] This proposal was not unanimously welcomed,[76] and its sensitivity is reflected by the strong amendments proposed by both the Council[77] and the Parliament.[78] The final formulation of the text will have to be analysed, as legal divergences may have an impact on trafficking flows and patterns,[79] as well as on police priorities and investigations. Furthermore, as the criminalisation of clients is a particularly sensitive issue for trafficking for the purpose of sexual exploitation, it has also an impact on trafficking for the purpose of labour exploitation, an area in which other EU legislative developments may further contribute to legislative discrepancies between the EU and the UK.

Lastly, further discrepancies may appear as the EU is engaged in a series of reforms in the field of social and labour laws that explicitly seek to reduce the risk of exploitation (including trafficking for the purpose of labour exploitation) of migrants who seek to access the EU labour market, and to ensure that Member States implement protection

[69] Council, Proposal for a Directive amending Directive 2011/36/EU – General Approach, Doc 9312/23, Art 1(6).

[70] European Parliament, *Report on the proposal for a Directive amending Directive 2011/36/EU*, A9-0285/2023.

[71] J Haynes, 'The Modern Slavery Act 2015: a Legislative Commentary' (2016) 37(1) *State Law Review* 38.

[72] Home Affairs Committee (n 2) Q45.

[73] European Commission (n 67) 22.

[74] GRETA, *Report concerning the implementation of the Council of Europe Convention on Action against Trafficking in Human Beings by the United Kingdom. Second Evaluation Round*, GRETA(2016)21, paras 126–134.

[75] European Commission (n 64), Preamble, recital 9 and Art 1(6) introducing a new article in the Directive.

[76] La Strada International, Statement on revision EU Anti-Trafficking Directive (19 December 2022).

[77] Council (n 69) Art 1(6).

[78] European Parliament (n 70) para 6.

[79] A di Nicola, *The differing EU Member States' regulations on prostitution and their cross-border implications on women's rights*, European Parliament, PE 695.394 – September 2021, 33–39.

measures for those who are victims of exploitation.[80] The former is a key objective of the recast Single Permit Directive 2011/98/EU[81] and the latter is central to the assessment of the Employers' Sanctions Directive 2009/52/EU.[82] However, such legislative evolutions are still in their early days.

## C. Informal Cooperation as a Safety Net

Operational cooperation often relies on informal mechanisms and networks, based on interpersonal contacts formed through common training, joint investigations, exchange of staff, etc. Mechanisms for cooperation in the EU, in which the UK often participated, offer additional occasions for law enforcement authorities to develop interpersonal contacts, in particular with units and services specialising in the countering of trafficking. The UK had also been engaged in a series of ad hoc bilateral forums of cooperation with some EU Member States,[83] such as the Common Travel Area Forum, allowing Irish and British colleagues to develop 'excellent cross-agency collaboration to tackle the trafficking of vulnerable people'.[84]

As a result, in the immediate post-Brexit context, British authorities could rely on long- and well-established interpersonal ties and a shared common history with their European counterparts to facilitate informal contacts.[85] Some initiatives allow such informal contacts to be maintained. For example, the UK has established a Europol Liaison Bureau, in which the different police forces of the country are represented,[86] thus facilitating direct and informal exchanges. Additionally, even though the UK can now only join a JIT at the invitation of an EU Member State, this evolution has not prevented the UK from remaining engaged in ongoing JITs.[87] The UK also participated

[80] European Commission, 'Communication on a New Pact on Migration and Asylum' COM(2020) 609 final.

[81] Directive 2011/98/EU of the European Parliament and of the Council of 13 December 2011 on a single application procedure for a single permit for third-country nationals to reside and work in the territory of a Member State and on a common set of rights for third-country workers legally residing in a Member State [2011] OJ L 343/1; European Commission (n 64).

[82] European Commission, 'Communication on the application of Directive 2009/52/EC of 18 June 2009 providing for minimum standards on sanctions and measures against employers of illegally staying third country nationals' COM(2021) 592 final.

[83] Shellaker, Tong and Swallow (n 53) 11–12.

[84] Northern Ireland Affairs Committee, *Cross-border co-operation on policing, security and criminal justice after Brexit* (HC 2019–21, 766) available at https://committees.parliament.uk/work/534/crossborder-cooperation-on-policing-security-and-criminal-justice-after-brexit/publications/ (last accessed 6 November 2024) para 26.

[85] Shellaker, Tong and Swallow (n 53) 11–12.

[86] Justice and Home Affairs Committee, Inquiry on Post-Brexit UK-EU security cooperation – follow up, Written evidence submitted by the Police Service of Scotland (PBS0009, 2023) available at https://committees.parliament.uk/work/7318/postbrexit-ukeu-security-cooperation-follow-up/publications/written-evidence/ (last accessed 6 November 2024).

[87] Eurojust, 'Eurojust assists Romania and UK in dismantling human trafficking network', Press Release (14 June 2022) available at www.eurojust.europa.eu/news/eurojust-assists-romania-and-uk-dismantling-human-trafficking-network (last accessed 6 November 2024); Europol, '9 arrested in crackdown on lover boy trafficking in Bulgaria and UK', Press Release (26 April 2023) available at www.europol.europa.eu/media-press/newsroom/news/9-arrested-in-crackdown-loverboy-trafficking-in-bulgaria-and-uk (last accessed 6 November 2024).

in Europe-wide coordinated actions days,[88] including those set up in the context of EMPACT,[89] recently turned into a permanent mechanism, in which third countries may participate in the operational implementation where appropriate, according to the identified threats and need.[90]

However, this has not prevented the appearance, post-Brexit, of new obstacles to informal cooperation. Staff mobility to new positions may contribute to the erosion of pre-existing informal networks and contacts. New administrative formalities have been reported, causing certain delays, notably for instruments substituting for European Arrest Warrants (EAWs) or European Investigation Orders (EIOs), transiting through different channels and/or requiring authorisations.[91] Recent legislative developments may even lead to a certain gap between the modalities of cooperation available to the UK and those applicable in the EU. The adoption in May 2023 of a new EU Directive on the exchange of information between law enforcement authorities[92] constitutes a relevant example. To facilitate direct exchange of information, it notably establishes a one-stop shop and time limits for processing and responding to requests (up to eight hours in case of urgent requests). The UK as a third country will not be able to benefit from these developments, potentially leading to a discrepancy in the modalities and speed of exchange of information, unless new arrangements are discussed under the TCA framework.

The obstacles and challenges discussed above could potentially be resolved through dialogue and negotiation of new arrangements. The TCA Specialised Committee on Law Enforcement and Judicial Cooperation could be a forum to address possible divergences and facilitate coordination between the UK and the EU; and the bilateral cooperation agreements between the UK and a Member State and/or the EU relevant agencies, possibilities foreseen under the TCA and EU law,[93] could also help to mitigate the consequences of Brexit on police cooperation in countering trafficking.

## IV. Conclusion

This chapter stressed how the UK's efforts in seeking to maintain control of borders and tackle illegal migration constitute a false narrative. They may in fact have the opposite

[88] European Labour Authority, 'EU authorities target labour exploitation in the fields', Press Release (14 October 2022) available at www.ela.europa.eu/en/news-event/newsroom/eu-authorities-target-labour-exploitation-fields (last accessed 6 November 2024).

[89] Europol, 'Violent labour exploitation gang busted in Romania and the UK', Press Release (29 April 2022) available at www.europol.europa.eu/media-press/newsroom/news/violent-labour-exploitation-gang-busted-in-romania-and-uk (last accessed 6 November 2024).

[90] Council, 'Conclusions on the permanent continuation of the EU Policy Cycle for organised and serious international crime' EMPACT 2022 +. Doc 7100/23.

[91] This is notably the case for the mechanism designed to replace EIOs. Instead of relying on a single instrument and a harmonised form, the UK authorities must now rely on the European Convention on Mutual Assistance in Criminal Matters, Strasbourg, 20 April 1959, ETS 30. In such a framework, their EU counterparts require an International Letter of Requests, which imposes on UK authorities to involve the Crown Prosecution Service.

[92] Directive (EU) 2023/97 of 10 May 2023 on the exchange of information between the law enforcement authorities of Member States [2023] *OJ* L134/1.

[93] Shellaker et al (n 50).

effect, by generating more opportunities for traffickers and criminal groups to engage in human trafficking and its closely related offence of human smuggling. Organised criminal groups conducting their activities across the UK and EU Member States remain active, justifying the need for sustained cooperation between the EU and the UK in countering trafficking.[94] Against this backdrop, the consequences of Brexit on such cooperation are real but should not be overestimated, especially considering that the UK has established long-standing cooperation with the EU, its agencies and the EU Member States. The challenge, then, may rather be for the UK authorities to develop cooperation mechanisms with new countries of origin, informal ties and knowledge, as national authorities must seek cooperation with countries without knowing much about their legislation, regulation or even corruption risk. These evolutions do not undermine the need for cooperation with the EU, where EU Member States are facing similar challenges, notably in light of the war in Ukraine and the trafficking risks associated with the displacement of Ukrainian refugees.[95]

To compensate for the loss of access to EU information databases, and to access information from new countries of origin, the UK places an emphasis on boosting global operational cooperation, notably through the increasing use of Interpol databases. This is in line with the priorities of the EU, in terms both of countering human trafficking and of police cooperation more generally. The latest EU strategy on trafficking in human beings reiterates the importance of international cooperation,[96] and the EU mobilises its foreign policy instruments and funding programmes to support specific counter-trafficking initiatives in countries of origin and transit. Additionally, the EU supports global operational cooperation, with its agencies being involved in worldwide coordinated investigations linked with EU operational plans;[97] and the envisaged cooperation agreement between the EU and Interpol would also facilitate cooperation, potentially placing Europol as the single point of contact for cooperation with non-EU countries.

As for bilateral EU–UK counter-trafficking cooperation, even though EU citizens' migration flows to the UK have reduced, such cooperation will remain a necessity, even if its modalities may evolve. It may shift to enhanced cooperation, for instance through the adoption of bilateral cooperation agreements reducing the formalities applicable

[94] See, eg, the explanation of Albanian criminal networks operating across Western Europe, including in the UK, discussed in GRETA (2020) *Report concerning the implementation of the Council of Europe Convention on Action against Trafficking in Human Beings by Albania: Third Evaluation Round*, GRETA. 09: para 12; US Department of State, *2022 Trafficking in Persons Report, Albania*; A Gentleman, 'Young Albanian men 'viciously exploited' after arriving in UK' *The Guardian* (5 March 2023) available at www.theguardian.com/uk-news/2023/mar/05/young-albanian-men-viciously-exploited-after-arriving-in-uk (last accessed 6 November 2024); G Evans, 'Lucrative Business: Albanian Criminal Exploitation of the UK Asylum System' *RUSI* (8 December 2022) available at https://rusi.org/explore-our-research/publications/commentary/lucrative-business-albanian-criminal-exploitation-uk-asylum-system (last accessed 6 November 2024).

[95] Europol, 'War in Ukraine: refugees arriving to the EU from Ukraine at risk of exploitation as part of THB' (March 2022) available at www.europol.europa.eu/publications-events/publications/early-warning-notification-war-in-ukraine-refugees-arriving-to-eu-ukraine-risk-of-exploitation-part-of-thb (last accessed 6 November 2024).

[96] European Commission (n 4) 17.

[97] Europol (n 47).

between the UK and the specific EU Member States from which trafficking flows persist, and/or also investigating the activities of transnational organised criminal groups active in the UK. Counter-trafficking cooperation may also focus on knowledge exchange with EU Member States that have dealt with trafficking flows coming from countries such as Vietnam, now becoming predominant in the UK as countries of origin of trafficking victims. However, for both parties, a crucial element would be to ensure a level playing field, particularly with regard to the protection of victims' rights and the prevention of trafficking.

# 22

# A Green Brexit? Post-Brexit EU–UK Cooperation in the Fight against Environmental Crime

AGATHE PIQUET

## I. Introduction

In July 2017, the then Secretary of State for the Department for Environment, Food and Rural Affairs, Michael Gove, made the promise of 'delivering a Green Brexit'.[1] This declared ambition was mostly a reaction to the growing fear among British society that Brexit would lead to some deregulation detrimental to the environment due to the United Kingdom's (UK's) leaving the European Union (EU) and its high environmental standards.[2] While concerns were mostly expressed regarding the future of environmental issues in relation with agriculture, fisheries, food or industry, they also emerged in respect with the fight against environmental crime.

In its most restrictive and *a minima* definition,[3] environmental crime covers any illegal activity that directly and seriously harms the environment, such as waste crime (eg, illegal trade in hazardous waste), wildlife crime (eg, illegal wildlife trade) and illegal resource extraction (eg, illegal logging, mining, fishing). Growing political attention is being paid to this form of crime at national and international levels, including at the EU one.[4] Diverse EU legislative and operational tools at the crossroads of environmental

[1] M Gove, 'The Unfrozen Moment – Delivering a Green Brexit', Speech at WWF Living Planet Centre Working (21 July 2017) available at www.gov.uk/government/speeches/the-unfrozen-moment-delivering-a-green-brexit (last accessed 6 November 2024).

[2] For instance, The Wildlife Trusts, 'Greener UK Coalition launches manifesto urging government to use Brexit to restore and enhance the environment' (22 February 2017) available at www.wildlifetrusts.org/news/greener-uk-coalition-launches-manifesto-urging-government-use-brexit-restore-and-enhance (last accessed 6 November 2024).

[3] For a more in-depth analysis of the debates about the definition of environmental crime see, eg, R White, *Crimes against Nature. Environmental Criminology and Ecological Justice* (Routledge, 2013); GM Vagliasindi, 'Legal Perspectives on Environmental Crime: The Transnational Dimension of Environmental Crime' in A Moiseienko, S. Hufnagel and V Mitsilegas (eds), *Research Handbook on Transnational Crime*. Cheltenham; Northampton: Edward Elgar Publishing, 2019) 142.

[4] PJ Cardwell, D French and M Hall, 'Tackling Environmental Crime in the European Union: The Case of the Missing Victim?' (2011) 23 *Environmental Law and Management* 113.

policies and Justice and Home Affairs (JHA) have thus been developed over time to ensure that Member States are effectively protecting the environment through criminal investigations and prosecutions.

Following Brexit, some questioned whether the UK would maintain a strong alignment with the existing EU legislation and preserve its operational commitment with its European counterparts in the fight against environmental crime. The 'Green Brexit' promise made by the UK Government could have let one assume that the UK–EU cooperation on that issue would be only marginally impacted by the withdrawal from the EU. This expectation was reinforced by the political messages sent by the Government that Brexit would not affect internal security, as exemplified by the successive British 'opt ins' in EU judicial and police cooperation tools after the 2016 referendum, and the parallel attempt of British negotiators to preserve the status quo regarding the use and access to EU instruments, agencies and databases.[5] Such cooperation appears even more valuable for the fight against environmental crime, predominantly framed as a transnational offence in its causes and consequences and as only efficiently dealt with through international exchanges of data and joint operations.[6]

However, at the same time, Brexit negotiations have led to some unprecedented politicisation of environmental issues with considerable uncertainty regarding the future of the EU acquis in UK legislation,[7] and the UK is now a third country whose engagement in EU JHA has been reduced,[8] as stipulated in Part Three of the Trade and Cooperation Agreement (TCA).[9] Therefore, this chapter investigates the extent to which Brexit has impacted UK–EU cooperation in the fight against environmental crime despite the political statements about the continuity of previous coordination mechanisms and policies. Section II considers the EU legislative and operational frameworks and the pre-Brexit participation of the UK in these. Section III highlights how, echoing the strong concerns from civil society, UK officials attempted to maintain their presence in the existing EU arrangements and venues to preserve their cooperation with the EU and its Member States. Finally, in section IV this chapter tackles the limitations and difficulties UK–EU collaboration could face, and pays attention to three main challenges for the future relationship.

## II. Environmental Crime, the EU and the UK

While acts that directly and seriously harm the environment are not new, they were defined as criminal offences by domestic and international laws only a few decades ago.

[5] S Wolff, A Piquet and H Carrapico, 'UK's Withdrawal from Justice and Home Affairs: A Historical Institutionalist Analysis of Policy Trajectories' (2022) 20 *Comparative European Politics* 604.

[6] T Spapens, R White and W Huisman, *Environmental Crime in Transnational Context: Global Issues in Green Enforcement and Criminology* (Routledge, 2016).

[7] C Burns and C Carter, 'Brexit and UK Environmental Policy and Politics' (2018) 23(3) *Revue Française de Civilisation Britannique*, doi.org/10.4000/rfcb.2385; C Burns et al, 'De-Europeanising or Disengaging? EU Environmental Policy and Brexit' (2019) 28 *Environmental Politics* 271.

[8] Wolff, Piquet and Carrapico (n 5).

[9] Trade and Cooperation Agreement between the European Union and the European Atomic Energy Community, of the one part, and the United Kingdom of Great Britain and Northern Ireland, of the other part [2021] OJ L149/10.

In comparison, while the EU has been very active in the protection of the environment since the 1970s, it appears as a latecomer in the field of environmental crime in comparison with other international organisations, such as the United Nations or the Council of Europe.[10]

In 1998, the latter adopted a Convention on the protection of the environment through criminal law.[11] Though innovative, as its objective was to criminalise acts causing or likely to cause environmental damage, the Convention never entered into force due to the insufficient number of national ratifications. Yet the discussions and intergovernmental negotiations created 'greater political momentum for the proposal of a supranational criminal law instrument to counter environmental harm'.[12] With the 1999 Erika oil spill, the political context became even more favourable for the European Commission to initiate legislative developments in the field. Reacting to this major environmental disaster, with more than 400 kilometres of French coastline being polluted by the wreckage of an oil tanker, the European Commission proposed in 2001 a Directive on the protection of the environment through criminal law.[13] Although that text was withdrawn due to unprecedented institutional struggles with the Council on the appropriate legal basis,[14] a similar Directive was nonetheless adopted in 2008. This 2008 Directive has become the primary EU instrument in the fight against environmental crime.[15] The text aims to protect the environment by requiring Member States to approach specific breaches of EU environmental legislation through criminal law, that is, to ensure that these unlawful activities are criminal offences and that individuals perpetrating them are sanctioned by 'effective, proportionate and dissuasive criminal penalties'.[16] Even though the EU was not competent at that time to determine the type and the level of sanctions, the Directive still sought to approximate national criminal laws by setting minimum standards of environmental protection.

The EU acquis in that domain also includes the transposition of many major international texts, such as Regulation 3626/82 implementing the 1973 Convention on international trade in endangered species of wild fauna and flora (CITES);[17] Directive 2005/35 integrating the international standards set by the 1973 Convention

[10] For a historical perspective, see MG Faure, 'A Paradigm Shift in Environmental Criminal Law' in R Sollund, CH Stefes Christoph and AR Germani (eds), *Fighting Environmental Crime in Europe and Beyond. The Role of the EU and its Member States* (Palgrave Macmillan, 2016) 17.

[11] Convention on the Protection of the Environment through Criminal Law, European Treaty Series 172, adopted on 4 November 1998.

[12] GF Perilongo and E Corn, 'The Ecocrime Directive and Its Translation into Legal Practice: EU Green Offences and Their Impact at National Level According to the Results of a Recent Survey' (2017) 8 *New Journal of European Criminal Law* 244.

[13] Proposal for a Directive of the European Parliament and of the Council on the protection of the environment through criminal law [2001] OJ C180E/20.

[14] E Herlin-Karnell, 'Commission v Council: Some Reflections on Criminal Law in the First Pillar' (2007) 13 *European Public Law* 47.

[15] Directive 2008/99/EC of the European Parliament and of the Council on the protection of the environment through criminal law [2008] OJ L328/28.

[16] For a detailed analysis of the text, see MG Faure, 'The Environmental Crime Directive 2008/99/EC' (2011) 1 *European Journal of Consumer Law* 193.

[17] Regulation (EEC) of the Council 3626/82 on the implementation in the Community of the Convention on international trade in endangered species of wild fauna and flora [1982] OJ L384/1. It was then replaced by Regulation (EEC) 338/97 of the Council on the protection of species of wild fauna and flora by regulating trade [1997] OJ L61/1.

on the prevention of pollution from ships (MARPOL);[18] or Regulation 1013/2006 implementing the 1989 Convention on the control of transboundary movements of hazardous wastes and their disposal (Basel Convention).[19]

Besides these legislative instruments, it is also worth paying attention to the diversity of 'soft law' tools developed by the European Commission over time to support the fight against environmental crime. One of them is the 2016 EU Action Plan against wildlife trafficking, with 32 measures to be jointly implemented by EU institutions and agencies and the Member States between 2016 and 2020.[20] These 32 measures covered three main objectives: the prevention of wildlife trafficking; the enforcement of existing legislation; and the establishment of a more global approach by further engaging with source, transit and consumer countries. The European Commission has also funded various initiatives to improve the existing knowledge on environmental crime, to assess national and EU policies and activities, to facilitate the encounters between practitioners and to provide recommendations (eg, the European Union Action to Fight Environmental Crime (EFFACE) or the so-called AMBITUS project). The financial support of the European Commission in the creation and maintenance of the EU-TWIX database is of specific interest to illustrate the range of EU activities. Indeed, this database has been developed by Belgian Federal Police and the non-governmental organisation (NGO) TRAFFIC to boost the fight against illegal wildlife trade in Europe by facilitating cooperation and the exchange of information.[21]

Furthermore, the EU is funding collaborative initiatives, such as the Network for the Implementation and Enforcement of Environmental Law (IMPEL) that started its activities in 1992, the Environmental Crime Network (EnviCrimeNet) set up in 2011, the EU Forum of Judges for the Environment (EUFJE) and the European Network of Prosecutors for the Environment (ENPE), the last two both created in 2012. By respectively gathering regulators, law enforcement officers, judges or prosecutors, these networks aim to boost the exchange of information, experience and best practices in order to offer a common and better understanding of environmental crime and of how to fight it effectively, including at EU level.[22]

Interestingly, relevant EU agencies have also been participating in these initiatives.[23] Both Europol and Eurojust are competent to deal with environmental crime, as made

[18] Directive 2005/35/EC of the European Parliament and of the Council on ship-source pollution and on the introduction of penalties for infringements [2005] OJ L255/11.

[19] Regulation (EC) 1013/2006 of the European Parliament and of the Council on shipments of waste [2006] OJ L190/1, then amended by Regulation (EC) 660/2014 of the European Parliament and of the Council amending Regulation (EC) 1013/2006 on shipments of waste [2014] OJ L189/135.

[20] Communication from the Commission to the European Parliament, the Council, the European Economic and Social Committee and the Committee of the Regions, 'EU Action Plan Against Wildlife Trafficking' COM(2016) 87 final, 26 February 2016.

[21] V Sacré, 'EU-TWIX: Ten years of Information Exchange and Cooperation between Wildlife Law Enforcement Officials in Europe' in LM Elliott and WH Schaedla (eds), *Handbook of Transnational Environmental Crime* (Edward Elgar Publishing, 2016) 478.

[22] L Smith and K Klaas, 'Networks and NGOs Relevant to Fighting Environmental Crime', Study in the framework of the Efface research project (Berlin: Ecologic Institute, 2015) available at https://efface.eu/sites/default/files/2.EFFACE_Networks%20and%20NGOs%20Relevant%20to%20Fighting%20Environmental%20Crime/index.pdf (last accessed 6 November 2024).

[23] V Mitsilegas and F Giuffrida, 'The Role of EU Agencies in Fighting Transnational Environmental Crime. New Challenges for Eurojust and Europol' (2017) 1 *Brill Research Perspectives in Transnational Crime* 1.

explicit by their respective Regulations.[24] Over the last decade, the two agencies have increased their internal capacity and expanded their operations in this field, especially after environmental offences became a priority of the 2018–21 and 2022–25 EU multiannual cycles to tackle organised crime.

Within Europol, contrary to what exists for counterfeit crime, drug trafficking or migrant smuggling for instance, there is no specific unit dedicated to the fight against serious damages to the environment at the moment. Yet some officials are specialised in that topic, particularly within the Europol Analysis Project EnviCrime set up in 2017. Already in 2013, environmental offences had been identified by the agency as one of the 'emerging threats, which require intensified monitoring'.[25] Consequently, for more than 10 years now, Europol has produced analytical reports and sent early-warning notifications to national authorities on this subject. It also set up specific communities on that very topic within the Europol Platform for Experts, to disseminate knowledge on environmental crime and inform about how to fight it effectively. This EU agency also provides support to transnational and international investigations on wildlife crime, waste trafficking, marine pollution, etc through the coordination of the national seizures and exchanges, operational and strategic analysis, technical expertise and the deployment of experts on the spot.[26] Furthermore, Europol facilitates the work undertaken by national authorities by liaising with a diversity of partners, including international organisations (eg, Interpol) and non-profit ones (eg, TRAFFIC, Wildlife Justice Commission). It is also collaborating with the EU networks mentioned above. For instance, Europol hosts the Secretariat of EnviCrimeNet, and together Europol and EnviCrimeNet launched the Intelligence Project on Environmental Crime (IPEC) in 2014 to improve knowledge of both green crime and green policing.

Similarly to Europol, Eurojust has over time acquired a degree of specialisation in environmental crime, and the contact point set up on that issue in 2014 has become a subgroup within Eurojust's College. This institutional change reflects the growing prioritisation of serious damage to the environment within the agency since 2013, in reaction to the report produced that same year by Europol, and then in accordance with the EU multiannual cycles. That specialisation has not gone unnoticed by national authorities, which have used Eurojust intensively to facilitate coordination meetings and to support joint investigation teams. Over the past few years, Eurojust staff have therefore provided legal advice, resolved conflicts of jurisdiction, ensured the exchange of information and evidence, and helped national judicial authorities to coordinate their activities in many cases.[27] In February 2023, for instance, the

[24] Regulation (EU) 2016/794 of the European Parliament and of the Council on the European Union Agency for Law Enforcement Cooperation (Europol) and replacing and repealing Council Decisions 2009/371/JHA, 2009/934/JHA, 2009/935/JHA, 2009/936/JHA and 2009/968/JHA [2016] OJ L 135/53 and Regulation (EU) 2018/1727 of the European Parliament and of the Council of 14 November 2018 on the European Union Agency for Criminal Justice Cooperation (Eurojust), and replacing and repealing Council Decision 2002/187/JHA [2018] OJ L295/138.

[25] Europol, 'Threat Assessment 2013. Environmental Crime in the EU'. available at www.europol.europa.eu/cms/sites/default/files/documents/4aenvironmental_crime_threatassessment_2013_-_public_version.pdf (last accessed 6 November 2024).

[26] For further information, see at www.europol.europa.eu/crime-areas-and-statistics/crime-areas/environmental-crime (last accessed 6 November 2024).

[27] Eurojust, *Report on Eurojust's Casework on Environmental Crime* (2021) available at www.eurojust.europa.eu/sites/default/files/assets/report_environmental_crime.pdf (last accessed 6 November 2024).

EU agency helped Italian and Germany authorities in setting up and funding a joint investigation team and coordinated a joint action leading to the arrest of 14 individuals suspected of illicit waste trafficking and 40 searches.[28] Eurojust is also liaising with many different actors, including other EU agencies (Europol is often involved in Eurojust's cases) and EU networks, such as ENPE and IMPEL, with which it has, for instance, organised joint conferences.

As a member of the EU, the UK had to comply with EU environmental requirements regarding environmental protection, and its domestic legislation has thus been intensively influenced by it. Directive 2008/99/EC is an interesting case study in that respect. As most of the environmental offences that Member States were required to criminalise were already legislated for in the UK before the Directive was adopted at EU level, no new national law resulted from this text, leading some scholars to analyse this process as an 'informal transposition'[29] through 'very scattered pieces of legislation'.[30]

In addition, even though broadly speaking environmental crime was not among the top priorities of the UK Government nor of its law enforcement agencies,[31] the country still acted as a driving force on some specific issues, particularly wildlife trafficking. For instance, in 2014 it organised a high-level international conference on illegal wildlife trade that led to the London Declaration with the proclaimed goal to end wildlife trafficking.[32] It also funded various initiatives in that respect, including the EU-TWIX database, and attempted to strengthen EU action in that domain, suggesting, for instance, that the 2016 EU Action Plan on wildlife trafficking include provisions on the full and effective implementation of the CITES.[33] British officials also engaged in cooperation with their European counterparts. They participated in different EU instruments, such as IMPEL, ENPE or EUFJE, of which the UK was a founding member.[34] They also took an active part in Europol operations related to environmental offences, particularly once

[28] Eurojust, 'Crackdown on a criminal network dealing with waste trafficking and money laundering' (16 February 2023) available at https://www.eurojust.europa.eu/news/crackdown-criminal-network-dealing-waste-trafficking-and-money-laundering (last accessed 6 November 2024).

[29] M Lennan, 'Evaluating the Effectiveness of the EU Environmental Liability and Environmental Crime Directives as Implemented by Scotland and the Rest of the United Kingdom' (2021) 24 *Journal of International Wildlife Law & Policy* 32. See also R Pereira, 'The Development of Environmental Criminal Law Enforcement in the European Union: From Institutional Fragmentation to European Environmental Criminal Justice Governance' in R Pereira, A Engel and S Miettinen (eds), *The Governance of Criminal Justice in the European Union* (Edward Elgar Publishing, 2020) 205.

[30] E Fasoli, 'Environmental Criminal Law in the United Kingdom' in A Farmer, M Faure and GM Vagliasindi (eds), *Environmental Crime in Europe* (Hart Publishing, 2017) 243.

[31] V Mitsilegas, M Fitzmaurice and E Fasoli 'Fighting Environmental Crime in the UK: A Country Report'. Study in the framework of the EFFACE research project (Queen Mary University of London, 2015) available at https://efface.eu/sites/default/files/EFFACE_Fighting%20Environmental%20Crime%20in%20the%20UK/index.pdf (last accessed 6 November 2024).

[32] Declaration of the London Conference on the illegal wildlife trade available at https://assets.publishing.service.gov.uk/media/5a7cbc2840f0b6629523b7c8/london-wildlife-conference-declaration-140213.pdf (last accessed 9 January 2025).

[33] A Ilhes, 'Wildlife Crime in the United Kingdom: In-depth Analysis for the ENVI Committee' (Report PE 578.963, 2016) available at www.europarl.europa.eu/RegData/etudes/IDAN/2016/578963/IPOL_IDA(2016)578963_EN.pdf (last accessed 6 November 2024).

[34] However, while the UK did not participate in EnviCrimeNet, it still contributed to some of its activities, for instance its joint project with Europol, IPEC: see at www.europol.europa.eu/cms/sites/default/files/documents/ipec_report_on_environmental_crime_in_europe_0.pdf (last accessed 6 November 2024).

again on wildlife trafficking[35] and animal abuse,[36] and referred at least one environmental crime case to Eurojust.[37] Taking into account these past developments during the UK's membership, the withdrawal from the EU appeared to be a potential turning point for the future of the UK's environmental protection and its cooperation with EU Member States and agencies.

## III. Brexit – Green Opportunity or Green Threat?

The environment, just like JHA, was not particularly debated nor did it have any determining issues in the 2016 referendum, especially in comparison with the economy or migration. Nonetheless, both became more prominent during the Brexit process.

Environmental policies in the UK have been profoundly shaped by the period that witnessed the UK's transition from the 'Dirty Man of Europe' in the 1970s, to a leading country on some green dossiers.[38] Consequently, voices emerged, especially from civil society and NGOs, about the risk of weaker environmental standards now that the UK was able to diverge from EU norms, especially in reaction to the strong politicisation of EU 'red tape' and the attacks against EU environmental norms based on Eurosceptic and anti-environment narratives. In that respect, for example, in 2017, 13 environmental organisations (including WWF, Greenpeace, Client Earth) launched a manifesto for a 'Greener UK', asking the Government, inter alia, to maintain the benefits of existing EU environmental legislation.[39]

These concerns were extended to the topic of environmental crime, where they were coupled with and amplified by the voices of practitioners worried about losing access to EU tools, agencies and databases, and its detrimental effect on law enforcement and criminal justice.[40] On that specific topic, a number of individual and collective actors publicly anticipated potential post-Brexit deregulation and, based on previous attempts to decriminalise low-level environmental offences,[41] pushed the UK Government to preserve its alignment with the EU and to keep cooperating with it.[42]

[35] See, eg, Europol, '3.4 tonnes of seized glass eels reintroduced into their natural habitat' (22 June 2018) available at www.europol.europa.eu/media-press/newsroom/news/34-tonnes-of-seized-glass-eels-reintroduced-their-natural-habitat (last accessed 7 November 2024); Europol, 'EU law enforcement step up efforts to protect the environment – 48 arrested for trafficking endangered species' (23 June 2017) available at www.europol.europa.eu/media-press/newsroom/news/eu-law-enforcement-step-efforts-to-protect-environment---48-arrested-for-trafficking-endangered-species (last accessed 7 November 2024).

[36] Europol, 'Police dismantle crime group trading horsemeat unfit for human consumption' (16 July 2017) available at www.europol.europa.eu/media-press/newsroom/news/police-dismantle-crime-group-trading-horsemeat-unfit-for-human-consumption) (last accessed 7 November 2024).

[37] Eurojust, *Report on Eurojust's Casework on Environmental Crime* (2021) available at www.eurojust.europa.eu/sites/default/files/assets/report_environmental_crime.pdf (last accessed 7 November 2024).

[38] Burns and Carter (n 7).

[39] The Wildlife Trusts (n 2).

[40] Wolff, Piquet and Carrapico (n 5).

[41] Pereira (n 27).

[42] For example, Wildlife and Countryside Link and UK Centre for Animal Law, 'Brexit: Getting the Best Deal for Animals' (January 2018) available at www.wcl.org.uk/docs/Link_A-Law_Brexit_Animal_Welfare_160118.compressed.pdf (last accessed 7 November 2024).

The Government aimed to appease these concerns with the promise of a 'Green Brexit'. Indeed, Brexiteers were keen to introduce Brexit as an unprecedented opportunity, a 'once-in-a-lifetime-change',[43] to achieve higher environmental standards that could not be reached within the EU. While retaining direct EU environmental legislation and EU-derived measures in domestic law, in 2018 the Government published a 25-year Environment Plan,[44] which included specific provisions on the political engagement to further prevent wildlife trade and waste crime.

At the same time, the Government tried to address public unease regarding internal security through the vision of a 'Secure Brexit' together with the 'Take back control' slogan, with the goal of enabling the UK to control who and what entered and exited its national territory. To achieve this goal, successive governments intended to maximise the UK's access to EU cooperation mechanisms and instruments. That option was discarded by EU negotiators as the UK refused to accept the jurisdiction of the Court of Justice of the European Union since it was no longer a Member State of the EU.[45] Nevertheless, the successive British opt ins to EU instruments before the start of the transition period, then Title V of the Withdrawal Agreement[46] and finally Part Three of the TCA still enabled some cooperation and exchange of information between the UK and the EU, including through Europol and Eurojust. Though not the exact continuity that applied previously, this arrangement still reflects the shared interests of the UK and the EU to fight crime together, including serious damage to the environment.

Indeed, since the UK's departure from the EU, British officials have taken part in several operations coordinated and supported by Europol to fight environmental crime. They contributed to the successive annual LAKE Operations, targeting glass-eel trafficking between 2019 and 2023,[47] and participated in coordinated seizures of illegal pesticides with 28 other European countries.[48] No specific data on Eurojust environmental crime cases involving the UK are publicly available. Nonetheless, the growing number of cases involving the EU agency, and the high number of new cases, coordination meetings and joint investigation teams in which the UK has been participating over the past few years,[49] allow us to assume that British authorities have been party to several of them.

This seems even more plausible taking into account the continuation of British membership of several relevant EU instruments on that topic. Even though no longer a

[43] HM Government, *A Green Future: Our 25 Year Plan to Improve the Environment* (11 January 2018) available at https://assets.publishing.service.gov.uk/government/uploads/system/uploads/attachment_data/file/693158/25-year-environment-plan.pdf (last accessed 7 November 2024).

[44] ibid.

[45] Wolff, Piquet and Carrapico (n 5).

[46] Agreement on the withdrawal of the United Kingdom of Great Britain and Northern Ireland from the European Union and the European Atomic Energy Community [2020] OJ L29/7.

[47] Europol, 'Law enforcement casts net over 256 eel smugglers' (29 June 2023) available at www.europol.europa.eu/media-press/newsroom/news/law-enforcement-casts-net-over-256-eel-smugglers) (last accessed 9 January 2025).

[48] Europol, 'Operation Silver Axe strikes for the fourth time seizing over 550 tonnes of illegal pesticides' (18 June 2019) available at www.europol.europa.eu/media-press/newsroom/news/operation-silver-axe-strikes-for-fourth-time-seizing-over-550-tonnes-of-illegal-pesticides (last accessed 7 November 2024).

[49] For the UK's current participation in Eurojust, see at www.eurojust.europa.eu/united-kingdom (last accessed 7 November 2024).

member of the EU, the UK is still participating in networks such as ENPE, EUFJE and IMPEL, and contributing to and funding the EU-TWIX database. Put together, this demonstrates a strong commitment from British authorities to keep exchanging and engaging with their European counterparts on a form of crime that is mainly framed as cross-border.

It should also be recalled that in addition to EU venues, British officials can exchange data and cooperate with European authorities at the international level. This includes Interpol, the international police organisation, the purpose of which is to connect police officers and enable them to work together. Following the loss of its direct access to Europol's Information System or to the Schengen Information System (SIS II), the UK has identified Interpol's I-24/7 database as a relevant alternative to mitigate the post-Brexit situation.[50] The Interpol channel is of particular interest with regard to environmental crime, as the organisation has over time acquired a strong expertise in this regard and has developed new capacities, setting up working groups and dedicated committees as early as the 1990s.[51] Interpol has also coordinated international investigations on that topic, the most important probably being the Thunder operations organised every year by Interpol and the World Customs Organisation as global crackdowns to enforce the CITES. The annual Thunder investigations have involved EU Member States and Europol, and the UK is still participating in these joint operations and even funding them, independently from its relations with the EU.[52]

Consequently, Brexit could be interpreted as having a limited impact on UK–EU cooperation in the fight against environmental crime in accordance with the promises made by British decision makers. Yet a more nuanced picture is needed in order to fully capture the implications of the withdrawal from the EU on this specific topic.

## IV. Assessing the EU–UK Post-Brexit Cooperation

Beyond the apparent continuity, some potential changes in UK–EU cooperation can be anticipated due to three main factors.

The first one relates to the legal framework. The TCA and the retained environmental EU law for the time being limit the divergence between the UK and EU Member States, including on the definition and approach to environmental crime. Yet this situation could evolve in the coming years due to parallel legislative developments happening in the EU and in the UK.

[50] House of Lords European Union Committee, *Beyond Brexit: Policing, Law Enforcement and Security* (25th Report of Session 2019–21, HL 250) available at https://publications.parliament.uk/pa/ld5801/ldselect/ldeucom/250/250.pdf (last accessed 7 November 2024).

[51] D Higgins and R White, 'Collaboration at the Front Line: INTERPOL and NGOs in the Same NEST' in G Pink and R White (eds), *Environmental Crime and Collaborative State Intervention* (Palgrave Macmillan, 2016) 101.

[52] Interpol, 'Global crackdown on illegal wildlife and timber trade: INTERPOL and World Customs Organization join forces' (6 December 2022) available at www.interpol.int/en/News-and-Events/News/2022/Global-crackdown-on-illegal-wildlife-and-timber-trade-INTERPOL-and-World-Customs-Organization-join-forces (last accessed 7 November 2024).

On the EU side, as part of the EU Green Deal Agenda, a Directive on the protection of the environment through criminal law was adopted in April 2024, replacing the 2008 Directive.[53] The new Directive brings changes to what is covered by 'environmental' crime, with new categories of offences added to the nine pre-existing ones (eg, illegal timber trade, illegal ship recycling, or serious breaches of EU chemicals legislation) that preceded Brexit. The 2024 Directive also requires more severe penalties for 'qualified criminal offences' to cover widespread and substantial damage caused to the environment, with an explicit reference to 'ecocide', a still very much debated notion at international level. Yet this crime does not exist in UK legislation, even though an 'Ecocide Bill' was introduced in the House of Lords in November 2023,[54] while a similar proposal was lodged in the Scottish Parliament one year later.[55] Furthermore, the 2024 Directive adds clarity to what constitutes an environmental offence, and to that end sets up some qualitative and quantitative thresholds that did not exist in the 2008 Directive, which was copy-pasted into UK law. Finally, the 2024 Directive introduces new provisions on minimum prison time and fine levels to dissuade such conduct effectively and to ensure approximation between national laws, elements that do not appear in the 'zombified'[56] version of EU legislation retained in UK legislation and that raise concerns about potential legal divergence between the EU and the UK.[57]

An additional challenge is that the divergence from EU definitions, standards and norms could increase further in the future, also due to a possible UK legislative evolution. While the initial decision to retain more than 1,000 EU environmental laws in domestic legislation was met with strong support from environmental groups and activists, recent discussions about the future of these rules and regulations have reactivated fears about post-Brexit environmental deterioration. During the debates about the Retained EU Law (Revocation and Reform) Bill, the commitment from the Government to retain those direct EU norms and EU-derived rules necessary to fulfil parallel international obligations could be interpreted as meaning that the environmental acquis would remain untouched.[58] This argument was strengthened by the final decision of the Government in May 2023 not to remove any important component of the environmental legislation introduced by the EU.[59] Nevertheless, some environmental groups and activists, such as Wildlife and Countryside Link,[60]

[53] Directive (EU) 2024/1203 of the European Parliament and of the Council of 11 April 2024 on the protection of the environment through criminal law and replacing Directives 2008/99/EC and 2009/123/EC.

[54] A Bill to introduce the crime of ecocide; and for connected purposes [2023] HL Bill 21.

[55] Proposed Ecocide (Prevention) (Scotland) Bill [2024] available at https://www.parliament.scot/bills-and-laws/proposals-for-bills/proposed-ecocide-prevention-scotland-bill (last accessed 10 January 2025).

[56] V Gravey and AJ Jordan, 'UK Environmental Policy and Brexit: Simultaneously de-Europeanising, Disengaging and (re)-Engaging?' (2023) 30 *Journal of European Public Policy* 2364.

[57] M Nicholson, 'A new EU Environmental Crime Directive – A diverging approach with the UK?' *Institute for European Environmental Policy UK* (November 2024) available at: https://ieep.uk/wp-content/uploads/2024/12/EU_Environmental_Crime_Directive_November_2024.pdf (last accessed 10 January 2025).

[58] J Grogan and C Barnard, 'The Retained EU Law (Revocation and Reform) Bill' *UK in a Changing Europe* (5 January 2023) available at https://ukandeu.ac.uk/the-retained-eu-law-revocation-and-reform-bill/ (last accessed 7 November 2024).

[59] CA Caine, 'Brexit and Environmental Law in England: Where Are We Now?' (2023) 41(4) *Journal of Energy & Natural Resources Law* 529.

[60] Wildlife and Countryside Link, 'Maintain UK nature laws or risk losing our iconic wildlife: warning as key nature talks at COP15 approach second week' (December 2022) available at www.wcl.org.uk/maintain-uk-nature-laws-or-risk-losing-our-iconic-wildlife.asp (last accessed 7 November 2024).

Client Earth[61] or Greener UK,[62] have expressed their concerns over possible future environmental deregulation based on past decisions of the Government to cut the budgets of environmental agencies and units (including the Department for Environment Food and Rural Affairs, National Parks and the National Wildlife Crime Unit of the Metropolitan Police), as well as governmental failures to comply with the Environment Act 2021 and the limited ambitions set by the Retained EU Law Bill.[63] Although the position of the recently elected Labour Government leaves open the question of regulatory alignment with the EU, these signals have been interpreted as demonstrating political willingness to diverge from the EU acquis, probably in the longer term, which could hinder cooperation between UK and EU officials on issues such as the fight against environmental crime.

Indeed, while differences in terms of definitions and sanctions do not fully prevent international cooperation, they do tend to complicate any exchange of information, coordinating action or the setting up of joint investigations. As highlighted by Colantoni et al,

> the absence of shared consensus on what constitutes an environmental crime, at least in the EU, is likely the greatest obstacle to the fight against such offenses … it prevents the alignment of enforcement strategies along common lines, the gathering of data and the establishment of standards – it is indeed rather complicated to consolidate information, if there is no mutual clarity among the sectors and players involved.[64]

The absence of a common definition also impacts operational cooperation, with, for instance, the use of advanced investigating techniques (eg, wiretapping) to fight environmental crime allowed in some countries and not in others, complicating joint operations and, at a later stage, national prosecutions.[65]

Second, UK–EU cooperation in the fight against environmental crime could suffer as a result of the current post-Brexit arrangements in the field of police and judicial cooperation, especially regarding Europol and Eurojust. While the UK has concluded a Working Arrangement with Europol and has posted a liaison prosecutor at Eurojust, by becoming a third country it lost some of the privileges reserved to EU Member States. As showed in section II, the current provisions have not made cooperation between UK and EU officials impossible, and the United States is a very relevant example of how a third country can contribute and benefit from the activities of EU agencies. Nevertheless, while it will be harder for British officials to preserve their influence and

[61] ClientEarth, 'REUL Act creates uncertainty for UK environmental protections' (6 July 2023) available at www.clientearth.org/latest/latest-updates/news/reul-act-creates-uncertainty-for-uk-environmental-protections/ (last accessed 7 November 2024).

[62] Greener UK, 'Retained EU Law (Revocation and Reform) Bill Consideration of Commons amendments' (20 June 2023) available at https://greeneruk.org/sites/default/files/download/2023-06/REUL_Bill_briefing_Lords_amendments_15_and_42.pdf (last accessed 7 November 2024).

[63] Gravey and Jordan (n 51).

[64] L Colantoni, GS Sarno and M Bianchi, 'Fighting environmental crime in Europe. An assessment of trends, players and actions' (Istituto Affari Internazionali, Rome – AMBITUS, 2022) available at www.iai.it/sites/default/files/ambitus_report.pdf (last accessed 7 November 2024) 19.

[65] L Colantoni and M Bianchi, 'Fighting environmental crime in Europe. Preliminary report' (Istituto Affari Internazionali, Rome – AMBITUS, 2020) available at www.iai.it/sites/default/files/ambitus_report.pdf (last accessed 7 November 2024).

their operational engagement, and to maintain similar access to the data collected by their EU counterparts, now that they have left the EU, and this loss will not be fully mitigated by their participation in other venues.

On the one hand, the different European practitioner networks dedicated to environmental crime (IMPEL, EUFJE, ENPE) favour the sharing of information and experiences and facilitate the establishment of contacts and of trust that are key to most operational cooperation dimensions. These exchanges, however, remain strongly dependent upon individuals' willingness due to these networks' limited internal capacity. As a result, the exchange of operational data and the launch of joint investigations emerge as bi-products of these formats of cooperation rather than as part of their primary goal.

On the other hand, the access of British officials to Interpol has not been impacted by Brexit and appeared as a relevant alternative venue for the Home Office to engage in multilateral cooperation with EU Member States. This is why, in addition to UK officials' now being strongly pushed to enter their data in Interpol databases, the Home Office is also encouraging the authorities of EU Member States to do the same in order for the UK to keep access to EU data in the name of shared interests. Yet this requires police officers of EU Member States to enter their data twice, once in EU databases and then in Interpol ones. Consequently, doubts have emerged as to the willingness and capacity of European law enforcement to duplicate efforts, as entering data has proved to be quite time-consuming for them and demands some familiarity with an additional information system, something already difficult to achieve with the Europol one.[66] Such uncertainty could thus to some extent affect the multilateral engagement of the UK with EU Member States.

Third, international cooperation to fight environmental crime is facilitated when a specialist unit or service exists and has staff who have acquired the required expertise and have access to enough financial and technical resources to deal mainly or exclusively with serious damage to the environment. Such specialisation reflects the importance and priority granted to environmental crime at the political and organisational levels, and is key to implementing international, regional and national legislation. This is because dealing with green crimes requires extensive practical knowledge of the diversity of environmental offences and their detection, given that they are often at the crossroads of licit and illicit economies, difficult to identify and to prove, and require liaison with a multiplicity of interlocutors (environmental agencies, veterinary services, etc). Consequently, the existence of a service or unit devoted to this form of crime puts together the resources required to tackle environmental crime and acts as the principal or unique action and contact point for external partners, including international ones.[67]

Such specialisation already exists in several EU Member States (eg, in Spain, Italy, France) and is strongly supported by EU institutions. For example, it was highlighted as good practice in the final report on the mutual evaluations on environmental

[66] V Mitsilegas and E Guild, 'Police and Criminal Justice Co-operation after Brexit' (2023) 30 *Journal of European Public Policy*. 2519; House of Lords European Union Committee (n 46).

[67] Farmer, Faure and Vagliasindi (eds) (n 28); Colantoni, Sarno and Bianchi (n 58).

crime led by the Council between 2016 and 2019.[68] In addition, Europol, Eurojust and the European Union Agency for Law Enforcement Training (CEPOL) also offer some training to national officials to support their specialisation and provide them with the expertise required to empower them and make them visible interlocutors for their European counterparts. Moreover, two articles in the 2024 Directive on environmental crime (Articles 17 and 18) now aim at ensuring that the relevant national competent authorities are trained, specialised and are granted the necessary human, financial, technical and technological resources to perform their activities by EU Member States.

The limited influence of EU soft power through recommendations, funding and training, and the legal divergence now that the UK has withdrawn from the EU have created uncertainty about the future of police specialisation on environmental crime, a political situation that is rendered more complicated given the difficult economic context faced by the UK. While there are no courts or tribunals specialising in environmental offences in the UK, some wildlife liaison officers or crime officers exist in certain police forces (Police Scotland, West Yorkshire Police, Police Service of Northern Ireland, etc). Further, the National Wildlife Crime Intelligence Unit (later the National Wildlife Crime Unit) was created in 2004 within the Metropolitan Police, to coordinate enforcement activity, collect intelligence and produce analytical reports. Although this unique Unit had limited human (fewer than 15 staff) and financial resources (less than £500,000 per year), its existence and funding were repeatedly put into question by the Government in the recent years, and the lack of public funding had to be partly compensated for by an NGO, World Animal Protection.[69] However, in June 2024 the Metropolitan Police announced the cutting back of the National Wildlife Crime Unit as part of the 'New Met for London plan', and the disbandment of this small but well-respected unit was met with strong criticism from civil society and NGOs.[70] Indeed, the closing down of this Unit could be detrimental to any future environmental law enforcement specialisation and hamper cooperation with EU national authorities, whose officers are encouraged to enhance their skills and knowledge in this area.

In conclusion, environmental crime was not one of the most salient issues during the referendum campaign, the negotiations of the Withdrawal Agreement or the negotiations regarding the TCA. Nonetheless, it is at the crossroads of two major concerns of citizens, the protection of the environment and that of internal security, with fears being expressed by civil society and practitioners about the future UK–EU arrangements and cooperation on that topic. The outcome of the negotiations, at first sight, suggests some degree of continuity, from both a legislative and an operational perspective. This is because, in addition to preserving the EU environmental acquis in domestic

[68] Council of the European Union, *Final report of the Eighth round of mutual evaluations on environmental crime*, Doc 14065/19, 15 November 2019.

[69] RA Sollund and J Maher, 'Illegal wildlife trade: A case study report on the illegal wildlife trade in the United Kingdom, Norway, Colombia and Brazil' *Efface–European Union Action to Fight Environmental Crime* (Ecologic Institute, 2015) available at http://efface.eu/illegal-wildlife-trade-case-study-report-illegal-wildlife-trade-united-kingdom-norway-colombia-and#overlay-context=case-studies (last accessed 7 November 2024).

[70] M Prior, 'Wildlife smugglers 'freer to offend' after police cuts' *BBC* (28 June 2024) available at https://www.bbc.com/news/articles/cv2g37zn9d5o (last accessed 10 January 2025).

legislation, UK officials have been willing to maintain their past operational commitment within multilateral venues, notably within relevant EU agencies and professional networks, playing a key role in the fight against environmental crime. Nonetheless, current arrangements do not exactly replicate pre-Brexit instruments regarding data exchange and joint operations, and challenges could appear in the long run. This scenario will strongly depend on the priority granted to the preservation of the environment in the UK, to the political willingness to keep upgrading domestic legislation and dedicated structures, and to the capacity of the UK and the EU to avoid diverging from each other and hampering future cooperation.

# 23

# Cybercrime in the TCA: Reduced Cooperation in an Environment of Regulatory Divergence?

BENJAMIN FARRAND

## I. Introduction

If there is one form of criminal activity that is not limited by physical proximity, borders or jurisdictions, it is cybercrime. Cybercrime is a considerable threat to the economy and well-being of individuals, as well as to the profitability of private business and security of critical infrastructures. From ransomware attacks against critical infrastructure in the United States (US), such as the Colonial Pipeline incident that left the East Coast with limited power supplies for a week until normal operations were restored,[1] to the massive increases in identify theft, phishing and fraudulent text messages harming consumers in the United Kingdom (UK) during the Covid pandemic,[2] cybercrime is a phenomenon that has significant implications for both the public and private sectors, individuals, companies and states. The purpose of this chapter is to explore how the EU regulates cybercrime, how relations between the EU and UK in tackling cybercrime have changed as a result of the UK's withdrawal from the EU and revised cooperation under the Trade and Cooperation Agreement (TCA),[3] and the potential pitfalls that continued cooperation faces.

In the discussion of cybercrime, it will also be necessary to briefly discuss cybersecurity. Cybercrime and cybersecurity are intertwined in such a way that speaking about one without the other is difficult, and even counterproductive. That there is no universally

[1] SM Kerner, 'Colonial Pipeline Hack Explained: Everything You Need to Know'. *TechTarget WhatIs.com* (22 April 2022) available at www.techtarget.com/whatis/feature/Colonial-Pipeline-hack-explained-Everything-you-need-to-know (last accessed 8 March 2023).

[2] National Crime Agency, 'Beware Fraud and Scams during Covid-19 Pandemic Fraud' (26 March 2020) available at https://nationalcrimeagency.gov.uk/news/fraud-scams-covid19 (last accessed 8 March 2023).

[3] Trade and Cooperation Agreement between the European Union and the European Atomic Energy Community, of the one part, and the United Kingdom of Great Britain and Northern Ireland, of the other part [2021] OJ L149/10.

accepted definition of 'cybercrime' is acknowledged by numerous academics,[4] which is also true of cybersecurity.[5] However, what can be clearly stated is that cybercrime constitutes the offensive side of this relationship, with cybersecurity representing the defensive side that seeks to prevent or mitigate the consequences of cybercrime, such as in the case of ensuring resilience (cybersecurity) against attacks on information systems (cybercrime). Cybersecurity, as this chapter will discuss, must be incorporated into analysis to truly understand the impact on EU–UK cybercrime cooperation. This is perhaps unsurprising, given that scholarly and policy focus on these issues transcends disciplinary boundaries and legal jurisdictions, with all the complexities that arise as a result.[6] In order to understand the place of cybercrime and cybersecurity in the TCA, this chapter will use the definitions arising from the EU's policy initiatives in this field. This will be expanded upon in the next section, but cybercrime for the purpose of this chapter refers to 'a broad range of different criminal activities where computers and information systems are involved either as a primary tool or a primary target'.[7]

This chapter is structured as follows: section II details the position on combating cybercrime and ensuring cybersecurity pre-Brexit, providing an overview of the relevant legislative frameworks, the nature of cooperation between Member States, and the fundamental role of bodies such as Europol and its European Cybercrime Centre, EC3; it details the ongoing cooperative efforts on joined-up cybersecurity and cybercrime initiatives, working with bodies such as the European Union Agency for Cybersecurity, ENISA.[8] Section III considers the current threat landscape and emerging trends in cybercrime, which have necessitated greater levels of cooperation and information sharing, before considering the cooperation provided for under the TCA. The final substantive section of the paper (section IV) explores the problems for continued cooperation in

[4] See, eg, DS Wall, 'Cybercrime, Media and Insecurity: The Shaping of Public Perceptions of Cybercrime' (2008) 22 *International Review of Law, Computers & Technology* 45; H Carrapico and B Farrand, 'The European Union's Fight against Cybercrime: Policy, Legal and Practical Challenges' in M Fletcher, E Herlin-Karnell and C Matera (eds), *The European Union as an Area of Freedom, Security and Justice* (Routledge, 2016) 459; EC Viano, 'Cybercrime: Definition, Typology, and Criminalization' in EC Viano (ed), *Cybercrime, Organized Crime, and Societal Responses: International Approaches* (Springer International Publishing, 2017) 3; S Broadhead, 'The Contemporary Cybercrime Ecosystem: A Multi-Disciplinary Overview of the State of Affairs and Developments' (2018) 34 *Computer Law & Security Review* 1180.

[5] See WA Wulf and AK Jones, 'Reflections on Cybersecurity' (2009) 326 *Science* 943; K Giles and W Hagestad, (2013) 'Divided by a Common Language: Cyber Definitions in Chinese, Russian and English', 5th International Conference on Cyber Conflict (CYCON), Tallinn (4–7 June 2013) available at www.researchgate.net/publication/261300676_Divided_by_a_common_language_Cyber_definitions_in_Chinese_Russian_and_English (last accessed 8 March 2023); R Collett, 'Understanding Cybersecurity Capacity Building and Its Relationship to Norms and Confidence Building Measures' (2021) 6 *Journal of Cyber Policy* 298; J Lewallen, 'Emerging Technologies and Problem Definition Uncertainty: The Case of Cybersecurity' (2021) 15 *Regulation & Governance* 1035.

[6] B Farrand and H Carrapico, 'The How and Why of Cybercrime: The EU as a Case Study of the Role of Ideas, Interests, and Institutions as Drivers of a Security-Governance Approach' in A Lavorgna and TJ Holt (eds), *Researching Cybercrimes: Methodologies, Ethics, and Critical Approaches* (Springer International Publishing, 2021).

[7] European Commission and High Representative of the European Union for Foreign Affairs and Security Policy, 'Cybersecurity Strategy of the European Union: An Open, Safe and Secure Cyberspace' JOIN (2013) 1 3.

[8] Established by Regulation 460/2004 establishing the European Network and Information Security Agency (ENISA) [2004] OJ L77/1, repealed and replaced by [2013] OJ L165/41, which in turn has now been repealed and replaced by Regulation 2019/881 on ENISA and on information technology cybersecurity certification (Cybersecurity Act) [2019] OJ L151/15.

this field, considering the impacts of reduced data sharing and strategic leadership, as well as the potential for increased regulatory divergence on issues such as human rights and data protection generally, through to substantive cybercrime laws specifically.

## II. The EU Approach to Cybercrime and Cybersecurity in the Context of International Cooperation

Since the negotiations over the Cybercrime Convention began in the late 1990s,[9] cooperation in combating cybercrime has been predicated on the understanding that it is largely a transnational and borderless phenomenon, often involving two or more jurisdictions.[10] For this reason, much of the work in this field has been in harmonising to an extent the criminal laws of states at a minimal level so as to ensure that cross-border investigation, arrest and prosecution might be facilitated.[11] The Cybercrime Convention was in essence a first step in this process, providing for states party to ensure that, at a minimum, attacks against information systems,[12] acts of computer-facilitated fraud[13] and certain forms of content[14] (often considered the movement of traditional 'offline' crimes to the 'online' environment)[15] were criminalised. The EU had already recognised the concerns raised by the potential for the Internet to be used for criminal purposes in the mid-1990s, with the European Council's Tampere Conclusions in 1999 stating that action needed to be taken to tackle 'high-tech crimes' through the establishment of common definitions and sanctions.[16]

The EU began work on this process of minimal harmonisation, focused on common definitions and minimum sanctions, operating under the then-Third Pillar of Justice and Home Affairs (JHA), implementing Framework Decisions on attacks on information systems,[17] on combating fraud and counterfeiting of non-cash means of payment,[18] and on combating the sexual abuse and sexual exploitation of children and child pornography.[19] Subsequent to the Cybercrime Convention Additional Protocol

[9] Council of Europe, Convention on Cybercrime, Budapest,23 November 2001 (CETS 185).

[10] S Schjolberg, 'The History of Global Harmonization on Cybercrime Legislation – the Road to Geneva' *Cyber Crime Law* (December 2008) available at www.cybercrimelaw.net/documents/cybercrime_history.pdf (last accessed 8 March 2023); see also SW Brenner and JJ Schwerha IV, 'Transnational Evidence Gathering and Local Prosecution of International Cybercrime' (2001) 20 *John Marshall Journal of Computer and Information Law* 347; DS Wall, *Cybercrime: The Transformation of Crime in the Information Age* (Polity Press, 2007).

[11] C Harding and JB Banach-Gutierrez, 'The Emergent EU Criminal Policy: Identifying the Species' (2012) 37(6) *European Law Review* 758; S Summers et al, *The Emergence of EU Criminal Law: Cyber Crime and the Regulation of the Information Society* (Hart Publishing, 2014). On EU efforts on criminal law harmonisation generally, see V Mitsilegas, *EU Criminal Law after Lisbon: Rights, Trust and the Transformation of Justice in Europe* (Hart Publishing, 2016).

[12] Convention on Cybercrime (n 7) Title 1.

[13] ibid Title 2.

[14] ibid Title 3.

[15] See generally J Clough, *Principles of Cybercrime*, 2nd edn (Cambridge University Press, 2015).

[16] European Council, 'Tampere European Council Conclusions' (15 and 16 October 1999) para 48.

[17] Council Framework Decision 2005/222/JHA on attacks against information systems [2005] OJ L69/67.

[18] Council Framework Decision 2001/413/JHA combating fraud and counterfeiting of non-cash means of payment [2001] OJ L149/1.

[19] Council Framework Decision 2004/68/JHA on combating sexual abuse and sexual exploitation of children and child pornography [2004] OJ L13/44.

that focused on the criminalisation of acts of a racist and xenophobic nature committed through computer systems,[20] the EU then implemented an additional Framework Decision criminalising hate speech in the form of racism and xenophobia.[21] After the entry into force of the Treaty of Lisbon,[22] the EU has developed criminal law competences that have allowed it to legislate in areas of identified concern,[23] and the regulation of cybercrimes in the EU has expanded beyond these initial actions. This has included the transposition of Framework Decisions into updated and codified Directives on attacks against information systems,[24] fraud and counterfeiting of means of non-cash payment,[25] and on child sexual exploitation.[26] Furthermore, the EU implemented a Directive on combating terrorism,[27] which made clear at recital 10 that the glorification and justification of terrorism online should also be considered an offence, with Article 5 of the Directive stating that Member States should take necessary measures to ensure that public provocations to commit a terrorist offence, 'whether online or offline', should be punishable as criminal offences. This had the impact of expanding the types of content offence that the EU sought to harmonise in the field of cybercrime, developing a position as an international actor in cybercrime and cybersecurity policies,[28] albeit one demonstrating significant difficulties in achieving a cohesive and coherent cybercrime approach.[29]

This was in fact a problem that the EU itself identified, and which the Commission made clear in a 2007 Communication.[30] The EU identified effective cooperation across borders as essential in the fight against cybercrime, noting a lack of engagement between national authorities,[31] which was seen as impeding speedy responses to cyberthreats. Europol was deemed as being central to the improvement of this coordination, with the establishment of the European Cybercrime Centre, or EC3, as a Europol unit in 2012.[32] As the Communication stated, EC3 was to deal with cybercrimes committed by organised crime groups (including where they were engaging in online acts of fraud), where

[20] Council of Europe, Additional Protocol to the Convention on cybercrime, concerning the criminalisation of acts of a racist and xenophobic nature committed through computer systems, 28 January 2003 (CETS 189).

[21] Framework Decision 2008/913/JHA on combating certain forms of racism and xenophobia by means of criminal law [2008] OJ L328/55.

[22] Treaty of Lisbon amending the Treaty on European Union and the Treaty establishing the European Community, signed at Lisbon, 13 December 2007 [2007] OJ C306/1.

[23] Mitsilegas (n 9); E Herlin-Karnell, *The Constitutional Dimension of European Criminal Law* (Bloomsbury Publishing, 2012); Harding and Banach-Gutierrez (n 9).

[24] Directive 2013/40/EU on attacks against information systems [2005] OJ L218/8.

[25] Directive 2019/713 on combating fraud and counterfeiting of non-cash means of payment [2019] OJ L123/18.

[26] Directive 2011/93/EU on combating sexual abuse and sexual exploitation of children and child pornography [2011] OJ L335/1.

[27] Directive 2017/541 on combating terrorism [2017] OJ L88/6.

[28] E Fahey 'The EU's Cybercrime and Cyber-Security Rulemaking: Mapping the Internal and External Dimensions of EU Security' (2014) 5 *European Journal of Risk Regulation* 46; H Carrapico and A Barrinha 'The EU as a Coherent (Cyber)Security Actor?' (2017) 55 *Journal of Common Market Studies* 1254.

[29] As discussed in H Carrapico and B Farrand, 'Cyber Crime as a Fragmented Policy Field in the Context of the Area of Freedom, Security and Justice' in A Ripoll Servent and F Trauner (eds), *The Routledge Handbook of Justice and Home Affairs Research* (Routledge, 2018) 146.

[30] European Commission, 'Towards a General Policy on the Fight against Cyber Crime' COM(2007) 267.

[31] ibid 4.

[32] European Commission, 'Tackling Crime in Our Digital Age: Establishing a European Cybercrime Centre' COM(2012) 140.

there was serious harm to individuals such as that inflicted by child sexual abuse and exploitation, or where cyberattacks were made against critical information systems of infrastructure within the EU.[33] It would help to combat these forms of criminal activity through information pooling and sharing, concentrating expertise and thereby assisting in Member State capacity building, providing support to national cybercrime investigations and engaging with other relevant stakeholders, such as civil society, researchers, private sector investigators and external organisations like Interpol.[34]

The Joint Cybercrime Action Taskforce, or J-CAT, was quickly established by EC3, with an initial pilot beginning in September 2014. The Taskforce was initiated by Member States Austria, France, Germany, Italy, the Netherlands, Spain and the UK, working in cooperation with Canada and the US, as a means of coordinating international investigations by both developing strategies as well as coordinating operational responses.[35] J-CAT has been considered to be an effective unit, particularly due to the agility and responsiveness facilitated by the semi-formalised network organisation and the ability to circumvent impediments imposed by strict legal or bureaucratic processes.[36] Indeed, one potential indicator of its success as a cooperation mechanism is that, despite beginning as a six-month-long pilot project, J-CAT still exists a decade later, with an expanded membership.[37] Europol has also formalised cooperation with other EU cyber-agencies,[38] including ENISA, the EU's cybersecurity agency;[39] CERT-EU, the Computer Emergency Response Team for the EU institutions, bodies and agencies;[40] and the European Defence Agency, intended to protect the Union from external threats by developing capabilities in the field of crisis management.[41] This cooperation is centred on the understanding that 'cybercrime' and 'cybersecurity'[42] are not strictly delimited fields,[43] but particularly when considering that attacks on information systems and computer-facilitated fraud are inextricably linked, and that the

[33] ibid 4.

[34] ibid 4–6.

[35] EC3, 'Expert International Cybercrime Taskforce Is Launched to Tackle Online Crime' *Europol* (September 2014) available at www.europol.europa.eu/media-press/newsroom/news/expert-international-cybercrime-taskforce-launched-to-tackle-online-crime-0 (last accessed 6 March 2023).

[36] T Reitano, T Oerting and M Hunter, 'Innovations in International Cooperation to Counter Cybercrime: The Joint Cybercrime Action Taskforce' (2015) 2 *The European Review of Organised Crime* 142; G Christou 'The Challenges of Cybercrime Governance in the European Union' (2018) 19 *European Politics and Society* 355.

[37] Europol, 'Joint Cybercrime Action Taskforce (J-CAT)' *Europol* (16 February) available at www.europol.europa.eu/operations-services-and-innovation/services-support/joint-cybercrime-action-taskforce (last accessed 8 March 2023).

[38] Memorandum of Understanding between ENISA of the first part, the EDA of the second part, Europol's EC3 of the third part, and CERT-EU of the fourth part, 23 May 2018.

[39] ENISA (n 3).

[40] Council Arrangement on the organisation and operation of a computer emergency response team for the EU's institutions, bodies and agencies [2018] OJ C12/1.

[41] Council Joint Action 2004/551/CFSP on the establishment of the European Defence Agency, which was repealed and replaced by Council Decision (CFSP) 2015/1835 defining the statute, seat and operational rules of the European Defence Agency.

[42] Initially dictated in EU law by Directive 2016/1148 concerning measures for a high common level of security and information systems across the Union [2016] OJ L194/1 (the NIS Directive), which has recently been replaced by Directive 2022/2555 on measures for a high common level of cybersecurity across the Union [2022] OJ L337/80 (the NIS2 Directive).

[43] See, eg, H Carrapico and B Farrand, 'Dialogue, Partnership and Empowerment for Network and Information Security: The Changing Role of the Private Sector from Objects of Regulation to Regulation Shapers' (2017) 67 *Crime, Law and Social Change* 245.

lines between 'public' and 'private', as well as 'internal security' and 'external defence', are inherently blurred when dealing with malicious cyber-activities.[44] For this reason, the development of expertise and sharing of practices is provided for in Article 3 of the Memorandum of Understanding, in the form of information exchange, education and training, cyber-exercises, technical and strategic cooperation, as well as 'any other areas identified as mutually important'. The tackling of cybercrime in the EU, then, has been predicated on effective cooperation across borders in an environment of minimal harmonisation. However, as will be discussed in section III, due to the highly uncertain threat landscape, there is a considerable desire on the part of the EU to go further in response to cyber-threats.

## III. Cybercrime and the TCA: Reduced Cooperation in the Face of a Broader, More Varied Threat Landscape

The perception of an increasingly threatening digital environment and the blurring of the types of actors engaging in a widening range of offences occurring online have in turn led to a sense of vulnerability on the part of the EU in the context of its broader 'poly-crisis'.[45] In a Communication from 2016,[46] written in the wake of Russia's actions in Crimea and concerns over disinformation being propagated in the online ecosystem, the EU considered that the EU was vulnerable to hybrid threats, comprising

> [t]he mixture of coercive and subversive activity, conventional and unconventional methods (ie diplomatic, military, economic, technological), which can be used in a coordinated manner by state or non-state actors to achieve specific objectives while remaining below the threshold of formally declared warfare.[47]

In this context, the EU considered that it required a strategic framework for EU initiatives on cybersecurity and cybercrime,[48] which the von der Leyen Commission has sought to realise through its priority area 'Promoting Our European Way of Life'.[49] Cybercrime features prominently in the EU's Security Union Strategy, with the Commission noting that 'cyber-attacks and cybercrime continue to rise'[50] and reiterating the increasingly complex threat landscape, with the blurring of boundaries between crimes committed by organised crime groups and malicious actions by foreign powers, as well as the blurring of lines between physical and digital spaces.[51]

[44] Memorandum of Understanding (n 35) 3.

[45] On the polycrisis of economic, legitimacy and security crises in the EU, see J Zeitlin, F Nicoli and B Laffan'Introduction: The European Union beyond the Polycrisis? Integration and Politicization in an Age of Shifting Cleavages' (2019) 26 *Journal of European Public Policy* 963.

[46] European Commission and High Representative of the Union for Foreign Affairs and Security Policy, 'Joint Framework on Countering Hybrid Threats' JOIN (2016) 18.

[47] ibid 2.

[48] ibid 10.

[49] European Commission: Directorate-General for Communication and U Leyen, *A Union that strives for more – My agenda for Europe – Political guidelines for the next European Commission 2019-2024* (Publications Office, 2019) 16.

[50] European Commission, 'Communication on the EU Security Union Strategy'. COM(2020) 605, 1.

[51] ibid.

So what are some of these threats? If we return to the three broad categories of attacks against information systems, online fraud and content offences, we have seen significant shifts in the threats posed since the adoption of the Cybercrime Convention, and particularly over the past five years. Attacks against information systems have become more sophisticated, ranging from attacks against infrastructure by states, such as those alleged to have been made by Russia in the context of its aggression against Ukraine, with knock-on effects on service provision in EU Member States,[52] to ransomware attacks perpetrated by professional organised crime groups either directly for personal profit[53] or as 'cybercrime as a service',[54] in which the perpetrators do not choose the target themselves but instead operate as a service provider on behalf of a third party. Furthermore, attacks are made not only against the intended target but also upon different organisations in that target's supply chain, allowing for multiple firms to be subject to ransom demands.[55] These attacks, often demanding transfers of cryptocurrencies for the decryption of infected files, have been estimated as resulting in payments of over USD $400 million between 2019 and 2020, a year-on-year increase of 300 per cent.[56] The increased move to remote/hybrid working and increased time spent online for both professional and personal reasons as a result of Covid-19 have also been pointed to by Europol as a reason behind the increased incidence of cybercrime.[57]

On the topic of cryptocurrencies, online fraud perpetuated through their use has continued to accelerate,[58] with high-profile scams and losses becoming typical of cryptocurrency exchanges, in addition to their use in laundering proceeds of crime.[59] Cryptocurrencies have also become a value-transfer medium of choice in facilitating other forms of fraud, such as investor fraud, business email compromise and CEO fraud,[60] increasing substantially while fraud such as 'card not present' schemes have levelled off in comparison.[61] They have also been identified by Europol as the main way in which financial transfers are made in the context of child sexual abuse material,[62] the

[52] Council of the European Union. 'Russian Cyber Operations against Ukraine: Declaration by the High Representative on Behalf of the European Union' (10 May 2022) available at www.consilium.europa.eu/en/press/press-releases/2022/05/10/russian-cyber-operations-against-ukraine-declaration-by-the-high-representative-on-behalf-of-the-european-union/ (last accessed 8 March 2023).

[53] S Mansfield-Devine, 'Ransomware: The Most Popular Form of Attack' (2017) 10 *Computer Fraud & Security* 15; J Hunt-Sharman, 'Transnational Organised Cyber Crime' (2022) 14 *Australasian Policing* 5.

[54] D Manky, 'Cybercrime as a Service: A Very Modern Business' (2013) 6 *Computer Fraud & Security* 9; TS Hyslip, 'Cybercrime-as-a-Service Operations' in TJ Holt and AM Bossler (eds), *The Palgrave Handbook of International Cybercrime and Cyberdeviance* (Springer International Publishing, 2020) 815.

[55] A Cartwright and E Cartwright, 'The Economics of Ransomware Attacks on Integrated Supply Chain Networks' (2023) 4(4) *Digital Threats: Research and Practice* 1.

[56] Europol, 'The Internet Organised Crime Threat Assessment (IOCTA)' (2021) 21–22.

[57] Europol, 'Catching the Virus: Cybercrime, Disinformation and the COVID-19 Pandemic' (2020).

[58] TA Anderson, 'Cryptocurrency: The Wild, Wild Web: Analogies to the American and Canadian Wild, Wild West – Will History Repeat?' (2018) 33 *Journal of International Banking Law and Regulation* 113; A Maurushat and D Halpin, 'Investigation of Cryptocurrency Enabled and Dependent Crimes' in D Goldbarsht and L de Koker (eds), *Financial Technology and the Law: Combating Financial Crime* (Springer International Publishing, 2022); J McCarthy, 'Cryptocurrencies, Digital Money and Regulatory Damage' (2022) 37 *Journal of International Banking Law and Regulation* 282.

[59] Europol (n 53) 18.

[60] ibid 32.

[61] ibid 33.

[62] ibid 27.

presence of which continues to increase on the Dark Web.[63] For this particularly insidious and harmful type of content, successful identification of the sources, perpetrators and Dark Web networks is utterly dependent upon effective private-sector and police cooperation, expertise pooling and data exchange, as well as ensuring careful debriefing and counselling for investigators.[64] Europol gives the example of the takedown of the Boystown sexual abuse website, which, it argues, was only possible as the result of cooperation within Europol, as well as externally with partners such as Australia, Canada and the US.[65]

It is somewhat unfortunate, then, that just when increased cooperation and collaboration are deemed essential in combating a vast array of different cyber threats, the UK has had to renegotiate its relationship with the EU agencies and institutions involved in combating cybercrime. In comparison to some other areas, however, the understanding that continued cooperation is imperative in combating cybercrime and ensuring cybersecurity appears to have had some influence in the shaping of the TCA. Title II of Part Four of the Agreement (which covers 'thematic cooperation') is dedicated to cybersecurity, with Article 703 stating:

> The parties shall endeavour to establish a regular dialogue in order to exchange information about relevant policy developments, including in relation to international security, security of emerging technologies, internet governance, cybersecurity, cyber defence and cybercrime.

Furthermore, Article 704 encourages cooperation in areas of mutual interest, through sharing of best practices and other 'cooperative practical actions',[66] and cooperation with each other in international venues both to strengthen global resilience to cyberthreats and to assist third countries in improving their effectiveness in fighting cybercrime.[67] Similarly, the UK may upon invitation be permitted to cooperate voluntarily with CERT-EU upon approval by its Steering Board under Article 705, with the Cooperation Group established under the NIS Directive under Article 706 and with ENISA under Article 707. Cooperation Group engagement is based around information exchange, particularly around standards of best practice, security exercises, emergent risks and incidents, training and education, and research and development; whereas ENISA engagement is based upon invitations to participate in specific activities relating to capacity building, knowledge and information provision, and awareness raising.[68] Interestingly, this engagement will be dependent upon a financial contribution and the drawing up of working arrangements by ENISA's Management Board,[69] with any exchange of information being considered purely voluntary.[70] At the time of writing, there is no evidence indicating whether these forms of cooperation have been pursued by the UK.

[63] ibid 26.
[64] SW Craun, ML Bourke and FN Coulson, 'The Impact of Internet Crimes Against Children Work on Relationships with Families and Friends: An Exploratory Study' (2015) 30 *Journal of Family Violence* 393; R Liggett et al, 'The Dark Web as a Platform for Crime: An Exploration of Illicit Drug, Firearm, CSAM, and Cybercrime Markets' in Holt and Bossler (eds) (n 51) 91.
[65] Europol (n 53) 27.
[66] TCA Art 704(1).
[67] TCA Art 704(2).
[68] TCA Art 706.
[69] TCA Art 707(2).
[70] TCA Art 707(3).

Given the importance of cooperation in combating cybercrime, activity that transcends traditional boundaries and borders, the relatively few substantive (aspirational, even) provisions dedicated to the topic in the TCA appear to represent a significant reduction in cooperation at a time when these threats are becoming more present in the minds of policy makers. Along with other areas of Europol cooperation governed under the general provision of Article 522 of the TCA,[71] operational engagement with Europol in the context of cybercrime[72] is provided for under Article 564, with cooperation being limited to the exchange of information such as specialist knowledge, general situation reports, the results of strategic analysis, information on criminal investigation procedures, participation in training, and the provision of advice and support in individual criminal investigations.[73] The UK has now concluded Working Arrangements for the cooperation of national authorities with Europol,[74] and while some cooperation is better than none, it is nevertheless a significant reduction in comparison to what was available before.

## IV. Problems for the Future and How to Prevent them?

As Arnell et al stated, 'the high level and intricate nature of cooperation between EU Member States was lost to the UK. Its maintenance was impossible. … [yet] a somewhat reassuring degree of cooperation and information exchange subsists under the TCA'.[75] That the UK can cooperate with Europol is positive, and the TCA provides for liaisons and points of contact, making that cooperation easier than would otherwise be the case.[76] Similarly, the UK continues to participate in J-CAT in a similar manner to states such as the US, which is also positive, given the effectiveness of J-CAT identified in section II. Similarly, engagement with ENISA is rendered feasible by the TCA, if at a somewhat basic level at present, with potential benefits for operational engagement, should opportunities arise. The UK has always been more enthusiastic about cybercrime cooperation than cooperation in other fields: even when pursuing opt outs from a variety of JHA instruments, the UK nevertheless continued to participate in all activities relating to cybercrime and cybersecurity.[77] However, at the level of *strategy*, a gap is more discernible, to the detriment of both the UK and EU. The UK, for example, has been a driver of an 'intelligence-led policing' approach to criminal investigations in Europe,[78] and was highly influential in the EU's strategic approach to cybercrime and cybersecurity.[79] Indeed, UK representatives frequently held leadership positions in

[71] Which has been discussed in other chapters in this volume and will not be reproduced here.
[72] TCA Art 566(1), which provides for cybercrime to be a subject for cooperation under Annex 41.
[73] TCA Art 567.
[74] Working and Administrative Arrangement establishing cooperative relations between the competent authorities of the United Kingdom of Great Britain and Northern Ireland and the European Union Agency for Law Enforcement Cooperation, concluded in September 2021.
[75] P Arnell et al, 'Police Cooperation and Exchange of Information under the EU–UK Trade and Cooperation Agreement' (2021) 12 *New Journal of European Criminal Law* 265, 266.
[76] ibid 272–73.
[77] S Wolff, A Piquet and H Carrapico, 'UK's Withdrawal from Justice and Home Affairs: A Historical Institutionalist Analysis of Policy Trajectories' (2022) 20 *Comparative European Politics* 604.
[78] V Mitsilegas, 'European Criminal Law After Brexit' (2017) 28 *Criminal Law Forum* 219.
[79] S Sweeney and N Winn, 'Do or Die? The UK, the EU, and Internal/External Security Cooperation after Brexit' (2022) 21 *European Political Science* 237.

taskforces such as J-CAT, as well as leading on European Multidisciplinary Platforms Against Criminal Threats projects,[80] meaning that while there have been significant losses for the UK as discussed, the EU also suffers as a result of reduced strategic leadership.

Potential regulatory divergence also presents possible risks for ongoing cooperation, or even for pursuing stronger links in the future. At the more general level, continued cooperation on security matters broadly is dependent upon respect for principles of democracy and the rule of law, as well as adherence to human rights laws.[81] Should the UK announce an intention to withdraw from the European Convention on Human Rights, Article 692 of the TCA permits the EU to terminate all law enforcement and judicial cooperation with the UK. To this extent, the TCA is dependent on the UK's continued participation in the European Convention,[82] and while there is nothing to suggest at this point in time that the UK will withdraw from it, the previous Conservative Government implied that it would 'consider' it in response to backbench Conservative MPs urging it in order to take actions in the context of immigration that would otherwise be in breach of Convention obligations.[83] While this is nevertheless unlikely to happen,[84] should this change, continued cooperation would not be possible. With the election of the Labour Government in July 2024, at the time of writing, there is nothing to suggest that this withdrawal from the Convention is likely to take place.

Similarly, continued cooperation and data flows are dependent on the UK's maintenance of its data protection adequacy position,[85] which is subject to regular review by the EU.[86] Europol cooperation is subject to strict requirements regarding the use of personal data,[87] and should the UK no longer found to be 'adequate' in its data protection policies, it may find that it is no longer part of the 'European privacy family'.[88] It is worth noting that the previous UK Government had expressed a desire to move away from the EU's 'overly cautious' data protection rules,[89] which could present a significant hurdle for either continued or deepening cooperation. Mazzi et al have argued that the proposed changes will have negative impacts upon data subjects' rights and harm prevention, and bring into question the regulatory and accountability dimensions of data protection law in the UK, which may in turn result in a potential loss of adequacy status.[90] It would be recommended for this reason that the UK Government think carefully about its reforms to existing data protection rules, or risk potential suspension

[80] V Mitsilegas and E Guild, 'Police and Criminal Justice Co-operation after Brexit' (2023) 30(11) *Journal of European Public Policy* 2519.

[81] TCA Art 524.

[82] Mitsilegas and Guild (n 77).

[83] J Elgot, 'Tory MPs to Push for UK Exit from European Convention on Human Rights' *The Guardian* (5 February 2023) available at www.theguardian.com/politics/2023/feb/05/tory-mps-to-push-for-uk-exit-from-european-convention-of-human-rights (last accessed 8 March 2023).

[84] Mallory, chapter 16.

[85] TCA Art 693(2).

[86] K McCullagh, 'Post-Brexit Data Protection in the UK Leaving the EU but Not EU Data Protection Law Behind' in G Gonzalez, R Van Brakel and P de Hert (eds), *Research Handbook on Privacy and Data Protection Law* (Edward Elgar, 2022) 36.

[87] TCA Arts 570–575.

[88] Mitsilegas and Guild (n 77) 16.

[89] Department for Digital, Culture, Media and Sport, 'Data: A New Direction – Government Response to Consultation' *gov.uk* (23 June 2022) available at www.gov.uk/government/consultations/data-a-new-direction/outcome/data-a-new-direction-government-response-to-consultation (last accessed 8 March 2023).

[90] F Mazzi et al, 'The UK Reform of Data Protection: Key Changes and Their Ethical, Social and Legal Implications' (2022) 30 *International Journal of Law and Information Technology* 269; see also I Lloyd, 'UK: Emerging Departures in IT-Law – Post Brexit' (2022) 23 *Computer Law Review International* 124.

of police cooperation in this area. At the time of writing, the Labour Government has proposed a Data (Use and Access) Bill,[91] which proposes modest reforms to existing data protection rules but does not relax existing controls over the use of personal data, meaning that the UK is currently unlikely to lose its adequacy status.

In terms of specific rules concerning cybercrime and cybersecurity, risks of divergence are also becoming greater. While the UK has implemented the Framework Decision on Racism and Xenophobia, as well as the Directives on attacks against information systems and child abuse online, questions arise as to whether Directive 2019/713 was incorporated into UK law. Under initial proposals for the Retained EU Law (Revocation and Reform) Bill, in clause 1, all retained EU law would have been revoked, unless a relevant national authority specifically specified retention (or assimilation, as referred to in clause 6) or implemented regulations to restate those laws before the end of 2023.[92] However, with the provisions of the Retained EU Law (Revocation and Reform) Act 2023 being significantly watered down in this respect, with *only* legislation explicitly listed in schedule 1 being revoked, cybercrime legislation was not rolled back, although areas for divergence in the future remain. As discussed briefly in section II on cybersecurity, the EU has passed the new NIS2 Directive,[93] as well as the EU Cybersecurity Act, neither of which was adopted in the UK, and both of which some commentators have suggested represent approaches that the UK may not see as being in its interests.[94] The previous UK Government has proposed an update to its existing NIS Regulations,[95] which, dependent upon their content, could also make cooperation with ENISA more difficult, should they represent a significant divergence. We are also seeing distinct divergences in the approach to the handling of illegal content in the EU and UK, with the EU's adopting a distinct 'regulated self-regulation' approach under the Digital Services Act,[96] in which service providers such as online platforms have retained existing immunity from liability provisions in exchange for judiciously moving to remove illegal content, with additional accountability and oversight mechanisms.[97] In comparison, the UK has approved the Online Safety Act,[98] which is much more prescriptive in terms of the obligations and forms of illegal content to be tackled, as well as the liabilities of both the platforms and their managers in the event that illegal content is not sufficiently handled.[99] Should the substance of criminal laws significantly diverge,

[91] Data (Use and Access) Bill, [HL] 157, 18 December 2024.

[92] Retained EU Law Bill, cl 12.

[93] Directive 2022/2555 (n 39).

[94] I Walden and JD Michels, 'Going It Alone? UK Cybersecurity Regulation Post-Brexit' (2021) 2 *International Cybersecurity Law Review* 19.

[95] HM Government, 'The NIS Regulations 2018' *gov.uk* (4 January 2023) available at www.gov.uk/government/collections/nis-directive-and-nis-regulations-2018 (last accessed 8 March 2023), which would reform the Network and Information Systems Regulations 2018 (SI 2018/506).

[96] Regulation 2022/2065 on a Single Market for Digital Services and amending Directive 2000/31/EC [2022] OJ L277/1.

[97] See, eg, B Farrand, 'The Ordoliberal Internet? Continuity and Change in the EU's Approach to the Governance of Cyberspace' (2023) 2 *European Law Open* 1; J Laux, S Wachter and B Mittelstadt, 'Taming the Few: Platform Regulation, Independent Audits, and the Risks of Capture Created by the DMA and DSA' (2021) 43 *Computer Law & Security Review* 105613; C Cauffman and C Goanta, 'A New Order: The Digital Services Act and Consumer Protection' (2011) 12 *European Journal of Risk Regulation* 758.

[98] Online Safety Act 2023.

[99] MR Leiser and E Harbinja, 'CONTENT NOT AVAILABLE: Why The United Kingdom's Proposal For A "Package of Platform Safety Measures" Will Harm Free Speech' (2020) *Technology and Regulation* 78; L Price, 'Platform Responsibility for Online Harms: Towards a Duty of Care for Online Hazards' (2021) 13 *Journal of*

as well as the processes and procedures by which liability is imposed (or not) for private sector action, this may in turn make future cooperation difficult to realise.[100]

## V. Conclusions

If there is one thing that this chapter has intended to demonstrate, it is that preventing cybercrime and ensuring cybersecurity are mutually reinforcing pillars of security more broadly, and fields of activity where cross-border cooperation, investigation and information sharing are essential. Since the late 1990s, states and the private sector have recognised cybercrime as constituting a transnational threat, in terms both of its origins and of its effects. Measures adopted by the EU have therefore focused on harmonising the substance of laws relating to cybercrime to make mutual assistance and cooperation possible, as well as providing for the establishment of agencies dedicated to effective intelligence and best-practice-led initiatives to provide for collective security. Europol's EC3 and ENISA are two examples of agencies set up to provide for this cooperation and collaboration, of which the UK has historically been both a strategic driver and operational leader.

Brexit, however, has reduced the scope of cooperation afforded through Europol and ENISA, with considerable downsides for both the EU and the UK. While the TCA provides for what cooperation is possible for a third country with EU agencies, such as through Europol Working Arrangements and continued cooperation through J-CAT, it remains to be seen how effective cooperation will be in the future. The potential for significant regulatory divergences in the fields of human rights and data protection in the UK could impact upon the consideration of the UK as subscribing to fundamental principles of democracy and the rule of law, as well as meeting the adequacy standards for the protection of data subjects. Specific initiatives launched by the UK Government could bring both into question. Furthermore, in terms of cybercrime and security substance, there is the potential for increased divergence as a result of distinct approaches to issues such as platform liability currently being adopted by the UK and EU, which could make certain forms of operational cooperation more difficult to realise. However, compared to the risk that the Law Enforcement and Judicial Cooperation chapter of the TCA could be suspended altogether as the result of regulatory drift on the part of the UK, even these questions of cybercrime substance become secondary. In order to maintain collaborative links, it is suggested that the UK should rethink regulatory reforms that take it out of the 'European privacy family', as well as taking up the opportunities to engage with ENISA, CERT-EU and the Cooperation Group on the basis of mutual interests in combating cybercrime and ensuring cybersecurity.

*Media Law* 238; A Phippen and L Street, 'Addressing Online Harms in Policy – Failing to Learn from the War on Drugs' (2023) 34 *Entertainment Law Review* 36.

[100] For more on this divergence, see B Farrand, 'How do we see online harms? The impact of conceptual divides on regulatory divergence between the Online Safety Act and Digital Services Act' (2024) *Journal of Media Law* 1.

# PART V

# Conclusion

# 24

# Understanding the Impact of Brexit on Police and Judicial Cooperation: Can Operational Deficits be Addressed in the Future?

GEMMA DAVIES AND HELENA CARRAPICO

## I. Introduction

The risks to the public had the United Kingdom (UK) left the European Union (EU) without any 'deal', causing all police and judicial cooperation to come to an immediate halt at midnight on 31 December 2020, would have been catastrophic.[1] The signing of the Trade and Cooperation Agreement (TCA)[2] only weeks before the end of the transition period meant that Part Three prevented the worst of the 'cliff-edge' consequences.[3] Early academic writings demonstrate that Part Three of the TCA has provided a good level of continuity in cooperation between the UK and EU.[4] As analysed by different authors in this edited volume, the UK and EU continue to exchange criminal records, DNA, and fingerprint and air passenger data using almost identical rules and processes.[5] The comprehensive provisions on

[1] House of Lords, *Brexit: future UK-EU security and police cooperation.* European Union Committee (7th Report of Session 2016–17, HL 77).

[2] Trade and Cooperation Agreement between the European Union and the European Atomic Energy Community, of the one part, and the United Kingdom of Great Britain and Northern Ireland, of the other part [2021] OJ L149/10.

[3] House of Lords, *Beyond Brexit: policing, law enforcement and security.* European Union Committee (25th Report of Session 2019–21, HL 250).

[4] W Schomburg and A.Oehmichen, 'Brexit: First observations on the EU–UK Trade and Cooperation Agreement in criminal law' (2021) 12(2) *New Journal of European Criminal Law* 193.

[5] P Arnell et al, 'Police cooperation and exchange of information under the EU–UK Trade and Cooperation Agreement' (2021) 21(2) *New Journal of European Criminal Law* 265; C Van de Heyning, 'Data protection and passenger name record in judicial criminal matters under the EU–UK Trade and Cooperation Agreement' (2021) 12(2) *New Journal of European Criminal Law* 257.

surrender/extradition have ensured that the process remained very familiar to those used to working with the European Arrest Warrant (EAW) and required very little amendment to domestic legislation.[6] Importantly, continued cooperation with Europol and Eurojust means that for most practitioners, their work has carried on seamlessly.[7] Whilst a generous transition period was needed for the UK to transform its technical capabilities to conform with new rules in relation to exchange of information, almost all aspects of the TCA are now fully operational and working as envisaged by the drafters.[8]

Throughout this edited volume, the authors' research has demonstrated that whilst the drafting of Part Three can be partly categorised as a political success story, the success of its implementation owes much to the dedication of practitioners working in the field. Numerous chapters repeatedly revealed the exceptional efforts made by practitioners and criminal justice organisations to ensure that strong working relationships continued.[9] Overwhelmingly, the focus has been on continuing to work together to 'get the job done'.[10] Trust between practitioners, notwithstanding the fraught political relationship, has astoundingly remained high.[11] This volume, however, also highlighted that, despite the apparent success of the TCA and its implementation, cooperation between the UK and the EU has undergone a 'downgrade' since Brexit. Section II of this chapter explores the nature and extent of this 'downgrade'. We map the key operational deficits and their impact. Brexit has led, at its worst, to impunity for serious crime. We demonstrate why evidencing the risks subsequently created for the public is challenging. The impact of Brexit in this area is often hidden and 'unknowable'. This does not mean that the impact is not real and that operational deficits should not be addressed wherever possible.

Understanding the impact of Part Three of the TCA is vital to addressing operational deficits. The TCA is due to be reviewed in 2026, and in section III of this chapter we set out what we believe the priorities should be for the future enhancement of the relationship between the UK and the EU. Section IV acknowledges the legal and political limitations surrounding the 2026 review. Overall, we hope that this edited volume has pointed at the need for a comprehensive and ambitious review to ameliorate current risks to public safety; a timid approach would be a missed opportunity to understand and address the operational deficits caused by Brexit.

[6] E Grange, B Keith and S Kerridge, 'Extradition under the EU-UK Trade and Cooperation Agreement' (2021) 12(2) *New Journal of European Criminal Law* 213.

[7] R Niblock, 'Cooperation with EU agencies and bodies under the EU–UK Trade and Cooperation Agreement: Eurojust, OLAF and the EPPO' (2021) 12(2) *New Journal of European Criminal Law* 277; see also G Davies and H Farrand Carrapico, *UK–EU Law Enforcement and Judicial Cooperation in Criminal Matters in Part Three of the Trade and Cooperation Agreement: The Impact on Scotland*, Scottish Parliament Policy Paper (2024).

[8] See minutes of the meetings of the Specialised Committee on Law Enforcement and Judicial Cooperation available at www.gov.uk/government/publications/specialised-committee-on-law-enforcement-and-criminal-justice-minutes (last accessed 9 October 2024).

[9] Davies and Farrand Carrapico (n 6).

[10] ibid.

[11] Marks, ch 5.

# II. Summary – TCA Implementation Challenges in Police and Judicial Cooperation

## A. Information Sharing

Title II of Part Three of the TCA provides for the automated exchange of DNA and fingerprint and vehicle registration data, and the provisions closely replicate the Prüm rules.[12] After a successful evaluation, the EU confirmed the UK was complying with most of the relevant TCA provisions.[13] However, the UK has so far indicated that it is not ready to be evaluated regarding the exchange of vehicle registration data.[14] This is not a Brexit loss, as the UK has never completed its technical preparations to build the vehicle registration data component of the Prüm system. Nevertheless, access to this part of Prüm can help police pursue foreign-registered vehicles of interest to law enforcement.[15] There was a 24.9 per cent increase in the number of vehicles stolen across England and Wales in 2022.[16] The UK National Vehicle Crime Intelligence Service, which manages three UK ports, identified £2.96 million worth of stolen vehicles in only the first nine months of 2021, destined primarily for Cyprus or Africa. This was a 112 per cent increase in comparison with the previous year.[17] The UK should develop its technical capabilities so that it can be evaluated and begin to share vehicle registration data with EU Member States, as already provided for in the TCA, as soon as possible.

Access to passenger name records (PNRs) for air travel departing from the EU is also importantly provided for in Title III of Part Three of the TCA, with rules that largely reflect the EU PNR Directive, although without the same oversight mechanisms.[18] However, there is one significant caveat. There is a new proviso that the UK must now delete PNR data of passengers after they depart the UK, unless objective evidence can be provided that certain passengers present a risk in terms of fighting terrorism and serious crime.[19] The deleting of data is an operational disadvantage and makes it more difficult

[12] Van de Heyning (n 4).

[13] This has been determined by the EU in a unilateral declaration set out in the Annex to Council Implementing Decision 2022/1014 [2022] OJ L170/68.

[14] Home Office, Second meeting minutes: Specialised Committee on Law Enforcement and Judicial Cooperation, 13 October 2022 available at www.gov.uk/government/publications/specialised-committee-on-law-enforcement-and-criminal-justice-minutes/second-meeting-agenda-specialised-committee-on-law-enforcement-and-judicial-cooperation-13-october-2022 (last accessed 11 October 2024).

[15] Home Office, *Prum Business and Implementation Case* (Cm 9149, 2015) 60.

[16] Office of National Statistics, *Crime in England and Wales: Appendix tables* (2024) available at www.ons.gov.uk/peoplepopulationandcommunity/crimeandjustice/datasets/crimeinenglandandwalesappendixtables (last accessed 11 October 2024).

[17] Direct Line Group, 'Cyprus, DR Congo and Ghana top destinations for stolen cars out of UK ports' (19 November 2021) available at www.directlinegroup.co.uk/en/news/brand-news/2021/cyprus--dr-congo-and-ghana-top-destinations-for-stolen-cars-out-.html#:~:text=In%20the%20first%20nine%20months%20of%202021%2C%20%C2%A32.96,on%20the%20value%20stolen%20in%202020%20%28%C2%A31.39%20million%29 (last accessed 11 October 2024).

[18] Fahey, ch 7. Directive (EU) 2016/681 of the European Parliament and of the Council of 27 April 2016 on the use of passenger name record (PNR) data for the prevention, detection, investigation and prosecution of terrorist offences and serious crime [2016] OJ L119/132.

[19] E Fahey et al, 'The novelty of EU Passenger Name Records (PNR) in EU Trade Agreements: On shifting uses of data governance in light of the EU–UK Trade and Cooperation Agreement PNR provisions' (2023) 8(1) *European Papers* 273.

to cross-check the names of persons of interest and their associates against historical flight data.

The National Police Chiefs' Council (NPCC) set out clearly the operational importance of access to the Second-Generation Schengen Information System (SIS II) in evidence to the House of Lords European Union Committee at an early stage of the Brexit negotiations:

> It provides the ability to understand whether somebody is wanted in another country, whether they are missing, whether the vehicle they are driving is stolen and so on. It is critical in allowing officers on the street to make decisions (for instance in relation to custody) to safeguard the welfare of people across the country.[20]

Despite its importance, the UK lost access to SIS II. Around 40,000 alerts on dangerous criminals and wanted suspects had to be deleted at the end of December 2020. Similarly, 5.7 million alerts originating from the UK were deleted at the end of 2021.[21] Early in the Brexit negotiations, law enforcement agencies accepted that they needed to mitigate against the loss of access to SIS II. The Interpol database I-24/7 was the only viable alternative system for circulating international alerts. There have been several problems with relying on I-24/7. First, it is not integrated into the police national computer (PNC). This means that, unlike with SIS II, there is no seamless integration. Both systems cannot be checked simultaneously. Similarly, alerts cannot automatically be circulated without separately putting them into both systems. This requires 'double keying' of information. Finally, there was, initially, a lack of I-24/7 licences and limited knowledge of the system.[22] To prepare for the impact of losing SIS II, the NPCC established the International Crime Cooperation Centre (ICCC), which was funded by the Home Office, to support and advise UK officers to make better use of the available international instruments. An extra 6,000 I-24/7 licences were also purchased. The ICCC's network of regional Single Point of Contacts (SPOCs) worked with forces across the UK to increase training on the use of international tools, including I-24/7, and provided 24-hour support. Force control rooms and custody staff were also trained to conduct I-24/7 checks.[23] Since Brexit, alerts and circulations generated in the UK are now created on the PNC. A secondary form is then completed and sent to the National Crime Agency's (NCA's) UK International Crime Bureau, where it is subsequently uploaded to the I-24/7 system. In 2021, this process was partly automated, using smart forms to limit the issue of double keying. Processes have improved since December 2020, and the time delay between receiving information and ensuring it is available on the PNC is now down to hours.[24] Overall, the UK's attempts to mitigate the loss of SIS II may be categorised as successful. However, the systems for sharing alerts are still not automatic and simultaneous, as was the case before the UK left the EU.

The successful use of I-24/7 requires reciprocity from EU partners. The UK is dependent on the creation of alerts and circulations on both SIS II and I-24/7 by law

[20] House of Lords (n 1) 90.
[21] Vavoula, ch 8.
[22] Pearson, ch 6.
[23] Thomson, ch 11.
[24] House of Lords (n 2) 25.

enforcement in EU countries. The UK has spent time persuading EU agencies to 'double key'.[25] Many states have responded well, but others less so. If a state is not consistently engaging in double keying, the operational consequence is that a criminal wanted throughout the EU on an EAW could travel to the UK undetected, if this information has not been dually circulated on I-24/7 as a red (wanted) notice. The degree of operational blindness that has resulted is unknown, as it is difficult to ascertain whether the UK has missed vital information to which it would have had access pre-Brexit.[26] The number of red notices coming through Interpol is said to be about 90 per cent of the number that were previously received through SIS II, and so it is hoped that the UK has been successful in persuading most EU Member States to use Interpol.[27] It is nevertheless very challenging to demonstrate the impact of a negative.

To resolve the problem of double keying permanently, the UK has been developing the International Law Enforcement Alert Platform (I-LEAP). Once in operation, this will provide a single platform – accessible via handheld devices – for UK law enforcement to access both the PNC and Interpol data. Phase one allows direct and real-time connection to Interpol data, which includes facial images on subjects of interest associated with Interpol notices and diffusions.[28] Successful roll outs are already underway. In phase two, the hope is to provide access to international partners, which will allow real-time sharing of alerts in the same way as SIS II does, but this technology is still in the early stage of development.[29]

## B. Cooperation with EU Agencies

Although the UK used to take part in the activities of multiple EU agencies working in the broad field of police and judicial cooperation (such as the European Union Drugs Agency and the EUIPO),[30] the TCA maintained access only to Europol and Eurojust.[31] Whilst the TCA provided for continued cooperation with both these agencies, there has been a degree of adaptation on the UK side to working on the sidelines of these institutions. In particular, the UK no longer sits on their management committees and has lost strategic influence.[32] In the case of Europol, UK officers cannot be employed in Europol's Operational and Analysis Centre, which may lead to a loss of expertise in the long term for both the UK and the EU.[33] The UK has also lost partial access to

[25] ibid 5.

[26] Pearson, ch 6.

[27] Vavoula, ch 8.

[28] Home Office, 'International Law Enforcement Alerts Platform Programme accounting officer assessment' (24 February 2023) available at www.gov.uk/government/publications/home-office-major-programmes-accounting-officer-assessments/international-law-enforcement-alerts-platform-i-leap-programme (last accessed 11 October 2024).

[29] C McGinn, 'Crime: Cross Border Cooperation. Question for Home Office' (15 October 2021) available at https://questions-statements.parliament.uk/written-questions/detail/2021-10-15/57131 (last accessed 09 October 2024).

[30] See Farrand, ch 23.

[31] The UK and Frontex also signed a Working Arrangement establishing operational cooperation in February 2024, which is contributing to the fight against smuggling of migrants.

[32] See Constantino and Cotroneo, ch 10.

[33] Davies and Farrand Carrapico (n 6).

intelligence information available to only EU Member States via the secure messaging service SIENA.[34] The UK can no longer initiate or lead a Joint Investigation Team (JIT).[35] Overall, officers have reported that police cooperation continues to take place at a similar level as pre-Brexit, but that this cooperation is now more resource-intensive given the necessary investment in bilateral relations. Regarding Eurojust, the UK is represented by a Liaison Prosecutor, supported by a team of up to five assistants. Participation in Eurojust operational meetings depends on the approval of the national members involved, which has not posed any major challenges for the UK to date. Although statistics show a slight decrease in UK activity within Eurojust, this reduction has been minimal, and the 2020 and 2021 figures were likely impacted by the pandemic.[36] In fact, the latest annual report shows an upwards trend in the number of coordination meetings initiated by the UK. Whilst overall cooperation with Europol and Eurojust has continued seamlessly for most practitioners, the long-term impact of loss of strategic influence, loss of expertise and loss of training opportunities may develop over time.

## C. Mutual Legal Assistance

The UK no longer participates in the European Investigation Order. Police and judicial authorities must obtain assistance through a Council of Europe 1959 Convention with some supplementation.[37] There is evidence that falling back on an outdated mutual legal assistance mechanism has made obtaining evidence more difficult post-Brexit, although further research is needed. Second, the domestic legislation of some EU Member States has created barriers to obtaining police-to-police cooperation, despite the signing of the TCA.[38] Sharing information with the UK may now require the approval of a prosecutor in the requested state, which means exchanges are now slower and the likelihood of refusal is increased. It also means that investigations are more time- and resource-intensive for the police.[39] The UK is attempting to mitigate this impact through bilateral negotiations with individual EU Member States.[40] The UK has signed over 20 bilateral declarations with EU Member States since 2021, which make reference to enhancing police and judicial cooperation.[41] For example, the UK is currently negotiating a law enforcement cooperation agreement with Belgium, which aims to improve cross-border

[34] Arnell et al (n 4).

[35] Davies and Farrand Carrapico (n 6).

[36] See Wade, ch 12.

[37] A Oehmichen and B Keith, 'Mutual legal assistance under the EU–UK Trade and Cooperation Agreement' (2021) 12(2) *New Journal of European Criminal Law* 222; European Convention on Mutual Assistance in Criminal Matters 1959, ETS 030.

[38] Davies and Farrand Carrapico (n 6).

[39] ibid.

[40] N Newson, *The future UK-EU relationship: Report by the House of Lords European Affairs Committee*, House of Lords Library (8 September 2023) available at https://lordslibrary.parliament.uk/the-future-uk-eu-relationship-report-by-the-house-of-lords-european-affairs-committee/ (last accessed 11 October 2024).

[41] S Wolff, H Carrapico and A Piquet, 'Out of Sight, Out of Mind? How UK bilateralism with European capitals in times of politicisation enables Europeanisation to continue' *JCMS* (29 September 2024), doi.org/10.1111/jcms.13690.

surveillance, data collection and sharing, and to encourage UK and Belgian teams to tackle serious and organised crime jointly.[42]

## D. Extradition

The UK can no longer extradite nationals from ten EU Member States and has limited ability to do so regarding three further states.[43] This has led to impunity for serious offences.[44] Dual criminality must be demonstrated in every surrender case, and some states have reintroduced a political offence exception.[45] After Brexit, there has been an increase in appeals caused by legal uncertainty and an increase in requests for assurances.[46] The Court of Justice of the European Union (CJEU) has made it clear that the UK no longer benefits from mutual trust.[47]

The Covid-19 pandemic significantly impacted extradition and has made it difficult to draw conclusions from comparison of data from before and after Brexit. There is no central record of the number of people the UK has been unable to obtain through surrender because of leaving the EAW.[48] When the UK is unable to request surrender for a known offender, or surrender is refused, prosecutors may request a formal transfer of proceedings.[49] The TCA provides that states in these circumstances are obliged to consider a domestic prosecution. There are no formal rules that govern transfer of proceedings in the TCA. In practice, transferring prosecutions has proved very difficult, and the authors of this volume are aware of no successful transfer of proceedings to date.[50] There is also no mechanism in the TCA to replicate the suite of Framework Decisions that facilitated transfer of custodial sentence, pre-trial bail or probation supervision between EU Member States.[51] Some Member States will surrender to the UK only temporarily and require nationals to be returned to serve their sentence. Without any rules governing the operation of temporary transfer, this process has been complex and time-consuming.

One of the most significant operational deficits caused by Brexit is the loss of the ability to circulate arrest warrants through SIS II. An EU Member State must now circulate an EAW through SIS II and, in addition, create a separate arrest warrant under the TCA (TCAAW), which it then circulates through Interpol's I-24/7 database. If an

[42] Home Office, 'Home Secretary meeting with Belgium Interior Minister' (23 March 2022) available at www.gov.uk/government/news/home-secretary-meeting-with-belgium-interior-minister (last accessed 11 October 2024).

[43] Home Office, 'Law enforcement and judicial cooperation notifications made under the UK-EU Trade and Cooperation Agreement' (18 March 2022) available at www.gov.uk/government/publications/law-enforcement-and-judicial-cooperation-notifications-made-under-the-uk-eu-trade-and-cooperation-agreement (last accessed 11 October 2024).

[44] Davies and Farrand Carrapico (n 6).

[45] See Arnell, ch 13.

[46] See Ryan, ch 14.

[47] Case C-202/24 *Alchaster*, ECLI:EU:C:2024:649.

[48] Davies and Farrand Carrapico (n 6).

[49] B de Jonge, 'Transfer of criminal proceedings: from stumbling block to cornerstone of cooperation in criminal matters in the EU' (2020) 21 *ERA Forum* 449.

[50] Davies and Farrand Carrapico (n 6).

[51] See Wilson, ch 15.

EU Member State is not uploading wanted notices to I-24/7, as well as to SIS II, then the operational consequence is that a criminal wanted throughout the EU on an EAW could travel to the UK undetected. Furthermore, TCAAWs are certified by courts in EU Member States only if there is a clear connection to the UK. This is not as effective as circulation through SIS II and decreases the likelihood of detection and prosecution of fugitives.[52] Demonstrating the significance of the impact is, however, difficult. Surrender figures are not yet a reliable mechanism for comparing post- and pre-Brexit surrender rates. If there are examples of dangerous individuals who would have been arrested on an EAW but have not been picked up under a TACAW, this is not in the public domain. Nevertheless, front-line officers have reported that the loss of the ability to circulate speculative warrants, as was possible with the EAW, has had a real impact on the number of people who have been identified and prosecuted.[53]

## III. Enhancing Cooperation between the UK and the EU in the Future

The TCA captures essential elements of police and judicial cooperation and instruments as they existed in December 2020. It is, therefore, not a living document but rather a snapshot in time. As technology develops and new crime threats emerge, both the UK and the EU will continue to develop new tools and update existing ones. Neither side will benefit from any new developments in EU and UK criminal law, and their cooperation capabilities could quickly become left behind. Even the tools available under the TCA may become obsolete, as EU Regulations and Directives are amended or become redundant, and the UK may paradoxically find itself in a position of having to align with EU law that it had no say in developing.[54] The UK will not benefit from any future developments within the EU without further amendment to the TCA. The UK Government should seek further development of the governance structures of the TCA to ensure greater transparency and accountability, as well as introducing political mechanisms that will enable the TCA to evolve in parallel with UK and EU domestic changes to police and judicial cooperation instruments over time.[55] This would need to be accomplished in a way that avoids extracting parts of EU criminal law from the EU's institutional framework.[56]

### A. Information Sharing

Even as the TCA was being negotiated, new developments were already occurring. In 2019, the EU signed an agreement to create a new database containing the past

[52] Pearson, ch 6.

[53] M Shellaker, S Tong and P Swallow, 'UK–EU law enforcement cooperation post Brexit: A UK law enforcement practitioner perspective' (2024) 24(4) *Criminology & Criminal Justice* 841.

[54] V Mitsilegas, 'European criminal law without the United Kingdom? The triple paradox of Brexit' (2017) 8(4) *New Journal of European Criminal Law* 437.

[55] Davies and Farrand Carrapico (n 6).

[56] A Wyembergh, 'Consequences of Brexit for European Union criminal law' (2017) 8(3) *New Journal of European Criminal Law* 284.

convictions of third-country nationals, called ECRIS-TCN. Once operational, the database will enable EU law enforcement, prosecutors and judges to find information on previous convictions of non-EU nationals.[57] The UK opted in to this measure whilst in the EU but exited before its implementation. The TCA, however, does not provide for access to ECRIS-TCN, as it is a centralised (rather than decentralised) database. The UK will be able to access such information only by making bilateral requests to Member States for data about third-country nationals. Making individual requests is resource-intensive and liable to result in blind spots. Access to ECRIS-TCN would be a significant operational benefit to the UK, and the UK should seek to negotiate access to the system so that UK law enforcement may have a complete picture of the criminal record of any third-country national who has spent time in the EU before entering the UK.[58]

The EU is also working towards a programme of interoperability of its large-scale IT systems.[59] The EU plans to make currently decentralised systems centralised and interoperable.[60] This process has already started for Prüm, which will connect to the centralised information systems. This will make the overall system more powerful and efficient, allowing authorities to consult multiple databases with ease. As Prüm II expands the categories of data exchange, it will be possible to share facial images, drivers' licences and police records, which would create the most extensive biometric surveillance infrastructure in the world. The proposals were agreed in March 2024 with the aim of promoting security, but the provisions have been criticised as creating serious risks for citizens' fundamental rights.[61] The proposed Regulation also provides for the creation of a new architecture that allows for easier and faster exchange of data between Member States. Centralisation is also planned for other databases, such as PNR. If Prüm and PNR become centralised, amendments to the TCA may be required for the UK to continue to have access to fingerprints, DNA and air passenger data.[62] The TCA foresees this and refers to future amendment. If Prüm is substantially amended, or 'is in the process of being amended substantially', the EU may notify the UK that it wishes to agree a formal amendment through the Specialised Committee for Law Enforcement and Judicial Cooperation. This notification will trigger a nine-month period of consultation, extendable for a further nine months, which could lead to suspension of cooperation if no agreement is reached.[63] Access to DNA, fingerprints and PNRs is a vital resource for the UK, and it is important that discussions take place as early as possible. Discussions internal to the UK are also important, as biometrics is a devolved matter in Scotland, and a joint UK position would need to be agreed before negotiations with the EU commence.[64]

[57] N Vavoula, *Immigration and Privacy in the Law of the European Union: The Case of Information Systems* (Brill, 2022).

[58] Davies and Farrand Carrapico (n 6).

[59] See Vavoula, ch 8.

[60] Vavoula (n 56).

[61] R Cavalli, 'Prüm II and the EPRIS Index in Europe: An Attempt to Balance People's Security and Privacy?' (2024) 14(7) *Computer Science and Information Technology* 57.

[62] Home Office, 'Explanatory Memorandum on European Union Legislation' (PE-CONS 75/23, 20 March 2024) available at https://assets.publishing.service.gov.uk/media/65faffda9316f5001164c415/2024-03-20_Prum_II_EM.pdf (last accessed 10 October 2024).

[63] See Vavoula, ch 8.

[64] Davies and Farrand Carrapico (n 6).

The EU is also planning to further develop SIS II, the largest data infrastructure supporting police cooperation and border controls in the EU.[65] Soon additional biometric data, including photographs, fingerprints, palm prints and DNA, will be available to police in EU Member States. This expansion will assist in the circulation of preventative alerts aimed at protecting vulnerable persons and disrupting terrorist activity,[66] from which the UK will not benefit. It is unlikely the UK will have access to SIS II in the near future, given the EU's position that access to this system must be reserved for EU Member States only.[67] However, one of the biggest impacts from the loss of SIS II is the inability to circulate arrest warrants to all EU Member States.[68] There is no legal reason why Europol could not upload TACAWs to SIS II on behalf of the UK. This would mean that, if there was a risk that a wanted person had left the UK, a warrant could be issued to all EU Member States immediately. This proposal would mitigate the risk that law enforcement in EU Member States might not have equivalent access to Interpol's I-24/7 as they do to SIS II.[69] This is in keeping with the Political Declaration, which stated that

> [t]he Parties should consider further arrangements appropriate to the United Kingdom's future status for data exchange, such as exchange of information on wanted or missing persons and objects … with the view to delivering capabilities that, in so far as is technically and legally possible, and considered necessary and in both Parties' interests, approximate those enabled by relevant Union Mechanisms.[70]

Another way of remedying the loss of capability created by the UK's leaving SIS II would be for the EU to agree to connecting Member States to the I-LEAP platform.[71] This could be a longer-term, stable solution to the problem. The Commission proposal in 2022 of a Regulation on a framework for reciprocal access to security-related information for front-line officers between the EU and third countries offers a legally stable way forward for the UK as a third country.[72]

[65] For criticism of SIS II, see R Bellanova and G Glouftsios, 'Controlling the Schengen Information System (SIS II): The Infrastructural Politics of Fragility and Maintenance' (2022) 27(1) *Geopolitics* 160.

[66] N Vavoula, 'Interoperability of EU information systems: The deathblow to the rights to privacy and personal data protection of third-country nationals?' (2020) 26(1) *European Public Law* 131.

[67] '[The European Parliament] stresses that the UK cannot have direct access to EU information systems data or participate in the management structures of the EU agencies in the area of Freedom, Security and Justice, while any sharing of information including personal data with the UK should be subject to strict safeguards, audit and oversight conditions, including an equivalent level of protection of personal data to that provided by EU law …', quoted in Shkurta Januzi, 'EU Parliament: UK Won't Have Access to Schengen Information System as of 2021' *Schengen News* (14 February 2020) available at https://schengen.news/eu-parliament-uk-wont-have-access-to-schengen-information-system-as-of-2021/ (last accessed 10 October 2024).

[68] Pearson, ch 6.

[69] Davies and Farrand Carrapico (n 6).

[70] European Commission, Political declaration setting out the framework for the future relationship between the European Union and the United Kingdom, 2019/C 384/ I/02, para 85.

[71] Home Office, *International Law Enforcement Alerts Platform (I-LEAP) Programme accounting officer assessment* (9 October 2024) available at www.gov.uk/government/publications/home-office-major-programmes-accounting-officer-assessments/international-law-enforcement-alerts-platform-i-leap-programme (last accessed 11 October 2024).

[72] European Commission, Commission proposal for a Regulation on a framework for reciprocal access to security-related information for front-line officers between the EU and key third countries to counter shared security threats, available at https://ec.europa.eu/info/law/better-regulation/have-your-say/initiatives/13243-Security-related-information-sharing-%E2%88%92-reciprocal-access-for-frontline-officers-in-the-EU-and-key-partner-countries_en (last accessed 5 November 2024).

## B. Mutual Legal Assistance

Further research is needed to understand the impact of the loss of the European Investigation Order on evidence and information exchange between the UK and all 27 EU Member States. There are reports that evidence exchange is taking longer and police-to-police exchange of information faces greater legal barriers in some cases.[73] As mentioned in section II.C, the UK and the EU are now operating under the provisions of the European Convention on Mutual Assistance in Criminal Matters, which was ratified in 1959, with limited supplementation. This treaty has long been recognised as being slow and out-of-date.[74]

The problems that law enforcement agencies have faced accessing electronic evidence (e-evidence) stored in a foreign jurisdiction are well documented.[75] The EU and the Council of Europe have developed legal instruments designed to simplify access to e-evidence and, in some instances, grant law enforcement the authority to directly request information from Internet service providers in other countries, bypassing the formal mutual legal assistance process. There are two pieces of recent EU legislation that provide for this direct law enforcement–service provider access to e-evidence between EU countries.[76] These provisions are referred to as the e-evidence package.[77] Although the UK opted in to the EU's e-evidence package before Brexit, this set of instruments is not provided for in the TCA. The UK should seek to negotiate an agreement on access to e-evidence now that the EU has finalised its own internal rules.[78] The EU has already opened negotiations with the United States, which should pave the way for UK–EU cooperation in this area.[79] This is particularly important, as the Council of Europe measure – the Second Protocol to the Budapest Convention – has significant limitations in its efficacy and reach.[80]

## C. Cooperation with Europol

Whilst it was inevitable that the UK's participation in Europol, as a third country, would be more limited than it was as a Member State, overall, cooperation with Europol is

[73] Davies and Farrand Carrapico (n 6).

[74] P Swire, JD Hemmings and S Vergnolle, 'A Mutual Legal Assistance Case Study: The United States and France' (2017) 34 *Wisconsin International Law Journal* 323.

[75] MA Biasiotti et al (eds), *Handling and Exchanging Electronic Evidence Across Europe* (Springer, 2018).

[76] S Tosza, 'All evidence is equal, but electronic evidence is more equal than any other: The relationship between the European Investigation Order and the European Production Order' (2020) 11(2) *New Journal of European Criminal Law* 161.

[77] S Tosza 'The E-Evidence Package is Adopted: End of a Saga or Beginning of a New One?' (2023) 9(2) *European Data Protection Law Review* 163.

[78] G Davies, 'Police Access to Electronic Evidence Stored Overseas: Cooperation between the EU and UK post Brexit' in L Heffernan (ed), *Criminal law and Justice in the European Union* (Clarus, 2022) 121.

[79] European Commission, 'EU-US announcement on the resumption of negotiations on an EU-U.S. agreement to facilitate access to electronic evidence in criminal investigations' (2 March 2023) available at https://commission.europa.eu/news/eu-us-announcement-resumption-negotiations-eu-us-agreement-facilitate-access-electronic-evidence-2023-03-02_en (last accessed 14 October 2024).

[80] Second Additional Protocol to the Convention on Cybercrime on enhanced co-operation and disclosure of electronic evidence (CETS No 224).

reported to be very good.[81] Practitioners are, however, concerned about the impact of the inability of UK police officers to be employed within the Operational and Analysis Centre, and the lack of access to Europol training and funding.[82] This negative impact is felt by both the UK and the EU, as both will feel the effect over time of the loss of expertise. Officers in the UK also report that the inability to initiate and lead JITs can cause delay and complexity. Concern has further been expressed about the UK's reduced capacity to shape the direction of Europol, having been instrumental in its development over the years. These are all issues that could be considered as the UK and the EU continue to work towards operational cooperation between the NCA and Europol.[83]

## D. Extradition

Due to the TCA's introduction of the nationality bar and the loss of mutual recognition, there has been an increase in the number of individuals who are wanted in the UK, sometimes for serious offences, but who cannot be surrendered/extradited from the EU Member State in which they reside.[84] As already mentioned, there is no formal agreement or set of rules governing the transfer of criminal proceedings and, to date, prosecutors have found this process challenging, with no case having yet been successfully transferred. The Commission has promised to 'continue working on a common legal framework for the efficient transfer of criminal proceedings between Member States, to step up the fight against cross-border crime'.[85] The UK and the EU should build on the EU's internal rules on transfer of proceedings once agreed, and seek to negotiate a multilateral agreement on the transfer of criminal proceedings when extradition/surrender is not possible or refused.[86] The EU has recognised that such rules could 'make it possible to avoid impunity for the accused person'.[87] Such impunity is currently occurring when extradition to the UK from an EU Member State is not possible on the ground of nationality, and therefore, *a fortiori*, an agreement between the UK and EU is needed.

Furthermore, the UK has yet to notify the Specialised Committee on Law Enforcement and Judicial Cooperation that, on the basis of reciprocity, the condition of dual criminality will not be applied to the offences listed in Article 599(5) of the TCA. Twelve EU countries have made such a notification, but to be effective this requires the

[81] Shellaker, Tong and Swallow (n 50).

[82] Davies and Farrand Carrapico (n 6).

[83] Europol, 'Conditional applicable to the cooperation with the UK since 1 January 2021', Press Release (29 April 2021) available at www.europol.europa.eu/media-press/newsroom/news/conditions-applicable-to-cooperation-uk-1-january-2021#:~:text=The%20EU-UK%20Trade%20and%20Partnership%20Agreement%20includes%20provisions,state%20already%20at%20the%20start%20of%20this%20year (last accessed 11 October 2024).

[84] P Arnell and G Davies, 'The new UK–EU extradition arrangements' (2021) 6 *Scots Law Times* 21.

[85] European Commission, 'Communication from the Commission to the European Parliament, The Council, The European Economic and Social Committee and the Committee of the Regions' COM (2021) 645 final, para 2.6.

[86] European Commission, 'Proposal for a Regulation on transfer of proceedings in criminal matters'COM(2023) 185 final.

[87] ibid.

reciprocity of the UK.[88] The effect of the UK's decision is that dual criminality must be established in all cases with all EU Member States.[89] The impact of this decision needs to be understood and revisited, as stakeholders have revealed that it is causing unnecessary complexity and delay during extradition hearings.[90]

Finally, the TCA does not include provisions replacing the suite of Framework Decisions that facilitated the transfer of custodial sentences, pre-trial bail or probation supervision between Member States.[91] Although the reasons for this exclusion remain unclear,[92] the UK should seek to include the transfer of custodial sentences, pre-trial bail or probation supervision in future TCA reviews or, alternatively, negotiate bilateral agreements directly with Member States. Such agreements would assist in the rehabilitation of foreign offenders and would facilitate smoother temporary transfers of prisoners for the purposes of trial.[93]

## IV. Review of the TCA in 2026 – What is Achievable?

The TCA foresees the possibility of a review every five years, with the first being scheduled for 2026, under Article 776. In addition, Part Three of the TCA contains its own review clause (Article 691), allowing for an earlier review of the Law Enforcement and Judicial Cooperation provisions, if both parties agree. The 2026 review is expected to be conducted by the Partnership Council or the Specialised Committees under it – specifically, the Law Enforcement and Judicial Cooperation Specialised Committee. Expected topics for the 2026 review include the operation of provisions regarding PNRs and the retention of notifications concerning surrender and extradition, as the current UK and EU Member States' notifications are set to expire in 2026. Although there was some initial uncertainty regarding the exact scope of the upcoming review, the European Commission has clarified that it will not entail a complete revision of the TCA's legal text. Instead, the focus will be on the practical implementation, interpretation and development of the provisions already contained in the Agreement. It also indicated that there is currently a lack of appetite to open TCA renegotiations, which it associated with current political priorities relating to the war in Ukraine and the conflict in the Middle East, as well as internal concerns over immigration and the rise of the far right.

The UK–EU relationship is neverthelesss evolving within a rapidly changing political landscape. The period following the 2016 Brexit Referendum was characterised

[88] Home Office, 'Law enforcement and judicial cooperation notifications made under the UK–EU Trade and Cooperation Agreement' (18 March 2022) available at www.gov.uk/government/publications/law-enforcement-and-judicial-cooperation-notifications-made-under-the-uk-eu-trade-and-cooperation-agreement (last accessed 14 October 2024).

[89] Grange, Keith and Kerridge (n 5).

[90] Davies and Farrand Carrapico (n 6).

[91] Wilson, ch 15.

[92] T Wilson, 'Prisoner Transfer within the Irish-UK Common Travel Area (CTA) after Brexit: human rights between politics and penal reform' (2021) 5(2) *The Journal of Criminal Law* 121.

[93] G Oancea and TED Ene, 'Transfer for rehabilitation?' in JA Branariz et al (eds), *Forced Mobility of EU Citizens: Transnational Criminal Justice Instruments and the Management of 'Unwanted' EU Nationals* (Routledge, 2024) 19.

by significant tensions in the relationship, which were particularly exacerbated by the negotiations of the Withdrawal Agreement and of the TCA. The discussion on the part of the UK Government regarding a possible departure from the European Convention on Human Rights, along with the proposals to replace the UK Human Rights Act 1998 with a Bill of Rights, and the Data Protection Act 2018 with the Data Protection and Digital Information Bill, further exacerbated these tensions. Under the Government led by Rishi Sunak, the relationship entered a more positive phase, marked by increased dialogue and a greater openness to closer cooperation. The former Prime Minister played an important role in de-escalating tensions by addressing post-Brexit issues through the signing of the Windsor Framework, a Memorandum of Understanding on financial services cooperation, and the UK's re-entry into the Horizon and Copernicus research programs.

Building on these initiatives, the current UK Government has committed to strengthening ties with the EU, as highlighted during the Labour Party's election campaign. While carefully navigating red lines related to the single market, customs union and free movement, the UK Government is actively pursuing negotiations to reduce trade barriers (sanitary and phytosanitary issues), secure mutual recognition of professional qualifications, expand touring opportunities for musicians, and establish a security and defence pact.[94] Despite its assertions that current political priorities lie elsewhere, the EU appears fairly open to advancing discussions in various areas. However, the EU remains particularly cautious to avoid a Swiss-style relationship, where the UK might selectively engage in cooperation while disregarding broader commitments.

The EU is keen to ensure that existing agreements with the UK are fully implemented and adhered to. In this context, the European Commission has issued several requests for the UK to demonstrate its commitment to closer relations. These include fully implementing the Withdrawal Agreement – particularly concerning the rights of EU citizens residing in the UK – and properly enforcing the Windsor Framework, especially in certifying animal and plant products and establishing a pet-checking scheme at the border.[95] Furthermore, the European Commission has signalled its readiness to refer the UK's infringements related to the Withdrawal Agreement, specifically regarding the rights of EU citizens and their families, to the CJEU if swift corrective action is not taken. The Commission's tough stance rests on the view that the change in UK Government has not translated to a real change in foreign policy towards the EU, as evidenced by the Prime Minister's rejection of key EU priorities, such as a youth mobility scheme.[96]

Overall, it is foreseeable that some of the issues highlighted could be addressed during the upcoming 2026 review of the TCA. Regarding law enforcement and judicial

[94] Prime Minister's Office, 'Prime Minister to hold Talks with EU Leaders in Brussels', Press Release (1 October 2024) available at www.gov.uk/government/news/prime-minister-to-hold-talks-with-eu-leaders-in-brussels (last accessed 5 November 2024).

[95] L O'Carroll, 'UK must apply existing Brexit deals before any reset in relations, says EU' *The Guardian* (1 August 2024) available at www.theguardian.com/politics/article/2024/aug/01/uk-must-apply-existing-brexit-deals-before-any-reset-in-relations-says-eu (last accessed 5 November 2024).

[96] J Stone and F di Sario, 'Leaked EU Document: Visas for under 30s essential to Brexit reset' *Politico* (30 October 2024) available at www.politico.eu/article/eu-uk-youth-mobility-essential-brexit-reset-leak-shows/ (last accessed 6 November 2024).

cooperation issues falling outside the scope of the TCA review, the outlook is more complex. While the EU has shown some openness to closer cooperation, it has also made it clear that a change in the UK Government alone is not seen as a pivotal shift in UK–EU relations. Given the EU's interest in ensuring the TCA functions effectively, the most pragmatic approach for the UK Government might be to work cooperatively and gradually with the EU, leveraging the existing TCA governance structures to highlight the growing number of issues arising from its implementation. This approach could open the door to emphasising the need to update Part Three of the Agreement to accommodate legislative and policy changes on both sides. Should cooperation between the UK and individual EU Member States begin to significantly exceed the framework of the TCA, this could also exert additional pressure to revise the Agreement.

## V. Conclusions

Part Three of the TCA can be seen as a success both politically and operationally. Its implementation since January 2021 has generally been smooth and the most important aspects of cooperation continued, in many cases seamlessly. This does not mean that Brexit has not resulted in significant operational deficits. While it remains difficult to quantify the exact impact of these challenges on security, there is clear evidence that changes to the UK–EU relationship are affecting the efficiency of the UK's criminal justice system and its ability to protect the public. Although some of these challenges may be difficult to overcome due to the UK's status as a non-Schengen third country, others are within reach. For instance, while direct access to the SIS II may be unlikely in the near future, negotiating the circulation of TACCAWs on SIS II could ensure that individuals are apprehended anywhere in the EU, even if frontline officers do not have access to I-24/7. The upcoming review of the TCA therefore presents a valuable opportunity to assess the impact of its implementation, address issues within the Agreement's scope and explore complementary agreements to tackle unresolved challenges. The key contribution of this book is to set out why a comprehensive and ambitious review of the TCA is needed to ameliorate current risks to public safety. We have shown that a conservative approach would be a missed opportunity to understand and address the operational deficits caused by Brexit.

# INDEX

www.ingramcontent.com/pod-product-compliance
Ingram Content Group UK Ltd.
Pitfield, Milton Keynes, MK11 3LW, UK
UKHW020237290926
15470UKWH00002B/590

9 781509 966448